Nonclinical Assessment of ABUSE POTENTIAL FOR NEW PHARMACEUTICALS

Nonclinical Assessment of **ABUSE POTENTIAL FOR NEW PHARMACEUTICALS**

Edited by

CARRIE G. MARKGRAF
THOMAS J. HUDZIK
DAVID R. COMPTON

ELSEVIER

Amsterdam • Boston • Heidelberg • London
New York • Oxford • Paris • San Diego
San Francisco • Singapore • Sydney • Tokyo
Academic Press is an imprint of Elsevier

Academic Press is an imprint of Elsevier
125 London Wall, London EC2Y 5AS, UK
525 B Street, Suite 1800, San Diego, CA 92101-4495, USA
225 Wyman Street, Waltham, MA 02451, USA
The Boulevard, Langford Lane, Kidlington, Oxford OX5 1GB, UK

Notices
Knowledge and best practice in this field are constantly changing. As new research and experience broaden our understanding, changes in research methods, professional practices, or medical treatment may become necessary.

Practitioners and researchers must always rely on their own experience and knowledge in evaluating and using any information, methods, compounds, or experiments described herein. In using such information or methods they should be mindful of their own safety and the safety of others, including parties for whom they have a professional responsibility.

To the fullest extent of the law, neither the Publisher nor the authors, contributors, or editors, assume any liability for any injury and/or damage to persons or property as a matter of products liability, negligence or otherwise, or from any use or operation of any methods, products, instructions, or ideas contained in the material herein.

ISBN: 978-0-12-420172-9

British Library Cataloguing-in-Publication Data
A catalogue record for this book is available from the British Library

Library of Congress Cataloging-in-Publication Data
A catalog record for this book is available from the Library of Congress

For information on all Academic Press publications
visit our website at http://store.elsevier.com/

Publisher: Mica Haley
Acquisition Editor: Kristine Jones
Editorial Project Manager: Molly McLaughlin
Production Project Manager: Lucia Perez
Designer: Matthew Limbert

Typeset by TNQ Books and Journals
www.tnq.co.in

CONTENTS

CONTRIBUTORS

Theodore J. Baird
Toxicology, Medivation Inc., San Francisco, CA, USA

Matthew L. Banks
Department of Pharmacology and Toxicology, Medical College of Virginia, Richmond, VA, USA

Michael T. Bardo
Department of Psychology and Center for Drug Abuse Research Translation, University of Kentucky, Lexington, KY, USA

Patrick M. Beardsley
Department of Pharmacology & Toxicology, School of Medicine, Virginia Commonwealth University, Richmond, VA, USA

Anton Y. Bespalov
Laboratory of Behavioral Pharmacology, Institute of Pharmacology, Pavlov Medical University, St. Petersburg, Russia

August R. Buchhalter
PinneyAssociates, Bethesda, MD, USA

Silvia Calderon
Center for Drug Evaluation and Research, Food and Drug Administration, Silver Spring, MD, USA

David R. Compton
Preclinical Safety, Sanofi US, Bridgewater, NJ, USA; Department of Pharmacology and Toxicology, Virginia Commonwealth University, Richmond, VA, USA

Edward J. Cone
PinneyAssociates, Bethesda, MD, USA

Paul W. Czoty
Department of Physiology and Pharmacology, Wake Forest School of Medicine, Winston–Salem, NC, USA

Michelle D. Ertischek
PinneyAssociates, Bethesda, MD, USA

Reginald V. Fant
PinneyAssociates, Bethesda, MD, USA

Charles P. France
Department of Pharmacology, The University of Texas Health Science Center, San Antonio, TX, USA

David V. Gauvin
Neurobehavioral Sciences, MPI Research Inc., Mattawan, MI, USA

Karen K. Gerlach
PinneyAssociates, Bethesda, MD, USA

Alessandra Giarola
Safety Pharmacology Department, GlaxoSmithKline, Ware, Hertfordshire, UK

Mausumee Guha
Medivation Inc., San Francisco, CA, USA

David Heal
RenaSci Ltd., BioCity, Nottingham, UK

Jack E. Henningfield
PinneyAssociates, Bethesda, MD, USA; School of Medicine, Johns Hopkins University, Baltimore, MD, USA

David B. Horton
Global Safety Pharmacology, Drug Safety Research and Development, Pfizer Research and Development, Groton, CT, USA

Thomas J. Hudzik
Development Sciences, Preclinical Safety, AbbVie Ltd., N. Chicago, IL, USA

Mary Jeanne Kallman
Preclinical Neuroscience, Covance Laboratories, Lead Optimization, Greenfield, IN, USA

Carrie G. Markgraf
Discovery Sciences Support, Merck and Co Ltd., Kenilworth, NJ, USA

Michael A. Nader
Department of Physiology and Pharmacology, Wake Forest School of Medicine, Winston–Salem, NC, USA

Sidney H. Schnoll
PinneyAssociates, Bethesda, MD, USA

Marta Sokolowska
Grünenthal USA Inc., Bedminster, NJ, USA

Michael D.B. Swedberg
Swedberg Preclinical Partner AB (Inc.), Trosa, Sweden

Greet Teuns
Janssen R&D, Janssen Pharmaceutica NV, Beerse, Belgium

Mark S. Todtenkopf
Life Sciences and Toxicology Department, Alkermes, Inc., Waltham, MA, USA

Suzanne K. Vosburg
Grünenthal USA Inc., Bedminster, NJ, USA

Justin R. Yates
Department of Psychology and Center for Drug Abuse Research Translation, University of Kentucky, Lexington, KY, USA; Department of Psychological Science, Northern Kentucky University, Highland Heights, KY, USA

FOREWORD

The epidemic of drug abuse has been studied and written about extensively for the past few decades. According to the Centers for Disease Control and Prevention (CDC)[1], drug overdose death rates in the United States more than tripled from 1990 to 2008. Overdose deaths involving opioid analgesics increased and exceeded deaths involving heroin and cocaine combined. The CDC analyzed rates of fatal overdoses, nonmedical use, sales, and treatment admissions for opioid analgesics. In 2008, drug overdoses in the United States caused 36,450 deaths. Opioids were involved in 14,800 deaths (73.8%) of the 20,044 prescription drug overdose deaths. Most abuse involves polypharmacy whereby abuse involves the use of opioids in combination with other central nervous system-active drugs for enhanced effects or for otherwise altering the pharmacologic effect. During 1999–2008, overdose death rates, sales, and substance abuse treatment admissions related to opioids all increased substantially.

Other statistics describe the issue with details about regions of the country that are particularly affected by the current national drug abuse problem. Each manner in which data on abuse is presented makes the problem seem closer to all of us and more and more personal. Individual stories are routinely reported in newspapers about seemingly average people, including young people, who are affected by the availability of prescription and nonprescription drugs with abuse potential. In some cases, they are being treated with a medicine and begin abusing it, and then they take it for recreational purposes and become dependent. Such use may lead to addiction and overdose and, in the worst cases, death.

The abuse potential of a new drug needs to be assessed in controlled nonclinical and clinical studies before it is approved for marketing. The general public wants to know about the drugs that they take and they want to be informed about their risks and likelihood for abuse before they become a problem. Drug developers and regulators need to acquire this information as early as possible. Many types of prescription drugs are abused (opioids, sedatives, hypnotics, stimulants, and hallucinogens) and abuse in the US is primarily in the form of polypharmacy. These drug classes comprise most substances that are listed in the schedules of the Controlled Substances Act (CSA)[2]. A single drug for abuse appears to be an infrequent event, though confirmatory and specific data describing an abuse incident is not often available. In 2011, the Drug Abuse Warning Network (DAWN)[3] ceased to collect data related to actual drug abuse encounters reported in

[1] Morb Mortal Wkly Rep 2011 Nov 4; 60(43):1487–92. Vital signs: overdoses of prescription opioid pain relievers–United States, 1999–2008. http://www.ncbi.nlm.nih.gov/pubmed/22048730.

[2] Title 21 Food and Drugs Chapter 13: Drug Abuse Prevention and Control.

[3] http://www.encyclopedia.com/doc/1G2-3403100175.html.

hospital emergency departments and medical examiners. A compilation of DAWN reports once provided annual national statistics on abuse, often of specific drug products and the combinations of drugs that are abused. Since 2011, a greater reliance on this type of information has fallen to a variety of surveys and other sources of data, including poison control center reports to identify drug abuse problems. Oftentimes, abuse and diversion data are not systematically acquired and the reliability of such data is questioned. These sorts of data also cannot be trended from year to year, so they do not allow us to interpret with accuracy the meaning of any observed annual changes in patterns of use, extent of drug use, and new drug abuse fads. Determining whether things are getting better or whether regulatory efforts are successful is difficult if one relies on such data. We are limited in our ability to know whether new approaches have been successful and where future efforts should be applied when successes are based on data that are not systematically collected.

Anticipated problems and needed risk management can be predicted by the assessment of the drug's abuse potential. Rigorous scientific studies and a logical approach to conducting studies on the abuse potential of drugs are needed prior to approval and marketing. Drug regulators can make a risk benefit calculation of the drug and ensure that appropriate risk management strategies are in place to address anticipated problems.

Several years ago, I was told by a pharmaceutical industry representative that the abuse potential assessment of a drug is arcane—a mysterious and obscure process known only to a few. To him and many others, assessing the abuse potential of a drug seemed to rely more on anecdotal reports of abuse than on scientific data and analysis. One inherent problem with the assessment of abuse potential was that it relied on a random consensus of nonclinical and clinical interdisciplinary scientific data from a variety of studies. The sort of studies and the Food and Drug Administration (FDA) standards and expectations from these studies were not widely known. The investment of capital (intellectual and otherwise) into conducting these studies and developing an abuse potential assessment and integrating it into the entire drug development process was largely unheard of. Such efforts needed to be justified and directed such that not only were meaningful scientific results produced but that the appropriate studies were performed at the appropriate times and on a fair playing field for all companies. Companies were limited in their ability to perform a successful program in this area prior to the FDA publication of the draft *Guidance for Industry: Assessment of Abuse Potential of Drugs*[4] in January 2010. The Guidance provided a framework for assessing abuse potential. In addition to describing the types of studies and data that are needed, the Guidance laid out a stepwise scientific approach, offering a logical sequence and timeline for performing certain studies before others, whereby later studies could build on results from earlier

[4] http://www.fda.gov/downloads/Drugs/GuidanceComplianceRegulatoryInformation/Guidances/UCM198650.pdf (Published January 27, 2010).

studies as new information about the new drug is obtained. Today, the assessment of abuse potential is a part of the FDA's Twenty-First Century Drug Review Process in the Center for Drug Evaluation and Research (FDA/CDER). For drugs with abuse potential, expert regulatory reviewers participate in all milestone meetings and prepare reviews of the studies with recommendations prior to approval.

The assessment of the abuse potential of a drug—whether new or well-known and already on the market—is part of the evaluation of the overall safety profile of a drug. The safety profile evaluation for a drug relates to the medical use of a drug and is primarily applicable to patient populations. In this context, the risk benefit determination for the drug can be made, since all drugs offer risks and potential therapeutic benefits. A unique feature of a drug's abuse potential is that the "abuse" of a drug affects a wider population of individuals than patients. Different populations are affected (or at risk) and studies in different populations often show a range of effects to the drug. For this reason, the pivotal human abuse potential study is carried out in experienced or recreational drug abusers, rather than drug-naïve healthy subjects or patient populations who are prescribed a drug for intended therapeutic purposes.

When a company submits a new drug application (NDA) to the FDA for review and approval, if the drug has a potential for abuse, the company must submit in the NDA an analysis of studies and other information related to the potential abuse and dependence liability of the drug and propose scheduling under the CSA, if appropriate, and drug product labeling that is supported by study data. The company project management should ensure that the drug development process addresses all pertinent nonclinical and clinical study data related to biochemistry, pharmacology, animal behavior and dependence, pharmacokinetics, chemistry, and drug formulation. An adverse events profile that includes events such as euphoria and hallucinations that are related to abuse potential are relevant. The nonclinical data informs us early in development of the likely mechanism of action of the drug and is highly predictive of how the drug should be studied further in humans. The early safety pharmacology and in vitro binding studies are useful in informing us about the drug's possible central nervous system activity and similarity to other known drugs of abuse. We gain from these studies an understanding of the relationship of the drug's pharmacology to neurotransmitters that may be associated with the mechanism of action leading to abuse. Importantly, the nonclinical studies are useful in the design of other behaviorally related animal studies (such as the drug discrimination and self-administration paradigms) in the selection of appropriate positive controls and doses. Importantly, the nonclinical study results assist in designing human abuse potential studies and provide assurance of safety in the conduct of clinical studies so that the necessary safeguards are in place at the start of the clinical studies. A thorough knowledge of the nonclinical data of the new drug assists in interpreting adverse events related to abuse that are reported in Phase 3 of development and postmarketing as well.

This book presents numerous contributions on the nonclinical assessment of abuse potential for new pharmaceuticals by expert scientists from industry, academia, and government. It contains a wide range of information on scientific laboratory studies that are used in acquiring data on drug abuse for new drugs. Finally, the book contains vital information beneficial to pharmaceutical companies, researchers, policymakers, and all others who are engaged in areas of drug development and drug abuse issues.

Michael Klein, PhD[5]
Director Controlled Substance Staff

[5] The opinions and information in this presentation are those of the author and do not necessarily reflect the views and policies of the FDA.

PREFACE

As undergraduate and then graduate students, many can recall being captivated by the idea, presented by B.F. Skinner and others, that animal behavior could represent, with high fidelity, the behavior of humans. The early work of Peter Dews showed us that the operant behavior of pigeons, responding under a particular schedule of reinforcement, provided a baseline from which to assess the adaptation of the organism to the schedule, as well as a stable baseline to understand the effects of drugs. The measured behaviors, as well as drug responses, were remarkably conserved across all species, up to and including humans.

This growing field of behavioral pharmacology was quickly adapted to the study of drugs of abuse, and along with it came the revelation that any given animal would engage in behavior that resulted in administration of drugs of abuse, the topic of some seminal reviews. That drugs could be seen as reinforcers of behavior, and that many behaviors were conserved among species caused a shift in thinking about drug addiction from some type of character flaw or moral weakness to a pathophysiological continuum from normal, biologically typical (and acceptable) seeking behaviors to abnormal, atypical (and unacceptable) behavior(s) resulting from over-activation of reward pathways in brain pathways highly conserved across species; just as animal behavioral responses occurring under schedules of positive reinforcement.

As a result, models of abuse potential covered in this volume are among the most predictive to humans of all animal models. However, the current challenge is that industry and regulatory scientists need to learn how to apply these well-described and long-established models to a new purpose: to profile the potential for abuse of new pharmaceuticals and, where possible, to mitigate the potential negative human health consequences of medication misuse and/or abuse. The focus of this book is to review current knowledge of the state of these models from the perspective, when possible, of pharmaceutical drug development and to demonstrate how the models are applicable to this problem presented by novel chemical entities.

Carrie Markgraf, PhD
Thomas Hudzik, PhD
David Compton, PhD

ACKNOWLEDGMENTS

We would like to thank Mark Ammann (and the CCALC), without whom we would not have started on this particular adventure. We would also like to acknowledge our professors, advisors, and colleagues who have inspired and guided us along our career paths toward improving human health and safety, notably from DRC: Kenneth M Johnson, and collaborator, mentor, and dear friend Billy R Martin (deceased); from TH: George Wagner, John Falk, Don McMillan, Galen Wenger, Bob Balster and Bob Schuster; and from CGM: Bob Osborne and Bruce Kapp. A special thank you also to Mary Jeanne Kallman: a colleague, friend, and inspiration to so many.

CHAPTER 1

Nonclinical Assessment of Abuse Potential for New Pharmaceuticals in a Regulatory Space

Thomas J. Hudzik[1], Carrie G. Markgraf[2]
[1]Development Sciences, Preclinical Safety, AbbVie Ltd., N. Chicago, IL, USA; [2]Discovery Sciences Support, Merck and Co Ltd., Kenilworth, NJ, USA

Contents

Abuse of prescription pharmaceuticals is a common media topic and has been described as an epidemic. Data from the 2010 National Survey on Drug Use and Health show that an estimated 2.4 million Americans used prescription drugs nonmedically for the first time within the previous year [1]. This nonmedical use of prescription drugs has led to a dramatic increase in emergency department visits and deaths [2]. However, when used as intended, these drugs are beneficial and have met current regulatory standards for safety and effectiveness. Overly restrictive scheduling of such products can cause patients difficulty in obtaining their medications and physicians to be burdened with questionable, extra record-keeping and potentially unwarranted and/or excessive scrutiny. It is incumbent on the pharmaceutical industry to determine as accurately as possible the relative abuse potential of new pharmaceuticals. That challenge is currently of great interest to regulators and pharmaceutical companies, as both seek to accurately characterize the abuse potential of new drugs in order to protect the public's safety [3]. In light of this responsibility to public safety, a high degree of regulatory oversight as well as guidance has been required, which has been a product of an ongoing dialogue among subject matter experts and scientists from both the Food and Drug Administration (FDA) and the industry. Scientists speak a common language regarding abuse liability assessment as most have received similar degrees of advanced training in the area of addiction. For example, there is agreement on definitions of addictive behavior, while owing to minor variations in emphasis; we can define it as a set of behaviors leading to the repeated, excessive self-administration of a substance, despite the resultant appearance of negative

Nonclinical Assessment of Abuse Potential for New Pharmaceuticals
http://dx.doi.org/10.1016/B978-0-12-420172-9.00001-1

consequences to one's health, wealth, or well-being, including one's social circle. Addiction is not a state. It is a process—indeed a disease. For those of us who work in or regulate the healthcare industry, incorrectly predicting abuse potential is quite the opposite of what we consider to be our public health mission.

1. TERMINOLOGY

The evaluation of the possibility that a drug could be addictive draws from many fields of study, including, among others, physiology, neuroscience, psychology, animal learning, and animal behavior. Each of these fields has its own terminology or may use similar terms with slightly different definitions. Since the authors of each of the chapters in this book were selected based on their expertise in the relevant field of study, terminology is not consistent throughout the book. Rather than force a common lexicon, each chapter stands on its own and reflects the terminology of that scientific area.

One common—and important—distinction is between the terms "abuse liability" and "abuse potential." Abuse potential is the ability of a drug to produce positive rewarding or reinforcing effects, which is thought to be predictive of risk for "addiction" [4]. Therefore abuse potential is more closely aligned to a property of the drug itself. Abuse liability, on the other hand, refers not only to abuse potential, but in a regulatory context, it is used to include all factors impacting the risk of misuse or abuse of a drug. These are factors that include therapeutic indication, availability, ease of synthesis, context of use, and risk for misuse or diversion. Abuse liability also includes the potential for negative outcomes resulting from abuse (e.g., addiction, overdose, or toxicity) [5].

2. ANIMAL MODELS OF ABUSE POTENTIAL

Using animal models to assess the potential for a substance to cause addiction is complex, in part because addiction is a multifaceted process that involves factors as diverse as physiology, social behavior, behavioral history, and learning, among others. Theories of drug addiction based on these processes range from focusing primarily on the hedonic (pleasure), or withdrawal and opponent processes, to the dysfunction of frontal cortical systems in decision-making. These theories are beyond the scope of the present book but have been well-reviewed and discussed elsewhere [6–10].

Animal models of "drug addiction" reside on a solid scientific base. Characterization of known drugs of abuse in rats, mice, pigeons, dogs, and monkeys of various species has provided validation of these models for identifying addictive substances. Modeling drug addiction in animals has evolved considerably since the late 1930s when the prevalent beliefs were summarized by a leading sociologist of the time, Alfred R. Lindesmith. Lindesmith argued that "only those to whom the drug's effects can be explained can become addicts," and went on to state: "Certainly from the point of view of social science it would be ridiculous to include animals and humans together in the concept of addiction" (Lindesmith, quoted by Spragg [11]). Clearly, the pharmacologists were not in full agreement with the sociologists of the time, and researchers such as Tatum and colleagues [12] were already modeling aspects of opioid addiction in the dog. S.D. Shirley Spragg was the first researcher to show that chimpanzees would "work" (i.e., learn specific behaviors) to get a dose of morphine [11]. In doing so, he challenged the thinking of the time and opened the door for various ways to model drug addiction in animals, which allowed exploration of specific factors that support and maintain addiction.

Spragg's work grew out of the sociology field, looking for ways to explain patterns of uniquely human behavior. He was enough a product of his time that he believed that while chimps would work for morphine, "lower" species (on the phylogenetic tree) such as rats never would. He wrote

> *...Since morphine addiction seems to depend essentially upon forming an association between the administration of the drug and the alleviation of withdrawal symptoms, and since this sequence involves a time lag of 10-15 minutes or more, the value of using subjects high enough in the phyletic scale to be able to make a delayed association of this nature is obvious. By this token, animals such as the rat, for example, could probably never become addicted to morphine, simply because they are not capable of forming associations of this order.... (p. 126 [11])*

Similar goals for explaining addiction were approached from an entirely different scientific view by learning theorist B.F. Skinner. Skinner's novel approach relied heavily on the concept of reinforcement. A positive reinforcer is a stimulus that increases the probability of occurrence of a preceding behavior [13], a concept that is easily adapted to the study of addictive drugs. Skinnerian or operant conditioning is the learning paradigm in which reinforcement (or punishment) can be systemically applied to engender, maintain, modify, or eliminate behavior. The behavior, or response, studied is usually a lever press and can be performed by most laboratory species. Headlee's [14] work with rats disproved Spragg's hypothesis and showed that species other than primates are capable of working to obtain a drug.

This important conclusion helped to open the door for further exploration of mechanisms of addiction and has provided an understanding of the basis of addiction, answering the question "what makes drugs addictive?" Collective work from many labs has helped identify three main properties that can define an addictive substance, and these properties should apply whether the drug is a known illicit drug of abuse or a new pharmaceutical compound targeting a novel central nervous system (CNS) mechanism. Those properties include reinforcement, stimulus effects, and dependence/withdrawal as primary factors, which can be heavily influenced by genetics, social pressure, or prior experience as well has mental health status. But first and foremost an addictive drug will possess reinforcing properties, as defined by Skinner. That is, administration of an addictive drug will increase the probability that the user will take the drug again. An addictive drug produces internal cues and feelings (stimulus effects) that people—and most likely animals—experience as pleasurable. The third aspect, dependence, is characterized by a withdrawal syndrome. In the course of drug administration, especially repeated drug administration, physiological adaptations occur, usually in the direction opposite to the pharmacologic effect of the drug. When the drug is absent, these adaptations become most apparent. Furthermore, it is important to consider how the state of withdrawal can affect the discriminative stimulus and reinforcing effects of drugs. Each of these main properties of an addictive substance can be accurately modeled in animals using the methods reviewed in the chapters of this volume as well as "state of the art" techniques that can be applied to further enhance the resolution of the methodologies. Additionally, a chapter on modeling abuse-related effects in humans is included and demonstrates the excellent forward translatability of the preclinical models.

3. REGULATION OF DRUGS OF ABUSE

The purpose of studying addictive properties of drugs has been to understand the disease of addiction, to help people with addiction, or to prevent addiction. There is another aspect of addictive drugs: regulation of their approved medical use. Regulations vary in different regions of the world. In the United States, federal restriction of the use of drugs is fairly recent: less than 100 years old. Prior to that time, restrictions were formed and enforced at the state or local level. The earliest regulation started in the 1830s with the prohibition of the selling of alcohol to Native Americans [15]. By 1855, 13 states had passed alcohol prohibition laws. In 1875, laws were passed banning the visitation of opium dens in San Francisco [16]. These early laws were aimed at the drug user rather than at the drug itself.

By 1935, some of the first laws aimed at regulating drug substances were enacted, banning the use of marijuana in 35 states. Initially, the control of drugs at the federal level was accomplished through taxation. Following the Great Depression and World War II, the view of the federal government changed to an increased role in protecting citizens, and the Food, Drug, and Cosmetic Act was passed in 1937 (15) with a key amendment in 1962 [17]. It was not until 1965 that the first direct prohibition of a drug was enacted. The Drug Abuse Control Amendment specifically created control over what were identified as "dangerous" drugs: amphetamines, barbiturates, and later, in 1968, LSD [18]. This amendment also gave the federal government the right to control any drug later deemed to be a "problem."

The Controlled Substances Act of 1970 defines our current approach to drugs. It states specifically that narcotics and other dangerous drugs are under direct federal jurisdiction, not controlled indirectly through taxation. This change moved the enforcement of controlled drugs out of the Treasury to the Justice department and gave rise to the Drug Enforcement Agency (DEA). The FDA is in charge of defining what substances need to be controlled, but the DEA is in charge of enforcement. Characteristics that define a controlled substance include

1. pharmacologic actions;
2. other scientific knowledge about it and related drugs;
3. risk to public health;
4. dependence (psychic or physiologic) potential; and
5. whether the drug was a precurser for other drugs listed.

Alcohol, nicotine, and caffeine are excluded from the act.

Around this time period, the United Nations (UN) created several treatises on addictive drugs: in 1961 the UN Single Convention on Narcotic Drugs and in 1971 the UN Convention on Psychotropic Substances. These documents, together with the 1988 UN Convention on Illicit Trafficking, form the basis for the European Union (EU) member states' restriction of controlled drugs, although each EU country has slightly different restrictions. Japan, in 1953, had four separate laws on controlled substances: one each for marijuana, stimulants, opiates, and narcotics/psychotropics. These were rewritten to be similar to the 1988 UN Convention.

Collectively, these laws seek to protect the public from drugs deemed to be dangerous by virtue of having abuse potential qualities. Among worldwide regulatory agencies, there is clear agreement as to which drugs have addictive properties. More difficult is predicting whether a drug with a novel mechanism might be abused. Thus, as new CNS-active pharmaceuticals are developed, there is a need to evaluate them for abuse potential. The unique interaction of regulatory science and the long-standing investigation of drugs of addiction form the basis for the collective topics in this book. There are special nonclinical challenges in regulating drugs that cause changes in human behavior and even more so for an occurrence like addiction in which the drug user is—quite consciously and purposefully—not using the drug as intended or as indicated by the label.

4. SCHEDULING

The outcome of the nonclinical and clinical studies plus regulatory evaluation of the data results in a decision as to how strictly to control, or schedule, a new medication. In most countries, there are levels of increasing control over a medication's use based on the strength of its addictive properties and the medical need. In the US, a drug's schedule is determined by the DEA. Schedule I drugs are without accepted/approved medical use and are considered to be the most dangerous class of drugs with a high potential for abuse and potentially severe psychological and/or physical dependence. The drug schedule changes—Schedule II, Schedule III—based on the abuse potential, down to Schedule V medication, which represents the least potential for abuse. Scheduling of a drug is indicated by the results of the 8-factor analysis. As described in 21 U.S.C 811(h), the eight factors to be considered are

1. a drug's actual or relative potential for abuse;
2. scientific evidence of its pharmacological effects;

3. the state of current scientific knowledge regarding the substance;
4. the history and current pattern of abuse;
5. the scope, duration, and significance of abuse;
6. what, if any, risk there is to the public's health;
7. the psychic or physiological dependence liability; and
8. whether the substance is an immediate precursor to a substance already controlled.

The UN classifies drugs and precursors according to the three UN Conventions of 1961, 1971, and 1988, which control the legitimate scientific or medical use of the drug while taking into account risks to public or individual health. This organization results in two Schedules: one for narcotics and one for psychotropic substances. For psychotropic substances, Schedule I is for drugs with the most serious abuse liability; Schedules II, III, and IV represent decreasing abuse liability. For narcotics under UN scheduling, there are four Schedules, but the order of severity is not sequential; Schedules I and IV are the most restrictive. Within the EU, some member states split the classification of narcotics and psychotropics, and some do not. A table of each country's scheduling can be found at: http://www.emcdda.europa.eu/html.cfm/index146601EN.html. Examples of drugs that meet Schedule I requirements in both the US and the EU are LSD and MDMA. Examples of drugs that fall into the least restrictive category (Schedules IV or V) are diazepam and some preparations of codeine.

5. SUMMARY

It is interesting to note that although the schedules were developed independently, there is common agreement in the US, the EU, and with the UN on which drugs are considered "dangerous" due to their addictive properties. Not only do health authorities agree on which drugs are addictive, but there is also general agreement as to the degree of those addictive properties, that is, to which schedule a drug belongs. This commonality speaks to the widely recognized characteristics of addiction in humans, which in turn suggests that this behavior, once thought to be uniquely human, can be modeled in animals. The brain areas involved with pleasure and reward are highly conserved across species, as is detailed in Chapter 2 of this edition. Thus, the well-characterized models of self-administration (Chapters 3 and 4), drug discrimination (Chapter 6), and dependence/withdrawal (Chapter 5), which are described briefly in this chapter, *can* serve to provide regulators with data critical to making decisions regarding the abuse potential of a new substance. The nonclinical evaluation of abuse potential does not stop with these three models, even though these are the most commonly used. Circumstances for an individual compound may dictate a different approach, for which the chapters in this edition on intracranial self-stimulation (Chapter 8) and conditional place preference (Chapter 7) will be instructive. Nonclinical data are not generated and used in a vacuum.

The chapters in this book on clinical evaluation of abuse potential (Chapter 9) and regulatory aspects (Chapter 10) help to place preclinical data in an appropriate context within drug development. In summary, taken together, the chapters in this book provide a detailed evaluation of the current state of the science of preclinical abuse liability assessment in a regulatory environment.

REFERENCES

[1] Drug Facts; Nationwide Trends. http://www.drugabuse.gov/publications/drugfacts/nationwide-trends [accessed on 11.02.15].

[2] Centers for Disease Control and Prevention (CDC). CDC grand rounds: prescription drug overdoses – a US epidemic. Morb Mortal Wkly Rep 2012;61:10–3.

[3] Balster RL, Bigelow GE. Guidelines and methodological reviews concerning drug abuse liability assessment. Drug Alcohol Depend 2003;70(3):S13–40.

[4] Calderon-Gutkind SN. The assessment of abuse liability: the regulatory perspective. 2003. http://www.fda.gov/CDER/Offices/CSS/presentations/DIA2003Workshop%5F05%5F22%5F03Calderon/.

[5] Schoedel KA, Sellers EM. Assessing abuse liability during drug development: changing standards and expectations. Nature 2008;83:622–6.

[6] Tiffany ST. A cognitive model of drug urges and drug-use behavior: role of automatic and nonautomatic processes. Psychol Rev 1990;97(2):147.

[7] Robinson TE, Berridge KC. The neural basis of drug craving: an incentive-sensitization theory of addiction. Brain Res Rev 1993;18(3):247–91.

[8] Tatum A, Seevers M. Theories of drug addiction. Physiol Rev 1931;11(2):107–21.

[9] Di Chiara G. Drug addiction as dopamine-dependent associative learning disorder. Eur J Pharmacol 1999;375(1):13–30.

[10] Drummond DC. Theories of drug craving, ancient and modern. Addiction 2001;96(1):33–46.

[11] Spragg SDS. Morphine addiction in chimpanzees. Comparative psychology monographs, 1940.

[12] Tatum A, Seevers M, Collins K. Morphine addiction and its physiological interpretation based on experimental evidences. J Pharmacol Exp Ther 1929;36(3):447–75.

[13] Skinner BF. The operational analysis of psychological terms. Psychol Rev 1945;52(5):270–7.

[14] Headlee CP, Coppock HW, Nichols JR. Apparatus and technique involved in a laboratory method of detecting the addictiveness of drugs. J Am Pharm Assoc 1955;44(4):229–31.

[15] Law MT. History of food and drug regulation in the United States. EH.Net Encyclopedia. 2004. Available at http://eh.net/encyclopedia/history-of-food-and-drug-regulation-in-the-united-states/.

[16] Drug Enforcement Agency (DEA). The history of illegal substance use, abuse and enforcement in the US. 2013. Available at https://usdrugenforcement.wordpress.com/2013/09/15/san-franciscos-opium-den-ordinance/.

[17] FDA. Kefauver-Harris Amendments Revolutionized Drug Development. 2012. Available at http://www.fda.gov/ForConsumers/ConsumerUpdates/ucm322856.htm.

[18] Carpenter D. Reputation and power: orgainzational image and pharmaceutical regulation at the FDA. Princeton NJ: Princeton University Press; 2010. 340–342.

CHAPTER 2

Neurochemistry of Abuse Liability Assessment and Primary Behavioral Correlates

David R. Compton[1], Thomas J. Hudzik[2]
[1]Preclinical Safety, Sanofi US, Bridgewater, NJ, USA; Department of Pharmacology and Toxicology, Virginia Commonwealth University, Richmond, VA, USA; [2]Development Sciences, Preclinical Safety, AbbVie Ltd., N. Chicago, IL, USA

Contents

Nonclinical Assessment of Abuse Potential for New Pharmaceuticals
http://dx.doi.org/10.1016/B978-0-12-420172-9.00002-3

1. INTRODUCTION

1.1 Purpose

The primary intent of this volume is to provide those in the pharmaceutical, regulatory, and related fields with a basic understanding of some well-established areas of science (i.e., neuroscience, neuropharmacology, drug abuse) with the associated scientific methodologies (e.g., ligand binding and behavioral assessments) that are becoming integral to the current drug development process by the application of these "classical" fields in a novel fashion or for a novel purpose. That novel purpose is the abuse liability assessment of NCEs (new chemical entities) that is being developed for marketing as therapeutic agents. The many factors precipitating this change in the drug development and approval process over the past decade is of historical interest but will not be presented here, except for reference to sections of current or draft guidance documents that are relevant to considerations of the neurochemistry of drug abuse and drug abuse liability assessment (DALA).

1.2 Considerations from Regulatory Guidance Documents

Certain drug classes and related neurotransmitter systems have been specifically identified in guidance documents, based on historical precedent of human misuse/abuse, as being of concern with respect to abuse liability assessment during the development of novel therapeutic agents. The 2006 European Medicines Agency (EMA) (EMEA/CHMP/SWP/94,227/2004) "Guideline on the non-clinical investigation of the dependence potential of medicinal products" (http://www.ema.europa.eu/docs/en_GB/document_library/Scientific_guideline/2009/09/WC500003360.pdf) specifies various drug classes of concern. The 2010 Food and Drug Administration (FDA) Draft Guidance "Assessment of abuse potential of drugs" (http://www.fda.gov/cder/guidance/index.htm) specifies neurotransmitter systems of interest—generally those associated with one or more mechanisms of action of various drugs of abuse (Table 1).

During the development of potential therapeutic medications, it will be important, if an abuse liability assessment is necessary, to identify whether the development candidate NCE acts upon one (or more) of these neurotransmitter systems as a simple in vitro binding ligand (with no pharmacological activity) or as an agonist (either direct or indirect), inverse agonist, antagonist, partial agonist/antagonist, or as a mixed agonist/antagonist. However, for the purposes of this chapter, those considerations come later in the reiterative abuse liability assessment process. Now it is appropriate to briefly consider the various neuronal pathways of importance to the neurochemistry of drug abuse.

2. REWARD SYSTEM

2.1 Overview

The mammalian "reward" system is comprised of the set of neural substrates that are active (or activated) under a variety of normal physiological conditions, some of which are basic

Table 1 Drug Classes and Neurotransmitter Systems of Concern. A listing of both drug classes and neurotransmitters systems of concern with respect to abuse liability assessment as identified in regulatory guidances such as the 2006 EMA "Guideline on the non-clinical investigation of the dependence potential of medicinal products" and the 2010 draft FDA guidance "Assessment of abuse potential of drugs."

Drug Classes of Regulatory Concern	Neurotransmitter Systems of Concern
Monoamine uptake inhibitors and CNS stimulants (see Note 1)	Dopamine (DA), norepinephrine (NE), and serotonin (5-HT)
Anxiolytics and sedatives (see Note 2)	GABA (see Note 3)
NMDA antagonists	NMDA (ionotropic glutamate receptor subtype)
Cannabinoids	Endocannabinoid (e.g., anandamide)
Nicotine-like	Acetylcholine (ACh; see Note 4)
Opiates	Endorphins, enkephalins (see Note 5)
Novel pharmacologic classes	Novel system (e.g., melatonin in 2005 for a first-in-class sleep aid)

ADHD = attention deficit hyperactivity disorder; CNS = central nervous system; GABA = gamma-aminobutyric acid; NMDA = *N*-methyl-D-aspartic acid (or *N*-methyl-D-aspartate); SSRI = selective serotonin reuptake inhibitors.
Note 1: monoamine inhibitors including SSRIs and CNS stimulants including appetite suppressants and medicinal products for ADHD.
Note 2: includes benzodiazepines, barbiturates, and other sedative/hypnotics.
Note 3: gabaergic receptor subtype of concern is the $GABA_A$ receptor with one recognition site for the endogenous ligand and a second site sometimes referred to as the GABA-benzodiazepine-chloride ion channel complex, to refer to the allosteric binding site for benzodiazepines.
Note 4: cholinergic receptor subtype of specific concern includes the ionotropic nicotinic receptor (nAChR) and particularly the neuronal configuration defined by the specific subunits $\alpha4\beta2$; of some potential concern is the metabotropic muscarinic receptor (mAChR).
Note 5: opioid receptor subtypes of concern include MOP (mu [μ]), DOP (delta [δ]), and KOP (kappa [κ]) opioid receptors; the historical designation of the sigma (σ) subtype as an opioid is no longer considered applicable, and the sigma receptor is both a distinct receptor class but not necessarily one of potential abuse liability concern.

to life itself (e.g., food [especially "sweet" reinforcement] [1] and water [due in part to "oral cooling" reinforcement] [2]) and some which have played a key role in the evolution of humanity and the maintenance of the human population (e.g., sex [3]). Of course, some pleasures are more "rewarding" than others (e.g., chocolate and red wine versus satiation of basic hunger or thirst) and are therefore more sought after even if the reinforcement (sweet, cool) does not mitigate the physiological condition (hunger, thirst) precipitating the behavior but the range of reward-motivated pleasure-seeking behaviors are still within the range of normal physiological functioning for a given species. Note that this indicates reinforcers can be "rewarding" and sought after in and of themselves, not simply because they alleviate a certain condition. The combined set of neural substrates of this "reward" system have been referred to as the Reward System, Reward Pathway, or even the Pleasure Pathway [4–13]. Other synonyms of the Reward Pathway refer to more specific anatomical regions, to be further elucidated below. First it is appropriate to understand some superficial aspects of "how" the Reward System has been identified.

Human studies utilizing fMRI (functional magnetic resonance imaging) and PET (positron emission tomography) scans after the administration of 2-DG (2-deoxy-glucose) provide data on increases in neuronal activity in scenarios where a reward (something considered desirable or pleasurable) is offered (or at least promised). In animals, data on neuronal activity under conditions of a reward scenario have also been gathered by more invasive techniques such as either ICSS (intracranial self-stimulation) following electrode implantation in various brain regions or the implantation of cannulas in various brain regions capable of delivering various chemical stimuli. Additionally, a combination of these and other techniques (e.g., drug discrimination, self-administration) have been combined with ablation/lesion studies to define brain structures necessary for a cue/stimulus–action–reward scenario.

Under conditions in which humans are offered any one of a variety of tangible rewards (i.e., money, luxury item, food, or drink) or a potential reward that is not guaranteed (e.g., money in a chance scenario [i.e., gambling]) or even the anticipation of a reward that will not be provided (e.g., sex) due to moral and ethical concerns during a human study, one region of the brain that becomes highly active includes the nucleus accumbens (NAc) of the limbic portion of the brain, which may also be referred to as the ventral striatum (which then includes the olfactory tubercle). In cases in which the reward is actually received, there being no moral or legal limitations, then another area that becomes highly active is the prefrontal cortex (PFC). It is clear from the sum total of all data available that the primary (but not only) regions involved in the Reward System are the target areas of the limbic brain (e.g., NAc) and PFC that receive a significant portion of their neuronal inputs from the ventral tegmental area (VTA) of the midbrain (mesencephalon). Note that in classical anatomic nomenclature, the VTA is also identified as the A10 nucleus (in contrast to the adjacent A9 region of the substantia nigra, part of the nigrostriatal pathway). Thus, using anatomical descriptors, the Reward System can also be referred to as the Mesolimbic Reward Pathway, or the Mesocorticolimbic Reward Pathway. The latter term properly incorporates the role of the PFC in the overall reward process and recognizes that many projections from the VTA impinge directly and separately upon limbic regions and the PFC. It may be of some importance to note, due to original research literature on this subject, that the bulk of fibers (axons) from the VTA reach target regions via an anatomical structure known as the medial forebrain bundle (MFB), as it was identified decades ago as being critical to the Reward System. In an attempt to be more inclusive in the identification of specific brain nuclei that are known to be involved in the Reward System, those additional regions are identified separately and without further discussion in Figure 1 and Tables 2 and 3.

The pharmacologically perturbed Reward System that is critical to considerations during an abuse liability assessment can be affected beyond normal neurophysiological functioning by multiple classes of drugs with a multiplicity of molecular mechanisms of action. The impacts of selected abused substances impinging upon the Reward System are depicted in Figure 2.

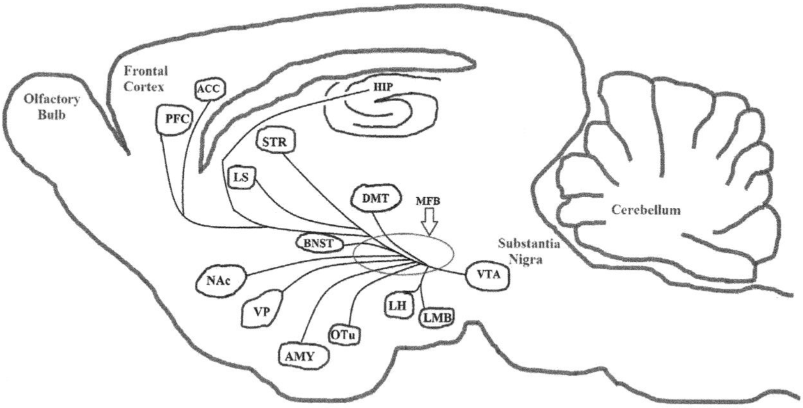

Figure 1 Primary neural substrates of the reward system. The mesolimbic dopaminergic projections via the medial forebrain bundle (MFB; arrow/circle) from the ventral tegmental area (VTA or A10 of the midbrain [mesencephalon]) to the primary neural substrates of the mesocorticolimbic reward system and the approximate anatomical locations of those nuclei among other indicated anatomic regions (i.e., olfactory bulb and frontal cortex to substantia nigra [A9] and cerebellum) within a depiction of a sagittal view of a rodent brain. *Mesencephalon (midbrain)*: VTA, ventral tegmental area. *Diencephalon*: LH, lateral hypothalamus; LMB, lateral mammillary body. *Telencephalon*: ACC, anterior cingulate cortex; AMY, amygdala (including both blAMY [basolateral amygdala] and meAMY [medial amygdala]); BNST, bed nucleus of the stria terminalis; DMT, dorsomedial thalamus; HIP, hippocampus; LS, lateral septum; NAc, nucleus accumbens; OTu, olfactory tubercle; PFC, prefrontal cortex; STR, striatum; VP, ventral palidum. Figure represents composite anatomical and connectivity information from multiple sources [12–14,16,17].

Table 2 Primary Neural Substrates of the Mesocorticolimbic Reward System. A listing of the three primary brain nuclei and/or regions integral to the Reward System, with associated descriptive neuroanatomical information

Ventral tegmental area (VTA, A10) of the midbrain (mesencephalon)	Nucleus accumbens (NAc) of the forebrain (telencephalon) and part of the limbic system	Prefrontal cortex (PFC) of the forebrain (telencephalon)

However, all known drug classes are typically considered to be misused or abused in large part due to some direct effects on the Reward System. In one sense or another, the use/abuse is considered pleasurable. Regardless of the direct versus indirect nature of the abuse, such drugs are scheduled (or controlled) by the US Drug Enforcement Agency (DEA) (in conjunction with the FDA for novel therapeutic agents), and the level of control (C-1 to C-5) is determined based on many factors that will not be discussed in this text. Some representative examples of drug classes which pose regulatory and abuse liability concerns, are controlled or scheduled and affect the Reward System, are provided in Table 4.

Table 3 Additional Nuclei of the Mesocorticolimbic Reward System (Located in the Mesencephalon, Diencephalon, and Telencephalon). A listing of 13 secondary brain nuclei and/or regions integral to the Reward System, with associated descriptive neuroanatomical information

blAMY (basolateral amygdala; see Note 1)	meAMY (medial amygdala; see Note 1)	BNST (bed nucleus of the stria terminalis)
DMT (dorsomedial thalamus)	HIP (hippocampus)	LS (lateral septum)
OTu (olfactory tubercle)	STR (striatum; see Note 2)	VP (ventral palidum)
LH (lateral hypothalamus)	LMB (lateral mammillary body)	ACC (anterior cingulated cortex)
MFB (medial forebrain bundle; see Note 3)		

Note 1: the amygdala (basolateral; medial) may be considered distinct as presented here; some anatomical descriptions of the Reward System instead identify the central nucleus of the amygdala plus the medial nucleus of the amygdala (also as distinct entities).
Note 2: the most appropriate term for certain species (e.g., rat, mouse) is "striatum," while this same anatomical region in other species (e.g., human) can be more correctly identified separately as the caudate plus putamen, which can be distinguished by the visible presence of the internal capsule; the STR is sometimes referred to as the "dorsal striatum" while the "ventral striatum" refers to the NAc plus OTu; the entire striatum (caudate-putamen) is not generally considered part of the Reward System, but some do consider the mediolateral portion of the STR with inhibitory striatothalamic projections regulating thalamocortical pathways (including PFC) to be of the Reward System.
Note 3: technically, the MFB is not a nuclei but rather is a "bundle" of over 50 sets of projection fibers (i.e., white matter) of both ascending and descending axons, however due to the large amount of data generated on this anatomical structure during the historical investigations of the Reward System and since it is considered a component of the mesolimbic pathway, it was considered appropriate to emphasize the structure in this table of nuclei.

Separate brief descriptions of the various specific neurotransmitter systems of concern during an abuse liability assessment will be provided in a subsequent section.

At this point, without addressing the complex issues of abuse, tolerance, dependence, and addiction, a clear differentiation should be made between the role of the Reward System under normal (or even extreme) physiological conditions and those situations in which the neural substrates of the Reward System are affected by acute or chronic exposure to pharmacological stimuli. Once the human condition is sufficiently altered to qualify as a diagnosis of "substance abuse disorder" per the Substance-Related and Addictive Disorders section (http://dx.doi.org/10.1176/appi.books.9780890425596.190656; http://dsm.psychiatryonline.org/content.aspx?bookid=556&sectionid=41101782) of the Diagnostic and Statistical Manual of Mental Disorders (Fifth Edition; DSM-5; American Psychiatric Association; Arlington, VA, 2013; http://dsm.psychiatryonline.org), then clearly the Reward System is no longer functioning within the bounds of neurophysiology as evolved in mammals for the purposes of evaluating and selecting, reinforcing, or rewarding behaviors such as foraging/appetite, procreation/reproduction, or child-rearing in settings of which environmental reward/feedback are critical to evolutionary success.

2.2 Conserved Homology

Homologous structures are conserved across species with a structural correspondence and have been derived from a common ancestor with a similar evolutionary or developmental origin [14–16]. However, homologous structures may not perform identical

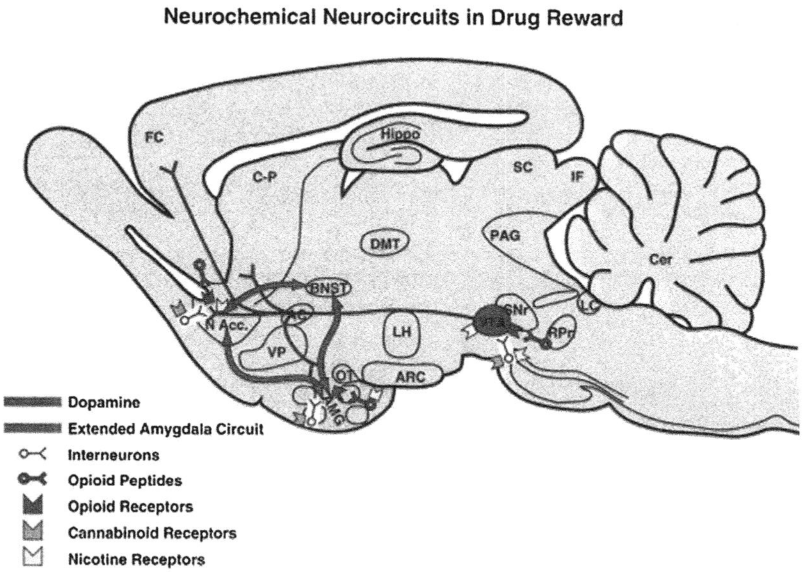

Figure 2 Neurochemical neurocircuits in drug reward. Sagittal view through a representative rodent brain illustrating pathways and selected receptor systems implicated in the acute reinforcing actions of drugs of abuse. Cocaine and amphetamines activate the release of dopamine in the nucleus accumbens and amygdala via direct actions on dopamine terminals. Opioids activate opioid receptors in the ventral tegmental area, nucleus accumbens, and amygdala via direct actions on interneurons. Opioids facilitate the release of dopamine in the nucleus accumbens via an action either in the ventral tegmental area or the nucleus accumbens but also are hypothesized to activate elements independent of the dopamine system. Alcohol activates γ-aminobutyric acid-A ($GABA_A$) receptors in the ventral tegmental area, nucleus accumbens, and amygdala via either direct actions at the $GABA_A$ receptor or through the indirect release of GABA. Alcohol is hypothesized to facilitate the release of opioid peptides in the ventral tegmental area, nucleus accumbens, and central nucleus of the amygdala. Alcohol facilitates the release of dopamine in the nucleus accumbens via an action either in the ventral tegmental area or the nucleus accumbens. Nicotine activates nicotinic acetylcholine receptors in the ventral tegmental area, nucleus accumbens, and amygdala, either directly or indirectly, via actions on interneurons. Nicotine also may activate an opioid peptide release in the nucleus accumbens or amygdala independent of the dopamine system. Cannabinoids activate cannabinoid CB_1 receptors in the ventral tegmental area, nucleus accumbens, and amygdala via direct actions on interneurons. Cannabinoids facilitate the release of dopamine in the nucleus accumbens via an action either in the ventral tegmental area or in the nucleus accumbens but also are hypothesized to activate elements independent of the dopamine system. Endogenous cannabinoids may interact with postsynaptic elements in the nucleus accumbens involving dopamine and/or opioid peptide systems. The blue arrows represent the interactions within the extended amygdala system hypothesized to have a key role in psychostimulant reinforcement. AC, anterior commissure; AMG, amygdala; ARC, arcuate nucleus; BNST, bed nucleus of the stria terminalis; Cer, cerebellum; C-P, caudate-putamen; DMT, dorsomedial thalamus; FC, frontal cortex; Hippo, hippocampus; IF, inferior colliculus; LC, locus coeruleus; LH, lateral hypothalamus; N Acc., nucleus accumbens; OT, olfactory tract; PAG, periaqueductal gray; RPn, reticular pontine nucleus; SC, superior colliculus; SNr, substantia nigra pars reticulata; VP, ventral pallidum; VTA, ventral tegmental area. *Reproduced with permission from Koob, Clinical Neuroscience Research, Volume 5, Issues 2–4, 2005, 89–101.*

Table 4 Drug Classes of Concern with Abused/Scheduled Representative Examples. A listing of both drug classes of concern with respect to abuse liability assessment (as identified in regulatory guidances) and representative examples of those drug classes that are abused and/or scheduled by the US Drug Enforcement Agency (DEA)

Drug Class of Concern	Abused and/or Scheduled Drugs
Monoamine uptake inhibitors and CNS stimulants (see Note 1)	Amphetamine, cocaine, MDMA, modafinil, methylphenidate, some "bath salts," phenylethylamines
Anxiolytics and sedatives (see Note 2)	Alprazolam, diazepam, lorazepam, temazepan, phenobarbital, zolpidem, zopiclone, GHB, ethanol (abused though not scheduled)
NMDA antagonists	Ketamine, PCP
Cannabinoids	Marihuana, cannabis, Δ9-THC, CP-47497, JWH018, "bath salts"
Nicotine-like	Tobacco products, nicotine delivery systems (abused though not scheduled)
Opioids	Morphine, hydrocodone, diphenoxylate, codeine, fentanyl, methadone, oxycodone, propoxyphene
Other and/or novel pharmacological classes (see Note 3)	Pentazocine, ketamine, LSD, DOET, psilocybin, lorcaserin testosterone, stanozolol Ramelteon (not scheduled; not abused; example of novel first-in-class therapeutic in 2005)

ADHD = attention deficit hyperactivity disorder; CNS = central nervous system; DOET = dimethoxy-ethylamphetamine; GHB = gamma hydroxybutyrate; LSD = lysergic acid diethylamide; MDMA = XTC, ecstasy, methylenedioxy-methylamphetamine; NMDA = *N*-methyl-D-aspartic acid (or *N*-methyl-D-aspartate); PCP = phencyclidine; SSRI = selective serotonin reuptake inhibitors; THC = tetrahydrocannabinol.
Note 1: therapeutic classes include appetite suppressants and medicinal products for ADHD.
Note 2: includes benzodiazepines, barbiturates, and other sedative/hypnotics.
Note 3: includes sigma (σ) receptor, serotonin (5-HT) receptors (too numerous to elucidate), and anabolic steroids; may include any first-in-class therapeutic with a novel mechanism of action (e.g., melatonin receptors in 2005).

functions in each species, though a common ancestral origin can be identified. In mammals, it is known that the Reward System is highly conserved across species. This conservation allows for the high level of predictability of the assays described in this text with respect to an abuse liability assessment in animals providing meaningful data regarding the potential human condition. The Reward System has been described sufficiently to indicate its importance in both modernity and in an evolutionary context. To further expand upon the topic of conserved homology of the Reward System, it is relevant to briefly consider nonmammalian species in order to fully appreciate the importance of these phylogenetically ancient neural substrates. A comprehensive review of this topic [14–16], with some well-considered critiques and suggested modifications [14–16], provides strong evidence that the Reward System is conserved across five major vertebrate lineages: mammals, birds, reptiles, amphibians, and fish. These conclusions are based on analyses of brain regions (i.e., 10 of those listed in Tables 2 and 3; all except the PFC and OTu) and utilizing preexisting data on comparative neuroanatomy combined with morphological criteria (brain topographical position), hodology (pathways and interconnections to other brain structures), gene expression (developmental and neurotransmitter genes), and neurochemical profile. Additionally, when data from lesion or stimulation studies were available, brain regions (which were possibly homologous) that regulated similar behavioral processes were considered examples of functional homology. The neurochemical profiles evaluated included the enzymes choline acetyltransferase (of the cholinergic system), dopamine beta hydroxylase (of the [nor]adrenergic systems), and tyrosine hydroxylase (of the dopamine and [nor]adrenaline catecholaminergic systems) plus the transmitters norepinephrine and the enkephalins (of the endogenous opioid system). The assertion of a conserved homology of mesolimbic pathways generally, and the Reward System in particular, across vertebrates may be less certain with regards to fish.

However, the assertion of a strong conserved homology of the Reward System across species with respect to vertebrates including mammals, birds, reptiles, and amphibians is supported by the careful analysis of a large amount of data as well as being considered highly conserved across species of mammals. The homology between mammals and birds has, of course, long been recognized in this classical field of scientific research, given that the early work (see the introduction of this volume) demonstrated that the operant behavior of pigeons responding under a reinforcement schedule provided a method for understanding the effects of reinforcing (and abused) drugs.

2.3 Neuronal Pathways Impinging Upon the Reward System

In general, this text will address the neuroanatomy of pathways [17,18] and is intended for the general audience, not the neuroscientist and/or neuroanatomist, but of necessity a sufficient level of detail is introduced here to allow readers to evaluate the veracity of subsequent conclusions. The purpose is to demonstrate the overlap of nuclei (clusters of cell bodies) and/or projection fields of various neurotransmitter pathways and their associated receptors to the anatomy of the Reward System. To aid the reader in quickly identifying anatomical regions associated with the Reward System, those regions will appear in **bold** font below when describing brain regions and neurotransmitter pathways of importance for an abuse liability assessment during the drug development process. First, to review—the three basic regions of the brain are: 1) the forebrain or prosencephalon composed of both a) the telencephalon with cerebrum (including the cortex [cerebral cortex including the **PFC**] plus deep subcortical structures such as the **amygdala**, basal ganglia, **hippocampus**, and **nucleus accumbens**) and b) the diencephalon (containing multiple thalamic structures); 2) the midbrain or mesencephalon (including the A9 [substantia nigra] and A10 [**ventral tegmental area**] nuclei, plus periaqueductal gray); and 3) the hindbrain or rhombencephalon (containing the pons, cerebellum, and medulla oblongata).

In addition to a basic (and incomplete) neuroanatomical description with respect to nuclei and their respective projection fields, the neuronal pathways relevant to abuse liability assessment will be identified according to the primary neurotransmitter released and associated target receptors. All currently recognized neurotransmitter receptors, regardless of a specific role (known or not) with respect to abuse liability, will be identified according to the IUPHAR (International Union of Basic and Clinical Pharmacology) Committee on Receptor Nomenclature and Drug Classification designations (see http://www.guidetopharmacology.org/GRAC/).

In general, receptors can be classified as either ionotropic or metabotropic. These classifications refer to the mechanism by which the extracellular message or chemical signal (the endogenous ligand or agonist) is "transduced" (the transduction process) across the cellular plasma membrane into an intracellular signal subsequent to the initial recognition (binding) of the agonist and activation of the receptor. An ionotropic receptor is one in which the receptor, during the recognition–transduction–signaling process, results in the flow of ions through a molecular pore after the ion channel is activated (opened). As a group, ionotropic receptors are referred as the LGIC (ligand-gated ion channel) superfamily.

A metabotropic receptor is one in which the signal transduction mechanism involves the generation of a second (intracellular chemical) messenger. For example, following agonist recognition/binding to a cell surface receptor, the activated receptor then binds to a regulatory protein (e.g., G protein), allowing the subsequent activation of an enzyme (e.g., adenylyl cyclase) capable of generating the intracellular second messenger (e.g., cAMP [cyclic adenosine monophosphate]). Many, but not all, metabotropic receptors fall into a single group referred to as the GPCR (G protein-coupled receptor) class.

Of the five monoaminergic neurotransmitter systems known, three are of primary importance (dopamine, norepinephrine, and serotonin) and another of potential significance (histamine) that will be covered briefly, but the last (epinephrine) will not be discussed due to the limited distribution of neurons in the brain that have no significant projections to the Reward System, despite some data suggesting a possible role in reward-seeking behavior.

2.3.1 Dopamine

The DA (dopamine) pathway is one of the catecholaminergic (chemical) classes of monoaminergic systems [19]. The important features of the dopaminergic pathways are presented at http://www.cnsforum.com/imagebank/section/Normal_brain/default.aspx. Seven DA pathways have been identified in the central nervous system (CNS). The two most important pathways, relative to a discussion of the Reward System, are those cell bodies of dopaminergic neurons that are located in the A9 (substantia nigra) and the A10 (**ventral tegmental area [VTA]**) regions. The A9 neurons are most well-known due to their projection to the **striatum** (or caudate-putamen) of the basal ganglia and are referred to as the nigrostriatal pathway, which has been linked to various disorders (e.g., Parkinson's Disease). However, with respect to the neurochemistry of abuse liability, the

Table 5 Dopaminergic Receptors. A listing of dopaminergic receptor families, specific receptor subtypes within each family, and associated signal transduction mechanisms

Family	Receptors	Comment
D_1-like	D_1, D_5	Adenylyl cyclase (↑ cAMP)
D_2-like	D_2, D_3, D_4	Adenylyl cyclase (↓ cAMP)

A10 or **VTA** neurons are of more importance. The **VTA** neurons project (via the MFB) to the **NAc** and related **limbic** regions, establishing the **mesolimbic** DA pathways, as well as to the **PFC**, establishing the **mesocortical** DA pathways. DA neurons project to the **amygdala, lateral septum**, and **hippocampus**. Additionally, there are some DA projections to regions of the **thalamus**, though the cell bodies lie in the A14 region (not the VTA-A10 region).

Early studies exploring the reward pathway demonstrated such a profound role for the limbic and cortical DA innervation that the neural substrates of reward were once referred to as the Mesolimbic Dopamine Reward System or the Mesocorticolimbic Dopamine Reward System. However, it is known that many other neurotransmitter systems play roles in the pleasure-seeking, cue-response-reward mechanisms of the brain as well as possessing important roles in abuse, tolerance, dependence, and addiction. Therefore a more inclusive and conservative approach would be to refer to these neural pathways more generically as the Reward System.

The metabotropic DA receptors are part of the GPCR class. The subtypes of DA receptors fall into two categories: the D_1-like and D_2-like families. Of the five receptor subtypes, the D_1 and D_2 receptors are the most abundant. After DA binding, the signal transduction step for D_1-like receptors involves G protein coupling to activate the enzyme adenylyl cyclase, thus increasing concentrations of the intracellular second messenger cAMP. In contrast, the D_2-like family, via an inhibitory G protein, inhibits adenylyl cyclase and decreases cAMP (see Table 5).

2.3.2 Norepinephrine

The NE (norepinephrine) pathway is another of the catecholaminergic classes of monoaminergic systems, and the neurotransmitter has also been referred to historically as noradrenaline [20]. Thus the pathway is typically referred to as the noradrenergic system. The features of importance of the noradrenergic pathways are presented at http://www.cnsforum.com/imagebank/section/Normal_brain/default.aspx. The cell bodies of noradrenergic neurons are located in multiple locations, with the A6 nuclei of the locus coeruleus being of importance with respect to abuse liability. The locus coeruleus projects to the **amygdala**, cerebral cortex (including the **PFC**), **hippocampus**, **septum**, and **thalamus**.

Due to historical precedence, in which two chemically related transmitters were identified by different names, common current vernacular includes both the use of

Table 6 Adrenoceptors. A listing of adrenergic receptor families, specific receptor subtypes within each family, and associated signal transduction mechanisms with comments on defining characteristics

Family	Receptors	Comment
α_1	α_{1A}, α_{1B}, α_{1D}	Postsynaptic Potency: NE > epinephrine PLC (↑ IP_3/DAG)
α_2	α_{2A}, α_{2B}, α_{2C}	Presynaptic Potency: epinephrine > NE Adenylyl cyclase (↓ cAMP)
β	β_1, β_2, β_3	Postsynaptic Potency: variable Adenylyl cyclase (↑ cAMP)

adrenaline/noradrenaline as well as of epinephrine/norepinephrine pairs of terms. Thus, even if "NE" is the term used to refer to the neurotransmitter, as in this text, the receptors that are activated by these two transmitters are commonly termed "adrenergic" receptors. The metabotropic adrenoceptors are part of the GPCR class for which signal transduction may involve either adenylyl cyclase or phospholipase C (PLC). Stimulation (or inhibition) of adenylyl cyclase leads to an increase (or decrease) of cAMP. Similarly, stimulation of PLC can lead to the increase in the second messengers IP_3 (inositol trisphosphate) and DAG (diacylglycerol). As shown in Table 6, the two subtypes of adrenoceptors fall into two categories: the alpha (α) and beta (β) adrenergic families (and subfamilies).

2.3.3 Serotonin (5-HT)

The serotonin pathway is another monoaminergic system [21,22]. The neurotransmitter is also referred to by its chemical structure 5-hydroxytryptamine or 5-HT. The core features of importance of the serotonergic pathways are presented graphically at http://www.cnsforum.com/imagebank/section/Normal_brain/default.aspx. The cell bodies of 5-HT neurons are located in the caudal raphe nuclei and the rostral raphe nuclei. Of these two nuclei, the rostral one (in the region of the midbrain and pons [hindbrain]) is of relevance to abuse liability as these neurons project (via the MFB [as the DA neurons]) to almost the entire cortex (including the **PFC**) as well as the **hippocampus** and **thalamus**.

The subtypes of 5-HT receptors fall into seven classes. Most serotonergic receptors (Table 7) are part of the metabotropic GPCR family [21]. One exception is the ionotropic 5-HT_3 class [22]. Most 5-HT receptors (except 5-ht 1e and 5-ht 5a/5b) mediate functional responses.

2.3.4 Indirect Agonists, Transmitter Releasers, and Reuptake Inhibitors

As indicated in Tables 1 and 4, one concern with respect to abuse liability assessment is those drugs with a mechanism of action called "uptake inhibitors." Once a

Table 7 Serotonergic Receptors. A listing of 5-HT (serotonin) receptor classes, specific receptor subtypes within each class, and associated signal transduction mechanisms with comments on defining characteristics

5-HT class	Receptors	Comment
1	**5-HT_{1A}, 5-HT_{1B}, 5-HT_{1D}, 5-ht_{1e}, 5-HT_{1F}** Note: 5-HT_{1A} receptor targeted by the nonbenzodiazepine anxiolytic buspirone	Note: lower case "ht" indicates protein has not yet attained receptor status due to lack of a robust protein-mediated response Adenylyl cyclase (↓ cAMP); plus 5-HT_{1A} activates G-protein-gated inwardly rectifying K^+ (GIRK) channel
2	**5-HT_{2A}, 5-HT_{2B}, 5-HT_{2C}** Note: some hallucinogens display "biased agonism" at 5-HT_{2A} receptors Note: lorcaserin: agonist displaying ~15-fold selectivity for 5-HT_{2C} over 5-HT_{2A} Note: reciprocal interaction of 5-HT_{2A} and glutamate receptor ($mGluR_2$) in cerebral cortex; the activation of $mGluR_2$ inhibits 5-HT_{2A} receptor function when activated by hallucinogenic (e.g., LSD) but not nonhallucinogenic 5-HT_{2A} agonists	↑ hydrolysis of inositol phosphates and elevated cytosolic calcium; plus other transduction pathways apparent (e.g., PI3K/Akt and ERK)
3	**5-HT_{3A}, 5-HT_{3AB}** 5-HT_{3A} = homomeric (subunit 5-HT3A) 5-HT_{3AB} = heteromeric (subunits 5-HT3A and 5-HT3B) Note: there are close structural relationships between 5-HT_3 and nicotinic acetylcholine and $GABA_A$ receptors	Ionotropic LGIC receptor complex with 5 subunits Inwardly rectifying current; permeability to divalent cations Subunit 5-HT3A forms a functional homomeric receptor; subunits (5-HT3B, 5-HT3C, 5-HT3D, 5-HT3E) do not form functional homomeric receptors but do form heteromeric receptors with the 5-HT3A subunit
4	**5-HT_4**	Adenylyl cyclase (↑ cAMP)
5	**5-ht_{5a}, 5-ht_{5b}**	Note: lower case "ht" indicates protein has not attained receptor status
6	**5-HT_6** Note: selectively expressed in the CNS	Adenylyl cyclase (↑ cAMP)
7	**5-HT_7**	Adenylyl cyclase (↑ cAMP) Note: other transduction pathways (e.g., ERK)
Potential orphan	**5-HT_{1P}**	

monoaminergic (DA, NE, and 5-HT) neurotransmitter is released into the synaptic cleft from a nerve terminal under normal physiological conditions, the transmitters continue to activate (via recognition/binding) their respective receptors until the neurotransmitters are removed from the local environment [18]. Removal (for DA, NE, and 5-HT) occurs via transporter proteins located on the presynaptic membrane that are responsible for the reuptake of the neurotransmitter prior to subsequent storage into vesicles for possible future reuse (or the transmitter can be subjected to intracellular metabolism). The reuptake and storage allows for the future reuse of the transmitter and thereby decreases the cellular metabolic demands since the de novo synthesis of the new transmitter is not required. Certain drugs can alter the cycle of synthesis, storage (into intracellular vesicles), action potential, release (to the synaptic cleft), and reuptake in a fashion such that excessive amounts of neurotransmitter (relative to normal physiological conditions) produce excessive nonphysiological levels of monoaminergic receptor activation. Thus, while drugs that bind directly to the receptors of neurotransmitter systems are pertinent to abuse liability assessment, so too are drugs that *indirectly* activate neurotransmitter receptors. Drugs that directly bind and activate a neurotransmitter receptor are referred to as *direct* agonists. Drugs that do *not* bind directly to neurotransmitter receptors, but do enhance the activation of those receptors via increased synaptic levels of endogenous neurotransmitters, are referred to as *indirect* agonists. Indirect agonists can act through a variety of mechanisms: 1) by causing a nonphysiological release of the newly synthesized neurotransmitter from the intracellular pool (not yet stored in vesicles); 2) by causing a nonphysiological release of the neurotransmitter stored in vesicles (otherwise waiting for an action potential to precipitate physiologically mediated release); and 3) by inhibiting/blocking the reuptake of the neurotransmitter released into the synaptic cleft and preventing the normal termination of action of the transmitter. One key characteristic of the first two potential mechanisms of indirect agonist action is the fact that, under pharmacological (i.e., nonphysiological) conditions, the transporter that normally moves a transmitter *from* the extracellular space *to* the intracellular presynaptic space can be induced to work *in reverse*, effectively moving (or releasing) the neurotransmitter *into* the extracellular (synaptic) space. It is also possible, under pharmacological conditions, to cause the release of the neurotransmitter from its vesicular storage compartment into the presynaptic nerve terminal cytoplasm, which can then be released into the synaptic cleft. The normal physiological binding of the storage vesicle to the intracellular presynaptic membrane can also be abnormally accentuated, producing a "normal" release from the vesicle directly into the extracellular space of the synapse. Lastly, a drug can also be a substrate for the reuptake mechanism. In such cases, instead of removing the neurotransmitter from the extracellular space, the transport protein removes ("takes up") the indirect agonist, while allowing the endogenous transmitter to remain at higher than normal levels in the synapse.

Abused drugs that work via one or more of these mechanisms include the amphetamine related class of drugs, cocaine, MDMA, etc. Few drugs are highly specific and

Table 8 SLC6 Neurotransmitter Transporter Family: Monoamine Transporter Subfamily. A listing of the monoaminergic subfamily of solute carrier 6 (SLC6) transporters, and associated neurotransmitter for each reuptake transporter (carrier) subtype with comments on specific subfamily identification and a unique substrate characteristic

Transmitter	Reuptake Transporter	Comment
Norepinephrine (NE)	NET (norepinephrine transporter) Stoichiometry-1 norepinephrine: 1 Na^+: 1 Cl^-	SLC6A2 Substrate: amphetamine
Dopamine (DA)	DAT (dopamine transporter) Stoichiometry-1 dopamine: 1-2 Na^+: 1 Cl^-	SLC6A3 Substrate: amphetamine
Serotonin (5-HT)	SERT (serotonin transporter) Stoichiometry-1 serotonin: 1 Na^+: 1 Cl^- (in): 1 K^+ (out)	SLC6A4 Substrate: MDMA (XTC)

therefore poorly differentiate between the reuptake transporters for DA, NE, and 5-HT. However, in general, there are some drugs that belong to a class that is more specific to the 5-HT transporter, referred to as selective serotonin reuptake inhibitors (SSRIs). An example of the distribution of cocaine binding sites in the brain is presented graphically at a National Institute on Drug Abuse (NIDA)-sponsored Website: http://www.drugabuse.gov/publications/teaching-packets/brain-actions-cocaine-opiates-marijuana/section-iii-introduction-to-drugs-abuse-cocaine-opiat-0.

The monoamine transporters [23] are a subfamily that, along with the gamma-aminobutyric acid [24] and glycine [25] (as well as dietary neutral amino acid) subfamilies, comprise the solute carrier family of transporters (designated SLC6; see Table 8) as one of 53 transporter families of the superfamily of solute carriers (SLC). The monoamine transporters are technically cotransporters, as they are sodium- (and sometimes chloride-) dependent neurotransmitter transporters, requiring the presence of ions for transmitter reuptake. The cotransport mechanism is one reason that under nonphysiological conditions the transporters can be forced to "run backwards" (causing transmitter release instead of reuptake).

2.3.5 Histamine

The histamine pathway is the fourth, and last, of the monoaminergic systems to be considered [26–28]. Commonly used over-the-counter antihistamines are known to cause slight-to-mild sedation that in some instances may be a "desired" effect and/or produce minimal "reward" to the user. Additionally, there is evidence to suggest misuse/abuse of some antihistamines by humans and evidence that some (e.g., diphenhydramine, tripelennamine)—but not all—antihistamines produce reinforcement in an animal self-administration model. However, typically histaminergic drugs (agonists or antagonists) are not known to fall into the category of "highly abused" or "highly addictive" (though some variance must be allowed with such statements for the individual proclivities of

Table 9 Histaminergic Receptors. A listing of histamine receptor subtypes and associated signal transduction mechanisms

Subtype	Comment
H_1	PLC (↑ IP_3/DAG) Ca^{2+} mobilization
H_2	Adenylyl cyclase (↑ cAMP)
H_3 (autoreceptor)	Adenylyl cyclase (↓ cAMP)
H_4 (not found in brain)	Intracellular Ca^{2+} mobilization ↑ MAP kinase activity

any one human). For these and other reasons, during a DALA of a potential novel therapeutic agent, any interaction with the histaminergic system should be considered and, if necessary, properly evaluated.

The cell bodies of histamine neurons are located in the tuberomammillary nucleus. These neurons project to almost the entire cortex (including the **PFC**) as well as to the **amygdala, septum**, and **thalamus,** plus to the dorsal raphe (the location of 5-HT neuron cell bodies) and the locus coeruleus (the location of NE neuron cell bodies). There are four subtypes of metabotropic histamine receptors—H_1 to H_4, as shown in Table 9.

2.3.6 Gamma-aminobutyric Acid

GABA (gamma-aminobutyric acid) is the major inhibitory amino acid neurotransmitter in the brain [24,29,30]. It has been estimated that 50% of the inhibitory synapses in the brain are GABA-mediated and "…it is probable that most if not all neurons in the brain are contacted by GABAergic fibers" [29]. Core features of the gabaergic pathway are presented at http://www.cnsforum.com/imagebank/section/Normal_brain/default.aspx. Though technically an amino acid, it should be noted that (unlike alpha-amino acids) GABA is not incorporated into proteins. GABA is a neurotransmitter with widespread innervation throughout the brain and includes both projection neurons from numerous locations (too numerous to elucidate here) as well as neurons functioning on a local basis following release from interneurons (not projecting long distances), which makes this transmitter system quite ubiquitous. Gabaergic inhibition via receptors is present throughout the CNS, including regions such as the **hippocampus** and cerebral cortex, including the **PFC**. Gabaergic neurons in the **NAc** constitute a portion of the projection output signal of this limbic region. Additionally, GABA interneurons are extremely abundant, with very few areas of the brain being devoid of them. GABA interneurons are found in limbic regions such as the **amygdala**. The two subtypes of GABA receptors include the ionotropic $GABA_A$ [31] and the metabotropic $GABA_B$ [32] families.

$GABA_A$ receptors (see Table 10) are part of the LGIC family that includes 5-HT_3 and nicotinic cholinergic receptors. $GABA_A$ receptors are typically heteromeric pentamers of four transmembrane subunits that form an anion (Cl^-) selective channel. The

Table 10 Gabaergic Receptors. A listing of GABA (gamma-aminobutyric acid) receptor families and associated subunit families with associated signal transduction mechanisms and defining characteristics

Family	Subunits	Comment
$GABA_A$	**8 Families (19 members)** Alpha (α1 to α6) Beta (β1 to β3) Gamma (γ1 to γ3) Delta (δ) Epsilon (ε) Theta (θ) Pi (π) Rho (ϱ1 to ϱ3)	Ionotropic LGIC Heteromeric pentamer ↑ Cl^- conductance
$GABA_B$	**2 Subunits** $GABA_{B1}$, $GABA_{B2}$ *4 Auxiliary proteins* KCTD8, KCTD12, kcdt12b, KCTD 16	Metabotropic GPCR Heterodimer: 1:1 stoichiometry Presynaptic: ↓ Ca^{2+} conductance Postsynaptic: ↑ K^+ conductance Adenylyl cyclase effect: variable KCTD proteins associate as tetramers

KCTD = potassium channel tetramerization domain.

19 subunits (of the eight subunit families) include the alpha (α1 to α6), beta (β1 to β3), gamma (γ1 to γ3), delta (δ), epsilon (ε), theta (θ), pi (π), and rho (ϱ1 to ϱ3) subunits. Many $GABA_A$ receptor subtypes contain α-, β-, and γ-subunits. Eleven naturally occurring $GABA_A$ receptors have been identified (i.e., α1β2γ2, α1βγ2, α3βγ2, α4βγ2, α4β2δ, α4β3δ, α5βγ2, α6βγ2, α6β2δ, α6β3δ, and ϱ). However, the largest population of receptors in the CNS is the heteromeric α1β2γ2. The neurotransmitter GABA binds at the α/β interface while the α/γ (and possibly α/β) interface creates the benzodiazepine site. Benzodiazepines act as allosteric modulators binding on the receptor protein at a site distinct from the recognition/binding site of GABA and which may have full agonist, partial agonist, inverse agonist, or antagonist activity at the $GABA_A$ receptor. Other terms used to refer to this receptor include the "benzodiazepine chloride ion channel complex" or the "benzodiazepine chloride ionophore complex," among others.

The metabotropic (GPCR) $GABA_B$ receptors are heterodimers composed of the subunits $GABA_{B1}$ and $GABA_{B2}$ and are widespread within the CNS. Functionality is modulated by auxiliary KCTD (potassium channel tetramerization domain) proteins 8, 12, 12b, and 16 that associate as tetramers to the $GABA_{B2}$ subunit to modulate both kinetic and pharmacological properties of the receptor. There is little evidence that this receptor per se plays a significant role in producing an abuse scenario, though there is some evidence that the receptor may play a role in modulating or diminishing the abuse of certain abused drugs [33].

Table 11 Ionotropic Glutamatergic Receptors. A listing of ionotropic families of LGIC (ligand-gated ion channel) receptors of glutamate with subunits, associated signal transduction mechanisms, and defining characteristics

Family	Subunits	Comment
NMDA	**7 Subunits** GluN1, GluN2A, GluN2B, GluN2C, GluN2D, GluN3A, GluN3B	Na^{+} and K^{+} ion conductance Ca^{2+} ion conductance Functional receptors from heteromers only GluN1 and GluN2A receptors require both glutamate and glycine binding for function
AMPA	**4 Subunits** GluA1, GluA2, GluA3, GluA4	Na^{+} and K^{+} ion conductance Ca^{2+} ion conductance IF no Glu2 subunit present Functional receptors from either homo- or hetero-oligomers
Kainate	**5 Subunits** GluK1, GluK2, GluK3, GluK4, GluK5	Na^{+} and K^{+} ion conductance Cl^{-} conductance IF GluK2 present Functional receptors from either homo- or hetero-oligomers of GluK1, GluK2, or GluK3 GluK4 and GluK5 expressed individually form high-affinity binding sites without function but can form heteromers with GluK1–3
Orphan	**2 Subunits** GluD1, GluD2	Do not form functional receptors either as homo- or hetero-oligomers with other subunits GluD2 subunits bind D-serine and glycine

2.3.7 Glutamate

Glutamate (Glu; glutamic acid) is the major excitatory amino acid transmitter in the brain [18,29]. Unlike GABA, glutamate is incorporated into proteins (with the designation Glu or E) and has important roles in cellular metabolism. The Glu pathways are presented graphically at http://www.cnsforum.com/imagebank/section/Normal_brain/default.aspx. Neuronal cell bodies utilizing glutamate as their transmitter are distributed broadly throughout the CNS and include areas such as the neocortex (projecting to the **VTA**, **amygdala**, **NAc**, and **olfactory tubercle**), **hippocampus**, and **VTA** (projecting to the **PFC**, to the rostrocaudal extent of the **ventral palidum**, plus the **olfactory tubercle**, **NAc** and **amygdala** [38]). Glutamate receptors include both ionotropic [34] (Table 11) and metabotropic [35] (Table 12) subtypes [30,36–41]. Most glutamate signaling is via the ionotropic glutamate receptors that are subdivided into three groups: NMDA (*N*-methyl-D-aspartate); AMPA (α-amino-3-hydroxy-5-methyl-4-isoxazoleproprionic acid); and kainate receptors. A high degree of receptor heterogeneity exists within each group due to both homo- and hetero-oligomeric assembly from 19 distinct subunits to form a cation-selective tetramer.

There are also eight metabotropic (GPCR) glutamate receptors ($mGlu_1$ to $mGlu_8$) that are classified into three groups (I to III) which further modulate both excitatory and inhibitory neurotransmission as well as neurotransmitter release.

Table 12 Metabotropic Glutamatergic Receptors. A listing of metabotropic groups of GPCR (G protein-coupled receptors) of glutamate and associated signal transduction mechanisms

Group	Receptors	Comment
I	$mGlu_1$, $mGlu_5$	PLC (↑ IP_3/DAG)
II	$mGlu_2$, $mGlu_3$	Adenylyl cyclase (↓ cAMP)
III	$mGlu_4$, $mGlu_6$, $mGlu_7$, $mGlu_8$	Adenylyl cyclase (↓ cAMP)

2.3.8 Acetylcholine

ACh (acetylcholine) is a transmitter with widespread projections throughout the brain (and the periphery) as well as a neurotransmitter functioning in the brain on a local basis following its release from the interneurons (not projecting long distances), which makes this transmitter system quite ubiquitous [18,29,42].The cell bodies of ACh-releasing neurons that have projections to other brain areas are found in the medial septum (Ch1 group), the vertical and horizontal diagonal bands (Ch2 and Ch3), and the Meynert nucleus (Ch4), which send projections to the entire cerebral cortex (including the **PFC**, **hippocampus**, and **amygdala**).The cholinergic neurons from the Meynert nucleus, the substantia innominata, plus the diagonal band collectively reside in the basal forebrain. The **PFC** is the only cortical region in rodents and primates that is known to project back to the basal forebrain both directly and indirectly (through the **NAc**). Other cholinergic neurons are found in the Ch5 (laterodorsal tegmental nucleus) and the Ch6 (pedunculopontine nucleus) cell groups, both of which project to the **thalamus**. Additionally, cholinergic interneuron projecting locally within a brain region can be found in the **NAc**, **olfactory tubercle**, and locus coeruleus (the location of NE neuron cell bodies).

The postsynaptic receptors of the cholinergic system in the brain (as well as the periphery) include both muscarinic [43–45] and nicotinic [46] types, which are presented at http://www.cnsforum.com/imagebank/section/Dementia_Cholinergic/default.aspx. Ionotropic nicotinic receptors (nAChR) are of importance with respect to potential abuse. Nicotinic cholinergic receptors (Table 13), which are part of an LGIC family that includes 5-HT_3 and $GABA_A$ receptors, are pentamers composed of a combination of 16 (out of 17) possible different mammalian subunits (α1–10, β1–4, γ, δ, and ε), as the α8 subunit is avian, not mammalian. Muscles and neurons express different receptor types, distinguished and identified by the subunit composition, resulting in the classification of muscle-type (α1β1γδ-nAChR) and neuronal-type (α4β2- and α7-nAChR) receptors. Note that α7-nAChR is a homopentamer, while other receptors are heteromers. It is believed that two α subunits, and thus two agonist binding sites, must be present for a functional receptor and that both sites must be bound by an agonist for optimal channel opening. Unlike the muscle-type nAChR, the subunit stoichiometry of the neuronal-type nAChR is uncertain, though subunit composition does affect function. The (α4β2)2α4 nAChR (having three alpha subunits) gains a third binding site (which alters function) in contrast to the (α4β2)2β2 nAChR, which only has two

Table 13 Cholinergic Receptors. A listing of ACh (acetylcholine) receptor families and associated subunit families or receptor subtypes with associated signal transduction mechanisms and defining characteristics

Receptor Family	Subunits or Receptor Subtype	Comment
nAChR	**5 Subunit families (members)** Alpha (α1 to α10) Beta (β1 to β4) Gamma (γ) Delta (δ) Epsilon (ε)	Ionotropic LGIC Postsynaptic effect: inhibitory or excitatory ↑ cation (Na^+, K^+) conductance
mAChR	**Receptor subtype** M_1, M_2, M_3, M_4, M_5	Metabotropic GPCR; plus other non-G protein mechanisms M_1, M_3, M_5 couple with Gq/11-proteins and activate PLC (↑ IP_3/DAG) M_1: ↓ K^+ and ↓ Ca^{2+} conductance M_2, M_4 couple with Gi/Go-proteins and inhibit adenylyl cyclase (↓ cAMP) M_2, M_4: ↑ K^+ and ↓ Ca^{2+} conductance

binding sites. In the brain, the most common nAChR composition is the $\alpha4\beta2^*$ (asterisk indicating one or more additional subunits) and $\alpha7$ nAChR. However, the presence of $\alpha6$ and $\beta3$ subunits does occur in catecholaminergic neurons forming the $\alpha6\beta2\beta3^*$ nAChR. Additionally, the $\alpha2$ subunit is more common in the primate brain than the rodent brain.

Though nicotinic receptors are of primary importance with respect to potential abuse, a role for the five metabotropic (GPCR) muscarinic receptors (mAChR) with respect to the hallucinogenic properties of some alkaloid plant extracts should not be dismissed prematurely. Though some plant alkaloid extracts (or other toxins) are capable of producing hallucinations, typically this is not the primary effect of such compounds (unlike true hallucinogens [e.g., LSD]), and hallucinations are typically only produced at very high doses that could arguably be categorized as suprapharmacological and/or subtoxic. The mAChR receptor family is composed of five subtypes, all of which are found in the CNS with differing distribution patterns. Though the mAChR subtypes are sometimes subcategorized according to their specific G protein coupling, this receptor family can couple to multiple signaling pathways. This includes those that are G protein-independent, including activation of PLC (generating IP3 and DAG), producing increases in intracellular calcium. M_2 and M_4 inhibit adenylyl cyclase, thereby decreasing the production of the second messenger cAMP.

2.3.9 Opioids

Historically, the opioid receptors (see Table 14) were identified/hypothesized on the basis of the unique and distinct pharmacological effects observed with a series of drugs chemically related to the analgesic morphine [47]. One receptor was identified based on the in vivo properties of the prototypical drug morphine and another on the in vivo properties of the prototypical drug ketocyclazocine, while a third receptor was identified based on its presence in certain in vitro tissues assays, which included the mouse vas deferens. Eventually, the endogenous ligands of the opioid system were discovered and include the enkephalins (e.g., met- or leu-enkephalin), β-endorphin, and the dynorphins (dynorphin-A and -B, α-neoendorphin), plus two putative ligands (endomorphin-1 and -2) that are present in the brain but are not yet considered endogenous ligands [48,49].

Neurons that release endogenous opioids are widely distributed throughout the central (and peripheral) nervous system. Similarly, the opioid receptors are widely and heterogeneously distributed throughout the brain [50]. The heterotrimeric, metabotropic GPCR targets of the opiate system include the MOP or mu (μ) opioid receptor, the DOP or delta (δ) opioid receptor, and the KOP or kappa (κ) opioid [48]. Additionally, there is a single nonopioid (NOP) branch of this receptor family with a pharmacological profile and effects that are quite distinct from the other receptors that was originally identified as the nociception/orphanin FQ (N/OFQ)-sensitive receptor [48]. An example distribution of opioid binding sites in the brain is presented on the NIDA-sponsored

Table 14 Opioid Receptors. A listing of both the common (Greek) designations and IUPHAR nomenclature for opioid receptor subtypes with associated endogenous ligands, signal transduction mechanisms, and defining characteristics

Greek or IUPHAR (See Note 1)	Endogenous Ligand	Comment
Mu (μ) or MOP (opioid branch)	β-endorphin, enkephalins	From "morphine" Sensitive to naloxone antagonism Couples with Gi/Go-proteins;
Delta (δ) or DOP (opioid branch)	β-endorphin, enkephalins	From (vas) "deferens" Sensitive to naloxone antagonism Couples with Gi/Go-proteins;
Kappa (κ) or KOP (opioid branch)	Dynorphin-A and -B, α-neoendorphin	From "ketocyclazocine" Sensitive to naloxone antagonism Couples with Gi/Go-proteins;
NOP (nonopioid branch)	Nociceptin/orphanin FQ (N/OFQ)	Insensitive to naloxone Pharmacologically distinct from opioid branch

Note 1: terminology considered an interim status utilizing both the widely used, more traditional Greek nomenclature to be used "in addition" to the current IUPHAR proposed nomenclature.

Website: http://www.drugabuse.gov/publications/teaching-packets/brain-actions-cocaine-opiates-marijuana/section-iii-introduction-to-drugs-abuse-cocaine-opiat-6.

The μ receptors are distributed throughout the brain with a high density in regions such as the **thalamus**, caudate putamen, neocortex, **NAc**, and **amygdala** as well as (at a moderate density) in the raphe nuclei (the location of 5-HT neuron cell bodies). The δ receptors are discretely distributed in the CNS, with a density varying from high levels in forebrain structures to relatively low levels in most hindbrain regions. The highest densities are found in olfactory bulb, neocortex, caudate putamen, **NAc**, and **amygdala**, with more moderate density in the **thalamus** and hypothalamus. The κ receptors are located predominantly in the cerebral cortex, **NAc**, and hypothalamus. Lastly, NOP receptors are present in selected regions of the cortex, anterior olfactory nucleus, lateral septum, ventral forebrain, **hippocampus**, hypothalamus, **amygdala**, substantia nigra (the location of the A9 DA neuron cell bodies), **VTA** (the location of the A10 DA neuron cell bodies), and locus coeruleus (the location of the NE neuron cell bodies).

The coupling of μ, δ, and κ receptors to Gi/Go activates intracellular second messenger systems that regulate metabolic enzymes, transcriptional machinery, and ion channels (such as activating K^+ channels and inhibiting Ca^{2+} channels) [48,50]. This can result in decreased neuronal excitability and inhibition of neurotransmitter release. The Gi/o-coupling also produces an inhibition of adenylyl cyclase (decreasing cAMP) and affects enzymes such as phosphatates and kinases. Opioids have predominantly inhibitory effects on cells in the CNS, though disinhibition (of GABA neurons) can lead to "paradoxical" excitation/stimulation.

2.3.10 Cannabinoid

The endogenous ligands of the cannabinoid system include the endocannabinoids anandamide (*N*-arachidonoylethanolamine), *N*-homo-γ-linolenoylethanolamine, *N*-docosatetra-7,10,13,16-enoylethanolamine, and 2-arachidonoylglycerol [51,52]. However, other compounds that may also function as endocannabinoids include *O*-arachidonoylethanolamine (virodhamine), oleamide, *N*-arachidonoyl dopamine, and *N*-oleoyl dopamine.

The metabotropic (GPCR) proteins of the cannabinoid system are CB_1 and CB_2 [51,53,54]. The CB_1 receptor is responsible for the psychoactive effects of Δ^9-tetrahydrocannabinol (Δ^9-THC; found in marihuana) [55–90], plus the receptor has been cloned from rat, mouse, and human tissues and found to have 97–99% amino acid sequence identity across species. An example distribution of cannabinoid binding sites in the brain is presented at an NIDA-sponsored Website: http://www.drugabuse.gov/publications/teaching-packets/brain-actions-cocaine-opiates-marijuana/section-iii-introduction-to-drugs-abuse-cocaine-opia-10. Brain cannabinoid receptor distribution across multiple mammalian species, including human, is conserved and includes areas such as the outflow nuclei of the basal ganglia (the substantia nigra and globus pallidus), ventromedial **striatum**, **hippocampus**, cerebellum, **amygdala**, **thalamus**, and the forebrain cerebral cortex (including the **PFC**). Cannabinoid receptors are present in the mammalian brain at higher levels than most GPCRs. Whole-brain cannabinoid receptor density is comparable to that of Glu and GABA, with some regions similar to that of DA, and greatly exceeding that for neuropeptide receptors. In contrast, the CB_2 receptor is found primarily within tissues of the immune system. Both CB_1 and CB_2 receptors are phylogenetically restricted to the chordate branch of the animal kingdom.

At a molecular level, CB_1 receptors can couple to both Gs and Gi/Go proteins. The Gi/Go-coupling produces an inhibition of adenylyl cyclase (causing decreased cAMP), regulates Ca^{2+} and K^+ ion channel conductance, initiates intracellular Ca^{2+} flux, stimulates MAP (mitogen-activated protein) kinase, and induces immediate early gene expression. At a neuronal level, the primary role of CB_1 receptors is to inhibit the release of excitatory and inhibitory neurotransmitters.

Most CB_2 receptors expressed on immune cells (outside or within the brain) modulate cell migration and cytokine release. CB_2 receptors may be expressed by certain central and peripheral neurons; however, the role of these putative neuronal receptors has not been established and appears to play no major role in the psychotomimetic effects of marihuana or related drugs of abuse.

Endocannabinoids (e.g., anandamide), plant-derived cannabinoids (e.g., Δ^9-THC), and synthetic CB_1/CB_2 agonists (and antagonists) can activate (or block) a non-CB_1, non-CB_2 GPCR, LGIC, and/or nuclear (PPAR) receptors with potencies very similar to their ability to bind CB_1/CB_2 receptors. These "noncannabinoid" receptors mediate actions on Ca^{2+} and K^+ channels as well as receptors of the NMDA, 5-HT_3, and nAChR classes (discussed above with respect to abuse liability assessment).

2.3.11 Sigma Receptors

Like the opioid receptor class, the sigma receptor was first identified via pharmacological tools (drugs producing in vivo responses unique from any other known class) [47,91]. In fact, the sigma receptor was originally misclassified as one of the opioid receptors, and the distinction of this hypothesized receptor was due to the pharmacological response to SKF 10,047 (*N*-allyl-normetazocine), which was different from that of either morphine or ketocyclazocine. Compounds considered prototypical agonists, such as SKF 10,047 and cyclazocine, produced psychotomimetic effects that could not be explained via actions at other opioid receptors. Though these compounds bind to the sigma receptor [92], it is now known that the benzomorphan compounds are also NMDA antagonists, likely explaining in part their unique pharmacological properties [93]. Compounds as different as antihistamines to psychotomimetics to antipsychotics bind to the sigma site. Thus, it is now clear that the sigma receptor was never truly part of the opioid, or any other known, receptor system. In contrast to the opioid receptor system, despite current identification of a unique receptor protein, no clear endogenous ligand has been identified.

Although there is no known "sigma" system at this time, two known sigma receptors are expressed in both the CNS and the periphery and appear to be located in **intracellular** locations [91,94–102]. Sigma receptors are located in the microsomal fraction of nonsynaptic areas of the plasma membrane. According to current (IUPHAR) classifications, the two sigma receptors are identified as the "sigma nonopioid intracellular receptor 1" (σ1) and the σ2 receptor. There is only moderate pharmacological overlap between sigma receptors and known GPCRs (in fact the amino acid sequence is inconsistent with that of a classical GPCR), there is no structural homology to either opioid or neurotransmitter receptors, and clear evidence for the coupling of sigma receptors through known conventional second messenger signaling pathways is largely lacking or inconsistent. Thus, any signal transduction mechanisms through which sigma receptors produce effects have yet to be clearly established, though it appears classical membrane-associated second messenger systems are involved in the effects of sigma receptor activation. However, this apparently occurs via intracellular mechanisms distinct from the known and well-described interactions of membrane-bound receptor systems.

Sigma-1 receptors are concentrated in limbic regions of the brain and distributed within areas including the olfactory bulb, **frontal cortex**, **hippocampus**, **septum**, **thalamus**, **NAc**, hypothalamus, periaqueductal gray, dorsal raphe (the location of 5HT neuron cell bodies), substantia nigra (the location of A9 DA neuron cell bodies), **VTA** (the location of the A10 DA neurons cell bodies), and locus coeruleus (the location of NE neuron cell bodies). Sigma-1 receptor subcellular distribution includes the neuronal perikarya and dendrites, plasma membrane, mitochondrial membrane, and endoplasmic reticulum (ER). It is assumed that σ1 receptors translocate from the ER to plasma and/or nuclear membranes upon activation. Some σ1 ligands have been shown to alter adenylyl cyclase, but as a drug class the effects are inconsistent. There are data supporting a role for σ1 receptor modulation of NMDA-mediated changes in K^+ current in the **hippocampus**. Overall, it appears σ1 receptors are capable of modulating GPCR, ion channels, and other second-messenger systems. With respect to abuse liability, not only are the psychotomimetic effects of σ1 agonists relevant, since multiple drugs of abuse (cocaine, methamphetamine, MDMA, some opioids, PCP) bind to sigma receptors, but also some psychostimulant-mediated effects have been hypothesized to be mediated or modified via the σ1 receptor. The latter is supported by the fact that cocaine binds to σ1, and cocaine-mediated effects on locomotion, behavioral sensitization, conditioned place preference (CPP), gene expression, convulsion, and lethality can be attenuated by the administration of σ1 ligands [97–99]. It is possible that activation of σ1 is important for these short- and long-term effects of psychostimulants. Similarly, some amphetamine- and methamphetamine-mediated effects also appear to be modulated by σ1 ligands.

Sigma-2 receptors are distributed to regions of the brain different than that of the σ1 receptor. The subcellular distribution of σ2 receptors includes the mitochondrial membrane and endoplasmic reticulum (ER), where they appear to regulate Ca^{2+} release from ER stores [103,104]. Modulation of Ca^{2+} stores would be expected to affect neuronal excitability as well as muscle contraction [105]. Sigma-2 (but not σ1) receptors have been implicated in the production of cytotoxicity as well as cellular proliferation and viability. Though less clear than the case for σ1 receptors, σ2 receptors may also modulate some psychostimulant effects as they alter amphetamine-mediated DA release.

2.4 In vitro Ligand Binding

2.4.1 Evaluation of Data: Targets of Potential Concern

In order to fully characterize potential pharmacological activity for a small molecule NCE, during the discovery stage of the process data must be generated to evaluate the unintended, off-target binding of the candidate molecule, in addition to the data on the binding to the intended target molecule plus closely related molecules (receptors, enzymes, etc.). Subsequently, once metabolism is known, during the development process it may also be necessary to generate similar on- and off-target binding data of all potential CNS-active metabolites. With respect to the abuse liability assessment process, it is important to know the relative binding affinities of the NCE to those receptors presented in this volume. It is critical to understand that any evaluation is a reiterative process, which continues as more and more data are collected throughout the development process. It is equally critical to realize that binding alone does not indicate there is "a problem" for the development of the NCE but rather that there are data that need to be placed within context and evaluated throughout development. Binding does not always indicate that there will be a pharmacological effect. If there is a pharmacological effect, then binding (alone) does not (typically) indicate whether the NCE is an agonist, partial agonist, inverse agonist, or antagonist. More data, if deemed appropriate, would be gathered by subsequent separate studies. Eventually, any binding data should be evaluated in the context of the specific off-target receptor function (and relationship to abuse potential), the relative affinity of the NCE (i.e., the degree of radioligand displacement), and the in vitro concentration of the NCE at which displacement occurs in the binding study, which is then combined with knowledge of the therapeutic dose, human plasma levels at a multiple of the therapeutic dose, and the ability of NCE to cross the blood–brain barrier, in order to estimate in humans the peak brain concentration at a therapeutic multiple. Even after such a mathematical approximation, all relevant in vitro data and all in vivo human data (adverse events, etc.) and animal behavioral data (from discovery and toxicology studies) should be incorporated into the final analysis.

Many NCE project team members, not being overly familiar with the scientific background on abuse liability (as presented in this volume), ask a simple question: "What are the ligand binding targets that are of concern in regards to abuse liability assessment?" for which there is no simple answer, and "Can a list be provided of 'all' the ligand binding targets of concern regarding abuse liability assessment?" to assist the novice. A difficult question, but one this volume attempts to address. In 2014, Xie et al. [106] attempted to broadly explore the issue of "which" molecular mechanisms may play some role within

Table 15 Partial List of GPCR Families (Receptor Subtypes) Reportedly Related to Abuse (per the DA-KB Database of Xie et al. [106])

Adenosine [3]	**(nor)adrenergic** [7]	**Cannabinoid** [2]	Cholecystokinin [2]
DA [5]	**GABA$_B$**	**Histamine** [4]	Melanocortin [5]
mAChR [5]	Neurokinin [2]	Neuropeptide [5]	**Nociceptin**
Opioid [3]	**Serotonergic** [12]	**Metabotropic glutamate** [8]	

A list of 15 pertinent GPCR (G protein-coupled receptor) families (with number of receptor subtypes per family), not including transporters or LGIC (ligand-gated ion channel) receptors, that are potentially related to abuse per a chemogenomic analysis approach evaluating which molecular mechanisms participate in abuse liability.
GPCR families identified/discussed in this text are provided in **bold** font; note that nociceptin is discussed in this text with the opioid system (as a nonopioid receptor).

the drug abuse scenario. This has been evaluated by the generation of a centralized "chemogenomics" drug abuse-knowledge base (DA-KB) incorporating data on GPCR proteins and their tissue distribution, side effects of abused drugs, the use of computational algorithms to explore drug abuse targets, drug abuse mechanisms and pathways, plus the polypharmacology of GPCR ligands and GPCR-targeted drug abuse treatments. Additionally, the researchers utilized data on 396 genes previously reported to be related to drug abuse, plus additional genes subsequently identified by NIDA genetics experts. Though as of this writing limited to metabotropic receptors, the resulting "list of drug abuse related GCPRs" is of interest despite the exclusion of transporter proteins and ionotropic receptor mechanisms. The chemogenomics "list" includes 85 drug abuse related GPCRs. It is of interest that 84 (of 85) of these GPCRs are expressed in the **NAc** with a significant number (>55) found throughout the brain in areas such as the **cerebral cortex** and frontal lobe (**presumably including the PFC**), **amygdala**, **thalamus**, and **striatum** as well as the caudate, periaqueductal gray, hypothalamus, dorsal raphe (the location of 5HT neuron cell bodies), substantia nigra (the location of A9 DA neuron cell bodies), **VTA** (the location of the A10 DA neurons cell bodies), and locus coeruleus (the location of NE neuron cell bodies). A partial list of the various GPCRs families (and receptor subtypes) accounting for up to 65 (of 85 total) targets of "drug abuse" are provided in Table 15.

Combining this information on GPCRs related to drug abuse with three transporters (DAT, NET, SERT) plus ionotropic receptors discussed in this text (GABA$_A$, NMDA, two 5-HT$_3$ subtypes, and nAChR) provides a fairly thorough list of molecular targets of potential concern during a DALA.

2.5 In vivo Behavioral Correlates

The sections above have extensively examined the neurochemistry and neuropharmacology of drugs operating on neurotransmission. When assessing whether an NCE is operating upon the CNS, often the first line of study is upon its integrated output: the behavior of the intact organism. One of the simplest behaviors to measure (and yet more difficult to interpret) is locomotor activity. Locomotor activity is amenable to studying direct pharmacology, tolerance and sensitization, and correlates with neurochemical changes in the reward pathways.

2.5.1 Locomotor Activity: General Considerations

There are two broad categories of locomotor activity: induced and spontaneous. An example of induced activity is the rotarod test [107–109] in which animals are trained to walk on a rotating cylinder in order to stay upright (Figure 3). The ability of a drug to disrupt this behavior (measured as time on the cylinder) is often used as an index of ataxia or of sedation, but drugs may operate in other ways as well to disrupt this behavior. For example, alterations in stress [110], attention, kinesthetic/proprioception senses and repeated presentation to the paradigm, and training [111] can impact performance as well.

The remainder of this chapter will focus on spontaneous (i.e., voluntary or "volitional") locomotor activity such as open field behavior that likely reflects a hardwired behavioral sequence directed at exploratory activity [112] and/or foraging. This behavioral sequence can be altered in numerous ways that are described below, but as employed in safety pharmacology, use of automated, quantitative measurement of spontaneous locomotor activity can be an extremely sensitive indicator of drug action and is usually more sensitive to drug effects than the rotarod test [113]. While quantitative locomotor activity assessment is sensitive to drug action, it is not particularly specific in its ability to discriminate from among different classes of drugs. That is, drugs will increase, decrease, produce restricted, repetitive behavior (stereotypy), or have no effects upon locomotor activity. Unlike the rotarod test, the behavior requires no training and can be measured continuously over longer periods of time in this automated test, which allows for the detection of onset, peak, and offset of drug effects within a single session. It is important to consider that not all apparatus configurations or associated software can differentiate between inactivity and stereotypy when evaluating data. While the remainder of the chapter will focus upon spontaneous locomotor activity, it is important to consider that the same principals apply to the rotarod test or other means of assessing coordinated locomotion.

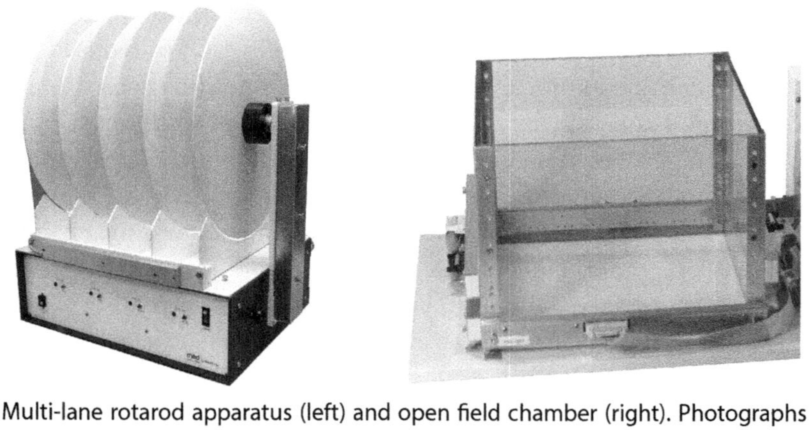

Figure 3 Multi-lane rotarod apparatus (left) and open field chamber (right). Photographs copyright Med Associates, used with permission.

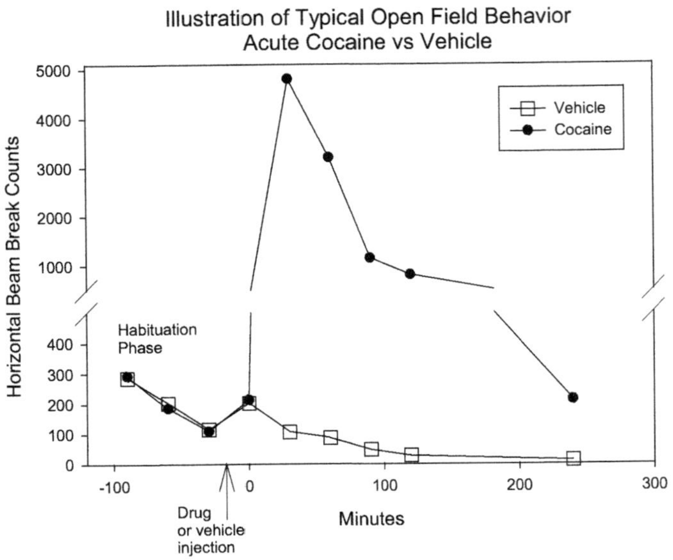

Figure 4 Typical open field behavior following vehicle administration (open squares) and cocaine (filled circles) following a habituation period. *X*-axis: minutes prior to and following drug administration (arrow); *Y*-axis: number of horizontal photobeam breaks—a gross estimate of overall locomotor activity. This number is often converted into distance travelled.

Figure 4 illustrates some fundamentals of locomotor activity and drug effects. When normal, undrugged animals are introduced to a locomotor activity chamber, there is an initial burst of exploratory activity that eventually subsides [114], resulting in a longer duration period of reduced locomotion sometimes referred to as general or nonspecific motor activity. Upon being returned to the apparatus after handling and injection, there is typically an additional spike in activity, which rapidly subsides over minutes under control conditions, and then activity further decreases over the recording period. After psychomotor stimulant administration, such as cocaine, there can be a rather dramatic and sustained increase in locomotor activity. The increase will be most marked when compared to the baseline or vehicle control during the period of reduced (habituated) general or nonspecific locomotor activity in contrast to similar testing during the period of heightened exploratory activity upon initial introduction to the novel environment of the testing paradigm. Conversely, when testing an NCE with sedative properties, such as gabaergic agonist, the experimenter can increase the sensitivity of the test to drug-induced decreases in activity by placing unhabituated animals into the chamber around the T_{max} of the compound. Under these conditions, the drug will reduce the initial exploratory burst and reduce the probability of a floor effect.

If a drug is given repeatedly prior to exposure to the open field assay, its effect can change over time. Figure 5 shows the effects of both acute (from the graph above) and repeated administration of cocaine. Under these conditions, spontaneous locomotion may actually increase prior to drug administration, during the habituation phase of the study.

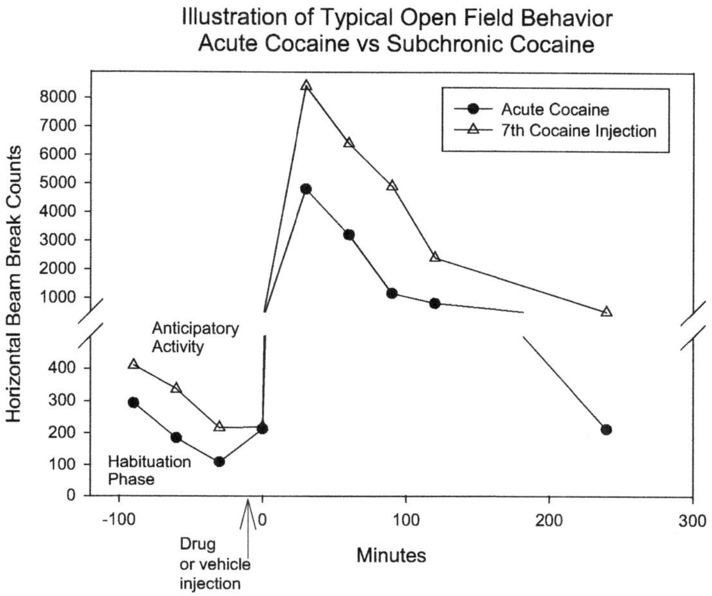

Figure 5 Typical open field behavior following acute cocaine (filled circles) or following the seventh injection of cocaine (open triangles). Other details are as described in the legend for Figure 4.

This phenomenon is referred to commonly as "anticipatory activity." Once the drug is administered repeatedly, both peak response and the area under the curve can increase (sensitization). Tolerance may also occur and would be represented graphically as a downward shifting in peak and area following repeated administration. To optimize the chances of detecting a drug-induced increase in locomotor activity, habituating the animals prior will lower variability.

A final principle is that what goes up must come down. All drugs will decrease locomotor activity at some dose, either through toxicity or through specific high-dose pharmacology, such as the stereotypy, as illustrated in Figure 6.

A very close relationship can be demonstrated between the activation of mesolimbic dopamine neurons and locomotor activity [115], as demonstrated in Figure 7.

This is not to say that all drugs that increase locomotor activity are drugs of abuse, nor that all drugs of abuse will increase locomotor activity. Nor does it mean that decreases in locomotion are a result of "sedative activity." Changes in locomotor activity are simply a flag for further follow-up. Another salient point is that qualitative differences between acute and subchronic administration can be demonstrated. For example, acute mu agonist opioids such as morphine often reduce locomotor activity, but upon repeated administration, tolerance develops to the sedating effects of the drug, unmasking motor stimulant activity [116].

2.5.2 Considerations on Animal Test Systems

Typically, male rats or mice are used for the in vivo efficacy models employed during discovery. Consideration of strain is important if comparison to the potency in the

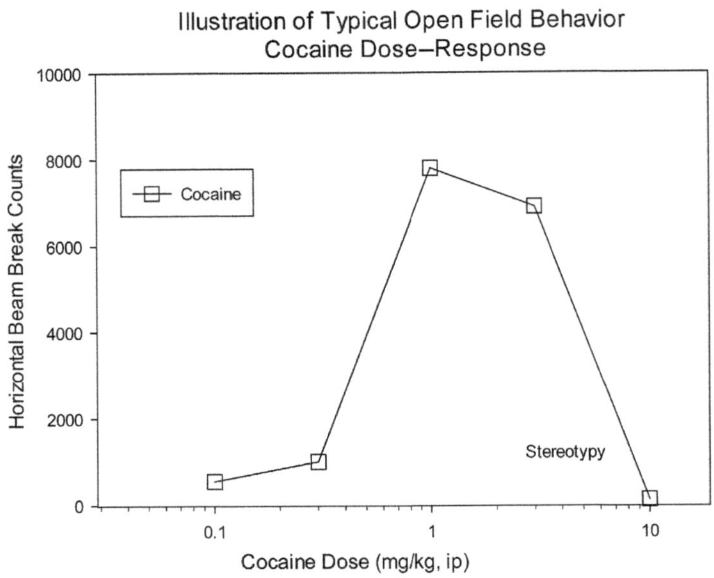

Figure 6 Typical dose–response function for cocaine. Increases in locomotion can occur abruptly or over several orders of magnitude, depending upon the drug administered, but eventually, high-dose behavioral toxicity results in a reduction in locomotion. Other details are as described in the legend for Figure 4.

efficacy models is desired, as different strains can occasionally produce not only potency differences in compounds, but also, although rarely, qualitative differences in drug effect. Wistar rats exhibit less exploratory motor activity than Long–Evans [117] rats. While rarely do safety pharmacologists stray from the use of the standard male rat because of the vast historical database on male animal data, it is important to consider that female rats can and do present qualitative and quantitative differences to the effects of drugs and locomotor activity [118–120]. Female rats tend to be more active than males. Age (and the associated weight) of a rat (e.g., 250 g, 8–9-week-old male) can also impact results in locomotor assessments [121]. In general, younger rats have overall higher levels of locomotor activity. In instances when other species are required for both efficacy and locomotor activity assessment (e.g., due to receptor homology), these methods can be easily adapted to species such as guinea pig [122,123], gerbil [124], zebra fish [125], etc. and are translatable to humans [126].

2.5.3 Considerations on Apparatus

The basic apparatus used to employ locomotor assessments are depicted in Figure 3. For the open field apparatus, photocells are arrayed on all sides of the chamber to assess horizontal activity via breaking the beams when crossed, and vertical activity, such as rearing, can be measured by including a second level of photocell arrays. Beam breaks are

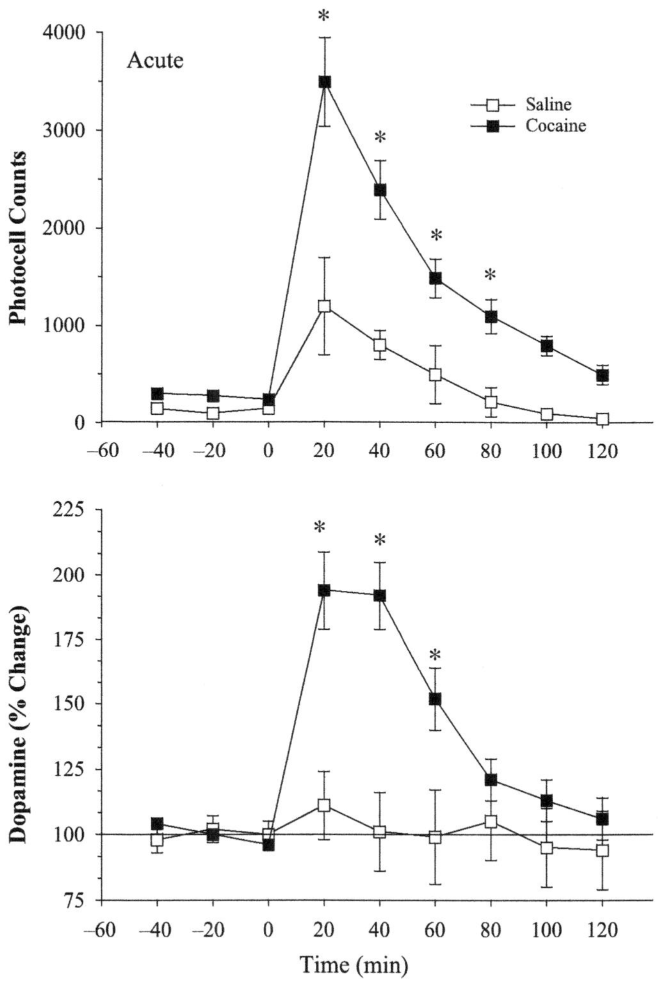

Figure 7 Data from Kalivas and Duffy [115] showing locomotor counts (above) and corresponding changes in dopamine release (below) as measured by a microdialysis probe.

recorded in real time by computers interfaced to the chambers. While the photocell apparatus is standard, there are other methods involving video analysis or use of running wheels that can be as useful and even offer advantages in terms of resolution of behaviors but are not as yet as commonly employed.

In terms of choice of open field apparatus, size matters. An open field which is too large or too small will tend to inhibit exploratory activity. When purchasing equipment, attention to the literature precedent will be useful in keeping to standardization, which will be useful in interlaboratory data comparison. Additionally, containing the open field apparatus in an enclosed, sound-attenuating chamber and cleaning the apparatus between uses are useful in helping to minimize variability.

2.5.4 Considerations on Data Interpretation

As mentioned earlier, increases in locomotion are often considered to be indicative of stimulant activity. However, one must consider that if, for example, a drug may disrupt working memory, it is possible that subsequent prevention of within-session habituation will result in increased locomotor activity [127], which is only an "apparent stimulation." One may interpret decreases in locomotion as indicative of sedation, but other mechanisms decreasing behavior in the open field may include decreases in appetitive behavior or increased anxiety by the drug [128], which may attenuate exploration in a novel environment. Indeed, it is well known that drugs which produce an anxiety-like state (e.g., negative modulators of gabaergic activity such as beta-carboline drugs) result in decreased crossings into the center of the open field arena as well as decreases overall in ambulation and/or freezing behavior [129].

2.5.5 Other Considerations

Table 16 summarizes some of the variables that can affect the behavioral baseline in spontaneous locomotion and consequently the magnitude of the drug-induced behavioral effects [130–133]. Many of these variables can be easily controlled by the experimenter but are often overlooked.

With the above caveats of interpretation in mind, we have attempted to summarize the locomotor effects of classes of drugs of abuse described above in Tables 1 and 4 to allow for a basis of comparison for NCEs that may have CNS activity but may not fall directly into any of the classes listed below (Table 17).

Catecholaminergics. Agents that enhance the effects of dopamine and norepinephrine include cocaine and phenylethylamines, including amphetamines. As demonstrated previously [134], these agents will increase spontaneous locomotion across much of the dose range and produce sensitization upon repeated administration [116]. Stereotypy is generally observed following administration of the highest doses, resulting in an overall decrease in ambulatory activity.

Gabaergics. Benzodiazepines increase the efficacy of GABA at the GABA-A receptor. The net effects of drugs that promote the activity of GABA on locomotion typically result

Table 16 Parameters that Can Affect Open Field Behavior

Lighting	Housing	Emotional state
Unpredicted sounds	Sickness behavior	Drug history
Temperature	Experimenter behavior	Tolerance
Season	Conspecific interactions	Sensitization
Time of day	Apparatus size	Habituation time
Deprivational state	Gender	Dose
Behavioral history	Method of dosing	Dose frequency
Strain	Species	Scent of previous animal

Table 17 Representative Drugs from the Classes Associated with Abuse. A listing of multiple neurotransmitter systems with the associated effect (either increase or decrease) most commonly produced on locomotor activity with representative drug examples for each system

Catecholaminergic ↑	**Gabaergic** ↓	**Serotonergic** ↓	**Cholinergic** ↑	**Opioid** ↓	**Cannabinoid** ↓	**Mixed Activity** ↑
Methamphetamine Cocaine MDPV Amphetamine β-Phenethylamine	Diazepam Phenobarbital GHB Choral Hydrate Ethanol	LSD Mescaline DOM	Muscarinics Nicotine	Oxycodone Morphine Heroin Hydrocodone	Δ^9-THC WIN-55,212	MDMA Tramadol MDPV

↑ Increase in ambulatory activity over most of the dose range.
↓ Decrease in ambulatory activity over the dose range.
DOM = 2,6-dimethoxy-4-methylamphetamine.
GHB = gamma hydroxyl butyric acid (or gamma hydroxyl butyrate).
LSD = lysergic acid diethylamide.
MDMA = 3 4-methylenedioxy-*N*-methamphetamine (Ecstasy; XTC).
MDPV = 3,4- methylenedioxypyrovalerone (MDPV).
Δ^9-THC = delta-9-tetrahydrocannabinol.

in a decrease in locomotor activity at higher doses and occasionally an increase in locomotor activity at lower doses where behavioral disinhibition (if not be masked by sedation) may occur or in which anxiolytic effects are pronounced, leading to a decreased "fear" of exploration. The effects of numerous similar agents are summarized elsewhere [128].

Serotonergics. The drugs of abuse within this class typically stimulate the 5-HT_{2A} receptor, which results in hallucinatory activity in humans. In rats, this can be registered as decreases in locomotor activity [135,136].

Cholinergics. The most notorious drug of abuse in this class is nicotine, and much of its pharmacology is driven by the $\alpha4\beta2$ subtype of the receptor. These agents will stimulate locomotor activity over much of the dose range (e.g., [137–138]).

Opioids. Like gabaergics, over lower doses μ- and δ-agonist opioids, especially after repeated administration, have been shown to stimulate locomotor activity but evoke a cataleptic-like state after higher doses [139]. Kappa agonists appear to only monotonically decrease locomotor activity.

This section summarized the application of spontaneous locomotor activity in the assessment of drug effects upon behavior. It is important to consider, however, that the assay is useful in many other regards, including as control for motor effects that may occur in efficacy assays, supplemental in physical dependence studies, drug screening, hypothesis testing in functional neuroanatomy and neurochemistry studies, and pharmacological dissection when antagonists are available as well as assessment of tolerance and behavioral sensitization, characteristics of many drugs of abuse.

2.6 Abuse Liability Assessment Process: Triggers for Additional Studies

As behavior is the output of the CNS, careful assessment of alterations in behavior by administration of the NCE is extremely important in understanding the pharmacology of a compound. In the course of late discovery or early development, either expected or unexpected CNS activity may be detected in an NCE, and at this point, consideration for advancing the compound to further investigation (as described in other chapters in this volume) must be made. CNS activity can be directly addressed (e.g., high brain/plasma ratios, via EEG or intracerebral microdialysis), but more commonly, safety pharmacology studies, such as changes in convulsive thresholds, alterations in barbiturate-induced sleep time, functional observational batteries, and clinical observations in the course of repeat-dose toxicology studies as well as alterations in spontaneous locomotor activity can all elucidate CNS activity, thus signaling the need for further specialized assessments.

REFERENCES

[1] Hoebel BG. Brain neurotransmitters in food and drug reward. Am J Clin Nutr November 1985; 42(5 Suppl.):1133–50.

[2] Wise RA. The role of reward pathways in the development of drug dependence. Pharmacol Ther 1987;35(1–2):227–63.

[3] Pfaus JG. Pathways of sexual desire. J Sex Med June 2009;6(6):1506–33.
[4] Arias-Carrion O, Stamelou M, Murillo-Rodriguez E, Menendez-Gonzalez M, Poppel E. Dopaminergic reward system: a short integrative review. Int Arch Med 2010;3:24.
[5] Bielajew CH, Harris T. Self-stimulation: a rewarding decade. J Psychiatry Neurosci September 1991;16(3):109–14.
[6] Bobzean SA, Denobrega AK, Perrotti LI. Sex differences in the neurobiology of drug addiction. Exp Neurol 2014;259:64–74.
[7] Ikemoto S. Involvement of the olfactory tubercle in cocaine reward: intracranial self-administration studies. J Neurosci October 15, 2003;23(28):9305–11.
[8] Rolls ET. The orbitofrontal cortex and reward. Cereb Cortex March 2000;10(3):284–94.
[9] Spanagel R, Noori HR, Heilig M. Stress and alcohol interactions: animal studies and clinical significance. Trends Neurosci April 2014;37(4):219–27.
[10] Wise RA. Forebrain substrates of reward and motivation. J Comp Neurol December 5, 2005;493(1):115–21.
[11] You ZB, Chen YQ, Wise RA. Dopamine and glutamate release in the nucleus accumbens and ventral tegmental area of rat following lateral hypothalamic self-stimulation. Neuroscience 2001;107(4):629–39.
[12] Koob GF, Nestler EJ. The neurobiology of drug addiction. J Neuropsychiatry Clin Neurosci 1997;9(3):482–97.
[13] Nestler EJ. Molecular basis of long-term plasticity underlying addiction. Nat Rev Neurosci February 2001;2(2):119–28.
[14] Alcaro A, Huber R, Panksepp J. Behavioral functions of the mesolimbic dopaminergic system: an affective neuroethological perspective. Brain Res Rev December 2007;56(2):283–321.
[15] Goodson JL, Kingsbury MA. What's in a name? Considerations of homologies and nomenclature for vertebrate social behavior networks. Horm Behav June 2013;64(1):103–12.
[16] O'Connell LA, Hofmann HA. The vertebrate mesolimbic reward system and social behavior network: a comparative synthesis. J Comp Neurol December 15, 2011;519(18):3599–639.
[17] Saper CB. Brain stem modulation of sensation, movement, and conscousness. In: Kandel ER, Schwartz JH, Jessell TM, editors. Principles of neural science. 4th ed. New York: McGraw-Hill; 2000. p. 890–910.
[18] Cooper JR, Bloom FE, Roth RH. The biochemical basis of neuropharmacology. 8th ed. New York: Oxford University Press, Inc.; 2002.
[19] Dopamine receptors. IUPHAR/BPS Guide to PHARMACOLOGY. http://www.guidetopharmacology.org/GRAC/FamilyDisplayForward?familyId=20 [accessed on 19.05.14].
[20] Adrenoceptors. IUPHAR/BPS Guide to PHARMACOLOGY. http://www.guidetopharmacology.org/GRAC/FamilyDisplayForward?familyId=4 [accessed on 19.05.14].
[21] 5-Hydroxytryptamine receptors. IUPHAR/BPS Guide to PHARMACOLOGY. http://www.guidetopharmacology.org/GRAC/FamilyDisplayForward?familyId=1 [accessed on 19.05.14].
[22] 5-HT_3 receptors. IUPHAR/BPS Guide to PHARMACOLOGY. http://www.guidetopharmacology.org/GRAC/FamilyDisplayForward?familyId=68 [accessed on 19.05.14].
[23] Monoamine transporter subfamily. IUPHAR/BPS Guide to PHARMACOLOGY. http://www.guidetopharmacology.org/GRAC/FamilyDisplayForward?familyId=176 [accessed on 20.05.14].
[24] GABA transporter subfamily. IUPHAR/BPS Guide to PHARMACOLOGY. http://www.guidetopharmacology.org/GRAC/FamilyDisplayForward?familyId=177 [accessed on 20.05.14].
[25] Glycine transporter subfamily. IUPHAR/BPS Guide to PHARMACOLOGY. http://www.guidetopharmacology.org/GRAC/FamilyDisplayForward?familyId=178 [accessed on 20.05.14].
[26] Histamine receptors. IUPHAR/BPS Guide to PHARMACOLOGY. http://www.guidetopharmacology.org/GRAC/FamilyDisplayForward?familyId=33 [accessed on 20.05.14].
[27] Brown RE, Stevens DR, Haas HL. The physiology of brain histamine. Prog Neurobiol April 2001;63(6):637–72.
[28] Haas HL, Sergeeva OA, Selbach O. Histamine in the nervous system. Physiol Rev July 2008;88(3):1183–241.
[29] The rat nervous system. 2nd ed. New York: Acadmic Press; 1995.
[30] Storm-Mathisen J, Leknes AK, Bore AT, Vaaland JL, Edminson P, Haug FM, et al. First visualization of glutamate and GABA in neurones by immunocytochemistry. Nature February 10, 1983;301(5900):517–20.

[31] $GABA_A$ receptors. IUPHAR/BPS Guide to PHARMACOLOGY. http://www.guidetopharmacology.org/GRAC/FamilyDisplayForward?familyId=72 [accessed on 20.05.14].
[32] $GABA_B$ receptors. IUPHAR/BPS Guide to PHARMACOLOGY. http://www.guidetopharmacology.org/GRAC/FamilyDisplayForward?familyId=26 [accessed on 20.05.14].
[33] Vlachou S, Markou A. GABAB receptors in reward processes. Adv Pharmacol 2010;58:315–71.
[34] Ionotropic glutamate receptors. IUPHAR/BPS Guide to PHARMACOLOGY. http://www.guidetopharmacology.org/GRAC/FamilyDisplayForward?familyId=75 [accessed on 20.05.14].
[35] Metabotropic glutamate receptors. IUPHAR/BPS Guide to PHARMACOLOGY. http://www.guidetopharmacology.org/GRAC/FamilyDisplayForward?familyId=40 [accessed on 20.05.14].
[36] Danbolt NC. Glutamate uptake. Prog Neurobiol September 2001;65(1):1–105.
[37] Dingledine R, Borges K, Bowie D, Traynelis SF. The glutamate receptor ion channels. Pharmacol Rev March 1999;51(1):7–61.
[38] Hnasko TS, Hjelmstad GO, Fields HL, Edwards RH. Ventral tegmental area glutamate neurons: electrophysiological properties and projections. J Neurosci October 24, 2012;32(43):15076–85.
[39] Meldrum BS. Glutamate as a neurotransmitter in the brain: review of physiology and pathology. J Nutr April 2000;130(4S Suppl.):1007S–15S.
[40] Platt SR. The role of glutamate in central nervous system health and disease–a review. Vet J March 2007;173(2):278–86.
[41] Pomierny-Chamiolo L, Rup K, Pomierny B, Niedzielska E, Kalivas PW, Filip M. Metabotropic glutamatergic receptors and their ligands in drug addiction. Pharmacol Ther June 2014;142(3):281–305.
[42] Sarter M, Parikh V, Howe WM. Phasic acetylcholine release and the volume transmission hypothesis: time to move on. Nat Rev Neurosci May 2009;10(5):383–90.
[43] Brown DA. Muscarinic acetylcholine receptors (mAChRs) in the nervous system: some functions and mechanisms. J Mol Neurosci July 2010;41(3):340–6.
[44] Haga T. Molecular properties of muscarinic acetylcholine receptors. Proc Jpn Acad Ser B Phys Biol Sci 2013;89(6):226–56.
[45] Acetylcholine receptors (muscarinic). IUPHAR/BPS Guide to PHARMACOLOGY. http://www.guidetopharmacology.org/GRAC/FamilyDisplayForward?familyId=2 [accessed on 20.05.14].
[46] Nicotinic acetylcholine receptors. IUPHAR/BPS Guide to PHARMACOLOGY. http://www.guidetopharmacology.org/GRAC/FamilyDisplayForward?familyId=76 [accessed on 20.05.14].
[47] Martin WR, Eades CG, Thompson JA, Huppler RE, Gilbert PE. The effects of morphine- and nalorphine- like drugs in the nondependent and morphine-dependent chronic spinal dog. J Pharmacol Exp Ther June 1976;197(3):517–32.
[48] Opioid receptors. IUPHAR/BPS Guide to PHARMACOLOGY. http://www.guidetopharmacology.org/GRAC/FamilyDisplayForward?familyId=50 [accessed on 20.05.14].
[49] Froehlich JC. Opioid peptides. Alcohol Health Res World 1997;21(2):132–6.
[50] Henriksen G, Willoch F. Imaging of opioid receptors in the central nervous system. Brain May 2008;131(Pt 5):1171–96.
[51] Cannabinoid receptors. IUPHAR/BPS Guide to PHARMACOLOGY. http://www.guidetopharmacology.org/GRAC/FamilyDisplayForward?familyId=13 [accessed on 20.05.14].
[52] Irving AJ, Rae MG, Coutts AA. Cannabinoids on the brain. Sci World J March 9, 2002;2:632–48.
[53] Herkenham M, Lynn AB, Little MD, Johnson MR, Melvin LS, de Costa BR, et al. Cannabinoid receptor localization in brain. Proc Natl Acad Sci USA March 1990;87(5):1932–6.
[54] Howlett AC, Bidaut-Russell M, Devane WA, Melvin LS, Johnson MR, Herkenham M. The cannabinoid receptor: biochemical, anatomical and behavioral characterization. Trends Neurosci October 1990;13(10):420–3.
[55] Adams IB, Compton DR, Martin BR. Assessment of anandamide interaction with the cannabinoid brain receptor: SR 141716A antagonism studies in mice and autoradiographic analysis of receptor binding in rat brain. J Pharmacol Exp Ther March 1998;284(3):1209–17.
[56] Adams IB, Ryan W, Singer M, Thomas BF, Compton DR, Razdan RK, et al. Evaluation of cannabinoid receptor binding and in vivo activities for anandamide analogs. J Pharmacol Exp Ther June 1995;273(3):1172–81.

[57] Compton DR, Martin BR. The effect of the enzyme inhibitor phenylmethylsulfonyl fluoride on the pharmacological effect of anandamide in the mouse model of cannabimimetic activity. J Pharmacol Exp Ther December 1997;283(3):1138–43.
[58] Compton DR, Aceto MD, Lowe J, Martin BR. In vivo characterization of a specific cannabinoid receptor antagonist (SR141716A): inhibition of delta 9-tetrahydrocannabinol-induced responses and apparent agonist activity. J Pharmacol Exp Ther May 1996;277(2):586–94.
[59] Compton DR, Johnson MR, Melvin LS, Martin BR. Pharmacological profile of a series of bicyclic cannabinoid analogs: classification as cannabimimetic agents. J Pharmacol Exp Ther January 1992; 260(1):201–9.
[60] Compton DR, Prescott Jr WR, Martin BR, Siegel C, Gordon PM, Razdan RK. Synthesis and pharmacological evaluation of ether and related analogues of delta 8-, delta 9-, and delta 9,11-tetrahydrocannabinol. J Med Chem November 1991;34(11):3310–6.
[61] Compton DR, Rice KC, de Costa BR, Razdan RK, Melvin LS, Johnson MR, et al. Cannabinoid structure-activity relationships: correlation of receptor binding and in vivo activities. J Pharmacol Exp Ther April 1993;265(1):218–26.
[62] Compton DR, Gold LH, Ward SJ, Balster RL, Martin BR. Aminoalkylindole analogs: cannabimimetic activity of a class of compounds structurally distinct from delta 9-tetrahydrocannabinol. J Pharmacol Exp Ther December 1992;263(3):1118–26.
[63] Compton DR, Prescott WR, Siegel CS, Gordon PM, Razdan RK, Martin BR. Evaluation of ether and free hydroxyl analogs of delta-8, delta-9, 11-THC as cannabinoid antagonists. NIDA Res Monogr 1990;105:297–8.
[64] Compton DR, Little PJ, Martin BR, Gilman JW, Saha JK, Jorapur VS, et al. Synthesis and pharmacological evaluation of amino, azido, and nitrogen mustard analogues of 10-substituted cannabidiol and 11- or 12-substituted delta 8-tetrahydrocannabinol. J Med Chem May 1990;33(5):1437–43.
[65] Compton DR, Martin BR. Pharmacological evaluation of water soluble cannabinoids and related analogs. Life Sci 1990;46(22):1575–85.
[66] Compton DR, Dewey WL, Martin BR. Cannabis dependence and tolerance production. Adv Alcohol Subst Abuse 1990;9(1–2):129–47.
[67] Dutta AK, Ryan W, Thomas BF, Singer M, Compton DR, Martin BR, et al. Synthesis, pharmacology, and molecular modeling of novel 4-alkyloxy indole derivatives related to cannabimimetic aminoalkyl indoles (AAIs). Bioorg Med Chem August 1997;5(8):1591–600.
[68] Huffman JW, Yu S, Showalter V, Abood ME, Wiley JL, Compton DR, et al. Synthesis and pharmacology of a very potent cannabinoid lacking a phenolic hydroxyl with high affinity for the CB2 receptor. J Med Chem September 27, 1996;39(20):3875–7.
[69] Lake KD, Compton DR, Varga K, Martin BR, Kunos G. Cannabinoid-induced hypotension and bradycardia in rats mediated by CB1-like cannabinoid receptors. J Pharmacol Exp Ther June 1997; 281(3):1030–7.
[70] Little PJ, Compton DR, Mechoulam R, Martin BR. Stereochemical effects of 11-OH-delta 8-THC-dimethylheptyl in mice and dogs. Pharmacol Biochem Behav March 1989;32(3):661–6.
[71] Little PJ, Compton DR, Johnson MR, Melvin LS, Martin BR. Pharmacology and stereoselectivity of structurally novel cannabinoids in mice. J Pharmacol Exp Ther December 1988;247(3):1046–51.
[72] Martin BR, Compton DR, Prescott WR, Barrett RL, Razdan RK. Pharmacological evaluation of dimethylheptyl analogs of delta 9-THC: reassessment of the putative three-point cannabinoid-receptor interaction. Drug Alcohol Depend March 1995;37(3):231–40.
[73] Martin BR, Compton DR, Semus SF, Lin S, Marciniak G, Grzybowska J, et al. Pharmacological evaluation of iodo and nitro analogs of delta 8-THC and delta 9-THC. Pharmacol Biochem Behav October 1993;46(2):295–301.
[74] Martin BR, Compton DR, Thomas BF, Prescott WR, Little PJ, Razdan RK, et al. Behavioral, biochemical, and molecular modeling evaluations of cannabinoid analogs. Pharmacol Biochem Behav November 1991;40(3):471–8.
[75] Martin BR, Compton DR, Little PJ, Martin TJ, Beardsley PM. Pharmacological evaluation of agonistic and antagonistic activity of cannabinoids. NIDA Res Monogr 1987;79:108–22.

[76] McLaughlin CR, Martin BR, Compton DR, Abood ME. Cannabinoid receptors in developing rats: detection of mRNA and receptor binding. Drug Alcohol Depend August 1994;36(1):27–31.
[77] Mechoulam R, Ben-Shabat S, Hanus L, Ligumsky M, Kaminski NE, Schatz AR, et al. Identification of an endogenous 2-monoglyceride, present in canine gut, that binds to cannabinoid receptors. Biochem Pharmacol June 29, 1995;50(1):83–90.
[78] Pertwee RG, Fernando SR, Griffin G, Ryan W, Razdan RK, Compton DR, et al. Agonist-antagonist characterization of 6′-cyanohex-2′-yne-delta 8-tetrahydrocannabinol in two isolated tissue preparations. Eur J Pharmacol November 14, 1996;315(2):195–201.
[79] Reggio PH, Wang T, Brown AE, Fleming DN, Seltzman HH, Griffin G, et al. Importance of the C-1 substituent in classical cannabinoids to CB2 receptor selectivity: synthesis and characterization of a series of O,2-propano-delta 8-tetrahydrocannabinol analogs. J Med Chem September 26, 1997; 40(20):3312–8.
[80] Reggio PH, McGaughey GB, Odear DF, Seltzman HH, Compton DR, Martin BR. A rational search for the separation of psychoactivity and analgesia in cannabinoids. Pharmacol Biochem Behav November 1991;40(3):479–86.
[81] Reggio PH, Seltzman HH, Compton DR, Prescott Jr WR, Martin BR. Investigation of the role of the phenolic hydroxyl in cannabinoid activity. Mol Pharmacol December 1990;38(6):854–62.
[82] Ryan W, Singer M, Razdan RK, Compton DR, Martin BR. A novel class of potent tetrahydrocannabinols (THCS): 2′-yne-delta 8- and delta 9-THCS. Life Sci 1995;56(23–24):2013–20.
[83] Seltzman HH, Fleming DN, Thomas BF, Gilliam AF, McCallion DS, Pertwee RG, et al. Synthesis and pharmacological comparison of dimethylheptyl and pentyl analogs of anandamide. J Med Chem October 24, 1997;40(22):3626–34.
[84] Showalter VM, Compton DR, Martin BR, Abood ME. Evaluation of binding in a transfected cell line expressing a peripheral cannabinoid receptor (CB2): identification of cannabinoid receptor subtype selective ligands. J Pharmacol Exp Ther September 1996;278(3):989–99.
[85] Smith PB, Compton DR, Welch SP, Razdan RK, Mechoulam R, Martin BR. The pharmacological activity of anandamide, a putative endogenous cannabinoid, in mice. J Pharmacol Exp Ther July 1994;270(1):219–27.
[86] Thomas BF, Compton DR, Martin BR, Semus SF. Modeling the cannabinoid receptor: a three-dimensional quantitative structure-activity analysis. Mol Pharmacol November 1991;40(5):656–65.
[87] Thomas BF, Compton DR, Martin BR. Characterization of the lipophilicity of natural and synthetic analogs of delta 9-tetrahydrocannabinol and its relationship to pharmacological potency. J Pharmacol Exp Ther November 1990;255(2):624–30.
[88] Wiley JL, Compton DR, Dai D, Lainton JA, Phillips M, Huffman JW, et al. Structure-activity relationships of indole- and pyrrole-derived cannabinoids. J Pharmacol Exp Ther June 1998;285(3): 995–1004.
[89] Wiley JL, Compton DR, Gordon PM, Siegel C, Singer M, Dutta A, et al. Evaluation of agonist-antagonist properties of nitrogen mustard and cyano derivatives of delta 8-tetrahydrocannabinol. Neuropharmacology 1996;35(12):1793–804.
[90] Yan G, Yin D, Khanolkar AD, Compton DR, Martin BR, Makriyannis A. Synthesis and pharmacological properties of 11-hydroxy-3-(1′,1′-dimethylheptyl)hexahydrocannabinol: a high-affinity cannabinoid agonist. J Med Chem August 5, 1994;37(16):2619–22.
[91] Sigma receptors. IUPHAR/BPS Guide to PHARMACOLOGY. http://www.guidetopharmacology.org/GRAC/FamilyDisplayForward?familyId=785 [accessed on 20.05.14].
[92] Compton DR, Bagley RB, Katzen JS, Martin BR. (+)- and (-)-N-allylnormetazocine binding sites in mouse brain: in vitro and in vivo characterization and regional distribution. Life Sci June 1, 1987;40(22):2195–206.
[93] Coan EJ, Collingridge GL. Effects of phencyclidine, SKF 10,047 and related psychotomimetic agents on N-methyl-D-aspartate receptor mediated synaptic responses in rat hippocampal slices. Br J Pharmacol July 1987;91(3):547–56.
[94] Guitart X, Codony X, Monroy X. Sigma receptors: biology and therapeutic potential. Psychopharmacol (Berl) July 2004;174(3):301–19.
[95] Hayashi T, Su T. The sigma receptor: evolution of the concept in neuropsychopharmacology. Curr Neuropharmacol October 2005;3(4):267–80.

[96] Liu Y, Matsumoto RR. Alterations in fos-related antigen 2 and sigma1 receptor gene and protein expression are associated with the development of cocaine-induced behavioral sensitization: time course and regional distribution studies. J Pharmacol Exp Ther October 2008;327(1):187–95.

[97] Matsumoto RR, McCracken KA, Pouw B, Zhang Y, Bowen WD. Involvement of sigma receptors in the behavioral effects of cocaine: evidence from novel ligands and antisense oligodeoxynucleotides. Neuropharmacology June 2002;42(8):1043–55.

[98] Matsumoto RR, Liu Y, Lerner M, Howard EW, Brackett DJ. Sigma receptors: potential medications development target for anti-cocaine agents. Eur J Pharmacol May 23, 2003;469(1–3):1–12.

[99] Matsumoto RR. Targeting sigma receptors: novel medication development for drug abuse and addiction. Expert Rev Clin Pharmacol July 2009;2(4):351–8.

[100] Maurice T, Martin-Fardon R, Romieu P, Matsumoto RR. Sigma(1) (sigma(1)) receptor antagonists represent a new strategy against cocaine addiction and toxicity. Neurosci Biobehav Rev June 2002; 26(4):499–527.

[101] Maurice T, Su TP. The pharmacology of sigma-1 receptors. Pharmacol Ther November 2009; 124(2):195–206.

[102] Mori T, Yoshizawa K, Shibasaki M, Suzuki T. Discriminative stimulus effects of hallucinogenic drugs: a possible relation to reinforcing and aversive effects. J Pharmacol Sci 2012;120(2):70–6.

[103] Torrence-Campbell C, Bowen WD. Differential solubilization of rat liver sigma 1 and sigma 2 receptors: retention of sigma 2 sites in particulate fractions. Eur J Pharmacol May 23, 1996;304(1–3):201–10.

[104] Bowen WD. Sigma receptors: recent advances and new clinical potentials. Pharm Acta Helv March 2000;74(2–3):211–8.

[105] Kinney GG, Harris EW, Ray R, Hudzik TJ. Sigma2 site-mediated inhibition of electrically evoked guinea pig ileum longitudinal muscle/myenteric plexus contractions. Eur J Pharmacol December 29, 1995;294(2–3):547–53.

[106] Xie XQ, Wang L, Liu H, Ouyang Q, Fang C, Su W. Chemogenomics knowledgebased polypharmacology analyses of drug abuse related G-protein coupled receptors and their ligands. Front Pharmacol 2014;5:3.

[107] Watzman N, Barry III H, Kinnard Jr WJ, Buckley JP. Influence of certain parameters on the performance of mice on the rotarod. Archives Int de pharmacodynamie et de Ther 1967;169(2):362–74.

[108] Watzman N, Barry III H, Buckley JP, Kinnard Jr WJ. Semiautomatic system for timing rotarod performance. J Pharm Sci 1964;53:1429–30.

[109] Plotnikoff N, Reinke D, Fitzloff J. Effects of stimulants on rotarod performance of mice. J Pharm Sci 1962;51:1007–8.

[110] Mizoguchi K, Yuzurihara M, Ishige A, Sasaki H, Tabira T. Chronic stress impairs rotarod performance in rats: implications for depressive state. Pharmacol Biochem Behav 2002;71(1–2):79–84.

[111] McIlwain KL, Merriweather MY, Yuva-Paylor LA, Paylor R. The use of behavioral test batteries: effects of training history. Physiol Behav 2001;73(5):705–17.

[112] Pinkston JW, Madden GJ, Fowler SC. Effects of white and infrared lighting on apomorphine-induced pecking in pigeons. Behav Pharmacol 2008;19(4):347–52.

[113] Lynch III JJ, Castagne V, Moser PC, Mittelstadt SW. Comparison of methods for the assessment of locomotor activity in rodent safety pharmacology studies. J Pharmacol Toxicol Methods 2011; 64(1):74–80.

[114] Denny BT, Fan J, Liu X, Guerreri S, Mayson SJ, Rimsky L, et al. Insula-amygdala functional connectivity is correlated with habituation to repeated negative images. Soc Cogn Affect Neurosci 2013.

[115] Kalivas PW, Duffy P. Time course of extracellular dopamine and behavioral sensitization to cocaine. I. Dopamine axon terminals. J Neurosci 1993;13(1):266–75.

[116] Kalivas PW, Stewart J. Dopamine transmission in the initiation and expression of drug-and stress-induced sensitization of motor activity. Brain Res Rev 1991;16(3):223–44.

[117] Moser VC, McCormick JP, Creason JP, MacPhail RC. Comparison of chlordimeform and carbaryl using a functional observational battery. Fundam Appl Toxicol: Official J Soc Toxicol 1988;11(2): 189–206.

[118] Forgie ML, Stewart J. Sex differences in amphetamine-induced locomotor activity in adult rats: role of testosterone exposure in the neonatal period. Pharmacol Biochem Behav 1993;46(3): 637–45.

[119] Simpson J, Ryan C, Curley A, Mulcaire J, Kelly JP. Sex differences in baseline and drug-induced behavioural responses in classical behavioural tests. Prog Neuro-psychopharmacol Biol Psychiatry 2012;37(2):227–36.
[120] Isiegas C, Mague SD, Blendy JA. Sex differences in response to nicotine in C57Bl/6:129SvEv mice. Nicotine & tobacco research. Official J Soc Res Nicotine Tob 2009;11(7):851–8.
[121] Koek W. Effects of repeated exposure to morphine in adolescent and adult male C57BL/6J mice: age-dependent differences in locomotor stimulation, sensitization, and body weight loss. Psychopharmacology 2014;231(8):1517–29.
[122] Evenden JL. The effect of 5-HT1A receptor agonists on locomotor activity in the guinea-pig. Br J Pharmacol 1994;112(3):861–6.
[123] Simmons MA, Werkheiser JL, Hudzik TJ. Acute nicotine and phencyclidine increase locomotor activity of the guinea pig with attenuated potencies relative to their effects on rat or mouse. Pharmacol Biochem Behav 2010;94(3):410–5.
[124] Mead LA, Hargreaves EL, Ossenkopp KP, Kavaliers M. A multivariate assessment of spontaneous locomotor activity in the Mongolian gerbil (*Meriones unguiculatus*): influences of age and sex. Physiol Behav 1995;57(5):893–9.
[125] Ingebretson JJ, Masino MA. Quantification of locomotor activity in larval zebrafish: considerations for the design of high-throughput behavioral studies. Front Neural Circuits 2013;7:109.
[126] Indic P, Salvatore P, Maggini C, Ghidini S, Ferraro G, Baldessarini RJ, et al. Scaling behavior of human locomotor activity amplitude: association with bipolar disorder. PloS One 2011;6(5):e20650.
[127] Schildein S, Huston JP, Schwarting RK. Open field habituation learning is improved by nicotine and attenuated by mecamylamine administered posttrial into the nucleus accumbens. Neurobiol Learn Mem 2002;77(3):277–90.
[128] Prut L, Belzung C. The open field as a paradigm to measure the effects of drugs on anxiety-like behaviors: a review. Eur J Pharmacol 2003;463(1):3–33.
[129] McAuley JD, Stewart AL, Webber ES, Cromwell HC, Servatius RJ, Pang KC. Wistar-Kyoto rats as an animal model of anxiety vulnerability: support for a hypervigilance hypothesis. Behav Brain Res 2009;204(1):162–8.
[130] Huynh TN, Krigbaum AM, Hanna JJ, Conrad CD. Sex differences and phase of light cycle modify chronic stress effects on anxiety and depressive-like behavior. Behav Brain Res 2011;222(1):212–22.
[131] Swiergiel AH, Dunn AJ. Effects of interleukin-1beta and lipopolysaccharide on behavior of mice in the elevated plus-maze and open field tests. Pharmacol Biochem Behav 2007;86(4):651–9.
[132] Laviola G, Renna G, Bignami G, Cuomo V. Ontogenetic and pharmacological dissociation of various components of locomotor activity and habituation in the rat. Int J Dev Neurosci: Official J Int Soc Dev Neurosci 1988;6(5):431–8.
[133] Remington G, Anisman H. Genetic and ontogenetic variations in locomotor activity following treatment with scopolamine or d-amphetamine. Dev Psychobiol 1976;9(6):579–85.
[134] Garrett BE, Holtzman SG. Comparison of the effects of prototypical behavioral stimulants on locomotor activity and rotational behavior in rats. Pharmacol Biochem Behav 1996;54(2):469–77.
[135] Wing LL, Tapson GS, Geyer MA. 5HT-2 mediation of acute behavioral effects of hallucinogens in rats. Psychopharmacology 1990;100(3):417–25.
[136] Krebs-Thomson K, Paulus MP, Geyer MA. Effects of hallucinogens on locomotor and investigatory activity and patterns: influence of 5-HT2A and 5-HT2C receptors. Neuropsychopharmacology 1998;18(5):339–51.
[137] Pawlak CR, Schwarting RK. Repeated nicotine treatment in rats with high versus low rearing activity: analyses of behavioural sensitisation and place preference. Psychopharmacology 2005;178(4):440–50.
[138] Brielmaier JM, McDonald CG, Smith RF. Immediate and long-term behavioral effects of a single nicotine injection in adolescent and adult rats. Neurotoxicol Teratol 2007;29(1):74–80.
[139] Iwamoto ET. Locomotor activity and antinociception after putative mu, kappa and sigma opioid receptor agonists in the rat: influence of dopaminergic agonists and antagonists. J Pharmacol Exp Ther 1981;217(2):451–60.

CHAPTER 3

Rat Self-Administration

David V. Gauvin[1], Mausumee Guha[2], Theodore J. Baird[3]
[1]Neurobehavioral Sciences, MPI Research Inc., Mattawan, MI, USA; [2]Medivation Inc., San Francisco, CA, USA; [3]Toxicology, Medivation Inc., San Francisco, CA, USA

Contents

1. INTRODUCTION

Early etiological theories of drug abuse emphasized its reactive processes. The development of the experimental analysis of drug-taking behaviors in laboratory animals had been previously responsible for a decisive shift in focus to the active, consequential control of drug self-administration [1]. Purpose-bred laboratory rats are the preferred species for preclinical assessment of new drugs (FDA) both in the United States and Europe [2,3].

One of the specific aims of abuse liability testing is to accurately predict whether a new chemical entity (NCE) will maintain patterns of nonmedical use that could result in the disruption of the activities of normal daily living or produce undesirable consequences in the patient given access to the compound through legitimate means. One role served by psychoactive drugs is that of a "reinforcer," defined as an event whose presentation, contingent upon a response, increases the future likelihood of that response. The demonstration that drugs can reinforce behavior, that is, can increase the likelihood of lever press responses having no consequence other than the recurrence of drug delivery, has supported the view that drugs themselves can act to shape the development of drug-seeking

Nonclinical Assessment of Abuse Potential for New Pharmaceuticals
http://dx.doi.org/10.1016/B978-0-12-420172-9.00003-5

and drug-taking behaviors [4]. Operant drug self-administration is considered to be the gold standard of preclinical abuse liability testing because of its high face and predictive validity. There is a relatively high correlation between drugs that are self-administered by laboratory animals and those that function as reinforcers in humans [5–8].

One important factor that must be kept in mind in understanding the dynamics of the self-administration paradigm is this:

> *To say that a drug is self-administered conveys as much information about the current and past behavioral and pharmacological contingencies in effect at the time of self-administration as it does about the physical chemical structure of the entity itself.*

Abuse potential assessment is accomplished through a series of laboratory-based procedures to determine the pharmacological activity of the NCE in assays sensitive to various correlates of, and contributors to, drug abuse in humans [9]. The demonstration that rats will exert work to earn a single delivery of an intravenously administered drug has provided convincing evidence to drug control agencies of the remarkable concordance and predictive validity between the range of chemical substances that are self-administered in the context of preclinical drug assessment models and those drugs abused by humans [6,10–12]. The demonstration of the initiation and maintenance of drug-taking behaviors by animals represents one of the major predictive assays used during the risk assessments conducted by both international [13–16] and national drug control policy makers [17–19].

Through active dialogue during a series of public meetings between the PhRMA and the Controlled Substances Staff (CSS) in the Center for Drug Evaluation and Research (CDER) at the US Food and Drug Administration (FDA), the rat self-administration assay has become the industry gold standard for the assessment of the reinforcing (rewarding) stimulus properties of new chemical entities. The findings from these studies have become an essential element of the data analysis that must be independently conducted by members of the Office of the Secretary of Health and Human Services and the US Attorney General's Office with respect to national and international drug control policies as part of every New Drug Application (NDA) submission process as defined in the Controlled Substance Act [19]. By standing letters of understanding, the Office of the Secretary of Health and Human Services has delegated the authority for the scientific analysis to the CSS staff at FDA, but experts from the National Institute on Drug Abuse (NIDA) give their input to the FDA as well. Under similar letters of understanding, the Attorney General Office has delegated its authority to set the legal schedule controls to the Administrator of the Drug Enforcement Administration.

During the public meetings between PhRMA and the FDA, specific features of the rat self-administration assay were set forth as industry best practices and published within the Question and Answer Documents [20] and the 2010 Draft Guidance document on abuse liability by the FDA [18]. The intent of this chapter is to set forth the details for the conduct of rat self-administration study that is designed to comply with the requirements of the Comprehensive Drug Abuse Prevention and Control Act (cf, 19: §811(c) and §812), the two international drug control treaties that govern the Schedule Control review of new drug applications [21,22], and the *Guideline on the Non-Clinical Investigation of the Dependence Potential of Medicinal Products* of the European Medicines Agency [23]. The study designs are also in compliance with the Food and Drug Administration's draft document titled, "Guidance for Industry: Assessment of Abuse Potential of Drugs" released on January 26, 2010 [18].

Because of the fluidity in regulatory required data sets for drug schedule control decisions by FDA and DEA, it is always highly recommended that ALL preclinical screening protocols for abuse liability assessments be reviewed by CSS staff prior to initiation of these studies. As regulatory agencies intimately involved in the process of schedule control actions of the new chemical entities, positioning the study design team with both the CSS staff at FDA and the Drug Diversion Team at DEA may significantly improve the review process early in development of the molecule and set the direction for the progress of preclinical to clinical trial advancement.

This chapter is intended to convey the current thinking of the drug control agencies on the standardization of the experimental parameters suggested for use in studies on preclinical abuse potential. The authors do not purport to speak for these agencies, although the current study design is set forth as the result of discussions and knowledge relevant to current policies and expectations. Acknowledging first that there are a variety of methodologies between and within laboratories that have been published in peer-reviewed scientific journals over the last five decades of research, the assay described in this chapter represents the current thinking of the agencies involved in drug control policies. No one study design has more regulatory weight or predictive power in the schedule control actions of either agency. These may in fact change over time, but studies being conducted contemporarily in multiple laboratories have based their strategy and study designs on the parameters set forth in this chapter. While this chapter describes the current thinking of the two regulatory agencies involved in schedule-control, pre-NDA meetings are not legally binding on the agencies. At the time of Phase II clinical trials, FDA may request a different study design than described here based on the known pharmacology of the NCE. As an example, the CSS staff may request all test article comparisons to be conducted from a saline-or an extinction-baseline when the known stimulus properties of the compound appear to predict weak reinforcing properties.

The rat self-administration procedure that has been adopted by the industry and FDA is described as a single-lever operant lever press response under a fixed-ratio 10 (FR10) schedule of cocaine deliveries with session lengths of at least 1-h duration. Once animals demonstrate day-to-day stability in responding for cocaine deliveries (e.g., less than 15–20% day-to-day variability in the total number of training drug deliveries for three consecutive days), rats are tested under multiple contiguous unlimited drug or vehicle access sessions over the ensuing 3–5 days. Complete dose–response functions should be conducted for the training drug (cocaine) and the test article for comparison. Additionally, for each dose of test article that has demonstrated reinforcing properties in this assay, a separate test for reinforcing efficacy should be included to understand the relative persistence of behaviors engendered by different experimental treatment conditions.

2. REGULATORY ISSUES

The first question in conducting preclinical safety studies is whether or not to conduct these studies in compliance with Good Laboratory Practice (GLP) guidelines [24]. Abuse liability studies are required to be submitted to the agency as part of an application for a research or marketing permit [25]; therefore, regulatory agencies have repeatedly stated that all abuse liability studies should be conducted per GLPs. As cited by Balster and Bigelow [26], FDA's position has been "regardless of whether abuse liability testing is designated as pharmacology or toxicology, the purpose of applying GLP regulations is to ensure application of top quality procedures and data quality control. FDA's experience in this area has been that laboratories must be handled equitably and that application of the GLP regulations must apply across the board in order to ensure maintenance of the high standards." Standard operant chambers used in these assays and the commercially available computer software packages used to control and collect the temporally stamped behavioral data are also amenable for full system validation under the GLPs. The recommendations of all current EMEA, ICH, and FDA guidance documents (listed previously) are to conduct these studies, to the extent feasible, under the Good Laboratory Practice Guidelines although GLP compliance is not required.

Critically important is the fact that these assays require the use of controlled substances. As such, a constant concern should be applied to the security measures in place maintaining restricted access to all controlled substances by the appropriately trained personnel running these studies and also limiting the access of other institutional personnel that may have admittance to areas in which these controlled substances are used on studies. Security manuals are available through the Office of Diversion Control at the DEA giving details for the security measures that should be in place while conducting these types of animal studies by laboratories with bona fide research registrations that will limit the possibilities for diversion and theft [27]. It is assumed that the controlled substances will be transported from one area within the institution to the testing environment such as from the pharmacy where the controlled substances are formulated to the rat operant testing room. This allows the controlled substance to be exposed to other employed personnel that are not directly involved in the dispensing, administration, or transport of the controlled substance. Therefore, most pharmacies and research institutions have implemented a two-person control system that requires two trained personnel to be in close proximity and visual contact of the controlled substance at all times that the formulations are not under locked control.

Within a secured environment, the use of restricted card-key (or equivalent) access to adjacent hallways and operant testing rooms must provide at least 30 man minutes against surreptitious entries (i.e., takes one man, 30 min to gain access or it takes 15 min for two men working in tandem to gain access). The use of remote video monitoring of hallways and access doors is also recommended to be able to clearly identify and document all personnel gaining entrance to the testing environment. For those directly involved in the conduct of the studies, further locking devices are required that provide at least 10 man minutes against forced entry or access to the drugs while the studies are conducted. Additionally, a controlled safe or locked-room should be available to store all prepared formulations if technicians are required to leave the immediate testing room for any reason. Laboratories have installed a series of controlled, double-coded, punch-key locked safes within or in close proximity to the testing rooms. With one technician having the pass code for panel A, and another technician has the code for panel B, both are needed to open the lockboxes.

3. THE OPERANT CHAMBER SET UP

Jim Weeks and John Davis [28] published the first report that described the manufacture and installation of chronic indwelling jugular catheters used to deliver drug as a positive reinforcer in standard lever-press operant tasks in rats. Many current suppliers provide a wide array of materials and designs for jugular catheters used in laboratories around the world, but the detailed analysis of materials, catheter parameters, such as length and diameter, were based on the seminal work of Jim Weeks at Upjohn Laboratories (Kalamazoo, MI). His "personal communication, number 1011" [29] was requested by many and was the standard reference guideline for the majority of laboratories conducting the early studies using rat self-administration.

Rats are surgically equipped with chronic indwelling jugular cannula under sterile surgical conditions. The catheters are tunneled to the mid-scapular region and exits for connection to a harness or jacket system. The stainless-steel tether system containing a catheter from the syringe drive pump system is connected to the harness or jacket just prior to each operant session. As a general rule, technicians are trained to never provide a negative pressure on the catheter system that may allow blood to enter into the subcutaneous catheter system in the jugular vein. The mid-scapular region of the exit site under the harness or jacket system is cleaned daily with a cleansing solution to minimize the risks of infection. The catheters are flushed prior to and at the completion of each operant session with a sterile heparinized saline solution. On days in which the animals are not run (i.e., washout periods), the catheters are also cleaned and flushed by the trained technicians. In the original Weeks and Davis [28] paper the authors stated, "Most cannulas are functional for many weeks." Indeed, catheter patency can be maintained for many months under the appropriate conditions.

Generally, the standard rat self-administration study design is based on a sample size of 32 rats. A Generalized Linear Mixed Model power analysis was conducted assuming a negative binomial distribution with a Treatment X Day repeated measures MANOVA design. Separate Cholesky factored unstructured variance-covariance matrixes were fitted for tests conducted with saline and the maintenance dose of cocaine in a pooled sample of 302 rats conditioned to self-administer 0.56 mg/kg/injection of cocaine. Ten thousand bootstrap samples were generated from the database, with samples ranging from four rats per test to 17 rats. Power for the various tests was calculated as the proportion of samples that were significant at the 5% level out of the samples that converged (roughly 91% of all samples converged). A sample size of four rats per test was required to provide a power of 90.0% for the Treatment × Day interaction. A sample size of five rats provided a power of >80% for significant differences between treatments on Day 3 of the 3-day substitution protocol.

All 32 rats are placed into a single group that will be trained as described below. Using 32 rats, each dose of a five-dose test article generalization function in a subset of six animals per dose can be tested without repeat. These same six animals can then be available if PK sampling is requested. At the end of the study, PK sampling by sublingual bleeds can be conducted following a special noncontingent playback session in which the rat is administered the same number and identical pattern of injections as was self-administered by each animal's computer-based session on Day 1 of substitution. In this playback session, the levers remain retracted. The animal receives noncontingent drug injections at the same speed, same time, and the same interval dose intervals. This provides accurate blood level concentration to that which was earned during the previous self-administration test, which can then be used to verify that animals are exposed to at least several multiples of the maximum clinical exposure. Day 1 of the 3-day substation session is selected because it generally provides the highest drug intake of the 3-day substitution, even if the drug is inert and is not considered to be reinforcing (i.e., an extinction burst). This animal use plan also allows for use of independent group statistical analyses instead of repeated measure designs to compare between test article doses on each study (Figure 1).

There are a number of manufacturers of the operant chambers that can be used for this assay. For self-administration sessions only a single lever and operant lamp can be used. The other installed lever and lamp that are used in drug discrimination studies are not activated by the computer software that controls experimental contingencies in this assay. The syringe drive pump is located above each chamber and is physically mounted to the sound-attenuating cubicle surrounding the operant chamber, and it is activated by computer software when the animal presses the active lever 10 times (FR-10). A single bolus of fluid is dispensed to the animal, and the lever is typically retracted. The stimulus

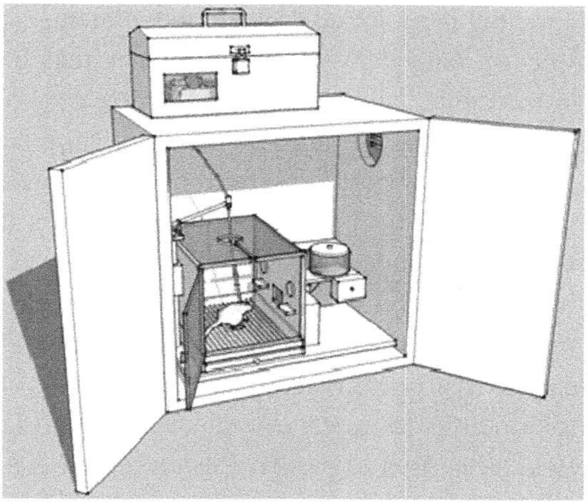

Figure 1 Standard operant chamber used for rat self-administration procedures. Each operant chamber (MedAssociates™, NH) is equipped with lever(s), stimulus lamp(s), pellet dispenser, house light, enclosure fan, spring tether catheter system, and a drug delivery pump. In most laboratories the chambers are used for both self-administration and drug discrimination operant paradigms, so two lever systems are most common. The syringe drive infusion pump is located in a locked metal storage cabinet that has been permanently mounted to the sound attenuating cubicle within which the operant chamber is maintained. The cubicle is also permanently mounted at the wall or base cabinet to avoid diversion.

lamp is darkened for a brief period during the drug delivery to avoid further lever press responding during and/or immediately following the drug delivery.

4. THE TRAINING

Tomoji Yanagita [30,31] was one of the first authors to detail the current FDA-guideline-suggested testing procedures in self-administration protocols. In the original report, Yanagita referred to the design as "cross self-administration test" but it is most often simply referred to as a "drug substitution procedure." A simple A-B-A study design compares the reinforcing effects of a new chemical entity (B) against a stable cocaine baseline (A). In the current procedure suggested by FDA, animals are first trained to lever press at fixed ratios of 1 to 10 (FR10). This is most typically conducted under food reward deliveries.

Rats are placed on a brief period of restricted access to food, such as meal patterning by supplying 15–20 g of food (versus ad libitum access) during a single delivery each day prior to operant conditioning trials. Alternatively, the animals may be food deprived to 85% of their free-feeding weights to motivate them to work for food during this conditioning phase of the study. Rats can be trained to press the lever using a shaping method commonly referred to as successive approximations [32,33], but are typically allowed a few acclimation trials conducted for 2 or 3 days before study initiation to allow the opportunity to explore the operant chambers for 30–60 min, during which many rats will press the lever spontaneously, without training, based on the demand quality of the lever itself (autoshaping).

Each rat's operant chamber is equipped with an operant panel containing two retractable levers (one for food or drug deliveries and another that may remain inoperable during the sessions) and stimulus lamps positioned over each lever and a house lamp. At the initiation of the drug delivery session, the stimulus lamp over the drug lever will be illuminated, and the drug lever will be inserted into the chamber for operations. Ten consecutive lever presses will deliver a single bolus of drug via the indwelling venous catheter that is connected to a syringe drive pump system located on the outside top of the cage. Following the drug session, the drug lever will retract, and the stimulus and house lamp will be darkened. Food may not be available during drug infusion sessions.

Training sessions usually last 60 min or 50 food deliveries, whichever occurs first. Once the rats are conditioned to routinely complete multiple FR10 schedule response requirements (e.g., they have learned to press the lever 10 consecutive times for delivery of a single 45-mg food pellet), a single operant session is planned in which both food and a single bolus of cocaine is delivered following the completion of the 10th response within the FR10 schedule. If an animal does not respond on the first day of cocaine-alone sessions, another food + cocaine day can be instituted into the series. To date, this laboratory has had less than 0.2% of all animals trained to continue on a second day of food + cocaine deliveries—cocaine is a rather robust positive reinforcing stimulus—one strong reason why it was selected by the PhRMA-FDA CSS review team.

Cocaine provides a rather robust stimulus that has repeatedly demonstrated to maintain stable day-to-day patterns of responding in rodents. The observation that behaviors originally reinforced by one drug (cocaine) may be maintained readily by a different drug has encouraged the development of substitution procedures as the standard procedure for the assessment of the reinforcing effects of novel compounds [4,34–37]. It is also important to note that the particular history used to establish a drug as a reinforcer does not appear to strongly control the later behavior maintained by a novel test compound [4]. Therefore, in most cases, the CSS and PhRMA staff have adopted cocaine as the reference or positive control article to be used for rat self-administration studies. It should also be noted that other common drugs-of-abuse may be selected as the maintenance drug based on the general therapeutic target of interest, or a specific pharmacologic effect (e.g., somnolence).

As stated previously, once animals have demonstrated day-to-day stability in responding for food, a single session is then scheduled in which each 10th lever press response is reinforced by a delivery of the expected food pellet as well as a simultaneous delivery of cocaine through the indwelling jugular catheter. The following figures depict the cumulative records of two rats during the transition between food-reinforced lever press responding to cocaine-reinforced lever press responding. A cumulative record is a running record of the pattern and rates-of-lever press responding automatically recorded by the software program controlling the behavioral contingencies during operant sessions. The computer software creates a pictorial representation of the accrual of lever presses (each lever press moves the pen upward) along the time continuum (horizontal plane) as well as the activation of the reinforcer delivery system, a downward blip of the pen, whether it is the food pellet dispenser or the syringe drive pump system.

As shown in Figure 2, the initial reinforcer, food, can be shifted to cocaine within a single session. Following this transfer of the primary stimulus used in the study to maintain lever press responding, cocaine will be the only delivered reinforcer for the rest of the training phase of the study.

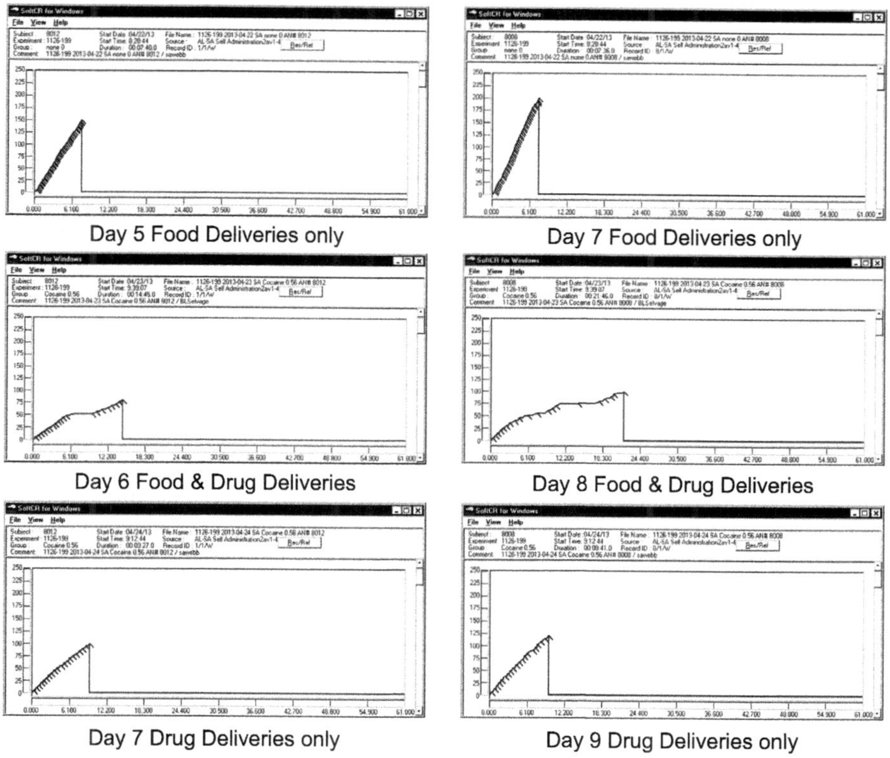

Figure 2 Cumulative records from two rats (left panels versus right panels) representing the moment-to-moment within session pattern of lever press responses emitted over three consecutive training days (top, middle, and bottom panels). Session duration is shown on the abscissa, and the sampling epoch was set for one-fifth of the session duration and shown on the ordinate. Had an animal reached the maximum height of the sampling epoch, the pen would have been reset to the baseline to continue recording the lever-press response topography. Top panels show the results of individual rats reinforced by the delivery of one 45-mg food pellet. The animals earned 50 food pellets within 7–8 min. The middle panel shows the two rat's lever-press responding when reinforced by the delivery of a 45-mg food pellet and a single bolus of 0.56 mg/kg/injection of cocaine. The session length was approximately 15 and 20 min for rats (left and right panels, respectively). The lower panels show the data from the third of three conditioning days in which only cocaine was delivered following the emission of 10 consecutive responses on the operant lever, and the animal earned the maximum number of 20 drug deliveries within 9–10 min.

5. THE DRUG CONTINGENCIES

Members of the PhRMA and CSS staff at CDER have expressed concerns regarding the use of equivalent volumes and infusion durations for all vehicle, positive control (maintenance drug), and test article dose administrations. Previous published reports have demonstrated that infusion speeds may be varied from immediate to 40s without any significant effects on the assessment of the reinforcing properties of intravenously administered drugs [38–40]. Other studies have shown that when infusions of cocaine or amphetamine were administered between 5 and 100s, there was very little, if any, effect on the acquisition or maintenance self-administration behavior, progressive ratio breakpoints, or the reinstatement of drug-seeking behavior [41–45]. Samaha, Minogianis, and Nachar [46] have more recently shown that conditioned reinforcing effects of drug cues are not critically dependent on the rate of dose administrations in rats using 5s versus 90s delivery intervals. The FDA has voiced concerns to ensure that similar volumes and infusion durations are used throughout the study plan for both positive and test article deliveries.

Daily training sessions are conducted in which an animal can receive 1) an unlimited number of injections of the drug during the session or 2) the daily compliment of total drug available is set at some predetermined limit (e.g., 10 to 20 injections). Session duration can be varied, but generally 1–2h sessions are sufficient to initiate and maintain consistent patterns of lever-press contingent drug deliveries. To avoid toxicity and to promote a rapid expression of day-to-day stability, most maintenance/training sessions are limited to 10–20 injections per session. This allows for a clear and distinct behavioral baseline to distinguish the maintenance of the lever press response being reinforced by the cocaine injections, but it prevents the possibility of overdose or toxicity during the initial training phases of the study. Once stable day-to-day operant lever-press responding has been established, usually defined as less than 15–20% day-to-day variability over three consecutive sessions, the rat can be tested.

6. THE TESTING

All novel doses and novel drug tests are conducted following the demonstration of stable self-administration with the reference/maintenance drug, cocaine. During test sessions, animals are given unlimited access to the drug unless there is evidence of a significant toxic or lethal dose that will set the upper limit for the total number of injections that can be earned during the session. Typically, lever press responding is self-limiting in that as toxicity is induced by drug delivered in the self-administration procedure, the animals tend to reduce their behavior and discontinue lever press responding to autoregulate the total dose consumed within a session. Each animal may press 10 consecutive times on a lever to deliver a single bolus of cocaine. There is no maximum number of injections earned during the 1-h session conducted for three consecutive days. A 10-s time out is generally scheduled between the end of the infusion and the opportunity to respond for the next injection to minimize the likelihood of overdose.

The primary dependent variables in self-administration assays are related to the drug that is delivered contingent upon the animal's behavior (lever press responding). The reinforcing properties of a drug are assessed by contingent drug administration, only.

Noncontingent drug administration (drug that is administered by the technician and not contingent upon any behavior of the animal) is documented in the study file but not included in the dependent variable data sets. Examples of noncontingent drug delivery are 1) the small amount of residual drug left in the catheter after the session that is flushed into the animal with heparinized saline or heparinized dextrose to clear the catheter and prepare it for heparinized lock conditions, 2) the priming injection at the start of the session to fill all catheter space between the outlet of the syringe and the cannula connection exiting the animals back, and 3) the methohexital tests that may be used to ensure catheter patency.

Once each animal demonstrates stable operant responding for cocaine infusion (0.56 mg/kg/injection) for three contiguous days of training or maintenance sessions, a series of test sessions are planned (A-B-A study design). The first series of test sessions are conducted with the maintenance dose of cocaine (0.56 mg/kg/injection)—in this session, the animal, for the first time, can respond for an unlimited number of injections over a 1-h access period on each of three consecutive days.

Following the completion of the maintenance dose tests, an extinction test with saline (vehicle) is scheduled. These operant-conditioning procedures make explicit use of the fact that drug-reinforced responding undergoes extinction and eventually decreases in probability when a reinforcing drug dose is replaced with vehicle (saline) or an ineffective drug reinforcer or drug dose.

In discussions between the PhRMA and the CSS staff in CDER at FDA, a general scheme for interpreting the results of a standard self-administration study was proposed:

Criteria for Establishment of the Test Item as an "Ineffective Reinforcer"

> If the total number of injections decline over the course of the 3-day substitution period or there is clear "vehicle-like" or "saline-like" response topographies during the course of testing (e.g., a downward staircase pattern), then the test article will be considered as an ineffective reinforcer.

Criteria for Establishment of the Test Item as a "Positive Reinforcer"

> *Full substitution* for cocaine is defined as drug-maintained lever-press responding for three consecutive days and the demonstration of between session stability of ≥ 80%. A dose of the test item is considered to *fully substitute for the maintenance dose* of cocaine if the total number of injections of a test article dose (expressed in mg/kg/injection) over three consecutive days of substitution is equivalent to the total number of injections engendered by the maintenance dose (0.56 mg/kg/infusion) of cocaine.

Criteria for Establishment of the Test Item as Demonstrating "Acute" Reinforcing Effects

a. If the test item maintains a stable number of injections across the three consecutive days of substitution in a single animal, then it is considered to be demonstrative evidence of a subject-specific, short-term, *acute reinforcing effect*.

b. If the test article maintains lever-press responding (equivalent to the maintenance dose of cocaine) throughout a session on Day 1 and/or Day 2, only, of the three day series of tests conducted in the study, the test item is considered to engender acute (short-lived) reinforcing effects.

Figure 3 shows the typical differential pattern of responding in rats conditioned to self-administer doses of 0.56 mg/kg/injection of cocaine in daily 1-h sessions. Day-to-day stability is maintained by the maintenance dose of cocaine with each animal delivering approximately 22 injections per day resulting in a total delivered daily dose of 12.3 mg/kg/session of intravenous cocaine. In trained animals exhibiting day-to-day stability for drug deliveries, the substitution of the normal maintenance drug dose with saline will produce an initial increase of (especially early session) lever-press responding during Day 1 of substitution, as if the animal is searching for his normal compliment of cocaine. This acute increase in responding is commonly referred to as an extinction burst. Generally, on the second and third day of a substitution test, rats will show a day-to-day decline in a downward staircase fashion demonstrating the vehicle lacks the reinforcing properties that have been established by the known drug of abuse, cocaine.

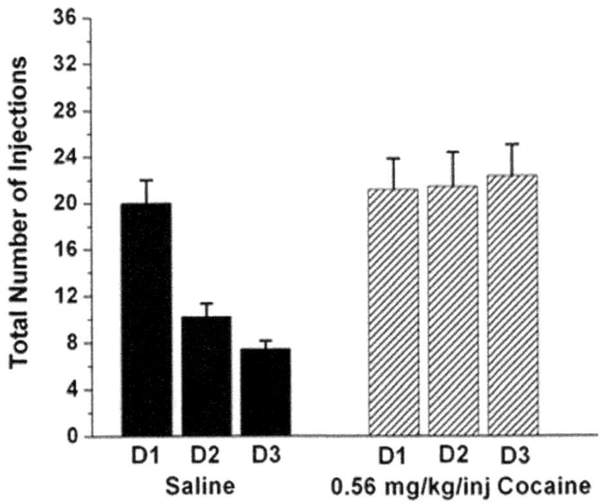

Figure 3 Total number of injections (mean ± SEM) earned during 1-h test sessions in which rats had unlimited access to the maintenance dose of cocaine (0.56 mg/kg/injection) or saline for three consecutive days (D1, D2, D3).

Failure to observe such extinction behavior when a benign, behaviorally inactive substance (i.e., Figure 4, saline) or a new drug, drug dose, or novel test condition is substituted for cocaine suggests that the test condition is reinforcing the continued responding. Following testing of the maintenance dose of cocaine (0.56 mg/kg/injection) and the extinction trial with saline, other doses of cocaine should be tested to demonstrate a full dose–response function for the maintenance drug (Figure 5).

Figure 6 shows the within-laboratory stability of cocaine self-administration studies. Over the last 4 years, 12 different groups of rats have been conditioned to self-administer 0.56 mg/kg/injection of cocaine. The group average intake over three consecutive days of testing in 12 different groups averaging 28 rats per study is shown, as follows:

The data depicted in Figure 3 demonstrate a clear ability to discriminate between saline and cocaine. The data depicted in Figures 5 and 6 illustrate further that a standardized procedure within a given laboratory can generate extremely stable and consistent intake of the maintenance dose of cocaine. Once this is achieved in a given experiment, a full cocaine dose response function can be generated.

7. DOSE–RESPONSE RELATIONSHIPS

Each study should include tests conducted with a full range of the reference or maintenance drug (cocaine) and ideally include demonstrative evidence of historical control data stability for the assay within the given laboratory (Figure 7).

All four graphs show the typical inverted U-shaped function generated in self-administration studies. All four studies also show the typical leftward peak shift in the dose response curve wherein lower doses engendered the highest daily intake of cocaine when compared to the maintenance dose used in each of the four study plans (0.56 mg/kg/injection). The studies depicted in the two top panels (A and B) used the same dose range and illustrate the characteristic dose response symmetry between independent studies. Dose response functions from Studies A, B, and C demonstrated the typical day-to-day stability and small within-sample variability for the 3 days the rats had unlimited access to each tested dose of cocaine. The final study (D) included even lower doses of cocaine to demonstrate that an extremely low, behaviorally inactive dose of the maintenance drug (0.01 mg/kg/injection) would engender the downward staircase pattern of responding typical of saline, or in this case, a nonreinforcing stimulus.

During discussions between the FDA and PhRMA, it was generally agreed that the test article dose effect function should be tested from low dose to high dose and target the terminal high dose test to be near the 3X the animal-equivalent efficacious dose (C_{eff}) or to the limits of solubility in the vehicle used on the study.

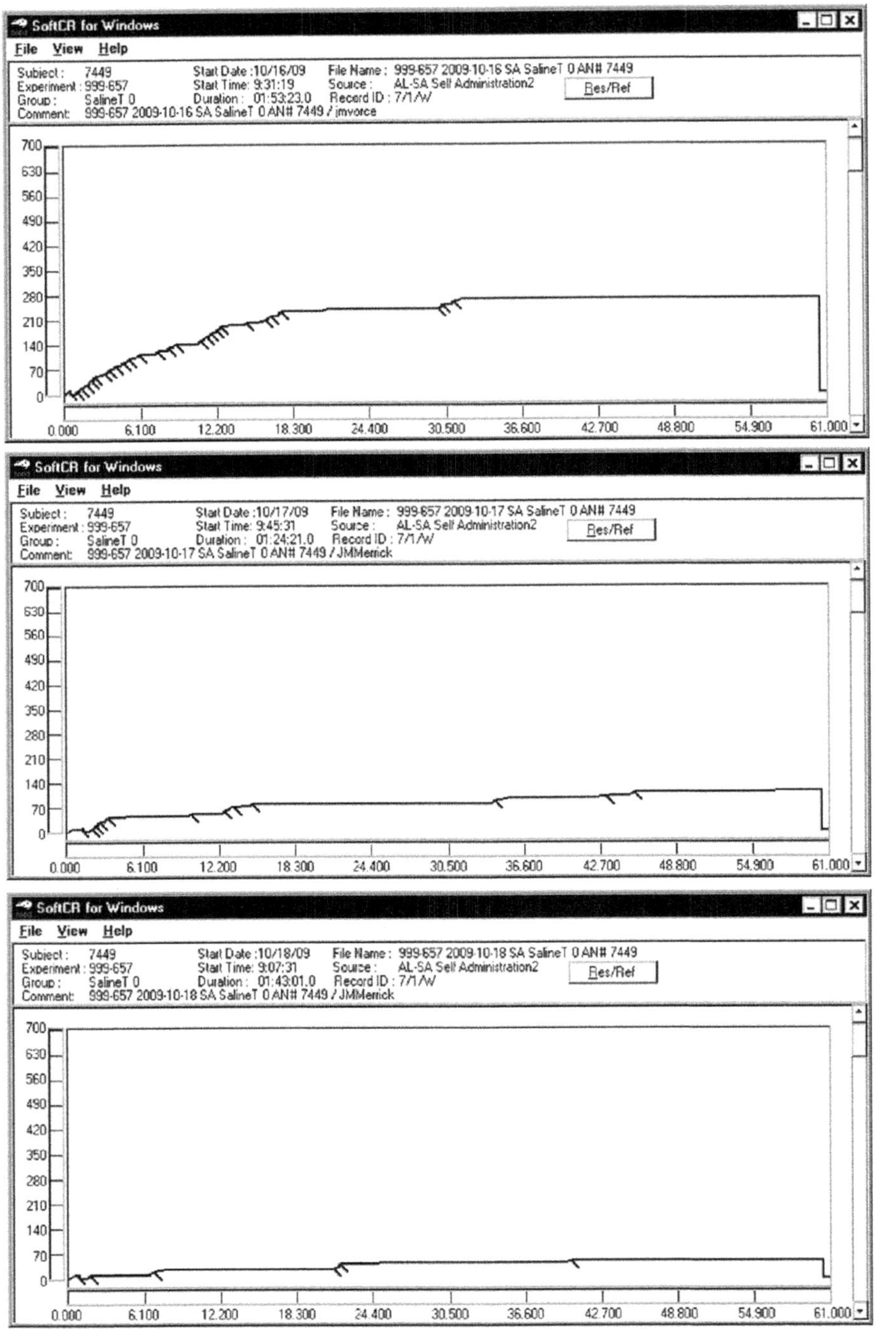

Figure 4 Cumulative records from one representative rat showing the within-session moment-to-moment pattern of lever press responses emitted over three consecutive test sessions with saline as summarized in Figure 3. Session length is shown on the abscissa. The rat completed responding for 27 injections on Day 1 (top panel), 12 injections on Day 2 (middle panel), and six injections on Day 3 (lower panel) representing the downward staircase pattern over the 3 days depicted in Figure 3. Note that on Day 1 (top panel), most responding occurred at the beginning of the session (extinction burst), but by Day 3 (bottom panel), the pattern of responding would best be described as "sampling behavior," as if the rat is periodically testing the system for the normal delivery of cocaine expected from its experimental history during these initial sessions.

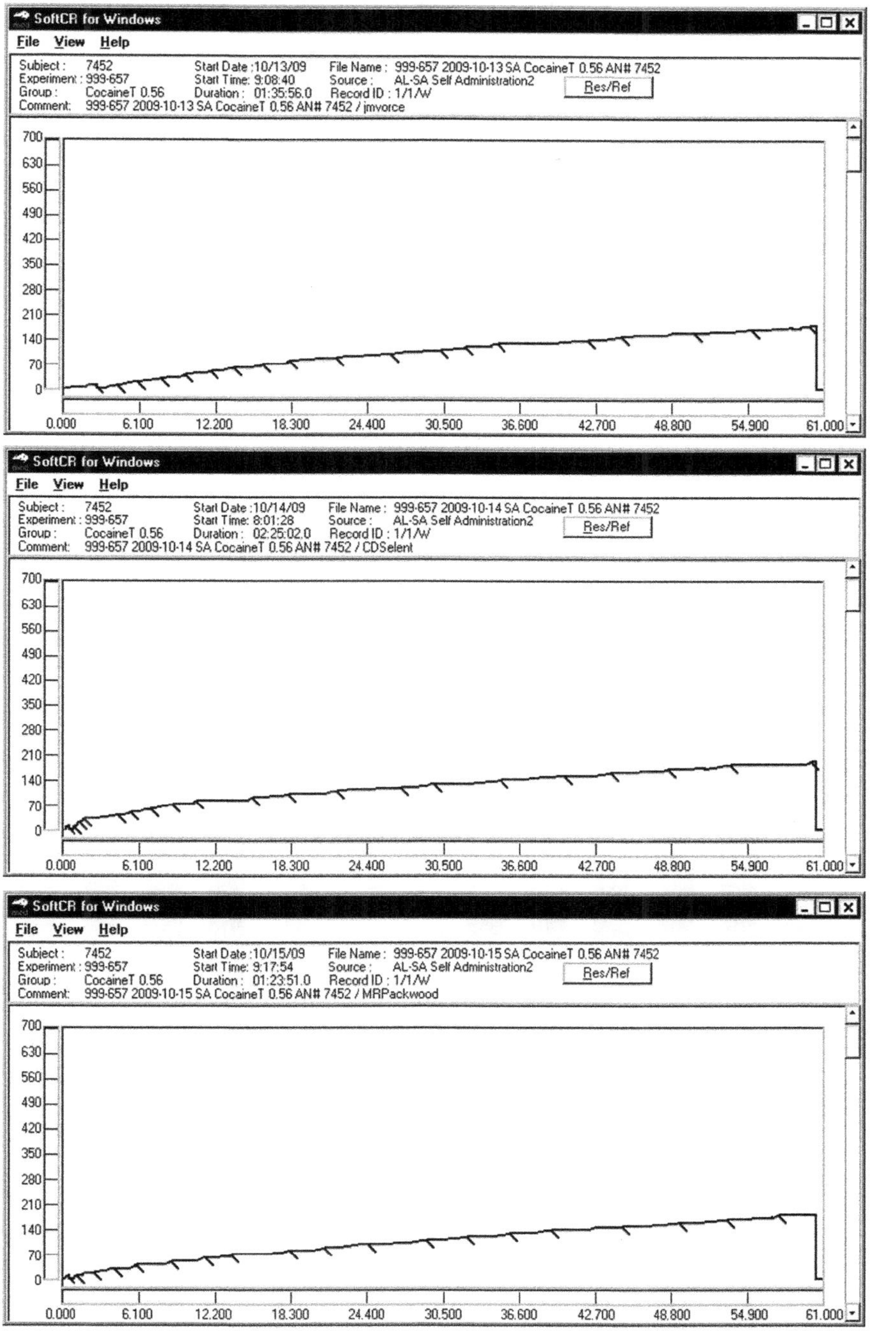

Figure 5 Cumulative records from one representative rat showing the within-session moment-to-moment pattern of lever press responses emitted over three consecutive test sessions with the 0.56 mg/kg/injection maintenance dose of cocaine as summarized in Figure 4. Session length is shown on the abscissa. The rat completed responding for 19 injections on Day 1 (top panel), 20 injections on Day 2 (middle panel), and 19 injections on Day 3 (bottom panel) representing very stable responding over the 3 days when compared to saline, depicted in Figure 4. Note that on all 3 days, the injections were distributed across the entire 1-h access period with very similar duration of pauses between earned drug deliveries.

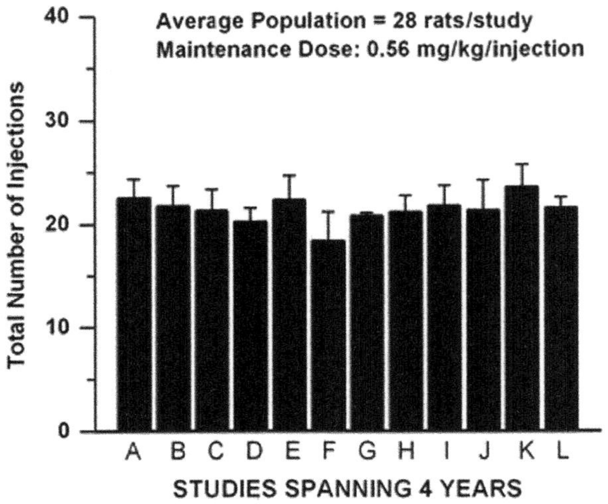

Figure 6 Group mean averages of cocaine intake assessed over three consecutive days of testing under unlimited drug access conditions in 12 different groups of male Sprague–Dawley rats tested over the course of 4 years. Standardized training procedures were used for all 12 groups of rats conditioned to self-administer 0.56 mg/kg/injection during daily 1-h access periods.

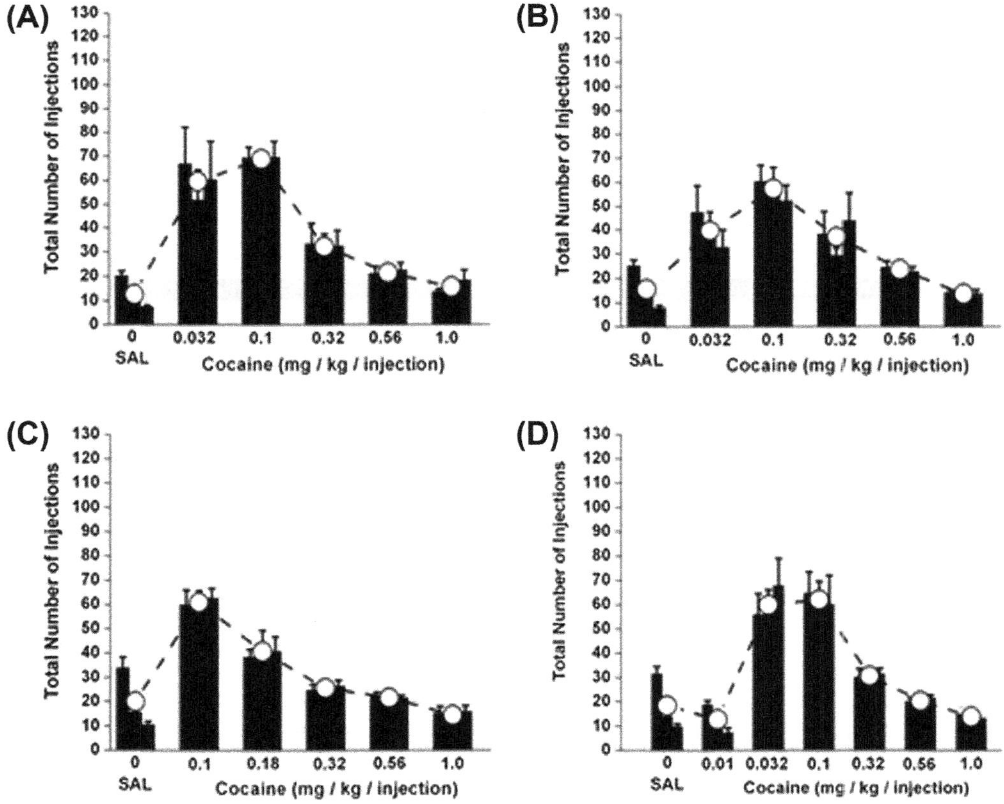

Figure 7 Cocaine dose–response functions from four independent studies conducted over 1 year. The total number of injections administered is plotted as a function of tested cocaine doses. Each bar represents the mean and standard error of the mean for 32 rats for both saline and the maintenance dose of cocaine (0.56 mg/kg/injection). All other data reflect the mean and SEM for doses that were tested for three consecutive days in a subset of six selected rats from the trained pool of subjects.

8. MAINTENANCE DRUG

For evaluation purposes, the standardized use of cocaine as the reference stimulus in self-administration studies in relation to the stimulus control of behavior maintained by another drug of abuse using rats as experimental subjects can be compared. However, based on the structure and function of the test article other positive control articles may be used. A detailed explanation for selecting the positive control in each study should be included in the protocol. Because schedule control action is based on the relative abuse liability to other known drugs of abuse, the positive control article must be selected from one of the many drugs listed in one of the five classes of scheduled drugs listed in the Controlled Substances Act. The positive control or maintenance drug must be a controlled substance. Unscheduled drugs, such as nicotine, ethanol, or dextromethorphan, that may give positive abuse liability signals in a group of rats may be included to provide context, limitations, or sensitivity of the model; however, an independent group of rats using a schedule control drug must also be included.

In the standardized design proposed by the guidance document, once rats are conditioned to self-administer cocaine, they can easily be transferred to another drug of abuse and maintain equivalent stimulus control of behavior. In one study (Panel A, Figure 8) rats were transferred from cocaine-maintained responding (0.56 mg/kg/injection) to self-administer hydrocodone (0.18 mg/kg/injection) based on the therapeutic targets of the test articles under evaluation in these experiments. Following approximately 3 weeks and the demonstration of less than 20% day-to-day variability for the total number of injections each rat administered, testing was initiated. Similar dose–response function tests were conducted with test doses of hydrocodone in animals initiated and maintained to self-administer cocaine (Panel B). The figures show that the dose–response function generated for hydrocodone in rats conditioned to self-administer 0.56 mg/kg/injection of cocaine (Panel B) compared to animals conditioned to maintain lever press responding by 0.18 mg/kg/injection of hydrocodone (Panel A).

Under the 8-factor analysis used to determine schedule control actions, using hydrocodone (Panel A) or cocaine (Panel B) as the maintenance drug in rats in standard self-administration assays would result in similar conclusions regarding the reinforcing properties of hydrocodone in rats. Hydrocodone has robust reinforcing properties in the rat. While some differences are evident in the day-to-day stability during testing between the two groups, there are marked similarities: 1) both groups demonstrated the inverted U-shaped dose response relationship and 2) both groups showed the leftward peak shift in responding for hydrocodone. The test dose of 0.032 mg/kg/injection of hydrocodone maintained the highest intake in both groups. And 3) the lowest tested dose of 0.01 mg/kg/injection of hydrocodone in both groups would be considered the threshold dose, demonstrating a 3-day downward staircase pattern of intake more similar to saline-based responding than the higher doses.

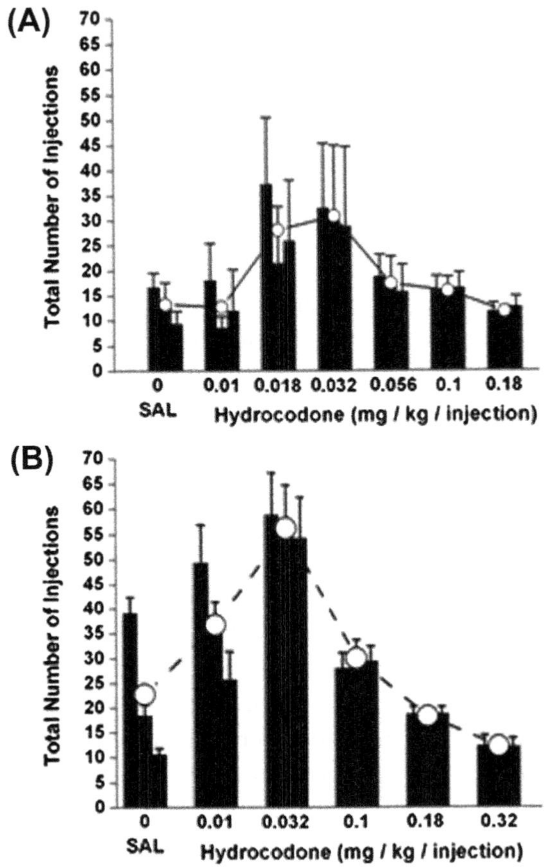

Figure 8 Hydrocodone dose–response functions generated in two groups of rats. Panel A shows the total number of injections of hydrocodone administered during 1-h unlimited drug access test sessions in rats conditioned to self-administer 0.18 mg/kg/injection of hydrocodone. Panel B shows the total number of injections of hydrocodone administered during 1-h unlimited access test sessions conducted in rats conditioned to self-administer 0.56 mg/kg/injection of cocaine.

9. GENDER

Current regulatory guidelines regarding preclinical safety assessments only require the use of one gender, while IACUC guidelines recommend a reduction in the number of animals on study. Generally, most of the published reports of self-administration studies appearing in peer-reviewed scientific journals have used male animals (Figure 9).

While trained male rats earned more drug deliveries at the 0.1 and 0.032 mg/kg/injection test doses of cocaine, both males and female rats, clearly demonstrated the

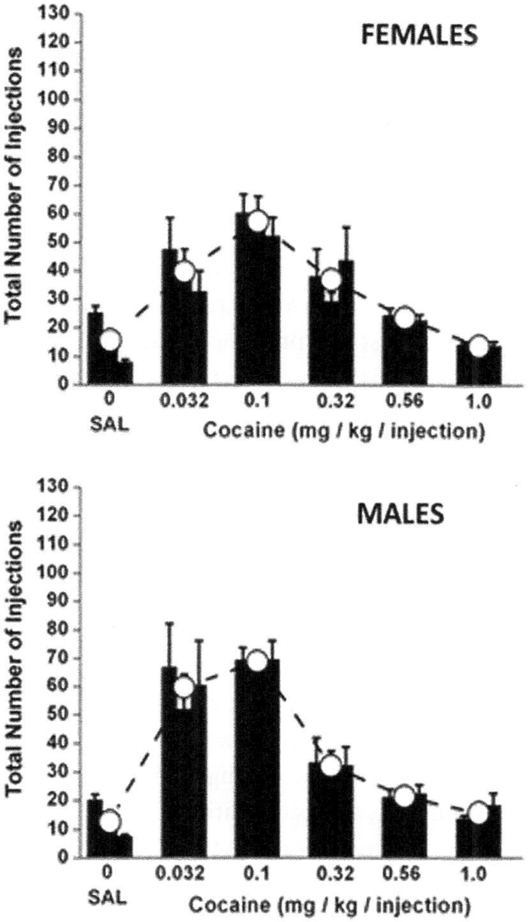

Figure 9 Cocaine dose–response functions generated in female (top) and male (bottom) rats conditioned to initiate and maintain lever-press responding for the delivery of a single bolus of 0.56 mg/kg/injection of cocaine. Unlimited drug access 1-h test sessions were conducted over identical cocaine dose ranges in both studies. Each bar and SEM for saline and 0.56 mg/kg/injection represent the total group means of 32 conditioned rats. Each bar and SEM for all other tested doses represent subgroups of six rats.

following: 1) the typical inverted U-shaped dose response relationship, 2) similar downward staircase patterns of responding when tested with saline, and 3) a leftward peak shift in responding with 0.1 mg/kg/injection engendering the largest number of injections in both groups. Therefore, under the guidelines for the assessment of the abuse liability of cocaine, similar conclusions would be drawn in both sexes—cocaine serves as a robust reinforcer in both male and female rats.

10. LIMITED VERSUS UNLIMITED ACCESS TO DRUG DURING TRAINING

As described previously, training or conditioning sessions conducted with the reference or maintenance drug can be scheduled to be delivered under limited or unlimited access conditions. Daily training sessions can be conducted 1) in which an animal can receive an unlimited number of injections of the drug during the session or 2) where the daily compliment of total drug available is set at some predetermined limit (e.g., 10–20 injections). To avoid toxicity and to promote a rapid expression of day-to-day stability, most maintenance/training sessions can be limited to 10–20 injections per session. This allows for a clear and distinct behavioral baseline to distinguish the maintenance of the lever press response being reinforced by the cocaine injections, but it prevents the possibility of overdose or toxicity during the initial training phases of the study. However, unlimited access sessions can be applied during conditioning to allow for tolerance to the rate-disruptive effects of the maintenance drug to develop over the course of initial training. In some cases, this may be advantageous if the test article has been previously shown to have rate-limiting effects already. Figure 10 shows a comparison between the cocaine dose–response functions generated in a group of rats that were trained under unlimited access conditions (top panel) in which no upper limit in the total number of injections was imposed during initial training and another group of rats that were conditioned with an upper limit of 10 injections per hour imposed during maintenance/conditioning days. Both drugs were tested under unlimited access conditions.

The three highest tested doses of cocaine 0.32, 0.56, and 1.0 mg/kg/injection engendered similar rates of cocaine self-injection regardless of the specific access conditions utilized during training. There were slightly larger numbers of injections self-administered for the two lowest threshold doses, 0.1 and 0.032 mg/kg/injection, in the group with a training history of unlimited access conditions (top panel) when compared to the limited access cohorts (bottom panel). In addition, the group having unlimited access training history tended to self-administer a greater number injections at the 0.032 mg/kg/injection dose in relation to the group having limited access during training. However, the general shape, patterns, and distribution of responding for cocaine and saline are quite similar regardless of the long history of access conditions during training. In regard to regulatory drug control policies, both groups would be considered demonstrative evidence of reinforcing properties of the reference drug.

To address the effects of limited and unlimited daily session access conditions of a known drug of abuse (cocaine) on the general health and well-being of the rats during both studies, Figure 11 depicts the bodyweight/growth charts for both groups of rats over the course of the studies.

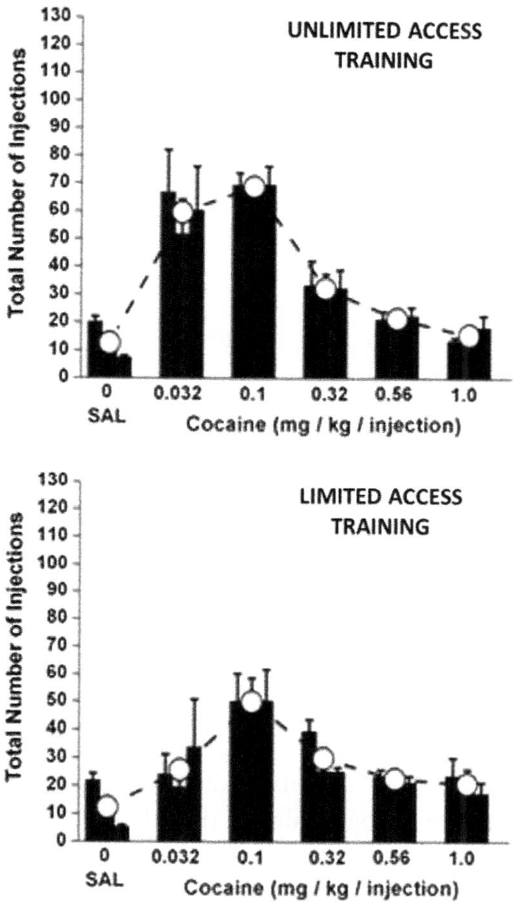

Figure 10 Cocaine dose–response functions generated under unlimited drug access test sessions in two groups of rats using 0.56 mg/kg/injection of cocaine as the maintenance dose. The top panel represents a group of rats that had unlimited access to cocaine during training, and the bottom panel represents a group of rats limited to 10 injections of cocaine during training.

11. RESPONSE TOPOGRAPHY

Cumulative records plotting the moment-to-moment patterns of reinforced responding for drugs typically show a series of closely spaced infusions (bursts) followed by a pause during which no infusions are taken. Records from nonhuman primates self-administering CNS depressants (barbiturates), for example, have been reported to show a series of bursts and pauses throughout the test session ([47], see Figure 12 top panel). In contrast, the moment-to-moment nature of responding for doses of psychomotor stimulants in nonhuman primates has been characterized as a regularly spaced pattern with large bursts of responding during the beginning of the session, with the time between infusions being increased as a function of increasing dose ([48,49], see Figure 12, bottom panel).

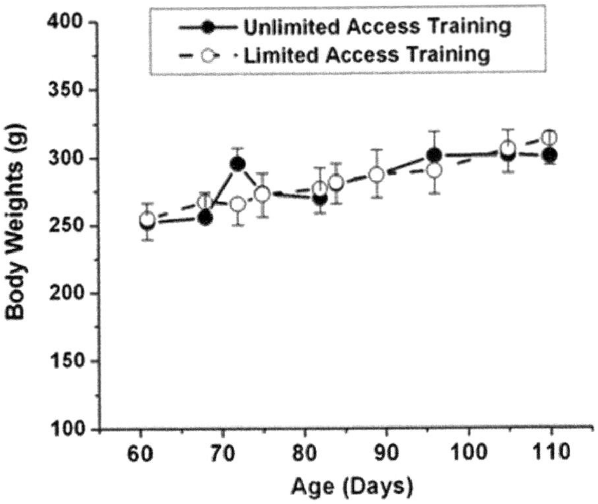

Figure 11 Group mean bodyweights of two groups of rats (N=32 rats/group) conditioned to self-administer 0.56 mg/kg/injection of cocaine in unlimited access (filled circles) and limited access (open circles) conditions during training and maintenance sessions over the last 40 days of the respective studies. No animal died in either group of rats over the 110 days of the studies. All rats were considered healthy and active, with patent catheters throughout the approximate 4-month period required to complete the studies.

Other within-session patterns of responding by nonhuman primates maintained by intravenous infusions of ethanol or opiates differ from the barbiturate-type or psychostimulant-type response topographies in that alcohol- and morphine-reinforced responding is rapid in the beginning of a session and slows as the session progresses ([50–52], see Figure 12, middle panel). For rats, these distinctions in within-session patterns of responding (response topography) for different classes of drugs are not as clear cut (Figure 13).

Both CNS stimulant (cocaine) and CNS depressant (hydrocodone) engendered a rapid intake at the beginning of the session and slower, consistent pauses as the session progressed. The characteristic, differential within-session patterns of responding for stimulant versus opiate drug types observed in monkeys may not generate similarly distinctive patterns of behavior in rats.

One potentially confounding drug property is that of altering response rates. Profound unconditioned and direct effects of drugs on the animals' rates of responding can be a misleading indicator of the reinforcing strength of the tested compound [35]. Under the standard fixed ratio schedule of drug deliveries, drug intake is a direct function of response rates [53]. Additionally, acute effects of the drug are critically dependent on the rate of ongoing behavior (rate dependency effect [54]). In actuality, under the FR10 schedule of drug deliveries, the response rates are similar to the distribution of the "total number of injections" earned in the session, presenting as an inverted U-shaped function

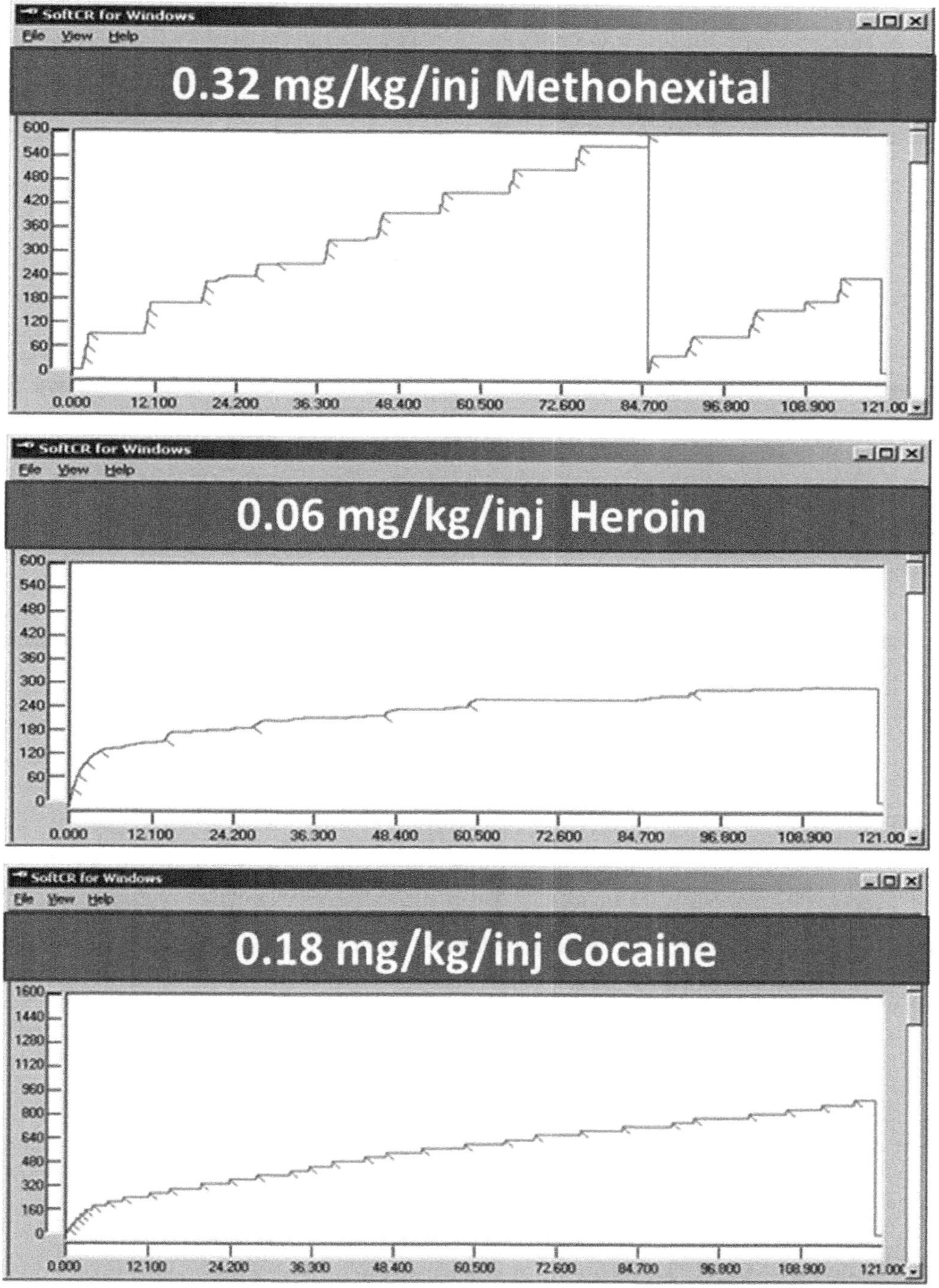

Figure 12 Cumulative records for one of three days of testing period from rhesus monkeys conditioned to self-administer a barbiturate (methohexital, top panel), an opiate (heroin, middle panel) or the psychomotor stimulant cocaine (bottom panels) in daily 2-h sessions. Monkeys were selected to demonstrate prototypic patterns of administration behavior in a meaningful way while trying to control for overall rates of responding based on the total number of injections earned in the sessions. The fast-acting barbiturate, methohexital, engenders a pattern described in the literature as "bursts and pauses," producing a step-like pattern over the full 2-h session in which the monkey earned 29 drug deliveries. Heroin, an opiate, engenders responding that is rapid in the beginning of a session and slows as the session progresses; the monkey shown took nine injections over the 2-h access period. In contrast, the psychostimulant, cocaine (bottom panel), is characterized as a regularly spaced pattern with large bursts of responding during the beginning of the session, with the time between infusions increasing as a function of increasing dose. Similar to the methohexital data (top panel), this monkey earned 30 injections over the 2-h session.

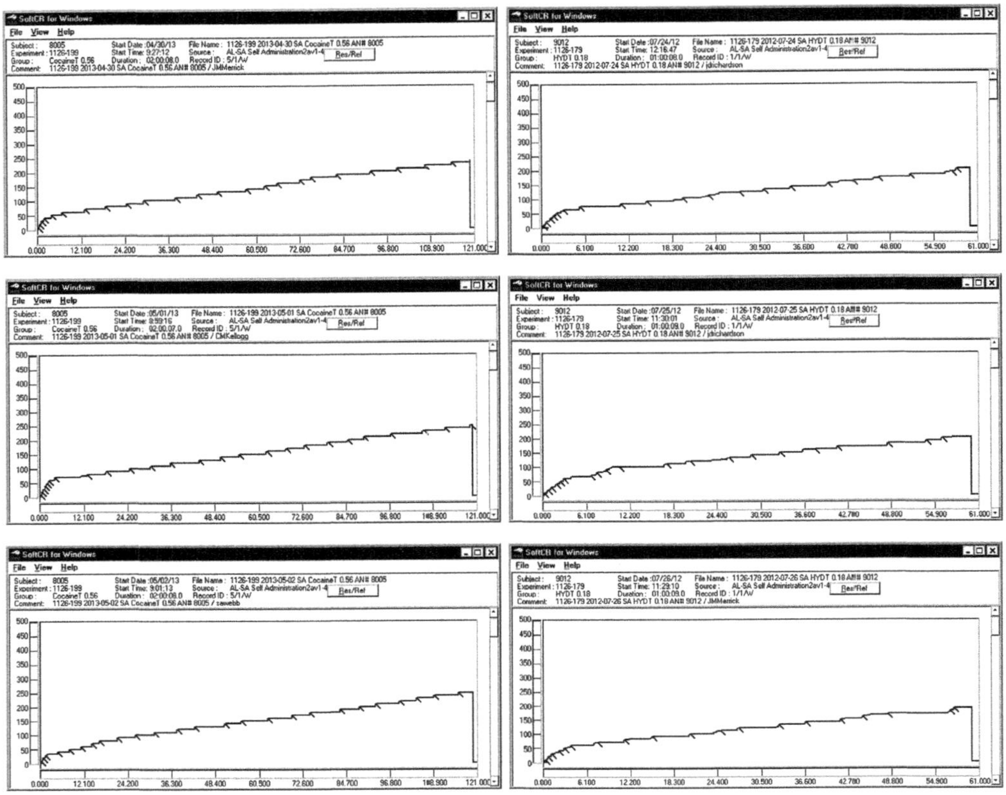

Figure 13 Cumulative records for a 3-day testing period from a single rat conditioned to self-administer the psychomotor stimulant cocaine (0.56 mg/kg/injection, left panels) and cumulative records from a 3-day testing period in a single rat similarly conditioned to self-administer the CNS depressant hydrocodone (0.18 mg/kg/injection, right panels). Rats were selected to evaluate patterns of administration behavior in a meaningful way while controlling for overall rates of responding based on the total number of injections earned in the three sessions. For cocaine (left panel), the rat earned 20, 21, and 21 injections on Day 1 (top, left panel), Day 2 (middle, left panel), and Day 3 (bottom, left panel), respectively. For comparison, the rat self-administering hydrocodone self-administered 20 injections on Day 1 (top right panel), 20 injections on Day 2 (middle, right panel), and 19 injections on Day 3 (bottom, right panel), respectively. Both CNS stimulant and CNS depressant engendered strikingly similar within-session moment-to-moment patterns of responding when the total number of injections earned within that session are controlled.

of drug dose [12,55,56]. Differences among drug classes in the temporal pattern of drug-maintained responding and drug intake under unlimited access conditions, as is typically used in this assay, have been observed consistently in different laboratories and different species. During the session, drug levels will rise, and the direct unconditioned effects of the drug will change the rates of ongoing behavior. The analysis of the raw response rates of lever-press responding has been considered an unreliable marker for the reinforcing properties of drugs [57]. The individual animals' rates of lever-press responding can be influenced by a number of factors, including drug and experimental history, present and past behavioral contingencies, the specific schedule of reinforcer delivery used during the test sessions, direct motor effects of the drug on ongoing behavior (toxicity), drug aversion, the induction of other behaviors not consistent with lever press responding (i.e., expression of stereotypy), or the lack of reinforcing properties of the test article itself [58,59].

12. REINFORCING EFFICACY

Inherent in any analysis of self-administration data determinative of drug control scheduling actions by both FDA and DEA is the assessment of abuse potential with respect to other known drugs of abuse already in the existing schedules. Part of each rat self-administration study should include an assessment of the relative reinforcing efficacy engendered by the maintenance drug (e.g., cocaine) and all doses of the test article that are determined to initiate or maintain self-administration in that study. The CSS staff at FDA has adopted a very conservative policy with respect to calling a "positive signal" in abuse liability studies during the 8-factor analysis conducted during NDA review.

Note: Under the current regulatory mindset, data from a single animal that initiates and maintains lever press responding for a single dose of test article during a single test in a multiple-day substitution test cycle *must be* considered to have some degree of abuse potential.

Relative reinforcing efficacy has been defined by Griffiths, Brady, and Bradford [35] as "the behavior-maintenance potency of a dose of drug which can be manifest under a range of different experimental conditions" (p. 192). According to Bickel, Marsch, and Carroll [60], reinforcing efficacy is a homogeneous construct that refers to a drug's ability to maintain behavior. Relative reinforcing efficacy is an intervening variable that summarizes empirical relationships [61].

At least two different techniques have been included on self-administration studies at the request of CSS staff at the FDA. Because the rate of self-administration is determined not only by reinforcing effects of a drug but also by the direct effects of the drug on motor behavior, to measure reinforcing effects in a quantitative way, it is necessary to use a procedure in which responding is determined by reinforcing effects uncontaminated with other drug effects.

For each dose of the test article that maintains self-administration of the compound over three consecutive days (15–20% variability) at levels that are similar to those levels maintained by cocaine, a second substitution test can be conducted under a progressive ratio (PR) schedule of drug delivery. Under this schedule, the animal responds on the lever for a delivery of test article. For each subsequent drug delivery, the total number of responses emitted on the lever as a requisite for drug delivery is incremented upward using a logarithmic (base e) scale using the following equation:

$$\textit{Response requirement} = 5^{*}e\ (\textit{response increment} * 0.2) - 5$$

The resulting progressive ratio schedule break point is defined as the highest number of responses emitted by the animal to earn a single reinforcer delivery of drug or vehicle. This break point is used as a behavioral marker of how much work will be expended by an experimental subject to earn a single reinforcer delivery. The amount of work expended to earn a single reinforcer is used to compare the efficacy of drug deliveries with respect to the hedonic valence induced by the drug injection, with the assumption that the subjective hedonic valence of a reinforcer determines its relative abuse liability (Figure 14).

Reinforcing efficacy has also been assessed using an extended substitution period above and beyond the initial extinction trials with saline (see Figures 3 and 4 and previous discussion). The term full extinction for the test article, saline, and the maintenance dose of cocaine is defined as a substitution or test session in which there are two or fewer infusion deliveries to each animal throughout the 2-h access session or over the duration of the saline extinction trial, whichever is shorter.

Following the generation of test article dose–response function, a data review in consultation with the sponsor usually takes place. The dose of the test article that demonstrated self-administration for 3 days and/or the highest total number of self-injections administered

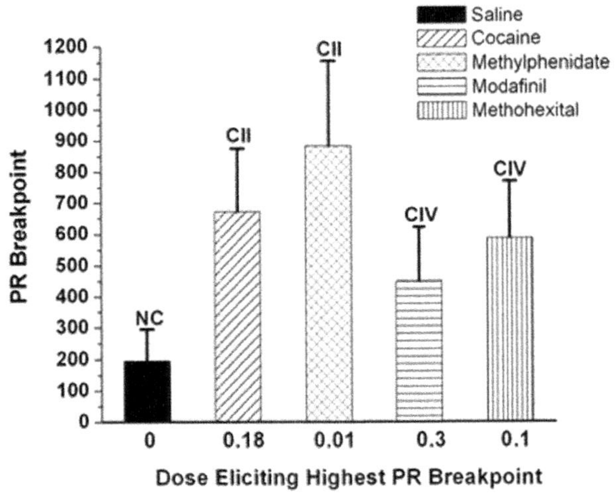

Figure 14 Progressive ratio break points established for various drug stimuli in rats conditioned to self-administer 0.56 mg/kg/injection of cocaine. The dose of test compounds that engendered the highest breakpoint is shown compared to saline and the dose of cocaine that also engendered the highest break point. All schedule controlled drugs engendered higher break points than saline (nonreinforcer), and Schedule II drugs (cocaine and methylphenidate) produced higher breakpoints than Schedule IV drugs (modafinil and methohexital) in similarly trained rats.

on Day1 of testing is subjected to an extended testing schedule to demonstrate the resistance to extinction for that dose. That is, the dose of test article that is determined to initiate and maintain self-administration for three consecutive days and/or represents the highest total self-administered injections on Day 1 of substitution testing are re-tested for a period equivalent to the saline extinction period (approx. 7–21 days duration) to show the resistance to extinction. In the event that no dose level of the test article demonstrated self-administration, the dose level that supports the highest total number of self-injections on Day 1 of substitution testing is usually assessed (Figures 15 and 16).

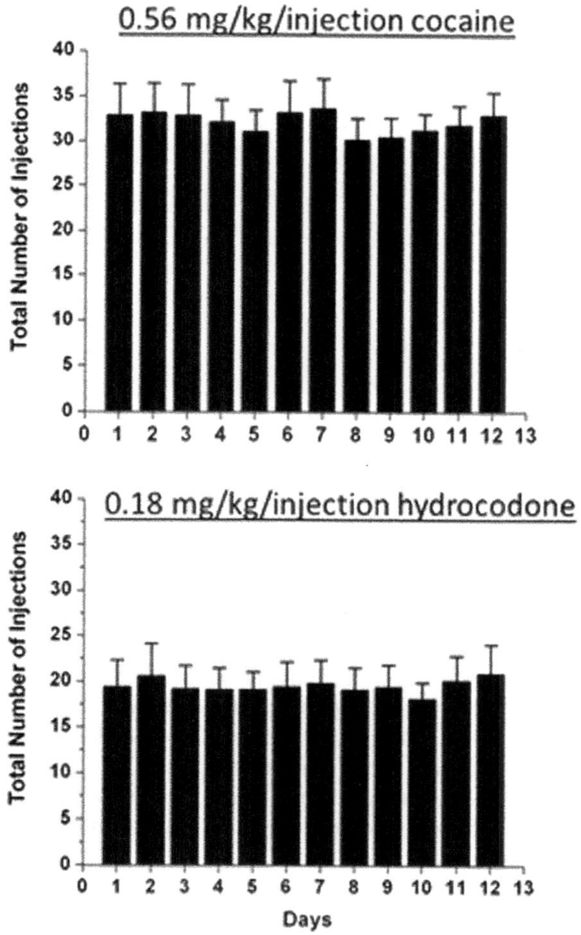

Figure 15 Extended daily test sessions used to quantify the total number of days of established stability of responding during repeated maintenance dose access periods in rats conditioned to self-administer 0.56 mg/kg/injection of cocaine (top panel) or 0.18 mg/kg/injection of hydrocodone (bottom panel). Relatively stable responding was demonstrated over 12 consecutive days of testing regardless of the drug or dose of controlled substance used to establish and maintain stimulus control of lever press responding in rats.

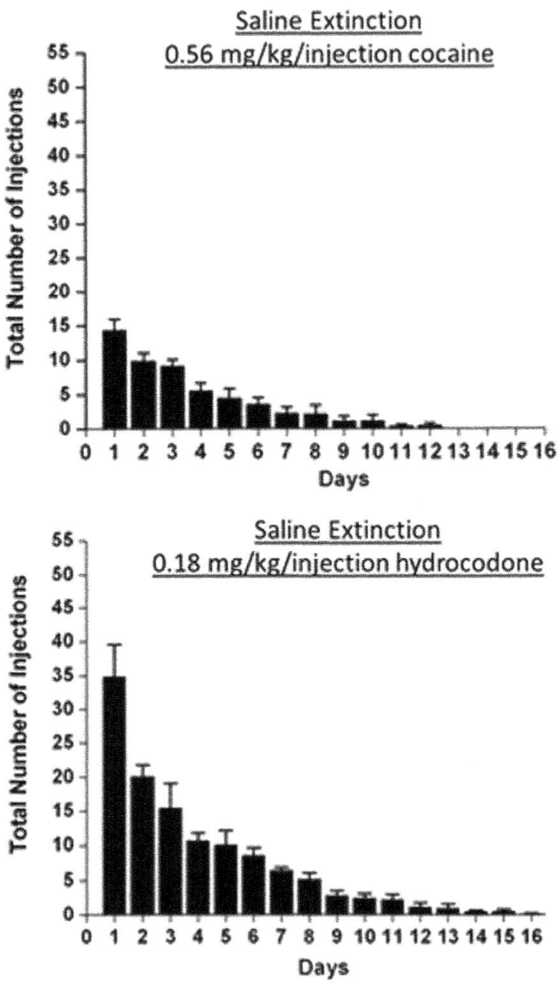

Figure 16 Extended daily test sessions used to quantify the total number of days needed to extinguish responding during repeated saline access periods in rats conditioned to self-administer 0.56 mg/kg/injection of cocaine (top panel) or 0.18 mg/kg/injection of hydrocodone (bottom panel). Extinction was defined as receiving ≤2 injections in the daily access period. Interestingly, 0.18 mg/kg/injection hydrocodone maintained higher extinction bursts during the initial extinction trials and a more pronounced resistance to extinction when compared to equivalently trained rats maintained on 0.56 mg/kg/injection of cocaine deliveries (12 versus 16 days).

Cocaine or hydrocodone, strong reinforcers, will maintain stable self-administration for weeks. A nonreinforcer, like saline, will engender diminished responding during the latter few days of an extended substitution period. This resistance to extinction is used for comparative purposes to help distinguish the strength of the reinforcing properties of any test article dose that may be relatively stable over three consecutive days, but may not maintain avid self-administration for longer durations of access.

13. CONCLUSION

Though there is a vast array of different self-administration paradigms that can validly assesses the reinforcing properties of drugs, the general international consensus on the preclinical assessment of a NCE's abuse liability is that it should be conducted in laboratory-bred rats. Additionally, the International Commission on Harmonization (M3), the European Medicines Agency, and the US FDA have all agreed on the use of 1) a simple, single-lever press operant self-administration assay, 2) using cocaine as the reference/maintenance stimulus, 3) under a fixed-ratio 10 schedule of drug deliveries, and 4) using a standard A-B-A substitution study design in laboratory rats.

The data presented here demonstrates the stability of this standard assay for the comparative analysis of the relative abuse liability of all new chemical entities that may have CNS activity, induce changes in mood or affect, or have clear stimulant, depressant, or hallucinogenic activity. The rat study may be conducted using venous catheterized male or female rats, and it can be trained using limited drug access or unlimited drug access conditions without any compromising effects on the face, construct, or predictive validity of the study plan. A second measure of reinforcing efficacy should be included in the study design for all doses of the NCE that initiate or maintain lever-press responding, even in a single animal.

The current zeitgeist within regulatory agencies requires the primary use of rat subjects. This should be maintained except in cases where metabolic, operational, or therapeutic target may require examination for the use of nonhuman primates. The results of preclinical self-administration studies are not the sole determinative factor in schedule control actions. The independent decisions of the two regulatory agencies (FDA and DEA) that conduct in-depth assessments of the abuse potential of all new chemical entities base their decisions on the totality of information [62] or weight of evidence [63] provided to them by the sponsor. There is no single positive predictor within the eight factors determinative of schedule control actions, and this includes self-administration assays. Caffeine, ethanol, ephedrine, and dextromethorphan have all shown patterns of abuse/misuse by humans and have shown positive signals in preclinical self-administration studies, but none are currently controlled substances. A positive signal in the self-administration assay should not be used as a go/no go screen for the advancement of new chemical entities in the pipeline. And, indeed, a negative signal in this assay should not be the interpreted as demonstrative evidence that the NCE will not be abused, once the drug has easy access to the general population (i.e., sibutramine, gamma hydroxybutyric acid [GHB], fenfluramine, LSD, etc.). The data set from this assay is but one piece of a complex puzzle related to the accurate prediction of abuse potential and should be considered as such during the NDA process.

REFERENCES

[1] Brady JV. Animal models for assessing drugs of abuse. Neurosci Biobehav Rev 1991;15:35–43.
[2] International Conference on Harmonisation of Technical Requirements for Registration of Pharmaceuticals for Human Use. Guidance on nonclinical safety studies for the conduct of human clinical trials and marketing authorization for pharmaceuticals. M3(R2). 2009. Available at: http://www.ich.org/fileadmin/Public_Web_Site/ICH_Products/Guidelines/Multidisciplinary/M3_R2/Step4/M3_R2__Guideline.pdf [accessed 18.04.14].
[3] International Conference on Harmonisation of Technical Requirements for Registration of Pharmaceuticals for Human Use. ICH harmonised tripartite guideline safety pharmacology studies for human pharmaceuticals, S7A. 2000. Available at: http://www.ich.org/fileadmin/Public_Web_Site/ICH_Products/Guidelines/Safety/S7A/Step4/S7A_Guideline.pdf [accessed 18.04.14].
[4] Young AM, Herling S. Drugs as reinforcers: studies in laboratory animals. In: Goldberg SR, Stolerman IP, editors. Behavioral analysis of drug dependence. New York: Academic Press; 1986. p. 9–67.
[5] Schuster CR, Thompson T. Self administration of and behavioral dependence on drugs. Annu Rev Pharmacol 1969;9:483–502.
[6] Griffiths RR, Bigelow GE, Henningfield JE. Animal and human drug-taking behavior. In: Mello NK, editor. Advances in substance abuse, behavioral and biological research: a research annual, vol. I. Greenwich, CT: JAI Press; 1980. p. 1–90.
[7] Haney M, Spealman R. Controversies in translational research: drug self-administration. Psychopharmacology (Berl) 2008;199:403–19.
[8] Carter LP, Griffiths RR. Principles of laboratory assessment of drug abuse liability and implications for clinical development. Drug Alcohol Depend 2009;105(Suppl. 1):S14–25.
[9] Henningfield JE, Hatsukami DK, Zeller M, Peters E. Conference on abuse liability and appeal of tobacco products: conclusions and recommendations. Drug Alcohol Depend 2011;116:1–7.
[10] Brady JV, Griffiths RR, Winger G. Drug-maintained performance procedures and the evaluation of sedative hypnotic dependence potential. In: Kagan F, Harwood T, Rickels K, Rudzik H, Sorer H, editors. Hypnotics: methods of development and evaluation. New York: Spectrum Publications; 1975. p. 221–35.
[11] Griffiths RR, Balster RL. Opioids: similarity between evaluations of subjective effects and animal self-administration results. Clin Pharmacol Ther 1979;25:611–7.
[12] Johanson CE, Balster RL. A summary of the results of a drug self-administration study using substitution procedures in rhesus monkeys. Bull Narc 1978;30:43–54.
[13] European Monitoring Centre for Drugs and Drug Addiction. Risk assessment of new psychoactive subtances. Operating guidelines. Lisbon: European Monitoring Centre and Drug Addiction (EMCDDA); 2009. Available at: http://www.emcdda.europa.eu/attachements.cfm/att_100979_EN_RiskGuidelines2010.pdf [accessed 18.04.14].
[14] WHO Expert Committee on Drug Dependence. WHO technical report series, 915, WHO expert committee on drug dependence: thirty-third report. Geneva: World Health Organization; 2003. Available at: http://whqlibdoc.who.int/trs/WHO_TRS_915.pdf [accessed 18.04.14].
[15] World Health Organization. Guidelines for the WHO review of dependence-producing psychoactive substances for international control. 2000. Available at: http://www.cpdd.vcu.edu/Pages/Index/Index_PDFs/GuidelinesForTheWhoReviewOfDependenceProducingPsychoactiveSubstancesForInternationalControl.pdf [accessed 18.04.14].
[16] World Health Organization. Guidelines for the WHO review of dependence-producing psychoactive substances for international control: proposed revision. 2009. Available at: http://apps.who.int/gb/ebwha/pdf_files/EB126/B126_21-en.pdf [accessed 18.04.14].
[17] US Food and Drug Administration (FDA). Controlled subtances staff, CDER, PhRMA-FDA dialogue session: abuse potential assessments. Available at: http://www.fda.gov/Cder/Offices/CSS/presentations/CSS_PHRMA_FDA_Dialogue_Session%20FINAL%20022508.pdf [accessed 18.04.14].
[18] US Department of Health and Human Services, Food and Drug Administration (FDA). Guidance for industry. Assessment of abuse potential of drugs; 2010. Available at: http://www.fda.gov/cder/guidance/index.htm [accessed 18.04.14].
[19] Title 21 USCA, Food and Drugs. Drug abuse prevention and control, as amendmended to February 15, 1996. [Chapter 1]. US Department of Justice; 1970. Available at: http://uscode.house.gov/download/pls/21C13.txt [accessed 18.04.14].

[20] US Department of Health and Human Services, Food and Drug Administration (FDA). PhRMA-fda dialogue session abuse potential assessments; 2008. Available at: http://www.fda.gov/downloads/AboutFDA/CentersOffices/CDER/UCM180769.pdf [accessed 18.04.14].

[21] United Nations. International Narcotic Control Board [INCB]. Single convention on narcotic drugs. As amended by the 1972 protocol amending the single convention on narcotic drugs (1961); 1961. Available at: http://www.incb.org/pdf/e/conv/convention_1961_en.pdf [accessed 18.04.14].

[22] United Nations, the Economic and Social Council. Convention on psychotropic substances, 1971. 1971. Available at: http://www.unodc.org/pdf/convention_1971_en.pdf [accessed 18.04.14].

[23] European Medicines Agency (EMeA). Guideline on the non-clinical investigation of the dependence potential of medicinal products. London: Committee for Medicinal Products for Human Use (EMEA/CHMP/SWP/94227/2004); 2006. Available at: http://www.ema.europa.eu/docs/en_GB/document_library/Scientific_guideline/2009/09/WC500003360.pdf [accessed 18.04.14].

[24] US Department of Human Services, Food and Drug Administration (FDA). Good laboratory practice (GLP) regulations, final rule, 21 CFR Part 58. September 4, 1987 Fed Regist 1978;52(172):33768–82. Washington, D.C.: US Government Printing Office.

[25] US Department of Human Services, Food and Drug Administration (FDA) Office of Regulatory Affairs. Guidance for industry: good laboratory practices; 1981. Questions and Answers. Question #4. Available at: http://www.fda.gov/downloads/ICECI/EnforcementActions/BioresearchMonitoring/ucm133748.pdf [accessed 04.14].

[26] Balster RL, Bigelow GE. Guidelines and methodological reviews concerning drug abuse liability assessment. Drug Alcohol Dep 2003;70(3 Suppl.):S13–40.

[27] Office of Diversion Control, Drug Enforcement Administration. Controlled substances security manual: security requirements for non-practitioner; 2014. Available at: http://www.deadiversion.usdoj.gov/pubs/manuals/sec/sec_non_prac.htm [accessed 18.04.14].

[28] Weeks JR, Davis JD. Chronic intravenous cannulas for rats. J Appl Physiol 1964;19:540–1.

[29] Weeks JR. (1983, personal communication). Personal Communication No. 1011, Cardiovascular techniques using unanesthetized and freely moving rats: a description and detailed instructions for intravenous injections, infusions, and measuring blood pressure. James R. Weeks, Ph.D., Experimental Biology Division, The UpJohn Company, Kalamazoo, MI 49001 (available upon request).

[30] Yanagita T. Methodological considerations in testing physical dependence potential of sedative-hypnotics in animals. In: Thompson T, Unna KR, editors. Predicting dependence liability of stimulant and depressant drugs. Baltimore: University Park Press; 1977. p. 47–56.

[31] Yanagita T. Drug dependence studies in laboratory animals. NIDA Res Monogr 1978;19:179–90.

[32] Michael J. Laboratory studies in operant behavior. New York: McGraw-Hill Book Company, Inc.; 1963.

[33] Tarpy RM. Basic principles of learning. Glenview, IL: Scott, Foresman and Company; 1975.

[34] Woods JH. Narcotic-reinforced responding: a rapid evaluation procedure. Drug Alcohol Dep 1980;5:223–30.

[35] Griffiths RR, Brady JV, Bradford LD. Predicting abuse liability of drugs with animal drug self-administration procedures: psychomotor stimulants and hallucinogens. In: Thompson T, Dews PB, editors. Advances in behavioral pharmacology, vol. 2. New York: Academic Press; 1979. p. 163–208.

[36] Johanson CE, Balster RL. A summary of the results of a drug self-administration study using substitution procedures in rhesus monkeys. Bull Narcotics 1979;30:43–50.

[37] Thompson T, Unna KR, editors. Predicting dependence liability of stimulant and depressant drugs. Baltimore: University Park Press; 1977.

[38] Crombag HS, Ferrario CR, Robinson TE. The rate of intravenous cocaine or amphetamine delivery does not influence drug-taking and drug-seeking behavior in rats. Pharmacol Biochem Behav 2008;90:797–804.

[39] Balster RL, Schuster CR. Fixed interval schedule of cocaine reinforcement: effect of dose and infusion duration. J Exper Analysis Behav 1973;20:119–29.

[40] Panlilio LV, Goldberg SR, Gilman JP, Jufer R, Cone EJ, Schindler CW. Effects of delivery rate and non-contingent infusion of cocaine on cocaine self-administration in rhesus monkeys. Psychopharmacology (Berl) 1998;137:253–8.

[41] Pickens R, Dougherty J, Thompson T. Effects of volume and duration of infusion on cocaine reinforcement with concurrent activity recording. In: Minutes of the meeting of the committee on problems of drug dependence. Washington, D.C: National Research Council, National Academy of Science; 1969. p. 5805–11.

[42] Liu Y, Roberts DC, Morgan D. Sensitization of the reinforcing effects of self-administered cocaine in rats: effects of dose and intravenous injection speed. Eur J Neurosci 2005;22:195–200.
[43] Kato S, Wakasa Y, Yanagita T. Relationship between minimum reinforcing dose and injection speed in cocaine and pentobarbital self-administration in crab-eating monkeys. Pharmacol Biochem Behav 1987;28:407–10.
[44] Wakabayashi KT, Weiss MJ, Pickup KN, Robinson TE. Rats markedly escalate their intake and show a persistent susceptibility to reinstatement only when cocaine is injected rapidly. J Neurosci 2010;30: 11346–55.
[45] Woolverton WOL, Wang Z. Relationship between injection duration, transporter occupancy and reinforcing strength of cocaine. Eur J Pharmacol 2004;486:251–7.
[46] Samaha A-N, Minogianis E-A, Nachar W. Cues paired with either rapid or sloer self-administered cocaine injections acquire similar conditioned rewarding properties. PLoS One 2013;6:1–9.
[47] Winger G, Stitzer ML, Woods JH. Barbiturate-reinforced responding in rhesus monkeys: comparisons of drugs with different durations of action. J Pharmacol Exp Ther 1975;195:505–14.
[48] Woolverton WL. Determinants of cocaine self-administration by laboratory animals. CIBA Found Symp 1992;166:149–61.
[49] Vanover KE, Nader MA, Woolverton WL. Evaluation of the discriminative stimulus and reinforcing effects of sertraline in rhesus monkeys. Pharmacol Biochem Behav 1992;41:789–93.
[50] Woods JH, Villareal JE. Patterns of cocaine, codeine, and pentazocine-reinforced responding in the rhesus monkey. Pharmacologist 1970;12:230.
[51] Schlichting UU, Goldberg SR, Wuttke W, Hoffmeister F. d-Amphetamine self-administration by rhesus monkeys with different self-administration histories. Proc Eur Soc Study Drug Toxic Excerpta Med Int Congr Ser 1970;220:62–9.
[52] Woods JH, Ikomi F, Winger G. The reinforcing property of ethanol. In: Roach MK, McIsaac WM, Creaven PJ, editors. Biological aspects of alcohol. Austin TX: University of Texas Press; 1971. p. 371–88.
[53] Howell LL, Wilcox KM. Intravenous drug self-administration in nonhuman primates. In: Buccafusco JJ, editor. Methods of behavioral analysis in neuroscience. Boca Raton, FL: CRC Press; 2001. p. 91–110.
[54] Thompson T, Dews PB, McKim WA, editors. Advances in behavioral pharmacology, vol. 3. New York: Academic Press; 1981.
[55] Woolverton WI, Nader MA. Methods for studying the reinforcing effects of drugs. In: Adler WM, editor. Testing and evaluation of drugs of abuse. New York: Liss; 1990. p. 165–92.
[56] Wise RA. Intravenous drug self-administration: a special case of positive reinforcement. In: Bozarth MA, editor. Methods of assessing the reinforcing properties of abused drugs. New York: Springer-Verlag; 1987. p. 117–41.
[57] Meisch RA, Lemaire GA. Drug self-administration. In: van Haaren F, editor. Techniques in the behavioral and neural sciences. Methods in behavioral pharmacology, vol. 10. Amsterdam: Elsevier; 1993. p. 257–300.
[58] Brady JV, Griffiths RR, Heinz RD, Ator NA, Lukas SE, Lamb RJ. Assessing drugs for abuse liability and dependence potential in laboratory primates. In: Bozarth MA, editor. Methods of assessing the reinforcing properties of abused drugs. New York: Springer-Verlag; 1987. p. 257–300.
[59] Katz JL. Drugs as reinforcers: pharmacological and behavioral factors. In: Liebman JM, Cooper SJ, editors. Neuropharmacological basis of reward. Oxford: Oxford University Press; 1989. p. 164–213.
[60] Bickel WK, Marsch LA, Carroll ME. Deconstructing relative reinforcing efficacy and situating the measures of pharmacological reinforcement with behavioral economics. A theoretical proposal. Psychopharmacology (Berl) 2000;152:44–56.
[61] MacCorquodale K, Meehl PE. On a distinction between hypothetical constructs and intervening variables. Psychol Rev 1948;55:95–107.
[62] Calderon SN, Klein M. A regulatory perspective on the abuse potential evaluation of novel stimulant drugs in the United States. Neuropharmacology 2014 (published online ahead of print). Available at: http://dx.doi.org/10.1016/j.neuropharm.2014.04.0001 [accessed 25.04.14].
[63] Weed DL. Weight of evidence: a review of concept and methods. Risk Anal 2005;25:1545–57.

CHAPTER 4

Nonhuman Primate Self-Administration in Assessments of Abuse Potential

Paul W. Czoty[1], Matthew L. Banks[2], Michael A. Nader[1], Charles P. France[3]
[1]Department of Physiology and Pharmacology, Wake Forest School of Medicine, Winston–Salem, NC, USA; [2]Department of Pharmacology and Toxicology, Medical College of Virginia, Richmond, VA, USA; [3]Department of Pharmacology, The University of Texas Health Science Center, San Antonio, TX, USA

Contents

1. ASSESSMENT OF ABUSE POTENTIAL IN LABORATORY ANIMALS

The focus of this chapter is the use of nonhuman primates (NHPs) for studying abused drugs and specifically for predicting the abuse potential of drugs. For studies of abuse potential the three most commonly used NHPs are squirrel monkeys, which are New World primates, and baboons and macaques (rhesus and cynomolgus monkeys), which are both Old World primates. Beginning with Spragg [1] there is a long history of using NHPs for assessing abuse potential due, in part, to the many advantages to using NHPs as subjects in studying the behavioral effects of drugs. First, the pharmacokinetic profile of drugs in humans is typically recapitulated more closely in NHPs than in any other species (e.g., [2]) Second, NHPs are the animals most similar to humans in terms of brain anatomy, physiology, and neurochemistry [3–5]. Third,

Nonclinical Assessment of Abuse Potential for New Pharmaceuticals
http://dx.doi.org/10.1016/B978-0-12-420172-9.00004-7

the long lifespan of NHPs allows for long-term longitudinal studies and within-subjects designs. Fourth, NHPs have an especially rich behavioral repertoire and can learn complex behaviors that can be ideal for assessing drug effects. Fifth, although not exclusive to NHPs, their relatively large brain size makes them especially useful for brain imaging studies that examine neuroadaptations following environmental and/or pharmacological manipulations (for review, see [6,7]). Sixth, monkeys are an excellent model for studying sex differences because female macaques have a 28-day menstrual cycle with similar hormone fluctuations as women [8]. Finally, research on drugs of abuse in nonhumans often uses adult subjects, in part because the relatively short duration of adolescence in rodents does not permit behavioral experiments requiring extended training. The comparatively slower development of NHPs permits examination of drugs in adolescents and young adults, two largely understudied populations in whom vulnerability to the abuse-related effects of drugs may differ from that of adults [9,10]. The objectives of this chapter are to highlight the use of NHPs as subjects in assessments of abuse potential and to describe important considerations regarding choice of experimental conditions for assessing physiological dependence. Throughout this chapter, it is stressed that experimental conditions can differentially influence behavioral effects of drugs and, ultimately, conclusions regarding a substance's abuse potential.

The guidelines proposed by the Food and Drug Administration (FDA) [11] dictate that before a drug with a potential for abuse is assigned to a schedule under the Controlled Substances Act, recommendations must be proposed to the Drug Enforcement Agency regarding the most appropriate schedule for the substance. The draft guidance document lists eight types of primary data that contribute to an overall assessment, ranging from information about the substance's chemical structure to clinical experience with the drug in the United States and around the world. Important among these data sets is "Animal Behavioral and Dependence Pharmacology." Of the behavioral procedures listed by the guidance document, the three that have been most frequently used to predict a drug's abuse potential are drug discrimination, drug self-administration, and assessment of dependence potential. This chapter will highlight techniques related to these three behavioral procedures.

2. RATIONALE FOR USING NONHUMAN PRIMATES IN ASSESSMENTS OF ABUSE POTENTIAL

Several different species are used to evaluate drugs for their abuse and dependence potential and each of those species has advantages and disadvantages. This discussion is restricted to the circumstances that justify the use of NHPs over other species for assessing abuse potential. We begin with pharmacokinetics to illustrate how duration of action can influence assessments of abuse potential. We then briefly describe neurobiological characteristics of NHPs. Of relevance to the focus of this chapter is that long-term drug use changes the brain in ways that may influence abuse potential. For example, chronic cocaine use increases dopamine transporter (DAT) densities in monkeys [12]; these increases might account for the changes in the reinforcing effects of other drugs including the long-acting cocaine analog 2-ß-propanoyl-3-ß-(4-tolyl)-tropane (PTT), which is self-administered by cocaine-experienced monkeys but not cocaine-naïve subjects [13]. Finally, we extend our description of NHP models to include opioids and benzodiazepines and the study of another important consideration in determining abuse potential—physiological dependence.

2.1 Pharmacokinetics

Pharmacokinetics refers to the absorption, distribution, metabolism, and elimination of a drug. Absorption is the process by which a drug enters the organism and the circulatory system. Distribution is the process of the drug being dispersed throughout the organism. Metabolism is the chemical modification of the drug to active and/or inactive entities. Excretion is the process of eliminating the drug and any metabolites from the organism. NHPs appear to be the most appropriate animal species for predicting human pharmacokinetics after either oral or intravenous routes of administration [14–16]. Significant pharmacokinetic differences between NHPs and rodents have been documented for several abused drugs. For example, 3,4-methylenedioxymethamphetamine (MDMA; Ecstasy) is widely abused and has qualitatively different effects in NHPs and rodents that are thought to be due, at least in part, to pharmacokinetic differences. The two primary metabolites of MDMA are 3,4-methylenedioxyamphetamine (MDA) and 3,4-dihydroxymethamphetamine (DHMA). No published data are available regarding MDA self-administration in NHPs or reinforcing effects of DHMA in either rodents or NHPs. Although both rodents and NHPs generate these MDMA metabolites, the two species differ markedly in the ratios of the metabolites that are produced. For example, MDA is the primary metabolite of MDMA in both rats and mice [17–21]. In contrast, MDA is not the major metabolite of MDMA in NHPs and humans; the amount of MDA that results from MDMA metabolism in NHPs is approximately 10-fold less than in rodents [22–24]. These differences in metabolism between species may partially explain reported difficulties in establishing MDMA self-administration in rodents [25] as well as the observation that MDMA functions as a positive reinforcer across different schedules of reinforcement in NHPs and in rodents [26–30]. This example highlights the need for basic pharmacokinetic data before abuse potential testing to inform which nonhuman species would be most appropriate and to use these pharmacokinetic data in the selection of the schedule of reinforcement.

2.2 Neurobiology

There are significant differences among species in the neurobiological substrates on which drugs act. Reviews on the use of NHPs in neuroimaging research illustrate the close correspondence between human and NHP brain structure as well as the similarity of effects of long-term cocaine use on the brain (e.g., [31–34]). This section highlights some examples involving NHPs in order to describe important neurobiological considerations that are relevant to the determination of the abuse potential of drugs.

The dopaminergic projections from the midbrain to the ventral striatum, particularly the nucleus accumbens (NAcc), play a prominent role in the reinforcing effects of drugs, with widespread involvement of frontal cortical areas in the long-term maintenance of addiction (e.g., [35]). Compared to rodents, NHPs have been shown to be more similar to humans in several aspects of the anatomy, neurophysiology, and neuropharmacology of these brain areas. For example, in rodents, the NAcc is delineated from surrounding tissue on the basis of cortical and subcortical fibers innervating the area. However, in NHPs, limbic afferent input from the cortex and thalamus and dopaminergic input from the midbrain are more broadly distributed across the ventromedial and medial striatum, whereas neurons from motor areas of the cortex and thalamus innervate the dorsolateral striatum [36]. Thus, in NHPs, a broad distinction has been made between striatal areas serving a limbic function (i.e., ventromedial striatum, including the NAcc, and central/medial striatum, including the caudate nucleus) and those that serve a sensorimotor function (i.e., dorsolateral striatum [36,37]). Likewise, there are differences among species in the number and localization of dopamine neurons in the basal ganglia [38,39], densities of DATs in the thalamus [40], and patterns of projections from the prefrontal cortex to the midbrain [41]. The cortical regions that mediate higher-order functions are more complex and more similar to humans in NHPs than in rodents. The cortex represents 80% and 72% of the brain in humans and rhesus monkeys, respectively, but only 28% in rodents [42]. The complexity in key cortical areas such as the prefrontal cortex does not exist in rodents (e.g., [43,44]). Taken together, important differences exist in the cortical and striatal areas that mediate the abuse-related effects of drugs that may render NHPs more predictive than other species on the abuse liability of drugs.

3. STUDYING DRUG SELF-ADMINISTRATION IN NONHUMAN PRIMATES

There are a multitude of drug self-administration procedures that are used in preclinical studies of abuse potential. The primary factor that characterizes these different procedures is the schedule of reinforcement—that is, the rules that describe the number or pattern of responses required by the subject to produce delivery of the drug injection (in the case of intravenous drug self-administration procedures). The FDA does not specify the schedule of reinforcement that should be used to test whether a drug functions as a reinforcer. Nonetheless, proper interpretation of studies of a drug's reinforcing effects requires an appreciation of the influence of experimental conditions—particularly the schedule of reinforcement—on the resulting amounts and patterns of behavior and, by extension, the determination of a drug's abuse potential.

3.1 Schedules of Reinforcement

All schedules of reinforcement are based on the classic 3-term contingency of operant conditioning describing the interactions between stimuli and behavior [45]. This 3-term contingency can be described as follows:

$$S^D \rightarrow R \rightarrow S^C$$

in which S^D designates a *discriminative stimulus*, R designates a response by the organism, and S^C designates a *consequent stimulus*. The arrows specify the contingency that, in the presence of the discriminative stimulus S^D, performance of the behavioral response R results in presentation of the consequent stimulus S^C. A common example in a preclinical laboratory is an NHP with a chronically indwelling venous catheter that is connected to an infusion pump containing a drug, placed within an experimental chamber that contains a visual stimulus (i.e., a light) and a response lever. When the stimulus light is illuminated (the S^D), depression of the response lever (R) results in the intravenous delivery of the drug (the S^C). Consequent stimuli that increase responding leading to their presentation are operationally defined as positive *reinforcing stimuli* (S^R), whereas consequent stimuli that decrease responding leading to their presentation are defined as *punishing stimuli* (S^P). The contingencies or rules that relate the S^D, R, and S^R or S^P are defined by the schedule of reinforcement or punishment, respectively [46]. Because the reinforcing effects of drugs are critical for determining their abuse potential, this discussion focuses on schedules of reinforcement rather than schedules of punishment.

3.1.1 *Simple Schedules of Reinforcement*

In the broadest sense, schedules of reinforcement are either ratio-based or interval-based. That is, delivery of the reinforcer occurs after either a certain number of responses have been emitted (ratio-based schedules) or when a response is made after a certain amount of time has elapsed (interval-based schedules). For example, if a single depression of the response lever is all that is required for intravenous delivery of the drug in the presence of the S^D, the schedule of reinforcement is operationally defined as a 1-response fixed-ratio (FR) or FR 1 schedule. FR schedules of reinforcement are the most common and easiest to train of all schedules used in behavioral pharmacology. Less common are variable-ratio (VR) schedules, under which a reinforcer is delivered after a number of responses that varies across a range of values but averages to a certain value within a session. For example, under a VR 5 schedule the number of responses required to receive successive reinforcers might be 3, 4, 5, 6, and 7, which average to 5.

The utility of FR schedules in preclinical drug self-administration research has been thoroughly reviewed elsewhere [47]. This discussion will briefly describe the dependent variables measured under FR schedules, the patterns of responding generated under FR schedules, and how this information is used to predict abuse potential. The primary dependent measure for FR schedules of reinforcement is either the rate of responding, defined as the number of responses emitted per unit of time (generally seconds or minutes), or the rate of reinforcement, defined as the number of reinforcers delivered per unit of time. When rates of operant responding are plotted as a function of the unit drug dose, the relationship between drug dose and behavior is a biphasic (inverted U-shaped) function [48,49]. Injection of a vehicle or very small doses of drugs maintains low rates of behavior; responding increases as a function of larger unit drug doses up to a maximum. This range of doses constitutes the ascending limb of dose-effect function. Further increases in unit drug doses do not lead to a further increase in responding. Rather, larger unit doses result in a dose-dependent decrease in both rates of behavior and the number of drug injections delivered and constitute the descending limb of dose-effect function. Although response rates and numbers of drug injections decrease with an increasing unit dose, total drug intake often increases over the entire range of doses constituting an inverted U-shaped function. However, under an FR schedule, several behavioral mechanisms combine to influence the location and slope of the descending limb. Animals might respond less because they are satiated or because larger unit doses have aversive effects. Alternately, large unit doses of some drugs can produce effects that are incompatible with operant responding; for example, large doses of some stimulant drugs produce stereotypies that prevent the animal from making a response. Consequently, the interpretation of self-administration data under FR schedules is made difficult by the integration of these effects into a single response-rate measure (see [50]).

When using fixed-interval (FI) schedules, the dependent variables and relationships between drug dose and behavioral output (i.e., inverted-U shaped function) are much the same as they are for FR contingencies. One important difference involves the pattern of responding generated under each type of schedule. Under FR schedules with response requirements higher than 1, after a pause, responding occurs at a consistent, high rate until a reinforcer is delivered. Thus there is a direct relationship between response rate and frequency of reinforcer delivery. However, under an FI schedule a reinforcer is delivered when a response occurs after a certain amount of time has passed; consequently, the frequency of reinforcer delivery is relatively independent of response rates. For example, under an FI 60-s schedule, the first response after 60 s results in delivery of a reinforcer; any responses made during the 60-s interval have no programmed consequence. Under appropriate responding, the response rate is not constant but rather increases through the 60-s interval.

Simple FR and FI schedules are commonly used to study drug self-administration and provide the most straightforward approach to abuse potential assessment, typically by comparing a new compound to both a drug that is an effective positive reinforcer with known abuse liability (e.g., cocaine or morphine) and to its vehicle (usually saline solution). If response rates leading to drug injection are significantly higher than response rates leading to injection of a vehicle, the drug is said to function as a positive reinforcer and likely to have abuse liability in humans. As described later in the chapter, the choice of which schedule, FR or FI, to use in an experiment depends on the pharmacokinetics of the drug and the research question. For example, studies investigating the neurobiological consequences of large drug doses may utilize FI schedules in order to obtain high drug intakes while having the animal self-administer those doses. A 2013 review by Horton and colleagues [51] empirically determined how well preclinical self-administration procedures using FR schedules of reinforcement predicted the schedule designation (I–V) of a drug according to the United States Controlled Substance Act. They reported that results from studies using FR schedules of reinforcement had statistically significant predictive value for both positive hits (drugs that are abused by humans that also function as positive reinforcers in nonhumans) and negative hits (drugs that are not abused by humans and do not function as positive reinforcers in nonhumans).

3.1.2 Complex Schedules of Reinforcement

FR and FI schedules can determine whether a drug functions as a positive reinforcer; however, reinforcing effects can vary quantitatively in a manner that can be important for predicting abuse. Differences in reinforcing effectiveness can be unmasked by using more complex schedules of reinforcement. Two general approaches have been used to estimate the strength of a reinforcer: progressive-ratio (PR) schedules and choice procedures.

One variation of the FR schedule is a PR schedule [52], in which the response requirement for delivery of each reinforcer is successively increased according to a predefined algorithm. For example, the first drug injection might be delivered after 50 responses, the second after an additional 62 responses, the third after an additional 77 responses, and so on. In addition to assessing whether a drug functions as a positive reinforcer, PR schedules provide a measure of how many responses subjects will emit in order to receive a drug injection before they cease responding. The value of this schedule for assessing abuse potential is that it can provide an empirical differentiation among drugs that all function as positive reinforcers. This in turn may be predictive of different degrees of abuse liability. The utility of PR schedules in preclinical drug self-administration research has been reviewed previously [53–55]. This discussion is limited to a brief description of the dependent variables measured under PR schedules and the patterns of responding generated under PR schedules and discussion of how these data inform abuse potential assessment. The primary dependent variable for PR schedules is the breaking point, defined as the final response ratio requirement completed either following a predetermined period of time without a drug injection or the end of an experimental session. Because the breaking point is not a continuous variable, the actual number of drug injections delivered is typically used to analyze the data (i.e., the number of injections plotted as a function of the unit drug dose). The dose-effect functions under PR schedules produce a more monotonic increase in responding compared to the inverted U-shaped function obtained with simple FR schedules. However, because the dependent measure is still a rate of operant behavior that integrates both reinforcement-dependent rate effects and reinforcement-independent rate effects, there is a unit drug dose that produces maximal responding. Further increases in unit drug doses do not generate more responding and can generate less responding, resulting in an inverted U-shaped dose response curve. The Horton et al. study [51] also examined data from PR schedules and, although the calculated predictions were similar between the PR and FR data, in contrast to the FR schedules, PR schedules did not significantly predict whether or not a drug was scheduled. However, given that few experiments using PR schedules were available for inclusion, it is possible that the analysis did not have adequate power for detecting a significant effect.

Another variation of the simples of reinforcement adds a second reinforcement schedule that results in delivery of a separate reinforcer. Under these programmed contingencies, there are two separate and independent discriminative stimuli, two separate responses, and two separate reinforcers. For example, in one scenario illumination of a white light above the left lever might indicate that responding on that lever under an FR contingency results in delivery of a drug injection whereas illumination of a green light above the other lever indicates that FR responding on that lever results in delivery of food. Because the schedule of reinforcement leading to delivery of a drug and the schedule of reinforcement leading to delivery of food are concurrently active, the term for this type of schedule is a concurrent FR:FR schedule of reinforcement. Such a schedule is also called a choice procedure because the subject can choose to respond for drug or food. Much work in NHPs has led to the development of various choice procedures which compare the relative reinforcing effectiveness of two drugs, two doses of the same drug, or drug combinations [56–58]. This feature of choice procedures has not frequently been exploited for abuse potential testing but could have great utility in understanding the abuse potential of drug combinations. For example, cocaine and opioids are frequently co-abused. Evidence from procedures in which monkeys could choose between injections of cocaine and injections of combinations of cocaine and the mu opioid receptor agonist remifentanil suggested that, although the combinations can increase potency, maximal reinforcing effectiveness of a combination is not generally greater than the component drugs [59].

Others have reviewed the utility of concurrent schedules in preclinical drug self-administration research [60–62]. The present discussion focuses on the dependent variables measured under a concurrent schedule, the patterns of responding generated under concurrent schedules, and ways that these patterns of responding can inform abuse potential assessment. In general, there are two primary dependent measures. One is the distribution of responses between the two alternatives. For example, in the drug versus food choice procedure, percent drug choice is calculated as the number of responses on the drug-associated lever divided by the total number of responses on both levers, multiplied by 100. Another method of calculating response allocation would be the number of FR requirements completed on the drug-associated lever divided by the total number of FR requirements completed on both levers, multiplied by 100. When percent drug choice is plotted as a function of unit drug dose, the dose-effect function generates a monotonic increase in choice for drug over the alternative reinforcer, up to a maximum of 100% drug choice. Larger unit drug doses typically maintain an exclusive choice for drug and only at the largest doses that suppress responding is it not possible to determine percent drug choice.

The other dependent measure of interest in choice procedures is the overall rate of responding. The main difference between choice procedures and simpler (single lever) drug self-administration procedures is that choice procedures do not rely on rates of responding to quantify reinforcement. Instead, response rates determined under concurrent schedules provide information regarding reinforcement-independent drug effects that might predict other effects, such as stimulation or sedation. One important consideration, and potentially a limitation, in using choice procedures is that drug preference is a relative measure and is, therefore, dependent on the magnitude and type of each reinforcer and is influenced by the schedule parameters. For example, a manipulation (e.g., potential new therapeutic drug) that decreases choice of drug versus food might do so because it decreases the reinforcing effects of the drug, increases the reinforcing effects of the food, or both. For such a result, the most conservative and appropriate conclusion would be that manipulation decreases the relative reinforcing strength of the drug compared to food.

In contrast to simple schedules of reinforcement, which primarily indicate whether or not a drug can function as a reinforcer, PR schedules and choice procedures provide information that can be more quantitative (beyond a yes/no determination) and potentially more relevant to clinical and to real-world situations. Choice procedures in particular encompass the clinical reality that drug use represents a choice to allocate time, effort, and resources toward obtaining drugs versus other potential reinforcers in the environment such as food, employment, family, or other enjoyable activities. Beyond simply determining whether a drug can function as a reinforcer, PR schedules and choice procedures can be used to compare and rank drugs according to their relative reinforcing effects, which can be used to predict relative abuse potential. This information goes beyond what is provided by self-administration procedures that characterize drugs according to response rates under simple schedules of reinforcement. In the context of this chapter, it is worth noting that because of the advantages described above—complex behavioral repertoire, ability to serve as subjects for a long period of time, etc.—using NHPs as subjects in these procedures permits great diversity in the experimental designs that are possible in studies of abuse potential.

3.2 The Influence of Experimental Conditions on Assessments of Abuse Potential

When initiating self-administration experiments with a new drug, several characteristics of the drug, including pharmacokinetics, duration of action, and direct effects on behavior, impact the selection of experimental conditions, which themselves can affect results and, ultimately, interpretations regarding abuse potential. For example, if an unknown drug has a long duration of action and/or has been shown to have significant rate-decreasing effects, studying the abuse potential of the drug under an FR schedule would likely result in very low rates of responding and low reinforcement frequency due to the accumulation of the drug over successive FR components (i.e., injections) and the suppressant effects of the drug on responding. The resulting low rates of responding might suggest that the drug has little or no abuse potential; however, the same doses of that drug might have robust positive reinforcing effects under other schedule conditions (i.e., that do not require as much responding as an FR schedule). The same drug studied under an FI schedule of reinforcement, when the passage of time and not the number of responses is most critical, might maintain responding that is significantly greater than responding that is maintained by a vehicle.

A specific example of how schedules of reinforcement can influence the interpretation of a drug's potential for abuse involves the behavioral effects of the long-acting DAT blocker 2beta-propanoyl-3beta-(4-tolyl)-tropane (PTT). Under an FI schedule of reinforcement in monkeys, PTT maintained rates of responding not different from saline [63]; thus, it did not function as a positive reinforcer. However, when studied under an FR schedule of reinforcement, PTT maintained responding that was significantly higher than responding for a vehicle but significantly lower than responding for cocaine [13,64,65]. What might account for the differences in measures of positive reinforcing effects between FI and FR schedules of reinforcement? Because the reinforcing effects of a drug are defined relative to the vehicle, it is possible that differences in rates of extinction could account for schedule differences. Another possibility involves the direct effects of the drug on the animal's ability to make a response. If a drug has response rate-decreasing effects, then it might result in lower responding and number of injections under FR schedules versus FI schedules. However, in the example above, it was the opposite—PTT functioned as a reinforcer under FR but not FI schedules. This suggests to a third possibility that the subject needs to receive several injections within a relatively short period of time in order for the drug to function as a reinforcer. If that were the case with the long-acting dopamine receptor indirect agonist PTT, then interval schedules would not allow for the increased frequency of injections.

The self-administration of phendimetrazine, a pro-drug for the monoamine releaser phenmetrazine, represents a specific example of the importance of the duration of the timeout between intravenous drug injections in determining interpretations regarding abuse potential. When the duration of the self-administration session was relatively short (2 h) and timeout periods between injections were brief (10 s), phendimetrazine functioned as a positive reinforcer in only one of four monkeys [66]. In contrast, phendimetrazine functioned as a positive reinforcer in all three monkeys when both the self-administration session and timeout between injections were longer (24 h and 3 h, respectively [67]). These differential results between the drug self-administration procedures suggest phendimetrazine has a long duration of action. This example illustrates the extent to which the schedule of reinforcement and other experimental parameters can influence assessments of abuse potential.

Each of these variables (rate of extinction, rate-decreasing effects, injection frequency, session and timeout duration) could be considered limitations of simple schedules of reinforcement. Many investigators feel that the use of more complex reinforcement schedules that assess measures of reinforcing effectiveness, such as PR schedules and drug choice procedures, provide a better measure of abuse potential. The use of PR schedules does not require any more time to determine a dose-response curve than using an FR schedule, but the information may be vastly different. The main consideration of this section is that the characteristics of the drug under study should guide the selection of experimental conditions, because they can influence the results and conclusions in studies of abuse potential.

4. STUDYING DRUG DEPENDENCE IN NONHUMAN PRIMATES

Early conceptualizations of addiction assumed that physical dependence was necessary for a drug to be abused [1,48,68] and that the effects of drugs were qualitatively unique in physically dependent individuals. This conceptualization was based, in large part, on the observations that significant physical dependence developed from repeated use of opioids (e.g., heroin) and that discontinuation of opioid use resulted in the emergence of withdrawal that was rapidly alleviated by administration of an opioid. It followed that drug abuse was perpetuated by the need to continually use drugs in order to avoid withdrawal. However, it became clear that not all drugs produced physical dependence and that some drugs (including drugs that are known to produce physical dependence) were abused under conditions that did not produce physical dependence (e.g., because of the comparatively smaller doses that were used and/or the low frequency of use). Thus, physical dependence was not a prerequisite for continued drug use, although it could be a significant contributing factor for the abuse of some types of drugs and some patterns of abuse. A further evolution of how drug abuse was conceptualized was prompted by the discovery that in the laboratory, nonhuman species would make an operant response to receive the same drugs that humans abuse (i.e., they served as positive reinforcers in self-administration procedures [1,69]). Importantly, it was shown that animals that were not physically dependent also self-administered many drugs that are abused by humans [49,70,71]. Not only was physical dependence not a prerequisite for drug abuse, but the effects of drugs in humans that appeared to be important for abuse (positive reinforcement) were also evident in nonhuman species. The similarities in the effects of abused drugs between humans and other species prompted what is still today an evolving effort to understand human drug abuse by studying nonhumans in the laboratory.

The use of self-administration procedures in NHPs for assessing abuse potential and the positive reinforcing effects of drugs were discussed above. Nonhuman species, NHPs in particular, have also been used to examine the dependence potential of new drugs. Although various species have been used to assess physical dependence potential, for some drugs and some types of studies NHPs provide the following advantages: (1) the very large literature that is available on the dependence-producing effects of known drugs of abuse, including opioids [72,73] and sedative/hypnotic drugs such as benzodiazepines [2,74,75] and barbiturates [76], in NHPs provides a rich context for and facilitates interpretation of results with new drugs; (2) for some drugs of abuse (e.g., opioids), the physical manifestations of withdrawal in humans are more similar in NHPs as compared with other species [77–80]; (3) the long life span of NHPs permits long-term dependence and withdrawal studies as well as repeated dependence-producing treatments and studies in the same subjects (within-subjects design); (4) the sophisticated behavioral repertoire of NHPs as well as the complex behavioral procedures that have been developed for NHPs (e.g., choice procedures in physically dependent subjects [81]) increase both the diversity and the human relevance of dependence studies in NHPs; and (5) the behavioral and physiological characteristics of NHPs allow for studies over a very broad range of conditions that are relevant to human substance abuse (e.g., active inhalation [smoking] of drugs [82]).

There are two general approaches by which physical dependence potential is studied in the laboratory. In one case, subjects receive a known drug of abuse under dosing conditions that produce physical dependence. Withdrawal occurs either by discontinuing chronic drug treatment (i.e., spontaneous withdrawal) or by administration of a pharmacological antagonist (i.e., precipitated withdrawal). Other drugs are assessed for their ability to reverse spontaneous withdrawal or prevent antagonist-precipitated withdrawal. Drugs that reverse or prevent withdrawal are assumed to themselves have dependence potential that is qualitatively (e.g., mechanistically) similar to the known drug of abuse that was administered chronically. A second approach for assessing dependence potential is to administer the test drug repeatedly. It is important in such a study that exposure to the test drug is sufficient to provide an adequate evaluation of dependence potential (i.e., sufficiently large doses administered sufficiently often and for a long enough period). Adequate blood levels following acute exposure can be confirmed by pharmacokinetic studies so long as there is some predetermined target blood concentration. Otherwise, physical dependence studies often administer the largest dose(s) that can be administered safely for an extended period of time (e.g., 4–8 weeks), as determined by a preliminary dose-finding study. Next, treatment is discontinued and subjects are observed for signs of withdrawal. Such a study might involve only directly observable changes in behavior or could also involve more sophisticated behavioral procedures (e.g., changes in operant behavior during discontinuation, including changes in response allocation in a choice procedure). Whatever effects are observed after discontinuation of treatment, a confirmation that those effects reflect withdrawal is made by again administering the test drug to see whether the presumed signs of withdrawal are reversed. Mechanisms mediating dependence can also be explored by administering pharmacological antagonists and by attempting to reverse withdrawal by administering other well-characterized drugs. For example, data showing that discontinuation of a test drug produces observable behavioral effects resembling those observed after discontinuation of an opioid receptor agonist (e.g., morphine), that an opioid receptor antagonist (e.g., naloxone) precipitates withdrawal in subjects treated with the test drug, and that an opioid receptor agonist reverses spontaneous withdrawal would collectively provide very strong evidence that the test drug has opioid-like physical dependence potential.

Relevant to this chapter is the matter of whether drug history, in general, and the development of physical dependence, in particular, modifies the abuse-related and positive reinforcing effects of drugs in a manner that impacts abuse potential. As noted above, evaluating the abuse potential of new chemical entities in the laboratory usually includes a self-administration study comparing a test drug to a known drug of abuse (e.g., cocaine) and to saline. Those evaluations often occur in subjects with little or no drug history, despite the fact that, arguably, the greatest risk of a new chemical entity (NCE) being abused is in current drug abusers. Though not always considered in a preclinical assessment of abuse potential, current and past drug history are potentially important factors that can impact the outcome of self-administration studies and, therefore, could provide insight into the abuse potential of drugs in particular populations. For example, self-administration of some drugs is more likely in subjects with a history of self-administering a drug from the same drug class. Self-administration of opioids was greater in NHPs with a history that included the self-administration of an opioid receptor agonist as compared with NHPs that had a history of self-administering cocaine [83]. Similarly, self-administration of an NMDA receptor antagonist was greater in NHPs with a history of NMDA receptor antagonist self-administration [84,85]. NHPs were more likely to self-administer a GABA-A receptor positive modulator (benzodiazepine) if they had a history of self-administering another GABA-A receptor positive modulator (barbiturate) as compared with a history of cocaine self-administration [86]. On the other hand, Δ^9-tetrahydrocannabinol self-administration was greater in drug-naïve, compared with cocaine-experienced, NHPs [87]. Thus, the reference (comparator) drug that is used for a self-administration abuse potential study can impact the likelihood that a new drug is self-administered. These examples showing how experience with a particular drug class can impact the likelihood that a new drug is self-administered are from studies that examined the acute effects of drugs in otherwise untreated subjects. However, it is clear that repeated drug treatment can significantly impact self-administration as well. The earliest studies on self-administration [48,68] used drug-treated subjects based, in part, on the notion that physical dependence was a core feature of drug abuse and a prerequisite for drugs to serve as positive reinforcers. While not typically considered in the design of preclinical studies of abuse potential, the impact of chronic drug treatment and, perhaps more importantly, the discontinuation of chronic drug treatment could be especially relevant for determining whether a new compound is likely to be abused, specifically by current drug users. Withdrawal resulting from either administration of an opioid receptor antagonist or discontinuation of chronic opioid treatment significantly increases self-administration of an opioid receptor agonist under a range of schedule conditions including FR and PR as well as in choice procedures [1,81,88–91].

5. CONCLUSIONS AND RECOMMENDATIONS

As discussed in this chapter, NHPs can offer specific advantages as research subjects in assessments of abuse potential. In general, we recommend the continued use of NHPs as research subjects in abuse-potential assessment based on their documented similarities to humans in pharmacokinetics and neurobiology, even if the abuse potential question is as simple as "does the drug function as a reinforcer?". Use of NHPs in self-administration and dependence studies is even more critical when aspects of the drug (e.g., pharmacokinetics or pharmacodynamics) require specific features of the experimental design to which NHPs are uniquely suited (e.g., long sessions in which injections can be separated in time). Based on these advantages, certain recommendations for the most appropriate and effective use of NHPs are presented.

First, compounds that have certain pharmacokinetic properties warrant the use of NHPs. For example, prodrugs (e.g., phendimetrazine) represent an important approach in reducing abuse potential of a possible pharmacotherapy. Prodrugs are most commonly metabolized into the pharmacologically active metabolite by either cytochrome P450 enzymes or esterase-catalyzed hydrolysis [92]. NHPs more closely model human prodrug metabolism compared to other preclinical models of these metabolic processes [93,94]. Similarly, as described above, studying a drug with a long duration of action necessitates alterations to the standard experimental design, such as providing subjects access to the drug several hours per day for many days. NHPs have a unique suitability to such studies.

Second, compounds that have novel mechanisms of action or target neurobiological systems where there are documented differences in receptor density or distribution between rodents and NHPs warrant the use of NHPs for preclinical abuse potential assessment. For example, species differences exist in the proportions and regional distributions of mu, kappa, and delta opioid receptors, with NHPs being most similar to humans [95]. Thus, NHPs might be the most appropriate species in which to test receptor-selective opioid agonists.

Third, the use of NHPs as research subjects affords greater experimental flexibility in the design of longitudinal assessments of abuse potential. Regarding choice procedures, NHPs have appropriate vascular anatomy to accommodate double-lumen catheters which permit sophisticated choice studies comparing the reinforcing strength of food, drugs, and drug combinations. Choice between a novel experimental drug and a nondrug reinforcer would build on data derived from simpler schedules in which responding to receive drugs is the only option. A drug may have positive reinforcing effects under those conditions that might be reduced or eliminated in the presence of an alternative reinforcer, such as food. Studying choice between a drug with known abuse liability and a novel drug could provide more quantitative information regarding the abuse potential of the novel compound. If a drug has positive reinforcing effects, but subjects choose it much less than a drug with known abuse liability, the novel drug may actually be less likely to support widespread abuse. Finally, studying drug combinations using choice procedures would generate unique data regarding the interaction of the component drugs' reinforcing effects.

Finally, because of the long experimental life of NHPs compared to other preclinical research subjects, comparisons could be made between experimentally naïve monkeys and monkeys with an extensive experimental history of drug self-administration or drug dependence with a reference abused compound. These types of assessments of abuse potential would allow for a better characterization and understanding of whether a drug is likely to be abused only by current drug abusers or also by drug-naïve individuals.

ACKNOWLEDGMENTS

Preparation of this chapter was supported, in part, by National Institutes of Health, National Institute on Drug Abuse grants R37 DA010584, R01 DA 017763, R01 DA026946, R01 DA031718, R01 DA005018, R01 DA029254, U01 DA034992, P50 DA06634, and K05 DA017918.

REFERENCES

[1] Spragg SDS. Morphine addiction in chimpanzees. Comp Psychol Mono 1940;15:1–132.

[2] Weerts EM, Ator NA, Kaminski BJ, Griffiths RR. Comparison of the behavioral effects of bretazenil and flumazenil in triazolam-dependent and non-dependent baboons. Eur J Pharmacol 2005;519:103–13.

[3] Berger B, Gaspar P, Verney C. Dopaminergic innervation of the cerebral cortex: unexpected differences between rodents and primates. Trends Neurosci 1991;14:21–7.

[4] Joel D, Weiner I. The connections of dopaminergic system with the striatum in rats and primates: an analysis with respect to the functional and compartmental organization of the striatum. Neuroscience 2000;96:451–74.

[5] Porrino LJ, Lyons D, Miller MD, Smith HR, Friedman DP, Daunais JB, et al. Metabolic mapping of the effects of cocaine during the initial phases of self-administration in the nonhuman primate. J Neurosci 2002;22:7687–94.

[6] Murnane KS, Howell LL. Neuroimaging and drug taking in primates. Psychopharmacology 2011;206:153–71.

[7] Nader MA, Banks ML. Environmental modulation of drug taking: nonhuman primate models of cocaine abuse and PET neuroimaging. Neuropharmacology 2014;76:510–7.

[8] Appt SE. Usefulness of the monkey model to investigate the role soy in postmenopausal women's health. ILAR J 2004;45:200–11.

[9] Gill KE, Pierre PJ, Daunais J, Bennett AJ, Martelle S, Gage HD, et al. Chronic treatment with extended release methylphenidate does not alter dopamine systems or increase vulnerability for cocaine self-administration: a study in nonhuman primates. Neuropsychopharmacology 2012;37:2555–65.

[10] Soto PL, Wilcox KM, Zhou Y, Kumar A, Ator NA, Riddle MA, et al. Long-term exposure to oral methylphenidate or dl-amphetamine mixture in peri-adolescent rhesus monkeys: effects on physiology, behavior, and dopamine system development. Neuropsychopharmacology 2012;37:2566–79.

[11] FDA guidance for Industry: assessment of abuse potential of drugs. US Department of Health and Human Services, Food and Drug Administration, Center for Drug Evaluation and Research; January 2010.

[12] Letchworth SR, Nader MA, Smith HR, Friedman DP, Porrino LJ. Progression of changes in dopamine transporter binding site density as a result of cocaine self-administration in rhesus monkeys. J Neurosci 2001;21:2799–807.

[13] Lile JA, Morgan D, Freedland CS, Sinnott RS, Davies HM, Nader MA. Self-administration of two long-acting monoamine transport blockers in rhesus monkeys. Psychopharmacology 2000a;152:414–21.

[14] Ward KW, Smith BR. A comprehensive quantitative and qualitative evaluation of extrapolation of intravenous pharmacokinetic parameters from rat, dog, and monkey to humans. I Clear Drug Metab Dispos 2004a;32:603–11.

[15] Ward KW, Smith BR. A comprehensive quantitative and qualitative evaluation of extrapolation of intravenous pharmacokinetic parameters from rat, dog, and monkey to humans. II. Volume of distribution and mean residence time. Drug Metab Dispos 2004b;32:612–9.

[16] Jolivette LJ, Ward KW. Extrapolation of human pharmacokinetic parameters from rat, dog, and monkey data: molecular properties associated with extrapolative success or failure. J Pharm Sci 2005;94:1467–83.

[17] Markert LE, Roberts DCS. 3,4-methylenedioxyamphetamine (MDA) self-administration and neurotoxicity. Pharmacol Biochem Behav 1991;39:569–74.

[18] Cho AK, Hiramatsu M, Distefano EW, Chang AS, Jenden DJ. Stereochemical differences in the metabolism of 3,4-methylenedioxymethamphetamine in vivo and in vitro: a pharmacokinetic analysis. Drug Metab Dispos 1990;18:686–91.

[19] Fantegrossi WE, Murai N, Mathúna BÓ, Pizarro N, de la Torre R. Discriminative stimulus effects of 3,4-methylenedioxymethamphetamine and its enantiomers in mice: pharmacokinetic considerations. J Pharmacol Exp Ther 2009;329:1006–15.

[20] Mueller M, Maldonado-Adrian C, Yuan J, McCann UD, Ricaurte GA. Studies of (±)-3,4-methylenedioxymethamphetamine (MDMA) metabolism and disposition in rats and mice: relationship to neuroprotection and neurotoxicity profile. J Pharmacol Exp Ther 2013;344:479–88.

[21] Concheiro M, Baumann MH, Scheidweiler KB, Rothman RB, Marrone GF, Huestis MA. Nonlinear pharmacokinetics of (±)3,4-methylenedioxymethamphetamine (MDMA) and its pharmacodynamic consequences in the rat. Drug Metab Dispos 2014;42:119–25.

[22] De La Torre R, Farré M, Ortuño J, Mas M, Brenneisen R, Roset PN, et al. Non-linear pharmacokinetics of MDMA ('ecstasy') in humans. Br J Clin Pharmacol 2000;49:104–9.
[23] Banks ML, Sprague JE, Kisor DF, Czoty PW, Nichols DE, Nader MA. Ambient temperature effects on 3,4-methylenedioxymethamphetamine-induced thermodysregulation and pharmacokinetics in male monkeys. Drug Metab Dispos 2007;35:1840–5.
[24] Goodwin AK, Mueller M, Shell CD, Ricaurte GA, Ator NA. Behavioral effects and pharmacokinetics of (±)-3,4-methylenedioxymethamphetamine (MDMA, Ecstasy) after intragastric administration to baboons. J Pharmacol Exp Ther 2013;345:342–53.
[25] Schenk S. MDMA self-administration in laboratory animals: a summary of the literature and proposal for future research. Neuropsychobiology 2009;60:130–6.
[26] Beardsley PM, Balster RL, Harris LS. Self-administration of methylenedioxymethamphetamine (MDMA) by rhesus monkeys. Drug Alcohol Depend 1986;18:149–57.
[27] Lile JA, Ross JT, Nader MA. A comparison of the reinforcing efficacy of 3,4-methylenedioxymethamphetamine (MDMA, "ecstasy") with cocaine in rhesus monkeys. Drug Alcohol Depend 2005;78:135–40.
[28] Schenk S, Hely L, Lake B, Daniela E, Gittings D, Mash DC. MDMA self-administration in rats: acquisition, progressive ratio responding and serotonin transporter binding. Eur J Neurosci 2007;26:3229–36.
[29] Banks ML, Sprague JE, Czoty PW, Nader MA. Effects of ambient temperature on the relative reinforcing strength of MDMA using a choice procedure in monkeys. Psychopharmacology 2008;196:63–70.
[30] Bradbury S, Bird J, Colussi-Mas J, Mueller M, Ricaurte G, Schenk S. Acquisition of MDMA self-administration: pharmacokinetic factors and MDMA-induced serotonin release. Addict Biol 2014; 19: 874–884.
[31] Howell LL, Murnane KS. Nonhuman primate positron emission tomography neuroimaging in drug abuse research. J Pharmacol Exp Ther 2011;337:324–34.
[32] Haber SN, Knutson B. The reward circuit: linking primate anatomy and human imaging. Neuropsychopharmacology 2010;35:4–26.
[33] Gould RW, Porrino LJ, Nader MA. Nonhuman primate models of addiction and PET imaging: dopamine system dysregulation. Curr Top Behav Neurosci 2012;11:25–44.
[34] Gould RW, Duke AN, Nader MA. PET studies in nonhuman primate models of cocaine abuse: translational research related to vulnerability and neuroadaptations. Neuropharmacology 2014;84:138–51.
[35] Koob GF, Volkow ND. The neurocircuitry of addiction. Neuropsychopharmacology 2010;35:217–38.
[36] Haber SN, McFarland NR. The concept of the ventral striatum in nonhuman primates. Ann NY Acad Sci 1999;877:33–48.
[37] Bradberry CW, Barrett-Larimore RL, Jatlow P, Rubino SR. Impact of self-administered cocaine and cocaine cues on extracellular dopamine in mesolimbic and sensorimotor striatum in rhesus monkeys. J Neurosci 2000;20:3874–83.
[38] Hardman CD, Henderson JM, Finkelstein DI, Horne MK, Paxinos G, Halliday GM. Comparison of the basal ganglia in rats, marmosets, macaques, baboons, and humans: volume and neuronal number for the output, internal relay, and striatal modulating nuclei. J Comp Neurol 2002;445:238–55.
[39] Duzel E, Bunzeck N, Guitart-Masip M, Wittman B, Schott BH, Tobler PN. Functional imaging of the human dopaminergic midbrain. Trends Neurosci 2009;32:321–8.
[40] Garcia-Cabezas MA, Martinez-Sanchez P, Sanchez-Gonzalez MA, Garzon M, Cavada C. Dopamine innervation in the thalamus: monkey versus rat. Cereb Cortex 2008;19:424–34.
[41] Frankle WG, Laruelle M, Haber SN. Prefrontal cortical projections to the midbrain in primates: evidence for a sparse connection. Neuropsychopharmacology 2006;31:1627–36.
[42] Passingham R. How good is the macaque model of the human brain? Curr Opin Neurobiol 2009;19:6–11.
[43] Petrides M, Tomaiuolo F, Yeterian EH, Pandya DN. The prefrontal cortex: comparative architectonic organization in the human and macaque monkey brains. Cortex 2012;48:46–57.
[44] Hutchison RM, Everline S. Monkey in the middle: why nonhuman primates are needed to bridge the gap in resting-state investigations. Front Neuroanat 2012;6:29.
[45] Skinner BF. The behavior of organisms. New York: Appleton-Century-Crofts; 1938.
[46] Ferster CB, Skinner BF. Schedules of reinforcement. New York: Appleton-Century-Croft; 1957.
[47] Katz JL. Models of relative reinforcing efficacy of drugs and their predictive utility. Behav Pharmacol 1990;1:283–301.

[48] Weeks JR. Experimental morphine addiction: method for automatic intravenous injections in unrestrained rats. Science 1962;138:143–4.
[49] Pickens R, Thompson T. Cocaine-reinforced behavior in rats: effects of reinforcement magnitude and fixed-ratio size. J Pharmacol Exp Ther 1968;161:122–9.
[50] Zernig G, Wakonigg G, Madlung E, Haring C, Saria A. Do vertical shifts in dose-response rate-relationships in operant conditioning procedures indicate "sensitization" to "drug wanting"? Psychopharmacology 2004;171:349–51.
[51] Horton DB, Potter DM, Mead AN. A translational pharmacology approach to understanding the predictive value of abuse potential assessments. Behav Pharmacol 2013;24:410–36.
[52] Hodos W. Progressive ratio as a measure of reward strength. Science 1961;134:943–4.
[53] Richardson NR, Roberts DC. Progressive ratio schedules in drug self-administration studies in rats: a method to evaluate reinforcing efficacy. J Neurosci Method 1996;66:1–11.
[54] Stafford D, LeSage MG, Glowa JR. Progressive-ratio schedules of drug delivery in the analysis of drug self-administration: a review. Psychopharmacology 1998;139:169–84.
[55] Rowlett JK. A labor-supply analysis of cocaine self-administration under progressive-ratio schedules: antecedents, methodologies, and perspectives. Psychopharmacology 2000;153:1–16.
[56] Iglauer C, Llewellyn ME, Woods JH. Concurrent schedules of cocaine injections in rhesus monkeys: variations under independent and non-independent variable-interval procedures. Pharmacol Rev 1975;27:367–83.
[57] Woolverton WL, Johanson CE. Preference in rhesus monkeys given a choice between cocaine and d,1-cathinone. J Exp Anal Behav 1984;41:35–43.
[58] Maguire DR, Gerak LR, France CP. Effect of delay on self-administration of remifentanil under a drug versus drug choice procedure in rhesus monkeys. J Pharmacol Exp Ther 2013;347:557–63.
[59] Freeman KB, Woolverton WL. Self-administration of cocaine and remifentanil by monkeys: choice between single drugs and mixtures. Psychopharmacology 2011;215:281–90.
[60] Johanson CE. Pharmacological and environmental variables affecting drug preference in rhesus monkeys. Pharmacol Rev 1975;27:343–55.
[61] Bergman J, Paronis CA. Measuring the reinforcing strength of abused drugs. Mol Interv 2006;6:273–83.
[62] Banks ML, Negus SS. Preclinical determinants of drug choice under concurrent schedules of drug self-administration. Adv Pharmacol Sci 2012;2012:281768.
[63] Nader MA, Grant KA, Davies HM, Mach RH, Childers SR. The reinforcing and discriminative stimulus effects of the novel cocaine analog 2beta-propanoyl-3beta-(4-tolyl)-tropane in rhesus monkeys. J Pharmacol Exp Ther 1997;280:541–50.
[64] Birmingham AM, Nader SH, Grant KA, Davies HM, Nader MA. Further evaluation of the reinforcing effects of the novel cocaine analog 2beta-propanoyl-3beta-(4-tolyl)-tropane (PTT) in rhesus monkeys. Psychopharmacology 1998;135:139–47.
[65] Lile JA, Morgan D, Nader MA. Single- vs. multiple-session substitution: an evaluation of the reinforcing effects of cocaine and the cocaine analog 2ß-propanoyl-3ß-(4-tolyl)-tropane (PTT). Exp Clin Psychopharmacol 2000b;8:424–33.
[66] Corwin RL, Woolverton WL, Schuster CR, Johanson CE. Anorectics: effects on food intake and self-administration in rhesus monkeys. Alcohol Drug Res 1987;7:351–61.
[67] Griffiths RR, Brady JV, Bradford LD. Predicting the abuse liability of drugs with animal drug self-administration procedures: psychomotor stimulants and hallucinogens. In: Thompson T, Dews PB, editors. Advances in behavioral pharmacology. New York: Academic Press; 1979. p. 164–208.
[68] Thompson T, Schuster CR. Morphine self-administration, food-reinforced, and avoidance behaviors in rhesus monkeys. Psychopharmacologia 1964;5:87–94.
[69] Headlee CP, Coppock HW, Nichols JR. Apparatus and technique involved in laboratory method of detecting the addictiveness of drugs. J Am Pharm Assoc Sci Ed 1955;44:229–31.
[70] Deneau G, Yanagita T, Seevers MH. Self-administration of psychoactive substances by the monkey. Psychopharmacologia 1969;16:30–48.
[71] Wilson MC, Hitomi M, Schuster CR. Psychomotor stimulant self-administration as a function of dosage per injection in the rhesus monkey. Psychopharmacologia 1971;22:271–81.
[72] Woods JH, Gmerek DE. Substitution and primary dependence studies in animals. Drug Alcohol Depend 1985;14:233–47.

[73] Woods JH, Smith CB, Medzihradsky F, Swain HH. Preclinical testing of new analgesic drugs. In: Beers Jr RF, Bassett EG, editors. Mechanisms of pain and analgesic compounds. New York: Raven Press; 1979. p. 429–45.
[74] Ator NA, Weerts EM, Kaminski BJ, Kautz MA, Griffiths RR. Zaleplon and triazolam physical dependence assessed across increasing doses under a once-daily dosing regimen in baboons. Drug Alcohol Depend 2000;61:69–84.
[75] Weerts EM, Ator NA, Grech DM, Griffiths RR. Zolpidem physical dependence assessed across increasing doses under a once-daily dosing regimen in baboons. J Pharmacol Exp Ther 1998;285:41–53.
[76] Yanagita T, Takahashi S. Development of tolerance to and physical dependence on barbiturates in rhesus monkeys. J Pharmacol Exp Ther 1970;172:163–9.
[77] Becker GL, Gerak LR, Koek W, France CP. Antagonist-precipitated and discontinuation-induced withdrawal in morphine-dependent rhesus monkeys. Psychopharmacology 2008;201:373–82.
[78] Katz JL. Effects of clonidine and morphine on opioid withdrawal in rhesus monkeys. Psychopharmacology 1986;88:392–7.
[79] Seevers MH. Opiate addiction in the monkey. I. Methods of study. J Pharmacol Exp Ther 1936;56:147–56.
[80] Seevers MH, Deneau GA. Physiological aspects of tolerance and physical dependence. In: Root WS, Hofmann FG, editors. Physiological pharmacology, Vol 1. New York: Academic Press; 1963. p. 565–640.
[81] Negus SS. Choice between heroin and food in non-dependent and heroin-dependent rhesus monkeys: effects of naloxone, buprenorphine and methadone. J Pharmacol Exp Ther 2006;317:711–23.
[82] Carroll ME, Krattiger KL, Gieske D, Sadoff DA. Cocaine-base smoking in rhesus monkeys: reinforcing and physiological effects. Psychopharmacology 1990;102:443–50.
[83] Hoffmeister F, Schlichting UU. Reinforcing properties of some opiates and opioids in rhesus monkeys with histories of cocaine and codeine self-administration. Psychopharmacologia 1972;23:55–74.
[84] Beardsley PM, Hayes BA, Balster RL. The self-administration of MK-801 can depend upon drug-reinforcement history, and its discriminative stimulus properties are phencyclidine-like in rhesus monkeys. J Pharmacol Exp Ther 1990;252:953–9.
[85] Young AM, Woods JH. Maintenance of behavior by ketamine and related compounds in rhesus monkeys with different self-administration histories. J Pharmacol Exp Ther 1986;218:720–7.
[86] Bergman J, Johanson CE. The reinforcing properties of diazepam under several conditions in the rhesus monkey. Psychopharmacology 1985;86:108–13.
[87] Justinova Z, Tanda G, Redhi GH, Goldberg SR. Self-administration of Δ^9-tetrahydrocannabinol (THC) by drug naïve squirrel monkeys. Psychopharmacology 2003;169:135–40.
[88] Gerak LR, Galici R, France CP. Self administration of heroin and cocaine in morphine-dependent and morphine-withdrawn rhesus monkeys. Psychopharmacology 2009;204:403–11.
[89] Goldberg SR, Woods JH, Schuster CR. Morphine: conditioned increases in self-administration in rhesus monkeys. Science 1969;166:1306–7.
[90] Goldberg SR, Woods JH, Schuster CR. Nalorphine-induced changes in morphine self-administration in rhesus monkeys. J Pharmacol Exp Ther 1971;176:464–71.
[91] Griffiths RR, Wurster RM, Brady JV. Discrete-trial choice procedure: effects of naloxone and methadone on choice between food and heroin. Pharmacol Rev 1975;27:357–65.
[92] Huttunen KM, Raunio H, Rautio J. Prodrugs–from serendipity to rational design. Pharmacol Rev 2011;63:750–71.
[93] Imai T. Human carboxylesterase isozymes: catalytic properties and rational drug design. Drug Metab Pharmacokinet 2006;21:173–85.
[94] Nishimuta H, Houston JB, Galetin A. Hepatic, intestinal, renal, and plasma hydrolysis of prodrugs in human, cynomolgus monkey, dog, and rat: implications for in vitro-in vivo extrapolation of clearance of prodrugs. Drug Metab Dispos 2014;42:1522–31.
[95] Mansour A, Khachaturian H, Lewis ME, Akil H, Watson SJ. Anatomy of CNS opioid receptors. Trends Neurosci 1988;11:308–14.

CHAPTER 5

Assessing Physical Dependence

Greet Teuns
Janssen R&D, Janssen Pharmaceutica NV, Beerse, Belgium

Contents

1. INTRODUCTION

The nonmedical use of prescription drugs is increasing continuously, in particular in young people (15–24 years old) in the Western world. In the US, prescription drugs are second only to marijuana as the drug of choice in substance abuse in teenagers [1,2].

Nonclinical Assessment of Abuse Potential for New Pharmaceuticals
http://dx.doi.org/10.1016/B978-0-12-420172-9.00005-9

In fact, seven of the top 10 drugs used by 12th graders (17–18 years of age) are prescription drugs. Prescription drugs are now contributing to far more fatalities than illegal drugs [2]. Antidepressants, analgesics, sedatives, cardiovascular drugs, and asthma medications account for half of the 10 most common poisonings that result in fatalities in the US [3]. The increase of the nonmedical use of methylphenidate (MPH) (prescribed for attention deficit hyperactivity disorder (ADHD)) by teens is another well-known example, with reports of fatalities due to intranasal administration [4].

This trend has raised an increased awareness of the abuse potential of central nervous system (CNS)-active drugs in development. This awareness has been translated into more stringent recommendations for the investigation, which have been released since 2006 (the European Medicines Agency (EMA) guideline [5]; the International Conference on Harmonization (ICH) guideline [6]; the Food and Drug Administration (FDA) draft guidance [7]; and the subsequent FDA's decision tree [8]). In particular, within the preclinical safety evaluation domain the need for drug abuse liability testing has become a major area of research, as all compounds in development (including their major metabolites [7,9]) exerting an activity in the brain (regardless of the therapeutic area) are subject to the regulatory requirements of drug licensing authorities on testing for abuse potential.

An abuse liability assessment aims to protect patients while they are being treated with medicines with CNS activity and to discourage healthy users from using these drugs in nonmedical situations (off-label, prescription misdirection, and recreational use). It provides data from highly predictive preclinical assays on the abuse potential of these new CNS-active drug candidates with a novel mechanism of action. Deterrence from nonmedical use of prescription drugs also requires support from chemists and formulation experts to modify the product form into a final commercial product, using abuse-deterrent formulations that are less suitable to misuse. Finally, it implies a demand for support from the regulatory staff to eventually prepare for scheduling of the final product based upon its abuse potential properties, thus influencing the prescription procedures and subsequently leading to a restricted availability of the drug product.

The complexity of testing new CNS-active drug substances in development for possible abuse potential often lies within the off-target pharmaco-toxicological profile, as the mechanism of action (MoA) of the majority of these new molecular entities (NMEs) is distinct from that of the known classes of abused drugs defined by the regulatory authorities worldwide (Table 1) and extensively investigated [10]. This complexity implies that the construct of the preclinical abuse liability assessment, in particular with regard to the relevance of the reference drug versus the new NME, is not straightforward and might even impose additional studies beyond the scope of the guidance, utilizing multiple different reference drugs.

The potential of a new CNS-active drug substance to induce physical dependence is one aspect that might contribute to the development of abuse, and the preclinical investigation hereof is a mandatory test within the abuse liability assessment. This behavioral model

Table 1 Specific Classes of Active Substances of Abuse According to the FDA and EMA Classifications

Specific Classes of Active Substances

FDA	EMA
Opioids	Opioids
Stimulants	Stimulants
Depressants	Sedatives and anxiolytics
Cannabinoids	Cannabinoids
Hallucinogens	NMDA-antagonists
	Nicotine-like active substances

evaluates the presence of withdrawal signs after abrupt cessation of the (sub)chronic dosing of a test substance. Although the conduct of this test is not as complex as those executed to investigate the psychological component of abuse potential, many factors have to be taken into account to ensure a proper study design and hence a correct interpretation of the results. The selection of a dose range to test several-fold of the maximum human efficacious dose (C_{eff} Hu) and the correct choice of a known psycho-active reference drug are the keys to a successful assessment that will be acceptable to regulatory authorities. The reference drug(s) are ideally relevant to the receptor binding profile and pharmacological properties or to the therapeutic class of the test substance. Development of the study design involves a thorough understanding and knowledge of the (neuro)pharmacology and the toxicological profile of both the test substance and the psycho-active reference drug(s).

In this chapter the basis of the nonprecipitated withdrawal study for testing physical dependence in preclinical drug development is described in detail. The Good Laboratory Practices (GLP) requirements and the timelines with regard to the conduct of this study type during drug development are discussed and a general view on the regulatory guidance of the drug licensing authorities is provided. Finally, general considerations adding to the high predictivity of this model are stipulated.

2. DEFINITIONS

2.1 Physical Dependence

Physical dependence is defined as a state of adaptation, manifested by a drug class-specific withdrawal syndrome produced by abrupt cessation, rapid dose reduction, decreasing blood level of the drug substance, and/or administration of an antagonist [11].

According to the Stedman's Medical Dictionary [12], the withdrawal or abstinence syndrome refers to "a constellation of physiologic changes undergone by people or animals that have become physically dependent on a drug substance or chemical who are abruptly deprived of that substance."

Physical dependence may occur with the chronic use of any drug substance, legal or illegal, even when taken as prescribed [13]. How the physical dependence or the withdrawal syndrome evolves is dependent on the drug class [14], the dose and duration of administration, and on the individual properties of the drug substance, but the symptoms are mostly opposite to the initial effects of the particular drug substance [15].

Withdrawal symptoms known to appear after cessation of drugs of abuse in humans may include insomnia, hallucinations and convulsions (barbiturates), anxiety, vomiting and diarrhea (opioids), irritability, shaking, nausea (alcohol), headaches, and difficulties in concentration (nicotine). However, some drugs of abuse do not produce clear-cut withdrawal symptoms upon cessation (cocaine, marihuana [16]; methylphenidate [17]).

Moreover, many drug substances that are not illicit drugs of abuse but are legally prescribed are also known to cause physical dependence, which is manifest upon cessation of (sub)chronic dosing [13]. These substances and their resulting potential side effects include corticosteroids (nausea, lethargy, and depression [18]); steroids (fatigue, loss of sex drive, and depressed mood [19]); antidepressants (dizziness, headache, nausea, and lethargy [20]); and cardiovascular medicines (beta blockers: beta-adrenergic hypersensitivity [21,16]), among others. For these drug substances, discontinuation of treatment needs careful tapering (gradual diminution of the therapeutic dose) in order to avoid a withdrawal syndrome.

Physical dependence is not equivalent to substance dependence/addiction, the latter of which has been described in the Diagnostic and Statistical Manual of Mental Disorders IV[1] of 2000 [22] as "a chronically relapsing disorder that is characterized by a compulsion to seek and take drug or stimulus, continued use despite harmful consequences, with loss of control in limiting intake, and emergence of a negative emotional state (e.g., dysphoria, anxiety, irritability) when access to the drug or stimulus is prevented". However, physical dependence can lead to craving for the drug to relieve or overcome the negative withdrawal symptoms upon cessation [23].

2.2 Tolerance

Tolerance is defined as a decrease in response to a given dose following the repeated administration of a drug substance. Metabolic or pharmacokinetic tolerance is an adaptation of the body by biological changes to the presence of the substance, to ensure a more rapid elimination of that substance from the body. An example is the metabolic tolerance to alcohol. Repeated dose administration induces a higher production of the liver enzyme alcohol dehydrogenase, allowing a faster metabolism of alcohol, as such increasing the clearance of alcohol from the body. This metabolic tolerance does not contribute to drug dependence or to withdrawal symptoms.

Functional or pharmacodynamic tolerance reveals an aspect of neuroadaptation, manifested by a decrease in sensitivity of the CNS to a drug substance [5] due to changes at the synaptic level [25]. A well-known example is the functional tolerance to alcohol: the response to alcohol (sensitivity) in the CNS is reduced, resulting in

[1] To avoid confusion of the terminology used, the recently released DSM-V of 2013 has combined the categories of substance dependence and substance abuse into one single term: "substance use disorder" [24].

an attenuated effect. These neuronal adaptations are protective mechanisms and occur to compensate for the increased alcohol concentration in the brain with chronic alcoholism. Thus to experience the same effect of alcohol when used chronically, the alcohol dose needs to be increased [26]. Similarly, the pharmacodynamic tolerance to opiates is well known, which explains why a dose sufficiently high to normally be lethal in (nondependent) humans can be used by an opiate tolerant addict without lethality. Sadly, this also explains some deaths of former addicts, who (after successful rehabilitation therapy) re-establish their opiate intake at a dose level known by them formerly to be without adverse effects or toxicity, only to experience that in the current nontolerant state the formerly used dose level is toxic and/or lethal.

Functional tolerance may contribute to the development of dependence but is not regarded as a robust marker.

2.3 Sensitization

Sensitization (the opposite of tolerance) to active substances is defined as an increased effect of the substance following repeated doses. In particular, behavioral sensitization or psychomotor sensitization can be observed in animals treated with stimulants, as evidenced by enhanced locomotor activity [27]. In such a sensitized state, there were corresponding increases in mesolimbic dopamine release/output (neuronal hypersensitivity) to levels greater than that produced previously, potentially leading to pathological wanting or incentive salience, even in the absence of increases in pleasure (reward) and as such resulting in increased drug seeking behavior [28–30]. This so-called incentive sensitization is considered to contribute to relapses of drug-taking behavior [31,32].

3. NEUROBIOLOGY OF WITHDRAWAL

For all drugs of abuse signs of acute withdrawal are driven by previous drug-induced neuroadaptations. These include a decrease in the dopaminergic activity of the mesolimbic dopamine system and a decrease in the serotonergic neurotransmission in the nucleus accumbens [33–35]. The corticotropin-releasing factor (CRF), present in the neurons of the amygdala, mediates the brain stress/aversive system and the hypothalamic–pituitary–adrenal axis, which are activated during withdrawal [35–37]. Other neuropeptides and neurotransmitters involved encompass dynorphin and neuropeptide Y, which also interact with CRF, and norepinephrine, whose level is increased during acute withdrawal [36,38].

4. WITHDRAWAL: PRECIPITATED AND NONPRECIPITATED

The physical dependence potential of a test substance can be investigated preclinically by means of a precipitated or nonprecipitated withdrawal test. Both tests include a repeated dose (RD) phase followed by a withdrawal period during which possible signs related to abstinence of the drug in the body might appear. In a precipitated withdrawal test an antagonist is administered after the last daily dose of the test substance, to rapidly induce the withdrawal symptoms. For known mechanisms, the precipitation of withdrawal signs via administration of such an antagonist can be useful due to the immediacy and magnitude of the responses (compared to observations for many days, as in the nonprecipitated withdrawal paradigm). For drugs with a very long half-life in a species (e.g., tetrahydrocannabinol,THC), the existence of withdrawal signs can be difficult to observe (or prove) unless precipitated by an antagonist (e.g., SR141716-rimonabant) [39]. Other examples include the use of naloxone in a mu opioid agonist withdrawal study or flumazenil with benzodiazepines testing.

However, as the precipitated withdrawal test can only be performed if a specific antagonist of the test substance is available, this model is less convenient for the investigation of the physical dependence potential of new NMEs with a novel mechanism of action and will not be further discussed in this chapter.

The nonprecipitated withdrawal test investigates the appearance of withdrawal symptoms after the cessation of subchronic drug exposure, coinciding with the elimination of the drug. Withdrawal symptoms may include a variety of behavioral effects and/or somatic or autonomic responses to occur, such as changes in body temperature or body weight and food consumption. The duration of the presence of withdrawal effects is largely independent of any particular mechanism and is related to the nature of the drug substance (physico-chemical and kinetic properties, receptor binding occupancy, biological half-life).

5. USE OF POSITIVE AND NEGATIVE CONTROLS IN THE WITHDRAWAL TEST

Positive and negative controls should be included in the withdrawal test [5,7].

The negative control could include a substance without abuse potential that is approved for treatment of the same condition as proposed for the new drug substance [7]; however, in practice, the control or vehicle formulations are used as negative controls [5].

The positive control should be a scheduled drug in the same pharmacological class or within the same therapeutic area as the test drug substance [7]. For example, morphine can be used as a reference drug within the same pharmacological class if the test substance has mu opioid properties. Using a marketed and scheduled drug as a positive control within the same therapeutic area may encompass morphine for a test substance with a totally different mechanism of action from that of opioids but both being indicated for the treatment of pain. An example could be the investigation of the physical dependence potential of severe gabapentin, a nonopioid for treatment of central neuropathic pain.

However, for testing NMEs with a novel mechanism of action the choice of a particular reference drug is not always straightforward. Considerable expertise on the pharmacology and on the toxicology of both the test substance and the various psycho-active reference drugs is needed and is achieved by assessing the receptor binding profile, the pharmacological action, and the toxicological effects of both in order to select a reference drug that is of relevance in view of the test substance's profile and its presumed therapeutic indication.

6. ANIMAL MODEL OF NONPRECIPITATED WITHDRAWAL

6.1 General Outline

The preclinical nonprecipitated or spontaneous withdrawal test comprises a RD phase and a withdrawal period. The RD phase allows the animal to develop a neuroadaptive response to the test substance as part of the homeostatic process. Sufficient exposure to the drug includes adequate receptor occupancy and/or brain penetration. For a drug candidate, this fundamental information is obtained during the phase prior to its selection and classically in the early drug development preclinical studies. The receptor selectivity of the drug candidate is investigated through functional in vitro assays for its agonist or antagonistic activity and for possible interaction with other targets. The binding profile of a drug candidate is evaluated on different receptor, ion channel, and transporter targets. Further, assays are designed to evaluate whether a drug candidate occupies the functional receptor in vivo through dose and time occupancy relationships after systemic administration. Besides these primary pharmacology data, the results of general pharmacological models (sleep wake architecture, specific drug target related CNS models, models related to additional body functions (autonomic nervous system, gastrointestinal system, etc.)) are also studied to ensure a proper dose selection with sufficient exposure in the brain.

The frequency of dosing (q.d., b.i.d., continuous dosing through IV infusion, etc.) and the route of administration (oral, subcutaneous, intravenous, etc.) determine brain and peak plasma exposures. Therefore, the kinetic profiles of the most stringent routes (often the oral and the intravenous route) are investigated as well for comparison of concomitant exposures.

A proper selection of the test dose range is not only based on the data of the above mentioned studies but also, very importantly, on the toxicological and concomitant toxicokinetic profile of the test substance, as the off-target toxicity is often actuating the selected dosages. Also adding to a scientifically based selection of various test dosages are the results of the tolerance studies, which are designed to determine the maximum tolerated dose; the repeated dose toxicity studies, which investigate possible effects due to repeatedly administrating the test substance (tissue accumulation, auto-induction, and target organ toxicity, among others); and the Modified Irwin's study or Functional

Observation Battery (FOB) test, in which the neurofunctional integrity in the rat is explored after single doses. The lowest dose of the test substance, situated within the range of the pharmacologically active dose, should not demonstrate behavioral effects, whereas the highest test dose should be within or approaching the toxic range. According to the recommendations [5–7], the highest dose tested must demonstrate plasma exposure levels that are multiples of the maximum human efficacious dose (expressed as C_{max}).

6.2 Choice of Species

The preferred species for testing physical dependence potential of NMEs in a nonprecipitated withdrawal test is the common, naive rat [5–7]. Whenever another species is selected a justification needs to be provided as well as the prior drug history of the individual animals included in the test. For example, nonhuman primates (NHP) can be preferred in limited cases when the rat is not predictive of human abuse [6,40,41]; in these cases, the macaque monkey (rhesus or cynomolgus strain), the marmoset, or the baboon are NHP strains that can be used [42,43].

In this chapter the rat model will be described, but this can be extended to other species if appropriate.

6.3 Rat Model

6.3.1 Animal Strain, Age, and Gender

Various strains can be used, including the albino Wistar and Sprague–Dawley rats or the pigmented Long Evans rat. The age of the rats at the start of the study varies from 6 to 9 weeks of age, in accordance with the common age of rats entering into general toxicity studies. Most often male rats will be used, although female rats or a combination of the two genders is an option, in particular when a clear gender difference is observed in previous pharmacological and/or toxicity studies, which is mostly related to pharmacokinetic (metabolism) dissimilarities.

6.3.2 Husbandry

Preferably an AAALAC-accredited (Association for Assessment and Accreditation of Laboratory Animal Care) testing facility is used for testing. Housing and experiments need to be conducted in accordance with the European [44] and the national guidelines (e.g., Belgian Law [45]) or with the US guidance on animal welfare [46] and with the principles of euthanasia, as stated in the Report of the American Veterinary Medical Association Panel [47].

As for behavioral studies, rats are preferably housed separately to exclude any attenuated or intensified effect(s) related to social behavior and/or social interactions [48]. Transparent polysulphone cages (floor area: 940 cm^2) with a wire mesh lid suspended in wheeled racks can be used.

Bedding material (Corn Cob size 12, Eurocob, France) and cage enrichment (wooden blocks, Sizzle nest, and/or transparent polycarbonate tunnels) are provided. There is a 12/12 light/dark cycle and illumination should not exceed 400 lux [46]. The test rooms are air-conditioned with their own supply of filtered fresh air. The standardized test conditions for temperature (20–23 °C), relative humidity (40–70%), and illumination are regularly controlled and recorded.

Rats are given free access to water, and food (e.g., R/M-H pelleted maintenance diet, Ssniff (Soest, Germany)) is provided ad libitum.

6.3.3 Route of Administration and Dose Groups

If feasible the intended clinical route is used for dose administration of the test substance. Various routes of administration ensuring systemic exposure (oral, intravenous (bolus or infusion), subcutaneous, intraperitoneal) can be employed in this type of study. The use of osmotic pumps is discouraged as the abrupt cessation of drug administration cannot be determined properly if pumps are not removed. Concurrently, surgical removal of the osmotic pumps after the RD phase needs to be conducted under anesthesia, followed by recovery and consequentially postsurgical medication. This will affect proper investigation of the subsequent withdrawal period after the dosing phase.

Typically, five groups of rats are used (n = minimum 5–8 rats per group), comprising a control/vehicle group (negative control), three test groups dosed/treated with different dosages of the test substance to enable investigation of a dose-effect curve, and a reference drug group (positive control).

The lowest dose of the test substance, situated within the range of the pharmacologically active dose, should not produce behavioral effects. As stated before, the highest test dose should be within or approaching the toxic range, demonstrating plasma concentrations (C_{max}) that are multiples of the human efficacious dose (C_{eff} Hu expressed as C_{max}) [5–7]. The dose volume for daily dose administration must be in accordance with the guidance "A Good Practice Guide to the Administration of Substances and Removal of Blood, Including Routes and Volumes" [49]. From the information obtained from the repeated dose toxicity studies, one may adapt the final doses in view of tolerance or sensitization to the test substance if this would be known to occur during the repeated dosing.

The control/vehicle group receives the test formulation but without any test substance included via the same route as proposed for the test substance. If liquid formulations are being prepared for dose administration of the test substance, the control/vehicle group receives the test formulation at the same volume but without any active compound included. If capsules are being used, an empty capsule will be given at the same dose regimen as for the test substance.

The route of administration and the dose of the reference drug (positive control) are selected according to the available data on the various feasible routes and according to its pharmaco–toxicological profile. Cocaine and amphetamine can be easily administered subcutaneously [50,17], whereas ethanol and chlordiazepoxide are classically dosed orally [51–53]. Morphine can be administered orally [53] or subcutaneously [54]. Some reference drugs are being employed intraperitoneally (e.g., ketamine [55]).

For drugs like morphine (100 mg/kg SC) or chlordiazepoxide (400 mg/kg b.i.d. OR) the administration of gradually increasing doses is needed before reaching the final test dose [56]. Amphetamine (0.8 mg/kg SC [17]); cocaine (20 mg/kg SC [57]); ethanol (1500 mg/kg OR [52]); and ketamine (30 mg/kg IP [55]) may be administered at their respective dose from the first day of dosing onwards.

6.3.4 Duration of the In Vivo Phase

6.3.4.1 Repeated Dose Phase

The length of the RD phase must be sufficiently long in order to obtain adaptation to the test substance by the body during subchronic drug administration as part of the homeostatic process, thus allowing the animal to develop a neuroadaptive response.

Classically the RD phase comprises 21 successive days to ensure both a steady-state level of the plasma exposures upon repeated dose administration and homeostatic neuroadaptation. The RD phase can be shortened (up to 2 weeks) or prolonged (up to 4 weeks).

6.3.4.2 Withdrawal Phase

The altered state of the neuronal circuitry, developed as a neuroadaptive response during the subchronic administration of a CNS-active test substance, might give rise to withdrawal signs when the active form of the test substance is removed from the body during the withdrawal (WD) phase. The toxicokinetic profile of the test substance determined during the former studies is one of the key factors to rely upon for determining the length of the WD phase. The maximum or peak plasma concentration (C_{max}) and the subsequent T_{max}, and the half-life ($T_{1/2}$) after single and repeated doses have to be taken into account for determining the length of the withdrawal period. The physico-chemical properties of the drug might also influence the ADME profile (Absorption/Distribution/Metabolism/Excretion), of which in particular the elimination phase is of importance during the withdrawal phase (e.g., morphine, a hydrophilic compound, is metabolized and eliminated more rapidly than diazepam, a lipophilic compound with a long half-life and accumulation properties [58,59]).

In a standard design the WD phase encompasses 7 days. However, this period can be prolonged based upon the compound's characteristics (e.g., if the test substance has a long $T_{1/2}$).

6.3.5 Parameters Investigated

It is important to consider the pharmacology of the NME and how it may impact the parameters described below both during the dosing phase, and during the WD phase of an experiment. Care is taken to avoid manipulation of the animals as much as possible throughout the study; as such, anticipating possible interference due to stress-related behavioral changes is necessary.

6.3.5.1 Behavioral Observations and General Clinical Observations

A number of specific behavioral observations alerting for possible physical dependence are included in Table 2. Some of the observations are known to be induced by psychoactive drugs (e.g., a wet dog shakes when mu opioids are administrated).

Table 2 List of Specific Behavioral Observations with Concomitant Scores and/or Grades

Observations	Scores	Description
Lethality	P, D, I or –	Preterminally killed, dead, incidental dead, or absent
Sniffing	+/–	Present/Absent
Abnormal licking	+/–	Present/Absent
Abnormal preening	+/–	Present/Absent
Grooming	+/–	Present/Absent
Wet dog shakes	+/–	Present/Absent
Twitches	0/4	0: no; 1: slight; 2: mild; 3: obvious; 4: severe
Tremors	0/4	0: no; 1: slight; 2: mild; 3: obvious; 4: severe Specific tremor: X if present
Convulsions	+/–	Present/Absent
Specific convulsions		X if present
• Clonic-type convulsions		Asymmetrical Running excitement Champing Popcorn Asphyxial
• Tonic-type convulsions		Opisthotonus Emprosthotonus
• Miscellaneous-type convulsions		Rock and roll Sitting up Praying
Locomotor activity	0/4	0: no; 1: slight; 2: mild; 3: obvious; 4: severe
• Abnormal biting	+/–	Present/Absent
• Restlessness	+/–	Present/Absent
• Writhing	+/–	Present/Absent
Body carriage		
• Straub tail	0/4	0: flat; 1: horizontal stretched; 2: 30° upwards; 3: 60° upwards; 4: 90° upwards
Dyspnoea	+/–	Present/Absent
Arousal		
• Excitation	0/4	0: no; 1: slight; 2: mild; 3: obvious; 4: severe
• Jumping	+/–	Present/Absent
• Sedation	0/4	0: no; 1: slight; 2: mild; 3: obvious; 4: severe
• Alertness	+/–	Present/Absent

Continued

Table 2 List of Specific Behavioral Observations with Concomitant Scores and/or Grades—cont'd

Observations	Scores	Description
Narrowing palpebral fissure	0/4	0: completely closed 1: narrowed; no reaction to stimuli 2: narrowed; half-closed eyelids 3: slightly narrowed; open after stimulus 4: open
Defecation	−2/2	−2: no feces −1: decreased feces 0: normal 1: increased feces 2: diarrhea
Lacrimation	+/−	Present/Absent
Catalepsy	+/−	Present/Absent
Abnormal gait		
• Ataxia	0/4	0: no; 1: slight; 2: mild; 3: obvious; 4: severe
• Tiptoe gait	+/−	Present/Absent
• Shuffling movements	+/−	Present/Absent
Salivation	+/−	Present/Absent

In order to obtain baseline values for comparison during the withdrawal period the incidence, severity, and duration of these observations are monitored and recorded for each individual animal during the RD phase on particular days at various daily time points. The selected days and the time points support the behavioral examination of the rats after a single and repeated (steady state) dose and at time points representing an exposure effect curve based upon C_{max}. In some cases, when there is a dose effect response but no exposure effect relationship, these factors must be taken into account as well for setting the appropriate time points. This might be the case when investigating pro-drugs or drug substances that trigger a molecularly based cascade within a certain pathway (e.g., allosteric modulators).

During the WD phase the behavioral observations are examined daily at the various time points, as defined during the RD phase.

Mortality and clinical observations are also recorded daily. It might be of interest to include several daily time points to observe the animals for general signs of toxicity if these are not included in the list of behavioral observations.

6.3.5.2 Body Temperature

Body temperature is another sensitive marker for detecting possible signs of physical dependence and is recorded throughout the RD and the WD period, usually at multiple time points per day. Indeed, some drugs, for example morphine, can increase body temperature or alter the diurnal body temperature pattern. Another detailed example is

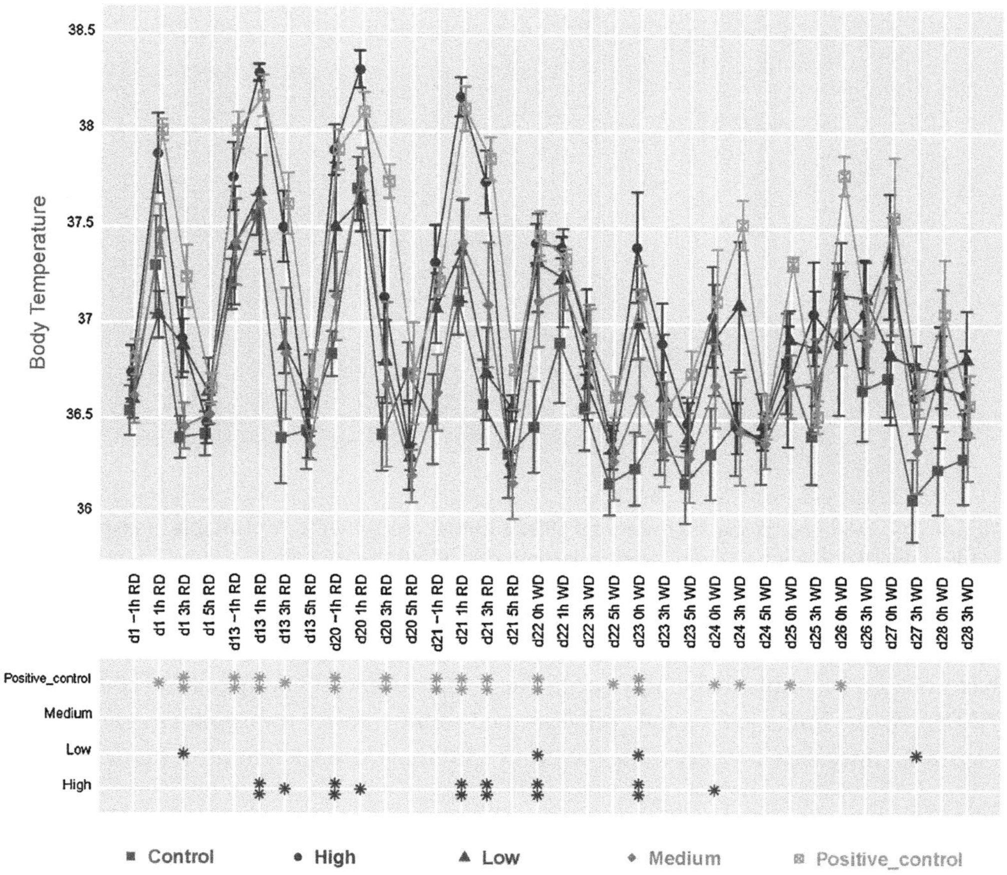

Figure 1 Body temperatures (BT, degree Celsius) recorded in animals dosed with NaCl 0.9% (control); methylphenidate (MPH) at 2.5 (low), 5 (mid), or 10 (high) mg/kg; D-amphetamine at 0.08 mg/kg SC (positive control) on specified days (days 1, 13, 20, 21 of the repeated dose (RD) phase and daily on days 21–28 of the withdrawal (WD) period) at various daily time points: 1 h: 1 h prior to dose administration (RD) or at a similar time (0 h) during WD; 1, 3, 5 h: 1, 3, 5 h post-dose or at a similar time during WD. Significance computed versus control by Mann–Whitney U (two-tailed): *$p < 0.05$, **$p < 0.01$, ***$p < 0.001$. *Reproduced with permission from Teuns* [17].

shown in Figure 1, where the body temperature was recorded in animals dosed orally with MPH at 0 (control), 2.5, 5, or 10 mg/kg or subcutaneously with D-amphetamine (AMP reference drug) at 0.08 mg/kg during 21 days, followed by a 7-day withdrawal period [17]. It was clearly demonstrated that a significantly higher body temperature (versus control) was recorded at 10 mg/kg MPH at 1 and 3 h during repeated dosing, returning to values comparable to control after 5 h, and that this effect remained present during the first days of withdrawal. The same pattern was present in the D-amphetamine group.

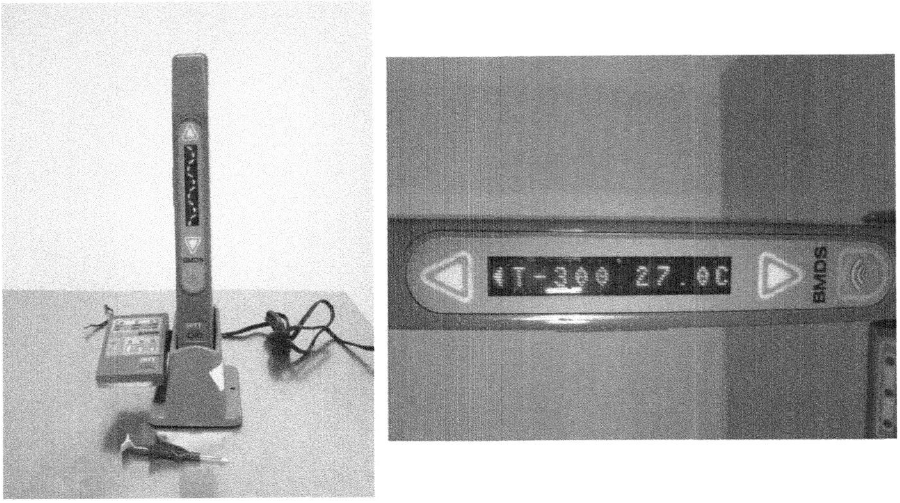

Figure 2 A validated probe thermometer (Plexx thermometer) with implantable transponders for reading the peripheral body temperature without disturbing the animals.

A probe thermometer is used for measuring the peripheral body temperature via subcutaneously implanted chips (e.g., Plexx thermometer: temperature reader (DAS 7007S) with implantable and programmed temperature transponders (IPTT-300), Figure 2), thus allowing recordings without additional manipulation of the rats.

6.3.5.3 Body Weight, Weight Gain, and Food Consumption

Body weight and food consumption are measured at various daily time points (based upon the toxicokinetic profile) on specified days during both the RD and the WD phase of the study. The so-called daytime measures (e.g., body weight and food consumption recorded over 5 h post-dose in the RD phase or during the same 5-h interval on the days of withdrawal) are of relevance for investigating possible effects on the diurnal rhythm (as for stimulants) or when compounds with a biphasic exposure profile are investigated (like opioids). They can also be compared with 24-h measures (e.g., body weight and food consumption recorded after 24 h post-dose, prior to the next daily dose during the RD phase or every 24 h during WD). An example is given in Table 3 where it was demonstrated that 24-h measurements of body weight and food consumption were comparable between all groups, but that daily 5–6-h measurements (so-called daytime measurements) of body weight gain and food consumption were higher (though not always significant) in the MPH and AMP groups compared with those of the control group, where a body weight loss and a lower food consumption were measured during daytime.

Table 3 Example of Mean Body Weight Gain Data and Food Consumption Recorded in Animals Dosed with NaCl 0.9% (Control); Methylphenidate (MPH) at 2.5 (Low), 5 (Mid), or 10 (High) mg/kg; D-Amphetamine (AMP) at 0.08 mg/kg SC (Positive Control) during the Repeated Dose Phase and during the Withdrawal Period, Calculated over Day Time (+5 h Post-Dose versus −1 h or versus 0 h) and over 24 h

MPH	Control 0 mg/kg	Positive Control 0.8 mg AMP/kg	Low 2.5 mg/kg	Mid 5 mg/kg	High 10 mg/kg
Mean Body Weight Gain					
Repeated Dose Phase					
• day 1: +5 h vs −1 h	−3 g	−12 g*	−8 g	−9 g	−10 g
• day 13: +5 h vs −1 h	−2 g	0 g	+2 g	+1 g	+3 g
• day 20: +5 h vs −1 h	−2 g	+2 g	+3 g	+2 g	+3 g
• day 21: +5 h vs −1 h	−1 g	+5 g	+2 g	+2 g	+5 g
• day 20: over 24 h	+4 g	−1 g*	+3 g	+4 g	0 g*
• day 21: over 24 h	+2 g	+6 g	+2 g	+1 g	+5 g
Withdrawal Phase					
• day 22: +5 h vs 0 h	0 g	+5 g	+6 g	+5 g	+6 g
• day 23: +5 h vs 0 h	−2 g	+6 g*	+5 g	+4 g*	+4 g
• day 24: +5 h vs 0 h	−4 g	+5 g	+6 g	0 g	+4 g*
• day 25: +5 h vs 0 h	−3 g	−1 g	+1 g	0 g	+5 g*
• day 26: +5 h vs 0 h	−2 g	−1 g	+1 g	−1 g	+2 g
• day 27: +5 h vs 0 h	−2 g	+3 g*	+2 g	+1 g	+3 g
• day 28: +5 h vs 0 h	−5 g	+2 g*	0 g*	0 g	+4 g**
• 24 h weight gain: min/max ranges over 24 h from day 22–28	+1 to 6 g	+1 to 6 g	+2 to 7 g	−1 to 9 g	+1 to 7 g
Food Uptake					
Repeated Dose Phase					
• day 13: +5 h vs 0 h	3 g	7 g	6 g	6 g	8 g*
• day 20: +5 h vs 0 h	5 g	9 g*	8 g	7 g	8 g
• day 21: +5 h vs 0 h	5 g	10 g	6 g	7 g	8 g
• day 13: over 24 h	26 g	30 g	29 g	28 g	29 g
• day 20: over 24 h	28 g	28 g	28 g	27 g	27 g
• day 21: over 24 h	29 g	32 g	28 g	27 g	30 g
Withdrawal Phase					
• day 22: +5 h vs 0 h	5 g	9 g	8 g	8 g	7 g
• day 23: +5 h vs 0 h	5 g	11 g*	8 g	8 g	8 g
• day 24: +5 h vs 0 h	4 g	9 g*	9 g	6 g	8 g*
• 24 h food uptake: min/max ranges over 24 h from day 22–28	28 to 31 g	30 to 32 g	27 to 31 g	28 to 31 g	28 to 31 g

Significance computed versus control by Mann–Whitney U (two-tailed): *$p < 0.05$, **$p < 0.01$, ***$p < 0.001$.
Reproduced with permission from Teuns [17].

6.3.5.4 Telemetry

Invasive methods such as telemetry [53,60] can be considered for continuous monitoring of the internal blood pressure, heart rate, and temperature using different probes. Froger et al. [53] described this procedure for studying the withdrawal effects of morphine and chlordiazepoxide in rats.

6.3.5.5 Toxicokinetics

Investigation of toxicokinetic parameters of the test substance and, if needed, of the major metabolite(s) (defined as CNS-active and circulating at a plasma level of >10% of parent exposure [6,9,61]) is included in the withdrawal test through separate satellite groups of male and/or female rats (3/sex/dose) that are dosed according to the main study design. A 24-h exposure versus time profile is determined after the first daily dose (single dose exposures) and after the last daily dose (repeated dose exposures). The time points for blood sampling are selected based upon the kinetic profile of the test substance demonstrated in previous toxicity studies. Depending on the test substance's kinetic profile, several samples can be collected during the WD phase (e.g., samples collected 24, 48, and 72 h after the last daily dose administration) to demonstrate the elimination of the test substance from the body upon cessation.

The parameters investigated comprise T_{max}, C_{max}, and $T_{1/2}$.

6.3.6 Other Tools to Enhance the Detection of Withdrawal Symptoms

The use of 24-h camera monitoring can be of added value, in particular during the last days of repeated dosing and the first days of withdrawal, to evaluate possible effects on behavior and on diurnal/nocturnal rhythms (as the rat is a nocturnal animal) or sleep wake patterns.

An example of the different parameters scheduled in a nonprecipitated withdrawal study is given in Table 4.

6.3.7 Termination of the Study

At the end of the WD phase, animals are euthanized.

7. GENERAL CONSIDERATIONS

The issue of whether this type of study could be integrated in a standard 1-month toxicity study, in order to reduce the number of animals needed, was investigated. Based upon careful evaluation of the withdrawal design and the 1-month design, it was concluded that incorporation of the assessment of physical dependence in toxicity studies is not encouraged. Behavioral studies per definition require an environment in which the animals should not be disturbed by various actions as performed in toxicity studies (e.g., manipulations at urine sampling) because these actions may influence the results of the various withdrawal parameters.

Table 4 Example of the Different Parameters Included in a Nonprecipitated Withdrawal Design as Scheduled during the Repeated Dose (RD) and Withdrawal (WD) Phase

	T_{-1} (−1 h)/T_0	1 h	3 h	5 h	7 h
Day −2	BW (randomization)				
Day −1	BT_{-24} $BObs_{-24}$				
Day 1 (first dose)	BT_{-1} $BObs_{-1}$ BW_{-1} TK_{-1}	BT_1 $BObs_1$ TK_1	BT_3 $BObs_3$ TK_3	BT_5 $BObs_5$ TK_5	BT_7 $BObs_7$ BW_7 TK_7
Day 2	TK_{24}				
Day 13	BT_{-1} $BObs_{-1}$ BW_{-1} FC_{-1}	BT_1 $BObs_1$	BT_3 $BObs_3$	BT_5 $BObs_5$	BT_7 $BObs_7$ BW_7 FC_7
Day 20	BT_{-1} $BObs_{-1}$ BW_{-1} FC_{-1}	BT_1 $BObs_1$	BT_3 $BObs_3$	BT_5 $BObs_5$	BT_7 $BObs_7$ BW_7 FC_7
Day 21	BT_{-1} $BObs_{-1}$ BW_{-1} FC_{-1} TK_{-1}	BT_1 $BObs_1$ TK_1	BT_3 $BObs_3$ TK_3	BT_5 $BObs_5$ TT_5	BT_7 $BObs_7$ BW_7 FC_7 KT_7
Day 22 (first day of WD)	TK_{24} BT_0 $BObs_0$ BW_0 FC_0	 BT_1 $BObs_1$	 BT_3 $BObs_3$ BW_3	 BT_5 $BObs_5$	 BT_7 $BObs_7$ BW_7 FC_7
Day 23	BT_0 $BObs_0$ BW_0 FC_0		BT_3 $BObs_3$ BW_3		BT_7 $BObs_7$ BW_7 FC_7
Day 24	BT_0 $BObs_0$ BW_0 FC_0		BT_3 $BObs_3$ BW_3		BT_7 $BObs_7$ BW_7 FC_7
Day 25, 26, 27, 28	BT_0 $BObs_0$ BW_0 FC_0		BT_3 $BObs_3$		 BW_7

BT: body temperature; BObs: behavioral observations; BW: body weight; FC: food consumption; h: hour(s); T_{-24}: 24 h prior to start of daily dosing; T_{-1}: time point prior to dosing; T_0: 0 h: 24 h after last daily drug treatment/actual hour defined on day 21; $T_{3/5/7}$: time points at 3, 5, or 7 h after 0 h.

Care should be taken to limit the number of persons entering the room in which the behavioral studies are performed to avoid disturbance of the behavior of the rats.

The possible impact of conditioning via the manipulation for daily treatment of the test substance (learned association of treatment procedure and effect of the drug) on the incidence and severity rate of the withdrawal symptoms was investigated (Teuns, unpublished data). Mimicking the drug treatment throughout the WD phase (sham treatment) resulted in less clear signs of withdrawal and should be avoided.

All scientific employees must be trained thoroughly to perform this type of study, enabling them to distinguish between the various behavioral observations and in particular to perceive changes in behavior during the WD phase which might be, in certain cases, very subtle [62,63]. All recorded differences from substance dosed animals versus control/vehicle dosed animals need to be examined carefully [63].

The investigation of Selective Serotonin Reuptake Inhibitors (SSRIs) and their physical dependence potential has been of special interest to the drug licensing authorities. Although such a type of compound is known not to induce abuse potential, a unique withdrawal syndrome occurs in humans that was not clearly defined in animals. To emphasize the risk/benefit assessment of this type of drug, a position paper was released by EMA in 2000 with a retrospective review of all relevant nonclinical data and with further actions of possible preclinical studies to investigate addiction and physical dependence potential related to the use of SSRIs [64,65]. Of special consideration was the length of the RD phase for this type of drug (2 months) and additional investigations on sleep, gross behavior, and locomotor activity.

Besides physical dependence, the psychological aspects of withdrawal can also be taken into account. This will require other models [5], such as the conditioned place avoidance test, to study conditioned withdrawal [35,41,66] or testing the sensitivity to anxiogenic stimuli via, for example, the elevated plus maze or the light-dark test [67].

Cross-dependence or cross-tolerance studies can be initiated through substitution of known drugs by a new test substance to verify a possible class effect on withdrawal or tolerance [5]. However, the added value of these types of studies is rather limited in view of testing new drug candidates with a novel mechanism of action.

Study Directors are trained to set up the correct design with regard to dose regimen, route of administration, and choice of positive control, to monitor the in vivo part and to interpret and report the observed behavioral changes properly.

An ethical protocol for the withdrawal test must be written and approved by the Ethics Committee or the Institutional Animal Care and Use Committee (IACUC). This is also of importance because animals are single housed to study the individual animal behavior for a period of time usually exceeding 2 weeks.

8. GOOD LABORATORY PRACTICES

The studies for testing the physical dependence potential are part of the safety evaluation of an NME and thus need to be conducted in compliance with GLP [5,7,68].

The study design and all the necessary equipment are made GLP-compliant. This includes the writing and subsequent approval of a Standard Operating Procedure (SOP), the technical validation of the probe thermometer described and the corresponding transponders, and the validation of any newly developed Information Technology (IT) systems to record all data according to the GLP requirements (state of the art: traceable and reproducible data). IT validation includes an inventory of the user requirements, execution of the various test scripts, and a validation report. A newly built IT system should include a system capable of capturing various time points per day on which specific parameters (body weight, body temperature, food consumption, behavioral observations) are measured and/or recorded. It must be made possible to differentiate within a specific behavioral observation as well (e.g., convulsions type: clonic; location: head). Care is taken to ensure easy input of electronic data and flexible reporting.

9. REGULATORY GUIDANCE AND GLOBAL REGULATORY FRAMEWORK

The investigation of physical dependence is part of the abuse liability assessment, needed for all new CNS-active substances and their major CNS-active metabolites [6,9,61], regardless of therapeutic area. This investigation is directed by guidances from drug licensing authorities worldwide. The most stringent regulatory documents comprise the EMA guidance [5], the international ICH M3(R2) guideline [6], and the FDA guidance [7]. The key objective of these recommendations embraces the dose range used in the preclinical studies, of which the highest dose must demonstrate a multiple of the human therapeutic dose, expressed as C_{max}.

In addition, an FDA Draft Decision Tree for Assessment of Abuse Potential was made public in 2011 [8]. This document gives an overview of the decision points, the type of preclinical studies to perform, and timelines within the drug development plan of NMEs (see also Section 10).

In the United Sates, the framework for abuse control is regulated by the Controlled Substances Act (CSA) [69], putting regulated drugs under federal jurisdiction. Substances with abuse potential are classified into five schedules by using an 8-factor analysis (Tables 5 and 6). This analysis is conducted by the Drug Enforcement Administration (DEA) who evaluates the scientific evidence relevant to scheduling of a drug, and is a component of the overall New Drug Application (NDA) process of the NME. This NDA file is evaluated by the FDA's Controlled Substances Staff (CSS) who uses the DEA's 8-factor analysis to assist them in their final scheduling decisions.

Table 5 8-Factor Analysis for Determination of Scheduling of a New Drug (DEA). Components of the 8-Factor Analysis[a] to Determine Whether Legal Scheduling Should be Recommended for a New Drug

1. Actual or relative potential for abuse
2. Scientific evidence of pharmacological effects
3. State of the current scientific knowledge concerning the substance
4. Historical and current patterns of abuse
5. Scope, duration, and significance of abuse
6. Potential or actual risk to public health
7. Potential of the substance to produce psychic or physiological dependence liability
8. Whether the substance comprises a precursor of a substance already controlled

[a]Specified in the US Food and Drug Code of Federal Regulations, Title 21, 811 (c) [70].

Table 6 US Scheduling of Drugs with Abuse Potential. The Various Schedules Implement Different Levels of Control over Substances with Abuse Potential, with Schedule I Having the Most Control (Most Restrictive and without Medicinal Use) While Schedule V Has the Least

Schedule I	• The drug or other substance has a high potential for abuse. • The drug or other substance has no currently accepted medical use in treatment in the US. • There is a lack of accepted safety for use of the drug or other substance under medical supervision.
Schedule II	• The drug or other substance has a high potential for abuse. • The drug or other substance has a currently accepted medical use in treatment in the US or a currently accepted medical use with severe restrictions. • Abuse of the drug or other substances may lead to severe psychological or physical dependence.
Schedule III	• The drug or other substance has a potential for abuse less than the drugs or other substances in schedules 1 and II. • The drug or other substance has a currently accepted medical use in treatment in the US. • Abuse of the drug or other substance may lead to moderate or low physical dependence or high psychological dependence.
Schedule IV	• The drug or other substance has a low potential for abuse relative to the drugs or other substances in schedule III. • The drug or other substance has a currently accepted medical use in treatment in the US. • Abuse of the drug or other substance may lead to limited physical dependence or psychological dependence relative to the drugs or other substances in schedule III.
Schedule V	• The drug or other substance has a low potential for abuse relative to the drugs or other substances in schedule IV. • The drug or other substance has a currently accepted medical use in treatment in the US. • Abuse of the drug or other substance may lead to limited physical dependence or psychological dependence relative to the drugs or other substances in schedule IV.

The European Union does not have its own scheduling system and typically follows the recommendations as stated in the international conventions of 1961 [71] and of 1971 [72], as supported by the World Health Organization.

10. TIMELINES

In general, preclinical abuse liability studies need to be finalized before the end of phase 2 [5–8]. The FDA encourages a consultation meeting before the end of phase 2 to discuss the preclinical data regarding abuse potential (including physical dependence) because for some compounds in development, a human clinical abuse liability study might be needed, which is typically executed in phase 3.

The preclinical studies investigating physical dependence potential can be conducted in an early phase of development to gain information on possible alerts. However, one needs to ensure a wide range of test doses. If the human efficacious dose is not covered at that time, the study will not be accepted by the drug licensing authorities.

11. PHYSICAL DEPENDENCE TESTING OF LARGE MOLECULES

The guidance worldwide describes the abuse liability testing of CNS-active substances [5–7]. This term implies substances penetrating the blood–brain barrier (BBB) to interact with brain receptors. For most large molecules it is known that they have a limited ability to cross the BBB [73]; as such, the risk for developing centrally mediated physical dependence is relatively low. However, the development of new large molecules capable of exerting activities in the brain (e.g., monoclonal antibodies to treat Alzheimer's disease [74]) is ongoing. Therefore, this type of molecule must be kept in scope whenever testing for abuse potential is considered.

12. PHYSICAL DEPENDENCE TESTING IN HUMANS

The Penn Physician Withdrawal Checklist (PWC-35 and the PWC-20 item version [75]) is one of the most frequently used scales for evaluating benzodiazepine-like discontinuation symptoms in clinical trials. It can also be helpful for detecting treatment discontinuation (withdrawal) symptoms caused by experimental anxiolytics of the nonselective SSRI type or by other CNS-active drugs. However, a systemic follow-up on discontinuation of treatment is not always performed and most withdrawal effects are reported as adverse effects [76]. Therefore, the preclinical investigation of physical dependence through a nonprecipitated withdrawal test has great added value to the safety evaluation of NMEs under drug development.

13. CONCLUSIONS

Preclinical investigation of the physical dependence potential of NMEs exerting an activity in the brain is part of the abuse liability assessment and a mandatory test contributing to the safety evaluation of a CNS-active drug candidate.

The nonprecipitated withdrawal test in rats studies the physical dependence potential and is proven highly predictive when the design is carefully considered. Preferably this test is conducted as a stand-alone study since the manipulations and procedures commonly executed in the classic 1-month repeated dose toxicity studies might give rise to stress-related behavioral changes that can disguise or interfere with drug-induced behavior and withdrawal symptoms. The length of the RD phase needs to be sufficient in duration to obtain neuroadaptive responses from the body to the test substance but usually does not exceed 3 weeks. Appropriate doses have to be selected to ensure sufficient plasma exposures and/or brain penetration during the RD phase. In addition, the high dose must demonstrate exposure levels that are multiples of human efficacious dose (C_{eff} Hu). If feasible, the clinical administration route is employed. The effects of subchronic administration of various doses of the test substance may differ in nature, duration, and severity from sometimes subtle changes in behavior or autonomic processes that might occur during the withdrawal period. The staff carrying out these observations must be trained thoroughly to distinguish from these discrete signs of withdrawal.

The choice of a relevant reference drug (positive control) requires extensive knowledge of both the test substance and the psycho-active drugs available in view of the pharmacological or therapeutic class of the test substance.

The nonprecipitated withdrawal study needs to be conducted in compliance with the GLP regulations, as the study is part of the safety evaluation of a test substance. Given the broad dose range that can usually be tested in this type of study, the timing for conducting this test may vary from very early on in drug development to identify possible alerts, up to the end of phase 2, when the human efficacious dose (expressed as C_{max}) is known. However, when the dose range selected for testing in a very early stage of drug development does not include a dose demonstrating a plasma exposure that is a multiple of the C_{eff} Hu, this early conducted study does not comply with the requirements of the drug licensing authorities and will need to be repeated.

Finally, if the rat, as the preferred species for testing physical dependence potential, would not be appropriate for testing a particular test substance, other laboratory animals can be used. Consequently, a rationale for the choice of the species selected needs to be written in accordance with the requirements of the regulatory authorities.

Drug-induced withdrawal may appear upon cessation of drugs that do not necessarily develop abuse potential but might nevertheless lead to craving to overcome the negative effects upon discontinuation of the medical treatment. In other cases the physical dependence of the NMEs will be indicative of abuse potential, in particular when positive signals of psychological dependence are also present. The data will thus provide safety information relevant to the patient and to the health care professional and also to the drug licensing authorities who will schedule a NME with abuse potential properties to protect healthy subjects from using these substances in nonmedical situations. In any case the risk/benefit of the drug candidate must be considered carefully in view of the aimed therapeutic indication.

Overall, considerable scientific knowledge and expertise is needed to perform the nonprecipitated withdrawal study and to ensure the translational approach of this highly predictive test in view of physical dependence testing as a possible indication of the development of abuse potential in humans.

LIST OF ABBREVIATIONS

AAALAC	Association for Assessment and Accreditation of Laboratory Animal Care
ADHD	Attention deficit hyperactivity disorder
ADME	Absorption/Distribution/Metabolism/Excretion
AMP	D-Amphetamine
BBB	Blood-brain barrier
b.i.d.	bis in die (twice daily)
BObs	Behavioral observations
BT	Body temperature
BW	Body weight
C_{eff} Hu	Human efficacious dose, expressed as C_{max}
C_{max}	Maximum (or peak) concentration that a drug achieves in a tested area after the drug has been administrated and prior to the administration of a second dose
CNS	Central nervous system
CRF	Corticotropin-releasing factor
CSS	Controlled Substances Staff
DEA	Drug Enforcement Administration
EMA	European Medicines Agency
EU	European Union
FC	Food consumption
FDA	Food and Drug Administration
FOB	Functional Observation Battery
GI	Gastrointestinal
GLP	Good Laboratory Practices
HPA	Hypothalamic-pituitary-adrenal
IACUC	Institutional Animal Care and Use Committee
ICH	International Conference on Harmonization
IP	Intraperitoneal
IT	Information technology
IV	Intravenous
MIST	Metabolites in Safety Testing
MoA	Mechanism of action

MPH	Methylphenidate
NDA	New Drug Application
NHP	Nonhuman primate
NME	New Molecular Entity
OR	Oral
PWC	Physician Withdrawal Checklist
q.d.	quaque die (once daily)
RD	Repeated dose
SC	Subcutaneous
SOP	Standard Operating Procedure
SSRI	Selective Serotonin Reuptake Inhibitor
$\mathbf{T_{1/2}}$	Half-life (amount of time required for a quantity to fall to half its value as measured at the beginning of the time period)
THC	Tetrahydrocannabinol
TK	Toxicokinetic(s)
$\mathbf{T_{max}}$	The time at which the C_{max} is observed
US	United States
WD	Withdrawal
WHO	World Health Organization

REFERENCES

[1] White House Office of National Drug Control Policy (ONDCP). Research on prescription drug abuse. 2014. http://www.whitehouse.gov/ondcp/prescription-drug-abuse.
[2] CDC US Centers for Disease Control and Prevention. A response to the epidemic of prescription drug abuse 2014.
[3] SPS Safety Pharmacology Society. Medical toxicology: an extension of the principals of safety pharmacology to a clinical setting [Markgraf C, Chair. Annual Meeting]. 2010.
[4] Morton WA, Stockton GG. Methylphenidate abuse and psychiatric side effects. Prim Care Companion J Clin Psychiatry 2000;2(5):159–64.
[5] EMA European Medicines Agency. EMEA/CHMP/SWP/94227/2004. Adopted by CHMP. Guideline on the non-clinical investigation of the dependence potential of medicinal products 2006.
[6] ICH International Conference on Harmonisation of Technical Requirements for Registration of Pharmaceuticals for Human Use. ICH harmonised tripartite guideline. Guidance of nonclinical safety studies for the conduct of human clinical trials and marketing authorization for pharmaceuticals 2009. M3(R2). Current step 4-version.
[7] FDA US Department of Health and Human Services Food and Drug Administration Center for Drug Evaluation and Research (CDER). Guidance for industry. Assessment of abuse potential of drugs. Draft guidance 2010.
[8] Bonson K, Sun S. Draft decision tree for assessment of abuse potential. Legacy Hotel, Rockville: Science of Abuse Liability Assessment, FDA Controlled Substance Staff, Center for Drug Evaluation and Research, US Food and Drug Administration; 2011 [Public information].
[9] FDA US Department of Health and Human Services Food and Drug Administration Center for Drug Evaluation and Research (CDER). Guidance for industry. Safety testing of drug metabolites 2008.
[10] NIDA National Institute on Drug Abuse. Research monograph 52. Testing drugs for physical dependence potential and abuse liability 1984.
[11] AAPM American Academy of Pain Medicine, APS American Pain Society and ASAM American Society of Addiction Medicine consensus document. Definitions related to the use of opioids for the treatment of pain 2001.
[12] Stedman's Medical Dictionary. Copyright © 2006 Lippincott Williams & Wilkins. All rights reserved.

[13] NIH National Institutes of Health: NIDA National Institute on Drug Abuse. The science of drug abuse and addiction. 2014. http://www.drugabuse.gov/publications/media-guide/science-drug-abuse-addiction.
[14] Eddy NB, Halbach H, Isbell H, Seevers MH. Drug dependence: its significance and characteristics. Bull World Health Organ 1965;32:721–33.
[15] Trujillo KA, Akil H. Excitatory amino acids and drugs of abuse: a role for *N*-methyl-D-aspartate receptor in drug tolerance, sensitization and physical dependence. Drug Alcohol Depend 1995;38(2):139–54.
[16] Nestler EJ. Molecular mechanisms of drug addiction. J Neurosci 1992;12(7):22439–50.
[17] Teuns GBA, Geys HM, Geuens SMA, Meert TF. Abuse liability assessment in preclinical drug development: predictivity of a translational approach for abuse liability testing using methylphenidate in four standardized preclinical study models. J Pharmacol Toxicol Methods 2014. http://dx.doi.org/10.1016/j.vascn.2014.02.002.
[18] Dixon RB, Christy NP. On the various forms of corticosteroid withdrawal syndrome. Am J Med 1980;68:224–30.
[19] Kanayama G, Brower KJ, Wood RI, Hudson JI, Pope Jr HG. Anabolic-androgenic steroid dependence: an emerging disorder. Addiction 2009;104(12):1966–78.
[20] Haddad PM, Anderson IM. Recognising and managing antidepressant discontinuation symptoms. Adv Psychiatr Treat 2007;13:447–57.
[21] Ross PJ, Lewis MJ, Sheridan DJ, Henderson AH. Adrenergic hypersensitivity after beta-blocker withdrawal. Br Heart 1981;7(45):637–42.
[22] American Psychiatric Association (APA). Diagnostic and statistical manual of mental disorders. Substance use disorders. 4th ed. Washington, DC: American Psychiatric Association; 2000 (DSM-IV), Text Revision.
[23] World Health Organisation (WHO). WHO expert committee on drug dependence Technical Report Series 836. Twenty-eighth report. 1993.
[24] American Psychiatric Association (APA). Diagnostic and statistical manual of mental disorders. Substance use disorders. 5th ed. Washington, DC: American psychiatric Association; 2013 (DSM-V).
[25] Littleton JM. Tolerance and physical dependence on alcohol at the level of synaptic membranes: a review. J R Soc Med 1983;76:593–601.
[26] NIH National Institutes of Health: National Institute on Alcohol Abuse and Alcoholism (NIAAA) No. 28 PH 356. Alcohol alert1995.
[27] Wise RA, Leeb K. Psychomotor-stimulant sensitization: a unitary phenomenon? Behav Pharmacol 1993;4(4):339–49.
[28] Kalivas PW, Sorg BA, Hooks MS. The pharmacology and neural circuitry of sensitization to psychostimulants. Behav Pharmacol 1993;4:315–34.
[29] Stewart J, Badiana A. Tolerance and sensitization to the behavioral effects of drugs. Behav Pharmacol 1993;4:289–312.
[30] Vanderschuren LJMJ, Pierce RC. In: Self DW, Staley JK, editors. Sensitization processes in drug addiction. Behavioral neuroscience of drug addiction, current topics in behavioral neurosciences 3. Springer-Verlag Berlin Heidelberg; 2009. http://dx.doi.org/10.1007/7854_2009_21.
[31] Robinson TE, Berridge KC. The incentive sensitization theory of addiction: some current issues. Phil Trans R Soc B 2008;2008(363):3137–46.
[32] Steketee JD, Kalivas Peter W. Drug wanting: behavioral sensitization and relapse to drug-seeking behavior. Pharmacol Rev 2011;63(2):348–65.
[33] Lingford-Hughes A, Nutt D. Neurobiology of addiction and implications for treatment. Br J Psychiatry 2003;2003(182):97–100.
[34] Christie MJ. Cellular neuroadaptations to chronic opioids: tolerance, withdrawal and addiction. Rev Br J Pharmacol 2008;154:384–96.
[35] Koob GF, Volkow ND. Neurocircuitry of addiction. Neuropsychopharmacol Rev 2010;35:217–38.
[36] Nestler EJ. Is there a common molecular pathway for addiction? Nat Neurosci 2005;8:1445–9.
[37] Koob GF, Le Moal M. Addiction and the brain. Antireward Syst Annu Rev Psychol 2008;59:29–53.
[38] Koob GF, Simon EJ. The neurobiology of addiction: where we have been and where we are going. J Drug Issues 2009;39(1):115–32.

[39] Tsou K, Patrick S, Walker J. Physical withdrawal in rats tolerant to delta 9-tetrahydrocannabinol precipitated by a cannabinoid receptor antagonist. Eur J Pharmacol 1995;280(3):R13–5.
[40] Bailey J. Non-human primates in medical research and drug development: a critical review. Biog Amines 2005;19(4–6):235–55.
[41] Lynch WJ, Nicholson KL, Dance ME, Morgan RW, Foley PL. Animal models of substance abuse and addiction: implications for science, animal welfare, and society. Comp Med 2010;60(3):177–88.
[42] Goodwin AK, Gibson KM, Weerts EM. Physical dependence on gamma-hydroxybutrate (GHB) prodrug 1,4-butanediol (1,4-BD): time course and severity of withdrawal in baboons. Drug Alcohol Depend 2013;132:427–33.
[43] Aceto MD, Bowman ER, Harris LS. Dextrorphan produces tolerance and physical dependence in rhesus monkeys. In: Conference on preclinical abuse liability testing: current methods and future challenges. Poster abstract. 2006.
[44] European Convention (ETS No. 123) for the protection of Vertebrate Animals Used for Experimental and Other Scientific Purposes. Council directive of November 24, 1986 (86/609/EEG) on the approximation of laws, regulations and administrative provisions of the member states regarding the protection of animals used for experimental and other scientific purposes, complemented with the commission recommendation of 18 June 2007 (2007/526/EC) on guidelines for the accommodation and care of animals used for experimental and other scientific purposes.
[45] Belgian Law. Protection of vertebrate animals used for experimental and other scientific purposes Royal Decree of November 14, 1993 for the protection of laboratory animals. October 18, 1991.
[46] US Department of Agriculture's (USDA) Animal Welfare Act (9 CFR Parts 1, 2 and 3). The guide for the care and use of laboratory animals, Institute of Laboratory Animal Resources. Washington, DC: National Academy Press; 1996.
[47] American Veterinary Medical Association (AVMA) Panel on euthanasia. 2000-Report. JAVMA 2001;218(5):669–96.
[48] Wang Y, Wang C, Lee C, Huang A. Effects of single and group housing conditions and alterations in social and physical contexts on amphetamine-induced behavioral sensitization in rats. Neurosci Lett 2010;486(1):34–37.
[49] Diehl K, Hull R, Morton D, Pfister R, Rabemampianina Y, Smith D, et al. A good practice guide to the administration of substances and removal of blood, including routes and volumes. J Appl Toxicol 2001;21:15–23.
[50] Gauvin DV, Briscoe RJ, Baird J, Vallett M, Carl KL, Holloway FA. Physiological and subjective effects of acute cocaine withdrawal (crash) in rats. Pharmacol Biochem Behav 1997;57(4):923–34.
[51] File SE, Zharkovsky A, Gulati K. Effects of baclofen and nitrendipine on ethanol withdrawal responses in the rat. Neuropharmacology 1991;30(2):183–90.
[52] Meert TF. Pharmacological evaluation of alcohol withdrawal-induced inhibition of exploratory behaviour and supersensitivity to harmine-induced tremor. Alcohol Alcoholism 1994;29(1):91–102.
[53] Froger-Colléaux C, Rompion S, Guillaume P, Porsolt RD, Castagné V, Moser P. Continuous evaluation of drug withdrawal in the rat using telemetry: effects of morphine and chlordiazepoxide. J Pharmacol Toxicol Methods 2011;64:81–8.
[54] Li YJ, Zhong F, Yu P, Han JS, Cui CL, Wu LZ. Electroacupuncture treatment normalized sleep disturbance in morphine withdrawal rats. Evid Based Complement Alternat Med 2011;2011. Article ID 361054, 8 pages.
[55] Becker A, Peters B, Schroeder H, Mann T, Huether G, Grecksch G. Ketamine-induced changes in rat behaviour: a possible animal model of schizophrenia. Prog Neuropsychopharmacol Biol Psychiatry 2003;27:687–700.
[56] File SE, Hitchcott PK. A theory of benzodiazepine dependence that can explain whether flumazenil will enhance or reverse the phenomena. Psychopharmacology August 1990;101(4):525–32.
[57] Ma Y, Ma H, Hong JT, Kim YB, Nam SY, Oh KW. Cocaine withdrawal enhances pentobarbital-induced sleep in rats: evidence of GABAergic modulation. Behav Brain Res 2008;194(1):114–7.
[58] Wells L. Fentanyl is superior to morphine. Fact or myth… Revised. Formulary Flash 2004;04(2B):1–2.
[59] Klotz U, Antonin K, bieck P. Pharmacokinetics and plasma binding of diazepam in man, dog, rabbit, guinea pig and rat. J Pharmacol Exp Ther 1976;199(1):67–73.

[60] Moser P, Wolinsky T, Castagné V, Duxon M. Current approaches and issues in non-clinical evaluation of abuse and dependence. J Pharmacol Toxicol Methods 2011;63:160–7.
[61] Robison TW, Jacobs A. Metabolites in safety testing. Regulatory focus. Bioanalysis 2009;1(7):1193–200.
[62] Moser P, Wolinsky T, Duxon M, Porsolt RD. How good are current approaches to nonclinical evaluation of abuse and dependence? J Pharmacol Exp Ther 2010;336(3):588–95.
[63] Swedberg MDB. Liability assessment strategy: a sponsor perspective. Behav Pharmacol 2013;24:396–402.
[64] European Medicines Agency (EMA). CPMP/2275/99. Background to the position paper on SSRIs and dependency/withdrawal reactions 2000.
[65] European Medicines Agency (EMA). CPMP/2278/00. Background to the position paper on possible pre-clinical studies to investigate addiction and dependence/withdrawal related to the use of SSRIs 2000.
[66] Myers KM, Carlezon Jr WA. D-Cycloserine facilitates extinction of naloxone-induced conditioned place aversion in morphine-dependent rats. Biol Psychiatry 2010;67:85–7.
[67] Kumar V, Bath ZA, Kumar D. Animal models of anxiety: a comprehensive review. J Pharmacol Toxicol Methods 2013;68:175–83.
[68] ICH International Conference on Harmonisation of Technical Requirements for Registration of Pharmaceuticals for Human Use. ICH harmonised tripartite guideline. Safety pharmacology studies for human pharmaceuticals. S7A. Current step 4-version 2000.
[69] FDA US Department of Health and Human Services Food and Drug Administration. Controlled substance act. Title 21-Food and drugs chapter 13-Drug abuse prevention and control. Subchapter I—control and enforcement 1970.
[70] Calderon SN, Klein M. A regulatory perspective on the abuse potential evaluation of novel stimulant drugs in the United States. Neuropharmacology 2014;XX:1–7.
[71] Single Convention on Narcotic Drugs. Final act of the United Nations Conference for the adoption of a single convention on narcotic drugs 1961.
[72] Convention on Psychotropic Substances. List of psychotropic substances under international control 1971.
[73] Vargas HM, Amouzadeh HR, Engwall MJ. Nonclinical strategy considerations for safety pharmacology: evaluation of biopharmaceuticals. Expert Opin Drug Saf 2012:1–12.
[74] Panza F, Frisardi V, Imbimbo BP, Seripa D, Solfrizzi V, Pilotto A. Monoclonal antibodies against β-amyloid (Aβ) for the treatment of Alzheimer's disease: the Aβ target at a crossroads. Expert Opin Biol Ther 2011;11(6):679–86.
[75] Rickels K, Garcia-Espana F, Mandos L, Case G. Physician withdrawal checklist (PWC-20). J Clin Psychopharmacol 2008;28(4):447–51.
[76] Brady KT, Lydiard RB, Brady JV. Assessing abuse liability in clinical trials. Drug Alcohol Depend 2003;70:S87–95.

CHAPTER 6

Drug Discrimination: Use in Preclinical Assessment of Abuse Liability

Michael D.B. Swedberg[1], Alessandra Giarola[2]
[1]Swedberg Preclinical Partner AB (Inc.), Trosa, Sweden; [2]Safety Pharmacology Department, GlaxoSmithKline, Ware, Hertfordshire, UK

Contents

Nonclinical Assessment of Abuse Potential for New Pharmaceuticals
http://dx.doi.org/10.1016/B978-0-12-420172-9.00006-0

1. FROM STATE DEPENDENCY TO DRUG DISCRIMINATION: A BRIEF HISTORY

In 1937, Girden and Culler [1] reported that dogs trained to produce a paw withdrawal response after having been treated with curare failed to do so when curare had not been administered. This was referred to as dissociation learning or state dependency and was considered the equivalent of altered states of consciousness as applied to humans. Hypnosis was considered a human equivalent of state dependence. Other examples are the state dependent effects of laudanum (opium), as described in the novel *The Moonstone* by Wilkie Collins in 1868 [2], in which a sacred diamond is removed under the influence of laudanum and only found when the person who removed it is again under the influence of laudanum. Another example is the "well-known" story of the porter who, after having lost a package while being drunk, was able to find it only after getting drunk again, given by Combe in 1830 [3] and again mentioned by Ribot in 1906 in *Diseases of Memory* [4]. For further historical accounts and overviews, readers are referred to previous literature on the subject (e.g., [5–9]). The Society for Stimulus Properties of Drugs (SSPD) was founded in 1977 and has since served to connect scientists interested in this field of research by regularly organizing international scientific meetings with a focus on drug discrimination. The SSPD also organized and maintains a database containing drug discrimination and self-administration studies (for more on rodent or primate self-administration, see Chapters 3 or 4, respectively).

Observations by Overton [10] and Barry and Krimmer [11] that high drug doses were required to cause state dependency and reports of frequent failures to demonstrate state dependency limited its use as an explanation for behavioral processes under the stimulus control of drugs. This was followed by Colpaert's hypothesis [12] that state dependency was an unconscious phenomenon, whereas drug discrimination was a conscious process. Early drug discrimination studies often used mazes requiring whole body movement transitions into one of two goal areas, such as go left or right [13] or swim left or right [14], rather than an operant behavior choice such as pressing the left or right lever, which is the most common discriminative task used today. Several volumes have been written based on international meetings and symposia, reflecting the development in the areas of state dependency and drug discrimination [15–18]. Conceptually, drug discrimination tasks are seen as the presence or the absence of the training drug at a certain dose, setting the occasion for which pressing the left or the right lever will be reinforced. For a drug to be able to serve as a discriminative stimulus, it needs to be able to cause a salient psychoactive effect, also termed interoceptive cue, that the animal can associate with a certain behavior. In an abuse liability assessment situation, it is important to realize that just because a drug can cause a salient psychoactive effect and maintain discriminative behavior does not by definition make it a drug of abuse.

2. METHODOLOGY

While recognizing that there are many variations in how drug discrimination methods can be applied in terms of species, schedules of reinforcement, etc., this section will describe a generic version of current methods commonly used in drug discrimination experiments in the area of abuse liability assessment of pharmaceuticals. For a technical review, see Ref. [19].

2.1 Species

Regulatory guidelines (see Strategic Placement of Drug Discrimination in the abuse liability assessment toolbox, and Chapter 10) suggest that the animal species used should be responsive to the pharmacological effects of the compound, sufficient documented experience with the chosen species in dependence potential testing should be available, and that the choice of species be justified.

The rat is a prevalent species in the pharmaceutical industry on which primary and safety pharmacology as well as pharmacokinetic and toxicology data are typically generated. Using the same strain of rat as in toxicology studies can be seen as an advantage and allows for comparisons and standardizations based on previously conducted pharmacological and pharmacokinetic studies. However, a different stain from that used in toxicology and other pharmacology studies may allow for a systematic replication, adding to the robustness of data [20]. Therefore, the rat is commonly used in drug discrimination studies, whereas nonhuman primates and humans are also used when appropriate. Nonhuman primates can, for example, be used when the rat is not a good choice due to their dissimilarities to humans on phylogenetic, neuroanatomical, metabolism, and pharmacokinetic parameters and when the nonhuman primate is considered more appropriate [21]. Regulatory agencies may ask for human data (Chapter 9) to be generated in studies that are not directly designed as drug discrimination studies but generate similar data in terms of identifying a development candidate as similar or dissimilar to known drugs of abuse (e.g., [22])—for example, methodological investigations on subjective effects and pharmacokinetics on standard drugs in preparation for investigational drugs [23], discriminative effects in humans [24], and subjective effects in recreational drug users as indicators of abuse potential [22,25].

2.2 Sex

Background data on novel compounds are generally available in rodents, particularly in the early stages of drug discovery and development. Typically, male rats have been more commonly used in pharmacology, pharmacokinetics, and toxicology studies, and consequently, a large amount of information has been generated in male rats. Primate studies tend to be mixed in terms of sex. The issue of sex differences in drug discrimination [26] has been addressed and this is an area which merits further investigation by using multiple groups of animals to further understand and characterize differences in various pharmacological mechanisms.

2.3 Group Size

A group size of six to eight rats per dose allows for reduced variability and for statistics to calculate ED_{50} values. If a novel drug tends to cause no drug-like effects, usually a total number of six, sometimes even fewer may suffice.

2.4 Apparatus

Operant procedures are by far more commonly used than, for example, mazes in drug discrimination studies for abuse liability assessment. The operant drug discrimination procedure was developed in the study of behavior and learning within experimental psychology. The standard equipment is an operant chamber, also known as a Skinner box (e.g., [27]), typically enclosed within a sound attenuating cubicle equipped with an exhaust fan that also serves as a source for white noise to mask potentially disruptive extraneous sound. Operant chambers are equipped with a house light, cue lights, and two response manipulanda: a left and a right response lever. A food cup or water source is placed equidistantly from the levers. Sometimes the chamber is also equipped to deliver an electrical stimulus from a shock generator via a grid floor. A drug discrimination system typically consists of several drug discrimination units connected via an interface to a computer that controls the experimental sessions and records data (see below).

2.5 Schedules of Reinforcement

A common source of motivation for an animal to respond is food deprivation to approximately 80% of free feeding weight. In other designs access to water, or the postponement or termination of an electrical stimulus, can be the motivator. The contingencies of reinforcement [28] in a dug discrimination study are: (1) a discriminative stimulus in the form of a selected dose of a certain drug administered by a particular route at a certain pretreatment time; (2) a response, typically a predetermined number of presses on the drug designated lever; and (3) the reinforcer (a "reward"), typically access to a small food pellet or a sip of water or in some designs the postponement or termination of an electrical stimulus. There are several schedules of reinforcement [28] governing how the response is reinforced. The ways they were technically implemented historically in an experimental setting such as the operant chamber were determined by the number of steps in electromechanical solid state steppers and clocks used to program earlier versions of drug discrimination equipment. The fixed-ratio 10 (FR10) schedule of reinforcement, in which 10 consecutive responses on the correct lever causes a reinforcer to be delivered, is a common schedule used in drug discrimination studies, although other operant schedules are also used (e.g., [29,30]).

2.6 Trials and Sessions

A trial is defined as the completion of the requirements for the delivery of a reinforcer, and a session describes how many trials are run per day. Training sessions are typically run 5 days per week, with drug and no-drug sessions scheduled according to single and double alternation schedules. Test sessions follow as the animals reach a predetermined criterion for discriminative behavior.

2.7 What Data to Record

Data recorded are responses on each lever in real time prior to each reinforcement, i.e., the completion of a trial. These data will allow for an analysis of response shifting, i.e., switching between levers, during the session. The distribution of responses between levers prior to the first reinforcement and the total distribution between levers during a session are measures typically combined to set criteria to determine whether the session was correct or not. The total number of reinforcements delivered is recorded, since if the number of reinforcements in a session was fewer than the maximum possible, this may be an indication of insufficient motivation via food deprivation (in food reinforced procedures) or of a drug affecting capacity to respond. The total session time and the total number of responses are important measures to calculate response rate.

3. SOFTWARE

Experiments are run and data collected by commercially available software. Data can be stored as text files, in calculation sheets, or in a secure database. Advantages with database storage include possibilities for retrieval of selected data and calculation of means and standard errors of the mean. Database storage sometimes also provides graphics. A database system software can also keep track of simultaneously run experiments, studies, drugs, doses, pretreatments and pretreatment times, and the progress of individual animals in studies. It can also keep track of individual animals' progress against preset criteria for when a particular animal is available for testing and what test to conduct (e.g., [31,32]). Another advantage of a database system is a "track changes facility" to record any changes made, when they were made, and by whom, information that will be essential if studies are run to Good Laboratory Practice requirements [31–33].

4. TRAINING DRUGS

In a drug discrimination experiment, any drug that causes a salient psychoactive effect can be used as a training drug. For the purpose of investigating the potential of drug abuse liability, commonly used training drugs are those that are known to be associated with abuse potential. However, as mentioned above, abuse liability is not a necessary condition for a drug to have discriminative properties. There are many examples of drugs with no known abuse potential that have been used as training drugs in drug discrimination experiments (see below).

4.1 Drugs Known to Have Abuse Liability Potential

For the assessment of abuse liability, common training drugs are representative drugs chosen from classes of drugs known to be abused and/or of regulatory concern (Chapter 2). These drugs are considered to mediate abuse liability of their respective type. Examples are morphine (opioid analgesics; e.g., [34]), cocaine (central nervous system (CNS) stimulants; e.g., [35]), chlordiazepoxide (benzodiazepines; e.g., [36]), PCP (NMDA antagonists [37,38]), (−)Δ^9-THC (cannabinoids [39]), nicotine (nicotinics; e.g., [40,41]), and others.

4.2 Central Nervous System Active Drugs with No Known Abuse Liability Potential

These compounds may include standard drugs for which salient psychoactive effects have been established in animals but for which abuse liability has not been demonstrated. This group of compounds includes, for example, selective serotonin reuptake inhibitors (SSRIs) and tricyclic antidepressants [42], 5-HT1A agonists [43], 5-HT1B agonists [44], alpha2-agonists [45], and antipsychotics [46]. It has been shown that drugs considered peripherally acting can cause discriminative effects [47]. However, even though these effects are considered to be of peripheral origin, they would still need to impinge on the organism in such a way as to cause a perceivable psychoactive effect, in ways similar to other stimuli of peripheral origin—for example, sound [48] and light [49]. Therefore, even though a primarily peripherally acting drug would cause discriminative effects, it would still be considered to have psychoactive effects and should be investigated accordingly.

4.3 Novel Proprietary Drugs of Unknown Abuse Liability Potential

Using novel, proprietary (in-house) drugs of unknown abuse liability potential as training drugs enables the characterization of the novel compound with known drugs of abuse. Although novel compounds may have psychoactive properties that prove dissimilar to those of known drugs of abuse based on testing in appropriate drug discrimination assays, the absence of discriminative (psychoactive) properties similar to those of known drugs of abuse is not a guarantee against the fact that the novel compound may possess heretofore unknown properties that may mediate psychoactive effects in humans and pose a potential risk of abuse. For example, in rats trained to discriminate the novel mGluR5 antagonists MTEP and AZD9272, novel psychoactive effects were discovered and characterized [31,32] and AZD9272 was shown to cause hallucinations in human studies (see Ref. [32]). Drug discrimination training with novel compounds to evaluate psychoactive effects has also been shown to elucidate mechanisms of action (e.g., [44,45]).

4.4 Training Doses, Routes of Administration, and Pretreatment Times

Training doses, routes of administration, and pretreatment times need to be adapted for each situation. If, for example, a cocaine versus no drug discrimination study is to be established, then there are many published reports that identify specific choices for various parameters of interest. Dosing parameters for novel test drugs can be selected from general toxicology and safety pharmacology behavioral studies such as the Irwin screen [50] or other behavioral studies [51]. It is of importance to include doses active in other behavioral models and to distribute doses to cover a wider range. If the novel test drug produces no drug-like discriminative effects, it is important to increase doses up to levels causing substantial effects on response rates in order to establish that behaviorally active doses have been tested. When selecting training doses it is important to realize that the sensitivity of the assay is typically dependent on the training dose level (see below: Dynamics of the Drug Discrimination Procedure).

5. DRUG DISCRIMINATION: TRAINING AND TESTING

Animals are trained in a two lever food reinforced operant procedure to discriminate a "training drug" at a selected dose by a certain route of administration at a predetermined pretreatment time, from no drug. Access to food is a typical reinforcer. The presence or the absence of the "training drug" signals whether pressing the left or right lever a predetermined number of times consecutively, for example 10 (a fixed ratio 10 schedule of reinforcement (FR10)), will give access to the reinforcer (see above). Depending on the saliency of the drug [52,53] training five days per week for about four to eight weeks will typically establish drug discrimination. In cases when the training drug has a prolonged duration of action such that the compound has not cleared the body by the next day, animals may be trained and tested every other day (e.g., [32]). Figure 1 shows a schematic overview of the training and testing situations.

The establishment of successful discrimination (generally >80% correct responding) is governed by a set of criteria that may differ between investigators and laboratories, and the reader is referred to published reports for further detail. Importantly, the establishment of a dose–response curve for the training drug is critical to determine the successful establishment of drug discrimination. To this end, animals are tested with the training drug at several doses to determine the dose–response curve and the specificity of the discrimination. An example of a dose–response curve for a training drug is shown in Figure 2. After the dose–response curve has been established a test phase starts. Test drugs are assessed at several dose levels; the extent to which the animals press the drug lever to gain access to the reinforcer is an indication of whether or not the test drug causes discriminative (psychoactive) properties similar to those of the training drug. As with the training drug, the test drug should be evaluated in a wide dose range, and in the absence of generalization (i.e., failure to obtain >80% drug lever responding) to the training drug, doses should be increased to levels sufficient to substantially affect the response rate.

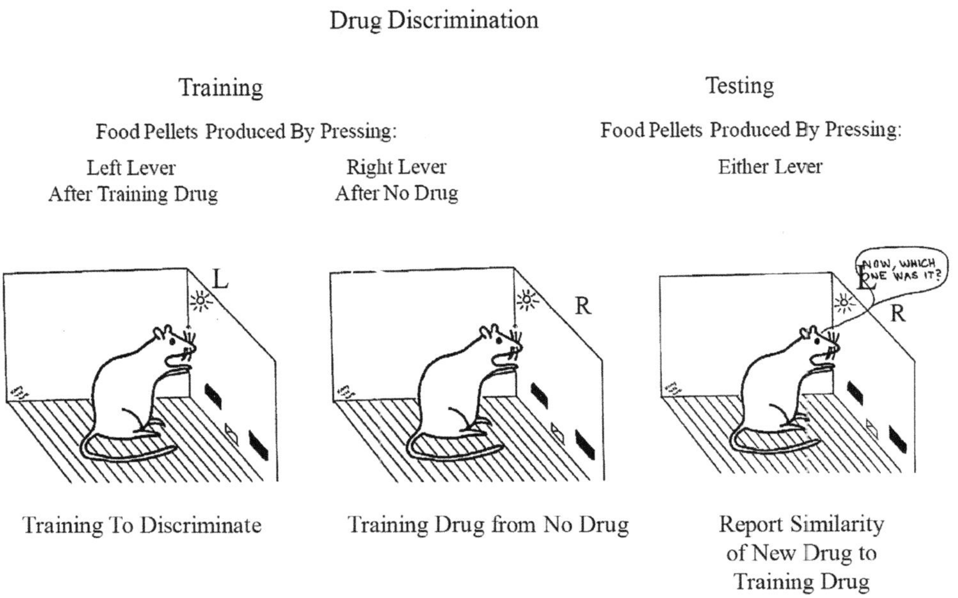

Figure 1 A schematic describing the basic idea of drug discrimination training and testing. *Reprinted with permission from the first author.*

Figure 2 shows a dose–response curve generated in male Wistar rats trained to discriminate Anpirtoline (D-16949), a 5-HT1B agonist in development for analgesia [44]. This is an example in which rats were trained on a novel proprietary compound (see above), rather than on a standard training drug (morphine, cocaine, or other).

5.1 Special Cases: Drug versus Drug and Three-Choice Paradigms

The most common drug discrimination procedure involves training an animal to discriminate the presence of a drug stimulus at a certain dose from no drug. Other drug discrimination procedures are Drug A versus Drug B procedures, in which animals have been trained to discriminate between two drugs, such that instead of a drug and a no drug condition, another drug has been used (e.g., [52]). In yet other procedures, three-choice discriminations, including two drug conditions and one no drug condition, have been utilized [53]. These procedures typically increase the sensitivity of the discriminations both versus the no drug condition as well as against other drugs but are principally used in a research setting and not typically used in abuse liability assessment of pharmaceuticals. Therefore, they will not be described here in further detail.

5.2 Administering the No Drug Condition

The "no drug" condition commonly involves administering saline or the vehicle alone. However, in order to reduce the number of injections an animal may receive, particularly in an industrial setting when animals may be trained and tested frequently, it is also

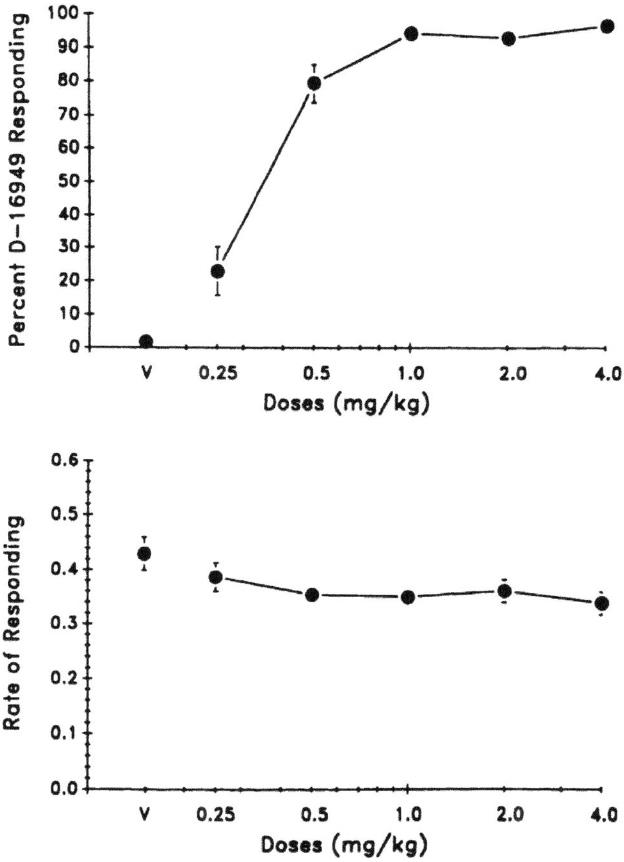

Figure 2 Dose–response curve in rats trained to discriminate D-16949 (anpirtoline) from no drug. Upper panel: percent D-16949 appropriate responding. Lower panel: rates of responding. *Reprinted from Ref. [44], with permission from The American Society of Pharmacology and Experimental Therapeutics, ASPET.*

possible to not give injections on "no drug" training days. Instead of administering saline or vehicle alone injections on no drug training days, so-called "acquisition test sessions" may be introduced to control for the potential that the mere absence of vehicle injections does not acquire discriminative cues or otherwise interfere with the acquisition of the discrimination. Acquisition test sessions are conducted by administering the training drug and dose, and the vehicle alone, respectively, as separate tests prior to the initiation of testing novel drugs (see Ref. [32] for a more detailed discussion).

6. DATA INTERPRETATION: LEVELS OF GENERALIZATION

The level of drug responding considered to constitute a drug effect is determined based on the mean percentage drug responding of a group of animals. A common way to determine the degree generalization is that drugs and doses producing less than 20%

training drug-appropriate responding are considered not to produce discriminative effects similar to those of the training drug. Drugs and doses producing between 20% and 80% training drug-appropriate responding are considered to produce discriminative effects partly similar to those of the training drug. Drugs and doses causing 80% or more training drug-appropriate responding are considered to fully share the discriminative effects of the training drug; drugs producing full training drug-like discriminative effects and having no significant effects on response rates (<50% reduction relative to the vehicle alone) are considered to produce discriminative effects identical to those of the training drug (e.g., [19,31,34]). When a dose-dependent generalization gradient is achieved an ED_{50} should be determined to allow potency comparisons with the training drug. In cases when a nondose-dependent generalization above 20% is achieved, a replication would be advised to ensure robustness of the data.

7. THE DISCRIMINATIVE EFFECT

7.1 Definition

The discriminative effect can be defined as a drug effect that an animal can attend to and use as an interoceptive signal to set the occasion for a certain behavior and is considered to be a psychoactive effect. A psychoactive effect is a prerequisite for a drug to be abused. Importantly, as mentioned previously, the fact that a drug causes a psychoactive effect is not in itself an indication of abuse liability but does suggest that the drug may have the potential to maintain drug self-administration and should be investigated further (see below: Strategic Placement of Drug Discrimination in the Abuse Liability Assessment Toolbox).

7.2 Pharmacological Selectivity

In drug discrimination studies, drugs are typically categorized by animals and humans according to the pharmacological mechanisms of action (for more on neurochemistry and receptor classes of interest, see Chapter 2). The literature provides many examples of pharmacological selectivity, showing that opioids, CNS stimulants, NMDA antagonists, nicotinics, and other types of pharmacologies tend to generalize within their pharmacological groups. For examples and discussion, see [38,54–57].

Antagonists, where available, also show that many pharmacological mechanisms that mediate discriminative effects can be reversed in a selective manner [58–60].

Novel discriminative effects can be determined by training animals to discriminate novel compounds—for example, the mGluR5 antagonists MTEP and AZD9272 [31,32].

An example of selectivity is provided by a study comparing compounds acting on ligand gated ionotropic glutamate receptors, evaluating the AMPA antagonist NBQX and the standard comparator NMDA antagonist MK-801 for PCP-like psychoactive effects [37]. In this study, using male Wistar rats trained to discriminate the NMDA

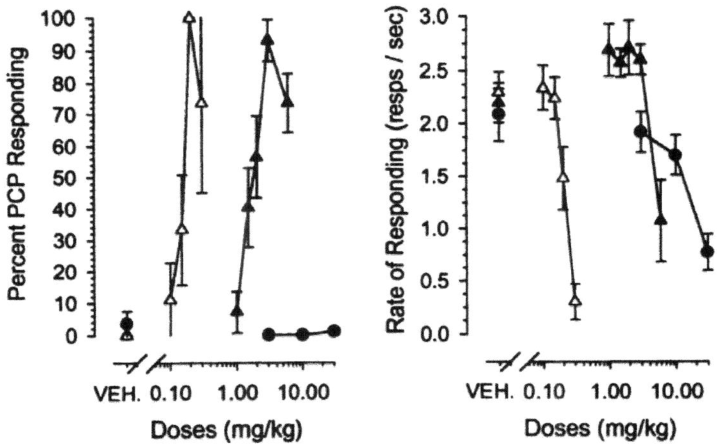

Figure 3 Dose–response curves of PCP, MK-801, and NBQX in rats trained to discriminate PCP from no drug. Left panel: percent PCP appropriate responding. Right panel: rates of responding. *Reprinted from Ref. [37], with permission from The American Society of Pharmacology and Experimental Therapeutics, ASPET.*

antagonist PCP from no drug and tested with NBQX and MK-801, results showed that MK-801 was approximately 10 times more potent than PCP and that NBQX was inactive up to dose levels that decreased response rates more than 50% (Figure 3).

7.3 Dynamics of the Drug Discrimination Procedure

The importance of generating dose–response curves cannot be overemphasized, as at the lower ends of the curve the selectivity will be lower and overlaps may occur. Dose–response curves will typically move leftwards with lower training doses and rightwards with higher training doses. The dynamic selectivity as a function of varying training doses in drug discrimination has been described by several authors. For example, Colpaert et al. [61] showed that reducing the training dose of fentanyl in a fentanyl versus saline discrimination task caused the generalization gradients to flatten and the fentanyl ED_{50}'s to decrease in a training dose-dependent way. In pigeons discriminating between two different drugs (cocaine and morphine) the training doses were important determinants for the shape of the generalization gradients [52]. When transforming a two-choice discrimination by the introduction of a third choice to a Drug A versus Drug B versus No Drug three-choice task, the pattern of responding changed not only to the training drugs but also to novel test drugs [53]. Further, in a Drug A versus Drug B discrimination procedure using two sedative/hypnotic drugs, it was shown that drugs that would generalize to each other in a standard Drug versus No Drug discrimination task were able to maintain robust discrimination, and the results in terms of drugs and doses generalizing changed predictably [62]. More recently, exploring potential NMDA antagonism involvement in the mediation of discriminative effects of mGluR5 antagonists, this dynamic feature of the drug discrimination task was utilized, hypothesizing that lowering the PCP training dose would create a more sensitive assay, enabling the detection of potential NMDA antagonist involvement in the psychoactive effects of the selective mGluR5 antagonists MTEP and AZD9272. In addition to the general dynamics of the drug discrimination procedure, this hypothesis was supported by specific data showing that training doses and ED_{50}'s of PCP correlated, such that a training dose of 3.0 mg/kg yielded an ED_{50} of 1.75 mg/kg [37], a training dose of 2.8 mg/kg yielded an ED_{50} of 1.55 mg/kg [31], and a training dose of 1.6 mg/kg yielded an ED_{50} of 0.6 mg/kg [32]. The mGluR5 antagonists did not generalize to PCP, demonstrating a lack of NMDA antagonist mechanisms in the discriminative effects of the selective mGluR5 antagonists.

7.4 Control for Confounding Drug-Induced Side Effects

A major advantage of discrimination procedures over other behavioral models is the simultaneous generation of a response rate measure that allows for the determination of the specificity of the behavioral response. Specifically, being a two lever operant choice model, the drug discrimination procedure is less sensitive to response rate reducing effects, as both choice alternatives require an equal amount of behavioral effort. Both response alternatives are therefore equally affected by any pharmacologically induced effect on response rates. Therefore, the discrimination design can provide control over factors that may influence the ability of an animal to respond on the levers either because of other behavioral (e.g., sedative) effects or because of a decreased motivation to work for the reinforcer. A drug that impairs motor performance or one producing a sensation of satiety, thereby reducing the motivation to eat, will affect responding on both levers equally and not confound the choice of levers. Therefore, drug side effects are not likely to influence the determination of a discriminative effect per se, except at very high doses when animals may cease responding altogether. This separation of effects will allow for higher doses to be tested while still maintaining the discriminative effect until such levels that responding is substantially suppressed.

8. TIME COURSE DETERMINATION

It has been shown that the pharmacokinetic c-max and the discriminative e-max do not necessarily co-occur. For example, Swedberg and Raboisson [32] showed that the discriminative effects occurred well before the pharmacokinetic c-max, which would therefore correspond to the ascending phase of the blood concentration curve. Similarly, the duration of the discriminative effect may follow a time course not necessarily predicted by the drug levels measured in the blood. For these reasons, the onset and duration of the discriminative effect can be useful for determining dosing conditions in drug self-administration (Chapters 3 and 4), physical dependence (Chapter 5), or other studies. Furthermore, such findings provide caution against a static interpretation of pharmacological effects in relation to blood levels and may predict psychoactive properties in humans at "unexpected" blood concentration levels [57].

Two different methods can be used to determine the discriminative time course. A time course can be generated in a fashion similar to when a dose–response curve is conducted, i.e., testing after different pretreatment times at different occasions. This may often be the case in an industrial situation when a higher throughput is needed and the equipment is continuously used for standard design studies. Another procedure that may be used when equipment can be reserved for a prolonged period of time during a particular day is a repeated tests procedure design in which the animals are tested at predetermined intervals after a single administration of the compound [63]. Two major advantages with a repeated tests procedure are that a time course can be determined in a very short period of time and the amount of compound needed is kept to a minimum. The repeated tests procedure was validated using (−)Δ^9-THC and run in parallel to a single tests procedure [63].

An example of a time course study is shown in Figure 4 [32]. In this study, the duration of action was compared between the two mGluR5 antagonists MTEP and AZD9272 in male Wistar rats trained to discriminate MTEP from no drug. Each time point test was conducted at separate occasions. The time points at which responding fell to 50% (t1/2) were determined to be 3.23 h for MTEP and 21.93 h for AZD9272. The prolonged duration of action was confirmed in a separate group of rats that had been trained to discriminate AZD9272 from no drug (not shown here) [32].

9. PHARMACOKINETICS

Blood samples can be collected immediately after a test session to verify blood levels and confirm the known pharmacokinetic characteristics. This way, both a pharmacodynamic and a pharmacokinetic data point are matched for each individual animal time point after the same drug administration. Alternatively, a satellite group of animals can be used to provide pharmacokinetic data.

10. STRATEGIC PLACEMENT OF DRUG DISCRIMINATION IN THE ABUSE LIABILITY ASSESSMENT TOOLBOX

The US Food and Drug Administration (FDA) and the European Medicines Agency have issued guidance to the industry on Abuse Liability Assessment [64,65], including recommendations on appropriate animal behavioral pharmacology studies to be conducted. Drug discrimination studies are part of these recommendations to assess whether a test drug produces psychic perceptions similar to those produced by known drugs of abuse. The drug discrimination procedure can be regarded as an analog to a human

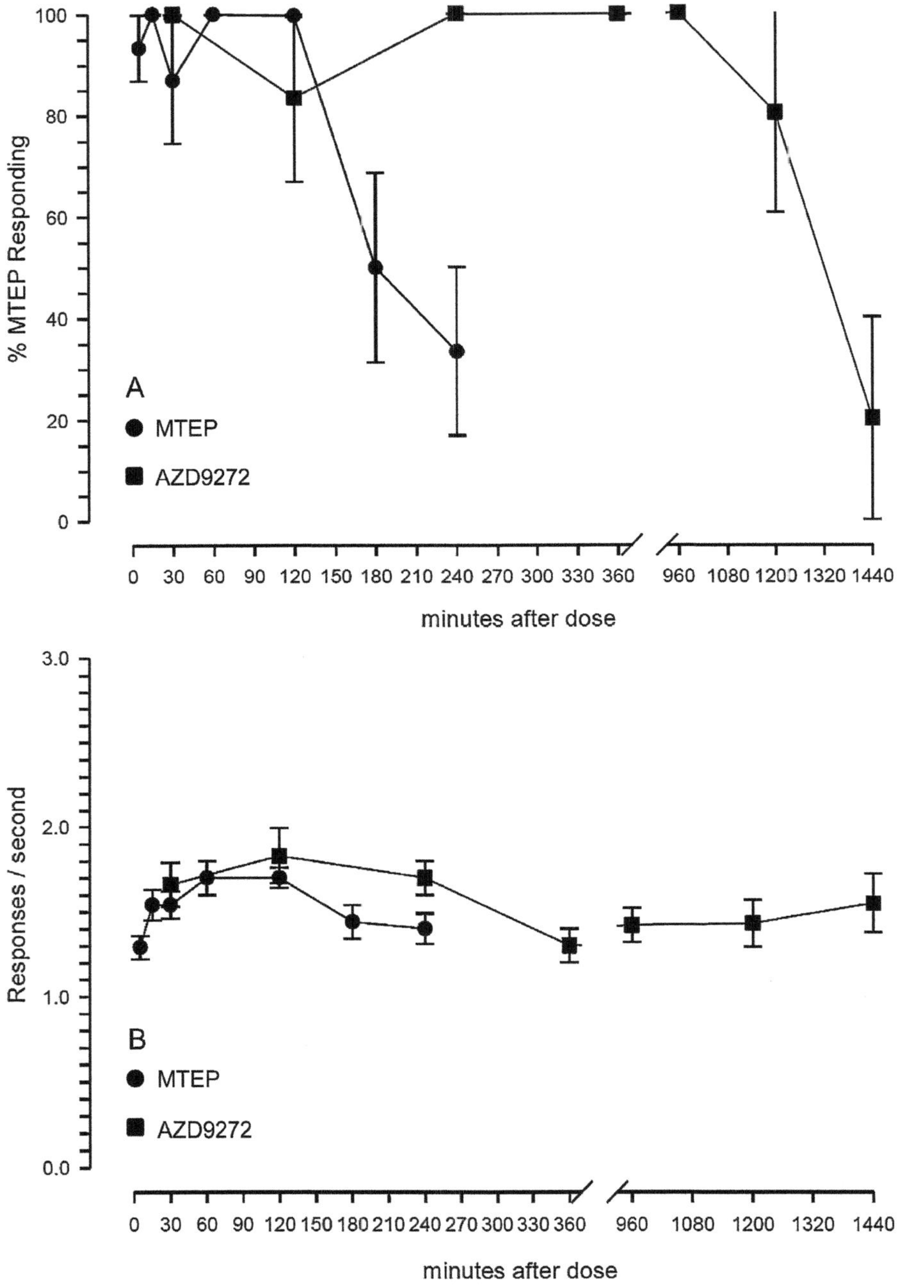

Figure 4 Time course of discriminative effects in rats trained to discriminate MTEP from no drug. Upper panel: percent MTEP appropriate responding. Lower panel: rates of responding. Circles: MTEP (2 mg/kg), squares AZD9272 (2 mg/kg). *Reprinted from Ref. [32], with permission from The American Society of Pharmacology and Experimental Therapeutics, ASPET.*

testing situation in which experienced recreational drug users can categorize test drugs as similar or dissimilar to drugs with which they have experience [66].

Strategies for nonclinical abuse liability assessment have been described by Moser et al. [56] and Swedberg [57], with the latter suggesting using drug discrimination as the primary technique among abuse liability assessment models by preceding drug self-administration and physical-dependence assessment. The major reason for using drug discrimination as the first line model in the cascade is based on established experience with its higher output, higher cost efficiency, and its utility to detect and isolate the psychoactive effects of a compound.

As mentioned above, by virtue of being generated in a two lever operant choice procedure, drug discriminative behavior is less sensitive to response rate reducing effects, as both response alternatives require equal amounts of response efforts. The drug self-administration procedure, on the other hand, is based on responding on a single lever and the choice is to respond or not to respond. Therefore, responding in a self-administration procedure is sensitive both to reinforcing effects as well as to other effects that may influence the willingness or ability to respond and thereby overshadow or disguise a positive self-administration effect. An additional advantage of placing the drug discrimination procedure early in abuse liability assessment cascade therefore, is to allow for dose escalation to levels above those feasible in a drug self-administration procedure.

Furthermore, in a drug discrimination test a novel drug can be conveniently given by any route of administration, such as intravenous (even in rats, e.g., [67,68]), intraperitoneal, intramuscular, subcutaneous, or oral, whereas in a self-administration model the standard route is intravenous (see Chapters 3 and 4).

Compared to self-administration studies in which animals need to be recatheterized over time and due to the limited use of a rat after multiple catheterizations, the longer productive time of a drug discrimination rat of up to two years confers a higher cost efficiency of a drug discrimination test.

Therefore, the drug discrimination test is well suited as a primary test and also serves dose finding purposes for further abuse liability assessment as well as other in vivo characterization.

11. DRUG DISCOVERY AND DEVELOPMENT STRATEGIC USE OF DRUG DISCRIMINATION

Swedberg [57] describes the placement of drug discrimination methodology as a primary model in a proactive abuse liability assessment strategy, based on the advantages and utility of this method relative to other models (see above) and on the experience and practice over several years of using drug discrimination as a behavioral screening model for psychoactive effects (a "psychoactivity indicator," Figure 5). The strategy outlines three different approaches.

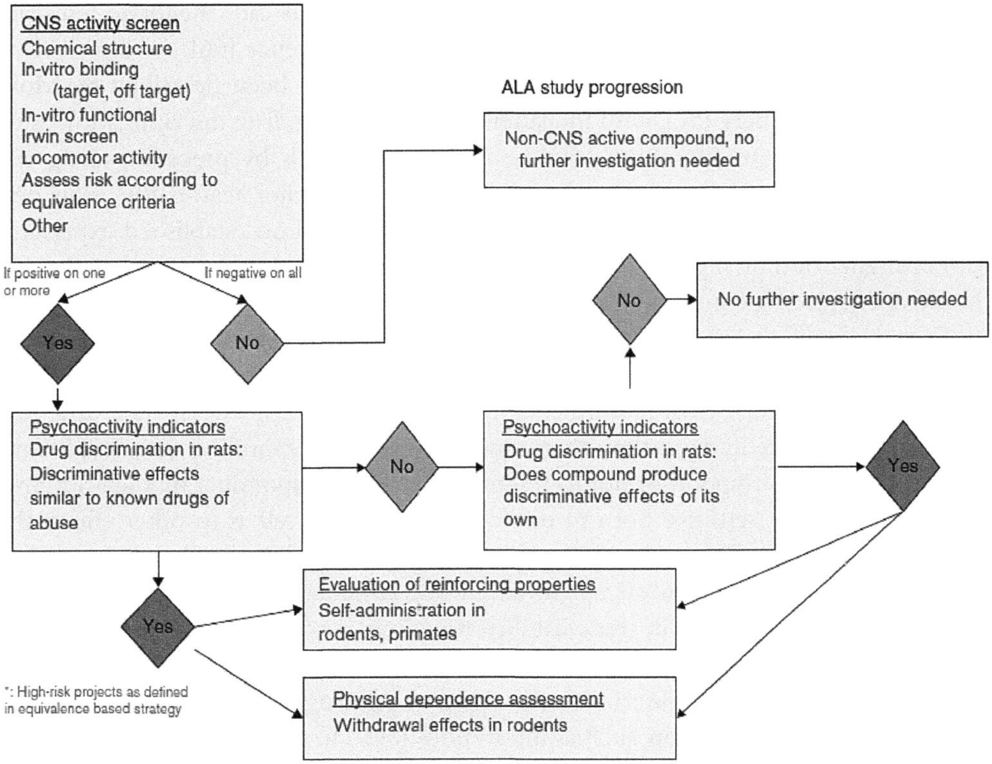

Figure 5 Example of drug abuse potential assessment strategy. *Reprinted from Ref. [57], with permission from Wolters Kluwer Health.*

The first approach is an assessment of a novel compound against a reference compound from a similar pharmacological group. For example, a μ-opioid agonist targeted for peripheral action was tested against morphine in a morphine versus no drug discrimination study. In order to maximize the possibility of discovering any unwanted central μ-opioid effects, the compound was administered intravenously and by different speeds of infusion [67,68].

The second approach is an assessment of a novel compound against a reference compound in use for the same therapeutic indication for which the novel compound is intended. For example, a δ-opioid compound intended for analgesia and anxiolysis, after testing negatively in a μ-opioid, i.e., morphine versus no drug discrimination study, was also tested in a cocaine versus no drug discrimination study due to its CNS-stimulant properties as discovered in other behavioral models and also against the benzodiazepine chlordiazepoxide in a chlordiazepoxide versus no drug study based on its anxiolytic properties [69]. Another example [70], which includes a histamine H3 antagonist that has been shown to possess cognitive-enhancing and wakefulness-promoting effects, was tested in an amphetamine versus no drug discrimination study.

The third approach is an assessment of the possibility of training a novel compound as a discriminative stimulus and then testing, to the extent available, with compounds with the same or related pharmacological mechanisms and with compounds in use for the same therapeutic indication(s). As discussed previously, and shown in Figure 2, rats could be trained to discriminate anpirtoline, a compound in development for analgesia [44], from no drug. The standard analgesics codeine, DL-pentazocine, or tramadol did not generalize to anpirtoline, nor did the μ-opioid antagonist naltrexone reverse anpirtoline discrimination. The psychoactive drugs PCP and D-amphetamine (AMP) failed to generalize, whereas the 5-HT1A agonist 8-OH-DPAT caused partial generalization and the 5-HT1B agonists TFMPP and RU-24969 caused full generalization, demonstrating 5-HT1B mechanisms of action. Similarly, rats were successfully trained to discriminate flupirtine, a compound in development for analgesia [45], from no drug. The standard analgesics codeine, DL-pentazocine, or tramadol did not generalize to flupirtine, nor did the μ-opioid antagonist naltrexone reverse flupirtine discrimination. The alpha1 adrenergic agonists phenylephrine and ST 587 did not generalize to flupirtine and the alpha1 adrenergic antagonist prazosin did not reverse the discriminative effects of flupirtine. The alpha2 adrenergic agonists clonidine and UK-14304 partially generalized to flupirtine and the mixed alpha1/alpha2 adrenergic antagonists as well as the more selective alpha2 adrenergic antagonists idazoxan and L-654,284 partially reversed the discriminative effects of flupirtine, suggesting an alpha2 adreneregic component in the discriminative effects of flupirtine. In other studies rats were successfully trained to discriminate between the selective mGluR5 antagonists MTEP [31] or AZD9272 [32], and no drug, respectively. MTEP data demonstrated that the mGluR5 antagonist discriminative effects were selective versus NMDA antagonists and other classes of psychoactive drugs [31]. AZD9272 generalized completely to MTEP, suggesting that AZD9272, like MTEP, caused selective discriminative effects. In rats trained to discriminate AZD9272 from no drug [32] this finding was confirmed, showing complete generalization with other mGluR5 antagonists but not with PCP. The discovery of the specific and selective mGluR5 antagonist discriminative properties [31,32] was followed by findings of dose-limiting anxiety and hallucinations in humans (see Ref. [32]).

In the three groups of examples given above, continuing safety pharmacology and clinical studies were able to gain valuable insight into the potential for psychoactive effects and at what exposure levels these could be predicted to occur in humans. Valuable information and data for the continuing nonclinical abuse liability assessment as well as for dosing and exposure regimens in clinical studies to follow were also gained.

11.1 Use as an Early Screening Tool to Determine In Vivo Relevant Central Nervous System Penetration

Drug discrimination studies are also suitable for application in early drug discovery programs as tools to determine the fit of a novel compound in a drug discovery project or portfolio. Since the discriminative effect is mediated via a psychoactive effect, compounds acting on the CNS via primary or secondary mechanisms may cause a discriminative effect, allowing for the identification of risk for abuse liability. It has been shown that drugs with primarily peripheral sites of action may cause discriminable effects (see above). However, even if the discriminative effects should be mediated by secondary mechanisms, the drug would still fall into the category of CNS-active drugs and should be treated accordingly.

In many drug projects, CNS effects are not acceptable and a mechanism to identify and discard them early in the drug development process is an advantage. Determining CNS penetration using in vitro methods or PK/PD modeling can serve as early tools but do not guarantee the absence of CNS effects (see Ref. [57] for discussion). Particularly for drugs with known central targets, data suggesting limited brain penetration do not eliminate the risk that a compound or its metabolites may reach the CNS in large enough quantities to cause behavioral effects [57]. In this context, an early assessment in an appropriate drug discrimination study may help in the process to identify and develop viable compounds while terminating the development of the nonviable ones.

REFERENCES

[1] Girden E, Culler EA. Conditioned responses in curarized striate muscle in dogs. J Comp Psychol 1937;23:261–74.
[2] Collins W. The Monstone. London (UK): Tinsley Brothers; 1868. Also published in 1979, J.M. Dent & Sons, Ltd. London.
[3] Combe G. A system of phrenology. 3d ed. Edinburgh: John Anderson Publishers; 1830.
[4] Ribot T. Diseases of memory. An essay in the positive psychology. 5th ed. Kegan Paul, Trench, Trübner & CO., Ltd; 1906.
[5] Overton DA. A historical perspective on drug discrimination. In: Glennon RA, Järbe TUC, Frankenheim J, editors. NIDA Research Monograph Series. Drug discrimination: applications drug abuse research. Research monograph, vol. 116. 1991. p. 5–24.
[6] Järbe TUC, Swedberg MDB. Discriminative stimulus properties of drugs: a brief history and a selective review. Scand J Psychol 1982;Suppl. 1:72–8.
[7] Siegel S. Drug dissociation in the nineteenth century. In: Colpaert FC, Slangen JL, editors. Drug discrimination: applications in CNS pharmacology. Amsterdam: Elsevier Biomedical Press; 1982. p. 257–61.
[8] Overton DA. State dependent learning and drug discriminations. In: Iversen LL, Iversen SD, Snyder SH, editors. Handbook of psychopharmacology, vol. 18. New York: Plenum; 1984. p. 99–127.
[9] Swedberg MDB. A model of discrimination learning with interoceptive stimuli. [Doctoral dissertation at the Faculty of Social Sciences]. Uppsala (Sweden): University of Uppsala; 1985.
[10] Overton DA. State dependent or "dissociated" learning produced with pentobarbital. J Comp Physiol Psychol 1964;57:3–12.
[11] Barry III H, Krimmer EC. Pharmacology of discriminative drug stimuli. In: Ho BT, Richards III DW, Chute DL, editors. Drug discrimination and state dependent learning. New York: Academic Press; 1978. p. 3–32.
[12] Colpaert FC. Drug-produced cues and states: some theoretical and methodological inferences. In: Lal H, editor. Advances in behavioral biology. Discriminative stimulus properties of drugs, vol. 22. New York: Plenum Press; 1977. p. 5–21.
[13] Swedberg MDB, Loman P, Järbe TUC. Effects of chlormethiazole (Heminevrin®) on drug discrimination and open-field behavior in gerbils. Psychopharmacology 1978;59:165–70.

[14] Järbe TUC, Sterner U, Hjerpe C. Conditioning of an interoceptive drug stimulus to different exteroceptive contexts. Psychopharmacology 1981;73:23–6.
[15] Lal H, editor. Discriminative properties of drugs. Advances in behavioral biology, vol. 22. New York: Plenum Press; 1977.
[16] Ho BT, Richards III DW, Chute DL, editors. Drug discrimination and state dependent learning. New York: Academic Press Inc.; 1978.
[17] Colpaert FC, Rosecrans JA, editors. Stimulus properties of drugs: ten years of progress. Amsterdam: Elsevier/North-Holland Biomedical Press; 1978.
[18] Colpaert FC, Slangen JF, editors. Drug discrimination: applications in CNS pharmacology. Amsterdam: Elsevier Biomedical Press; 1982.
[19] Solinas M, Panlilio LV, Justinova Z, Yasar S, Goldberg SR. Using drug discrimination techniques to study the abuse-related effects of psychoactive drugs in rats. Nat Protoc 2006;1:1194–206.
[20] Sidman M. Tactics of scientific research. Evaluating experimental data in psychology. New York: Basic Books Inc; 1960.
[21] Weerts EM, Fantegrossi WE, Goodwin AK. The value of nonhuman primates in drug abuse research. Exp Clin Psychopharmacol 2007;15(4):309–27.
[22] Shram MJ, Schoedel KA, Bartlett C, Shazer RL, Anderson CM, Sellers EM. Evaluation of the abuse potential of lorcaserin, a serotonin 2C (5-HT 2C) receptor agonist, in recreational polydrug users. Clin Pharmacol Ther 2011;89:683–92.
[23] Marsch LA, Bickel WK, Badger GJ, Rathmell JP, Swedberg MDB, Jonzon B, et al. Effects of infusion rate of intravenously administered morphine on physiological, psychomotor, and self-reported measures in humans. J Pharmacol Exp Ther 2001;299:1056–65.
[24] Johanson C-E, Lundahl LH, Lockhart N, Schubiner H. Intravenous cocaine discrimination in humans. Exp Clin Psychopharmacol 2006;14(2):99–108.
[25] Preston KL, Jasinski DR, Testa M. Abuse potential and pharmacological comparison of tramadol and morphine. Drug Alc Dep 1991;27:7–17.
[26] Craft RM. Sex differences in analgesic, reinforcing, discriminative, and motoric effects of opioids. Exp Clin Psychopharmacol 2008;16:376–85.
[27] Rachlin H. Behavior and learning. San Francisco: W.H. Freeman and Company; 1976.
[28] Skinner BF. Contingencies of reinforcement, a theoretical analysis. Englewood Cliffs (New Jersey): Prentice-Hall Inc.; 1969.
[29] Stolerman IP. Measures of stimulus generalization in drug discrimination experiments. Behav Pharmacol 1991;2:265–82.
[30] Kueh D, Baker LE. Reinforcement schedule effects in rats trained to discriminate 3,4-methylenedioxymethamphetamine (MDMA) or cocaine. Psychopharmacology 2007;189:447–57.
[31] Swedberg MDB, Ellgren M, Raboisson P. mGluR5 antagonist induced psychoactive properties: MTEP drug discrimination, a pharmacologically selective non-NMDA effect with apparent lack of reinforcing properties. J Pharmacol Exp Ther 2014;349:155–64.
[32] Swedberg MDB, Raboisson P. AZD9272 and AZD2066: selective and highly CNS penetrant mGluR5 antagonists characterized by their discriminative effects. J Pharmacol Exp Ther 2014;350:212–22.
[33] Good laboratory practices (GLP) for non-clinical laboratory studies. 21 CFR part 58.
[34] Dykstra LA, Preston KL, Bigelow GE. Discriminative stimulus and subjective effects of opioids with mu and kappa activity: data from laboratory animals and human subjects. Psychopharmacology 1997;130:14–27.
[35] Huskinson SL, Naylor JE, Rowlett JK, Freeman KB. Predicting abuse potential of stimulants and other dopaminergic drugs: overview and recommendations. Neuropharmacology 2014;87:66–80.
[36] Yasar S, Bergman J, Munzar P, Redhi G, Tober C, Knebel N, et al. Evaluation of the novel antiepileptic drug, AWD 131-138, for benzodiazepine-like discriminative stimulus and reinforcing effects in squirrel monkeys. Eur J Pharmacol 2003;465:257–65.
[37] Swedberg MDB, Jacobsen P, Honoré T. Anticonvulsant, anxiolytic and discriminative effects of the AMPA antagonist 2,3-dihydroxy-6-nitro-7-sulfamoyl-benzo(f)quinoxaline (NBQX). J Pharmacol Exp Ther 1995;274:1113–21.
[38] Nicholson KL, Mansbach RS, Menniti FS, Balster RL. The phencyclidine-like discriminative stimulus effects and reinforcing properties of the NR2B-selective N-methyl-D-aspartate antagonist CP-101 606 in rats and rhesus monkeys. Behav Pharmacol 2007;18:731–43.

[39] Hruba L, McMahon LR. The cannabinoid agonist HU-210: pseudo-irreversible discriminative stimulus effects in rhesus monkeys. Eur J Pharmacol 2014;727:35–42.

[40] Smith JW, Mogg A, Tafi E, Peacey E, Pullar IA, Szekeres P, et al. Ligands selective for α4β2 but not α3β4 or α7 nicotinic receptors generalise to the nicotine discriminative stimulus in the rat. Psychopharmacology 2007;190:157–70.

[41] Giarola A, Auber A, Chiamulera C. Acetylcholinesterase inhibitors partially generalize to nicotine discriminative stimulus effect in rats. Behav Pharmacol 2011;22:1–6.

[42] Dekeyne A, Millan MJ. Discriminative stimulus properties of antidepressant agents: a review. Behav Pharmacol 2003;14:391–407.

[43] Morgan D, Picker MJ. Discriminative stimulus effects of the 5HTIA agonist 8-OH-DPAT: attenuation by mu but not by kappa opioids. Psychopharmacology 1995;122:336–45.

[44] Swedberg MDB, Shannon HE, Nickel B, Goldberg SR. D-16949 (anpirtoline). A novel serotonergic (5-HT1B) psychotherapeutic agent assessed by its discriminative effects in the rat. J Pharmacol Exp Ther 1992;263:1015–22.

[45] Swedberg MDB, Shannon HE, Nickel B, Goldberg SR. Pharmacological mechanisms of action of flupirtine: a novel, centrally acting, non-opioid analgesic, evaluated by its discriminative effects in the rat. J Pharmacol Exp Ther 1988;246:1067–74.

[46] Millan MJ, Schreiber R, Monneyron S, Denorme B, Melon C, Queriaux S, et al. S-16924, a novel, potential antipsychotic with marked serotonin $_{1A}$ agonist properties. IV. A drug discrimination comparison with clozapine. J Pharmacol Exp Ther 1999;289:427–36.

[47] Colpaert FC, Niemegeers CJE, Janssen PAJ. Differential response control by isopropamide: a peripherally induced discriminative cue. Eur J Pharmacol 1975;34:381–4.

[48] Sederholm F, Swedberg MDB. Establishment of auditory discrimination and detection of tinnitus induced by salicylic acid and intense tone exposure in the rat. Brain Res 2013;1510:48–62.

[49] Carlsson MA, Swedberg MDB. A behavioural operant discrimination model for assessment and pharmacological manipulation of visual function in rats. Brain Res 2010;1321:78–87.

[50] Irwin S. Comprehensive observational assessment: Ia. A systematic, quantitative procedure for assessing the behavioral and physiologic state of the mouse. Psychopharmacologia 1968;13:222–57.

[51] Mattsson JL, Spencer PJ, Albee RR. A performance standard for clinical and functional observational battery examinations of rats. J Amer Coll Toxicol 1996;15:239–54.

[52] Swedberg MDB, Järbe TUC. Drug discrimination procedures: roles of relative stimulus control in two-drug cases. Psychopharmacology 1985;86:444–51.

[53] Swedberg MDB, Järbe TUC. Drug discrimination procedures: differential characteristics of the drug A vs Drug B and the drug A vs Drug B vs No drug cases. Psychopharmacology 1986;90:341–6.

[54] Bergman J, France CP, Holtzman SG, Katz JL, Koek W, Stephens DN. Agonist efficacy, drug dependence, and medications development: preclinical evaluation of opioid, dopaminergic, and GABA A -ergic ligands. Psychopharmacology 2000;153:67–84.

[55] Koek W. N-Methyl-D-aspartate antagonists and drug discrimination. Pharmacol Biochem Behav 1999;64:275–81.

[56] Moser P, Wolinsky T, Duxon M, Porsolt RD. How good are current approaches to nonclinical evaluation of abuse and dependence? J Pharmacol Exp Ther 2011;336:588–95.

[57] Swedberg MDB. A proactive nonclinical drug abuse and dependence liability assessment strategy: a sponsor perspective. Behav Pharmacol 2013;24:396–402.

[58] Bowen CA, Fischer BD, Mello NK, Negus SS. Antagonism of the antinociceptive and discriminative stimulus effects of heroin and morphine by 3-methoxynaltrexone and naltrexone in rhesus monkeys. J Pharmacol Exp Ther 2002;302:264–73.

[59] Jutkiewicz EM, Brooks EA, Kynaston AD, Rice KC, Woods JH. Patterns of nicotinic receptor antagonism: nicotine discrimination studies. J Pharmacol Exp Ther 2011;339:194–202.

[60] Shoaib M, Zubaran C, Stolerman IP. Antagonism of stimulus properties of nicotine by dihydro-β-erythroidine (DHβE) in rats. Psychopharmacology 2000;149:140–6.

[61] Colpaert FC, Niemegeers CJE, Janssen PAJ. Factors regulating drug cue sensitivity: limits of discriminability and the role of a progressively decreasing training dose in fentanyl-saline discrimination. J Pharmacol Exp Ther 1980;212:474–80.

[62] Järbe TUC, Swedberg MDB. Discriminative stimulus functions of CNS sedative drugs assessed by drug versus drug discrimination procedures in gerbils. Psychopharmacology 1998;135:201–12.
[63] Järbe TUC, Swedberg MDB, Mechoulam R. A repeated tests procedure to assess onset and duration of the cue properties of (-)Δ^9-THC, (-)Δ^8-THC-DMH and (+)Δ^8-THC. Psychopharmacology 1981;75:152–7.
[64] FDA. Guidance for industry, assessment of abuse potential of drugs, draft guidance. US Department of Health and Human Services, Food and Drug Administration, Center for Drug Evaluation and Research (CDER); 2010.
[65] EMA. Guideline on the non-clinical investigation of the dependence potential of medicinal products. European Medicines Agency (EMEA), Evaluation of Medicines for Human Use; 2006.
[66] Griffiths RR, Bigelow GE, Ator NA. Principles of initial experimental drug abuse liability assessment in humans. Drug Alc Dep 2003;70:S41–54.
[67] Swedberg MDB, Ståhlberg M, Velasquez C, Ericson A-C. The discriminative effects of morphine administered intravenously to rats as 2-min or 15-min infusions share similar efficacy and potency. Soc Neurosci Abstr 2001;27:2553.
[68] Swedberg MDB, Ståhlberg M, Velasquez C. Similarities in the discriminative effects of short and long duration intravenous infusions of morphine in the rat. Program No. 900.15. 2002 Abstract Viewer/Itinerary Planner. Washington (DC): Society for Neuroscience; 2002.
[69] Hudzik T, Pietras M, Caccese R, Bui K, Paronis C, Swedberg MDB. Effects of the ð opioid agonist AZD2327 upon operant behaviors and assessment of its potential for abuse. Pharmacol Biochem Behav 2014;124:48–57.
[70] Hudzik TJ, Basso A, Boyce-Rustay JM, Bracken W, Browman KE, Drescher K, et al. Assessment of the abuse liability of ABT-288, a novel histamine H 3 receptor antagonist. Psychopharmacology 2013;228: 187–97.

CHAPTER 7

Conditioned Place Preference as a Preclinical Model for Screening Pharmacotherapies for Drug Abuse

Michael T. Bardo[1], David B. Horton[2], Justin R. Yates[1,3]
[1]Department of Psychology and Center for Drug Abuse Research Translation, University of Kentucky, Lexington, KY, USA;
[2]Global Safety Pharmacology, Drug Safety Research and Development, Pfizer Research and Development, Groton, CT, USA;
[3]Department of Psychological Science, Northern Kentucky University, Highland Heights, KY, USA

Contents

1. INTRODUCTION

Conditioned place preference (CPP) is a method used widely for examining drug reward. While CPP has been demonstrated in humans [1], it is utilized primarily in preclinical research involving either mice or rats. A number of reviews have already provided coverage of the myriad theoretical and empirical details from this extensive literature [2–6] and the current chapter will not attempt to duplicate these previous reviews. Instead, the major emphasis here will be to underscore the important aspects of CPP as it relates to preclinical drug discovery and development of anti-addiction pharmacotherapies. We first will discuss the basic principles of CPP and then will apply this background specifically to work toward the development of novel pharmacotherapies for addictive disorders. Finally, a compilation of studies designed to reduce drug CPP will be provided to illustrate the host of potential molecular targets that may offer insights toward the development of novel pharmacotherapies to treat substance use disorders.

Nonclinical Assessment of Abuse Potential for New Pharmaceuticals
http://dx.doi.org/10.1016/B978-0-12-420172-9.00007-2

2. BASIC PRINCIPLES OF CONDITIONED PLACE PREFERENCE

2.1 Methodology

CPP is a Pavlovian procedure in which a distinct context serves as the conditioned stimulus (CS) and a drug serves as the unconditioned stimulus (US). After repeated CS–US pairings, the CS alone comes to elicit an approach response that is taken as evidence of a conditioned response (CR) indicative of reward. This effect is somewhat akin to a sign-tracking response when a discrete CS (e.g., lever) is paired with the presentation of the food US [7]. Although conditioned effects independent of drug reward may contribute to the approach response [8], the most likely and parsimonious explanation for approach to the CS is that the context accrues positive incentive salience due to its association with the rewarding effect of the drug. In fact, with few exceptions, all drugs that have abuse liability as assessed by operant self-administration (see Chapters 3 and 4) also produce CPP, whereas drugs that are not abused produce either no effect or conditioned place aversion (CPA) [2]. Although CPP reward is most commonly used to measure drug reward, this preparation also can be used to measure other natural rewards, including food [9,10], water [11], sexual activity [12,13], novel stimuli [14,15], social interaction [16–18], hypothalamic brain stimulation [19], and pain relief [20,21].

In essentially all drug CPP experiments, animals are given a drug paired with one context and a vehicle paired with a different context, and then they are allowed to choose between the two contexts while in a drug-free state. Although a host of procedural variations have been used [5,22], the most typical procedure is to pair the drug with one of two distinct contexts across four trials. On conditioning trials, animals are most often confined to one context immediately following the drug injection; depending on the pharmacokinetics of the drug, the duration may vary from 15 to 60 min. Drug conditioning trials typically occur once every other day, with four exposures to the other context also occurring on intervening days following an injection of the vehicle. Control animals are given a vehicle paired with both contexts. Importantly, the context paired with the drug is usually counterbalanced across animals within each group. On the day following the last conditioning trial, animals are tested for CPP by being allowed to choose between the two contexts. CPP is reflected as a preference for the drug-paired context, with the vehicle control group showing no preference for either context. The lack of preference in vehicle control animals is taken as evidence that animals have no inherent bias for one context over the other, thus indicating any preference observed is due to the effect of the drug.

A methodological variation used widely in CPP experiments is to include a preconditioning test in which animals are allowed to choose between two contexts prior to any drug conditioning trials. It has been argued that exposing animals to the CS context in the absence of the drug US may weaken CPP [2], a phenomenon known as the CS preexposure effect or latent inhibition [23]. However, the empirical evidence indicates that robust CPP is obtained even with preconditioning tests, perhaps because the free-choice exposure to the to-be-conditioned context does not generalize readily to forced exposure to the context on drug conditioning trials. Preconditioning testing is advantageous from at least two perspectives. First, a preconditioning test allows for determining whether any initial preference for the two distinct contexts exists. Any initial preference then can be used to counterbalance the to-be-conditioned context to avoid a strong bias (unbiased design) or can be used to select the least preferred context for pairing the drug (biased design). Second, a preconditioning test can be used to calculate if animals show a shift in preference from preconditioning to postconditioning tests. Using this within-subject shift in preference for the drug-paired context can be useful in reducing the number of animals needed, as each animal serves as its own control. However, in most cases, a between-subject vehicle control group remains the best strategy because it affords the most straightforward interpretation of CPP results.

Since CPP is a Pavlovian process, it is somewhat surprising that preexposure to the to-be-conditioned drug US appears to enhance conditioning. For example, it has been shown that preexposing rats to repeated injections of cocaine, amphetamine, nicotine, or morphine prior to conducting the first conditioning trial increases the magnitude of CPP [24,25]. These findings contrast with more traditional Pavlovian preparations in which preexposure to the US prior to the first learning trial tends to decrease acquisition of the CR [26]. One possible explanation for the enhanced CPP following US preexposure is that sensitization occurs to the rewarding effect of the drug. Alternatively, US preexposure may promote tolerance to any aversive drug effect that may be present with acute administration.

While assessment of the drug US is of primary interest for the vast majority of CPP studies, a few studies have demonstrated that the nature of the CS also needs to be considered. The CS used in most studies consists of multimodal sensory stimuli provided by the drug- and vehicle-paired compartments, including differences in wall colors/patterns, floor textures, and odors embedded under the floor. Little is known about whether each CS element becomes associated separately with the drug US or whether the mixture of elements is important. Nonetheless, it is clear that presentation of a unimodal CS element is sufficient to establish CPP under different procedures. For example, tactile cues alone can be used to establish morphine and ethanol CPP in rodents [27,28] and this CPP is not enhanced by the addition of visual cues, at least for ethanol reward [29]. In addition, visual cues alone can be used to induce CPP in avians [30].

Although there is excellent agreement between CPP and operant self-administration results about what drugs are rewarding [2], there is a general consensus that these two measures are not redundant. In particular, in contrast to CPP, drug self-administration is an operant conditioning procedure that measures the direct reinforcing effectiveness of drugs, with the response output being tightly regulated around a drug satiety threshold [31]. The dissociation between self-administration and CPP was illustrated in a study by Bardo and colleagues [32] in which individual rats were tested for both CPP and self-administration sequentially. Rats were first tested for single-trial CPP with amphetamine (1 mg/kg/intravenous) and then were tested for acquisition of self-administration with amphetamine (0.03 mg/kg/infusion) using a standard 2-lever training procedure in which one lever delivered amphetamine contingently on a continuous reinforcement schedule. Results showed no correlation between the strength of CPP and the subsequent number of amphetamine self-infusions, demonstrating a dissociation between these two measures of drug reward. Thus, while drug self-administration measures the direct reinforcing effect of drugs, CPP models the conditioned rewarding effects of contextual stimuli associated with exposure to the drug.

2.2 Advantages and Limitations

To illustrate the widespread use of CPP, we entered the term "conditioned place preference 2013" into PubMed.gov and obtained 315 references for that single year. This widespread use likely relates to the ease and utility of CPP for application to various research questions. In particular, as outlined in detail previously [2,5], CPP has multiple advantages over drug self-administration. First, relative to drug self-administration, surgical implantation of an intravenous catheter is not required; however, in cases where the intravenous route is needed, CPP also is readily amenable to catheter implantation [33–35]. Second, there is precise control over the drug dose; this may be especially advantageous for studying the neural mechanisms of drug reward because drug-induced changes in neurochemical and transcription factors obtained postmortem are not confounded by individual variation in drug exposure that is inherent in drug self-administration studies. Third, while small volumes of a drug can be self-administered directly into the brain [36], intracranial microinjections using CPP procedures are more practical for mapping the neural circuitry of drug reward. Fourth, dose response curves tend to be monophasic [3]; this contrasts with biphasic curves using fixed ratio responding for drugs, which may signify either an increase or decrease in reinforcer effectiveness. Fifth, in addition to drug reward, CPP is sensitive to drug aversion [37]. Sixth, locomotor activity also can be measured as an additional dependent measure to enrich the data set for analysis. Seventh, CPP is readily adaptable to multiple species, including humans [1], rats [38], mice [28], chickens [30], quail [39], crayfish [40], and zebrafish [41]. The utility of CPP with mice and zebrafish makes it highly advantageous for mapping genetic loci involved in drug reward.

There are several important concerns raised about interpreting CPP results that have been covered in detail elsewhere [5,22,28]. In the case of a biased design in which the drug is conditioned to the nonpreferred compartment, data interpretation is complicated because a shift in preference could be interpreted as either reward and/or anxiolysis. This problem is obviated by using a between-subject unbiased design. However, regardless of the design used, perhaps the most serious caveat with CPP is related to the so-called "novelty" interpretation [2]. Since it is well known that rodents prefer a novel compartment over a familiar compartment [14] and that entry into a novel compartment increases dopamine levels in the nucleus accumbens [42], it can be difficult to determine if CPP reflects drug reward or amnesia. That is, if the drug impairs habituation to a distinct compartment, that compartment may be relatively more novel than the vehicle-paired compartment on the test day. This interpretational problem can be ruled out by using a 4-compartment apparatus containing a middle choice compartment and three side compartments: drug-paired, vehicle-paired, and novel compartments [38]. While this procedure is relatively easy to perform in principle, it is used rarely.

Another limitation to using CPP to assess drug reward relates to establishing dose effect curves. CPP is relatively less sensitive than drug self-administration to small changes in the drug dose, perhaps because preference behavior is not effort-based. This contrasts with lever- or nose-poking responses engendered by fixed ratio and progressive ratio schedules in drug self-administration. Moreover, dose effect functions must use a between-subject design that requires a large number of subjects to establish full graded dose effect functions [3]. This limitation may be especially important when trying to determine the interactive dose effects of an agonist drug of abuse (ED_{50}) with a pharmacotherapy designed to inhibit the agonist (IC_{50}). Despite the limitations of CPP in yielding detailed pharmacological information, the overall advantages of this procedure make it amenable to medication development.

3. APPLICATION OF CONDITIONED PLACE PREFERENCE TO MEDICATION DEVELOPMENT

As detailed above, CPP exhibits numerous benefits in behavioral testing, making it a valuable tool in the preclinical drug discovery and development toolbox. CPP has value throughout the drug development process, ranging from early use in mechanistic investigations to use in later-stage drug safety studies. In this section, the use of CPP in two important aspects of drug development will be discussed, namely the use of CPP in (1) efficacy studies in developing novel pharmacotherapies for drug abuse and (2) preclinical safety assessments of the abuse liability of novel drugs.

3.1 CPP in Efficacy Studies

While drug abuse is a serious worldwide public health concern, there are relatively few pharmacotherapies available to help treat this complex disease. To address this unmet need, numerous academic laboratories and pharmaceutical companies are focused on the development of novel therapeutics aimed at treating drug addiction. Throughout this effort, CPP is one of the numerous preclinical tools research labs use in the discovery and optimization of novel compounds in treating drug abuse. The benefits of an amenable design, low resource requirements, and rapid data readouts make CPP a widely used and valuable tool in drug discovery.

One of the most straightforward uses of CPP in drug discovery efficacy studies is to determine the direct effect of the pharmacotherapy on drug-induced CPP. As detailed above, drugs of abuse readily induce CPP after a few conditioning sessions, which is a measure of drug reward. In the postconditioning test, the preference or approach response exhibited by the animal is thought to be due to the contextual cues associated with drug reward. This measure of drug seeking, once established, is a quantifiable behavioral endpoint and the inhibition of this effect by a potential pharmacotherapy can readily be assessed. The effect of a pharmacotherapy on CPP can be measured on two behavioral processes within the CPP paradigm: "acquisition" and "expression." Acquisition of CPP is the process involved in learning or training of the CR following repeated drug pairings, while expression represents the performance of the CR exhibited by the animal during the postconditioning "test" phase [43].

Assessment of the effect of a pharmacotherapy on CPP acquisition is performed by pretreating animals prior to exposure to the training drug of abuse during the conditioning phase. Typically, a single dose of the training drug is selected that is known to induce reliable CPP; however, multiple doses of the pharmacotherapy should be tested, if possible, to allow for characterization of a dose response on the acquisition of CPP. Of course, given the between-subjects design, this would require larger animal numbers. In addition to the drug-paired group, a control group that receives a vehicle paired with both contexts should also be included so that the pharmacotherapy can be profiled in both the drug- and vehicle-conditioned groups. The effect of the pharmacotherapy in the vehicle control group will reveal if the pharmacotherapy induces CPP or CPA alone, which could complicate interpretation of the CPP response in the drug-paired group. The doses of the pharmacotherapy should be chosen based upon a variety of factors including, but not limited to, pharmacokinetic/pharmacodynamic (PK/PD) relationships, target occupancy, and behavioral activity. The dosing pretreatment time and the route of administration of the pharmacotherapy prior to drug conditioning should be dependent upon the PK/PD characteristics of the pharmacotherapy to allow for adequate exposures to cover the entire conditioning session. Thus, a clear understanding of the PK/PD characteristics of the pharmacotherapy is vital to a proper study design.

CPP acquisition studies are typically useful for mechanistic studies to better understand the processes involved in acquiring the CR over repeated drug pairings. In early efficacy work for developing pharmacotherapies for addiction, research teams often look to models such as CPP to better understand the mechanism behind drug-induced reward, specifically with how their target of interest is involved in the manifestation of reward. The use of intracranial (local) drug administration and/or lesioning of specific brain regions in CPP acquisition studies offer researchers considerable advantages in determining the involvement of specific brain regions and neurotransmitter systems in the development of reward [6,22,44]. Furthermore, researchers can better understand the mechanism by which their target is involved in the association of drug reward with the contextual cues through assessing the acquisition of CPP while the target is blocked either genetically or pharmacologically with a selective tool compound throughout the conditioning phase. As such, genetically modified animals such as knock-out/knock-down rodents and transgenic zebrafish offer considerable value in the CPP model for their use in mechanistic studies.

Related to the novelty interpretation discussed previously, another caveat for interpreting the effect of a pharmacotherapy on acquisition of CPP is the potential for impairing learning or memory. One of the most well-known examples of this perturbation of learning or memory comes from the dissociative effects of *N*-methyl-D-aspartate (NMDA) antagonists. The NMDA receptor, an ionotropic glutamate receptor (see Chapter 2), plays an instrumental role in induction of long-term potentiation (LTP), a putative mechanism of learning [45]. Given the important role of NMDA receptors in LTP, it is not surprising that NMDA receptor antagonists can lead to deficits in learning and memory in both preclinical models and in the clinic [46–48]. In addition, the potential effect of the drug to modulate sensory thresholds that contribute to the salience of the contextual cues associated with the reward should also be considered [49]. For example, methamphetamine is thought to elicit its effect on CPP partly through alteration of sensory processing separate from its hedonic effects [50]. Thus, CPP studies involving drugs that affect learning and memory, such as NMDA antagonists, should be interpreted with this caveat in mind. One way to assess whether a pharmacotherapy alters learning and memory or sensory processing is to determine if the pharmacotherapy blocks the acquisition of CPP produced by a nondrug reward (e.g., food).

While assessment of a pharmacotherapy on acquisition of CPP behavior is useful primarily for mechanistic studies, this type of study design is less suitable for direct determination for the efficacy of a pharmacotherapy as a potential treatment for drug abuse [43]. Study designs examining CPP acquisition specifically measure the process by which the association is formed between contextual cues and drug reward and not the actual performance of the CR, thus lacking face validity to the clinical setting. In the clinical setting, the subject has already formed the cue reward associations, so administering the pharmacotherapy during the "acquisition phase" is not feasible. Instead, in the development of pharmacotherapies to treat drug abuse, the effect of the pharmacotherapy on the retrieval or performance of the conditioned approach response to the contextual cues associated with reward is of greater interest.

The effect of a novel pharmacotherapy on CPP expression can readily be assessed by administering the pharmacotherapy prior to the postconditioning test instead of during the conditioning phase. Similar to the study design of CPP acquisition studies, CPP expression studies are conducted using a between-subjects design. In this design, the pharmacotherapy is administered to both the drug-treated and vehicle-treated animals so that the effect of the pharmacotherapy on the expression of CPP can be compared to the vehicle. Administering the pharmacotherapy to the vehicle control animals can determine if any untoward side effects exist, such as changes in motor function (see

Chapter 2), which could confound interpretation of the data. By administering the pharmacotherapy prior to the CPP test session, one can determine the effect on choice behavior in animals without any drug conditioning. Similar to acquisition studies, multiple doses of pharmacotherapy are preferred to characterize the dose response effect on CPP expression; however, given the between-subjects design, this also requires a higher animal numbers. Doses, pretreatment times, and routes of administration of the pharmacotherapy should be selected with careful consideration of the PK/PD relationships of the pharmacotherapy to achieve adequate exposures prior to the postconditioning test.

As mentioned, one of the problems for interpreting results obtained from CPP expression studies is the effect of the pharmacotherapy on motor function. Since the determination of CPP or CPA is dependent upon approach or avoidance responses, respectively, the effect of the pharmacotherapy on locomotor activity must be considered. For example, if doses of the potential pharmacotherapy induce a pronounced decrease in locomotor activity, the effect of the pharmacotherapy on CPP expression could be misinterpreted as reward related and not due to motoric dysfunction of the approach response. This potential problem can be addressed by determining the effect of the pharmacotherapy on locomotor activity that can easily be assessed within most CPP paradigms since activity is routinely monitored throughout the study. Furthermore, potential pharmacotherapies that induce memory deficits or perturb memory reconsolidation could affect the ability of the animal to exhibit CPP based on previously learned associations. Thus, CPP studies involving potential pharmacotherapies that act upon mechanisms that could affect memory, such as NMDA [47] or beta-adrenergic antagonism [51], should be interpreted with this caveat in mind. In addition, the effect of pharmacotherapies on sensory thresholds should also be considered, as this effect could impair processing of the CS and potentially alter CPP results [49].

CPP also can be used to study context-dependent reinstatement of the CR following a period of extinction. Reinstatement of drug seeking using the self-administration paradigm is thought to be a model of context-induced relapse [52], although with some important shortcomings that may limit full translation to the clinical situation [53]. With CPP, two main procedures have been used to test for reinstatement [54]. The first method is to give repeated free-choice tests until CPP is extinguished, followed by a reinstatement test in which the drug is readministered immediately prior to the session. A major advantage of this method is that extinction of CPP is recorded across sessions, thus making it straightforward to determine when extinction is complete. The second method is to give repeated alternating exposures to the drug- and vehicle-paired contexts as during conditioning but without any drug, and then give a free-choice reinstatement test in which the drug is readministered immediately prior to a test session. While this method does not trace the loss of CPP across sessions, it controls for individual differences in exposure to the drug-paired context. Further, this method may reflect a more appropriate procedure for breaking the CS–US association formed on drug conditioning sessions, as the contextual cues experienced on free-choice test sessions are not identical to the CS experienced on conditioning sessions. In any case, both of these methods have been used to study the ability of pharmacotherapies to serve as potential antirelapse treatments [55]. However, similar to assessing the effect of a pharmacotherapy on CPP expression, interpreting CPP reinstatement results also requires consideration of potential motoric and sensory side effects.

In addition to determining the effect of pharmacotherapies on drug reward through the CPP model, place conditioning can also be used to examine the aversive effects of drugs through CPA. Repeated administration of a drug can lead to physical dependence, and cessation of drug use or antagonist treatment (e.g., naloxone) may induce a withdrawal syndrome characterized by various "negative" symptoms [56]. Physical dependence and withdrawal are fundamental features of drug addiction and amelioration or prevention of these negative symptoms represents a potential treatment option for developing addiction pharmacotherapies [57]. CPA can be utilized to characterize the negative motivational aspects of physical dependence and withdrawal; for example, CPA has been established in morphine-dependent rats following antagonist-induced precipitated withdrawal [6,58]. The ability of numerous compounds of various mechanisms of action have been demonstrated to significantly attenuate CPA following antagonist-induced precipitated withdrawal [6]. By modeling the withdrawal syndrome through CPA, the potential ability of the pharmacotherapy to attenuate the negative symptoms of withdrawal can be assessed.

One of the main benefits of the CPP model over other efficacy models used in the discovery of novel addiction pharmacotherapies is the relatively quick turnaround of results. Self-administration studies, for example, can take up to 14 weeks to provide a readout on the effect of a pharmacotherapy on drug reinforcement. In contrast, results from CPP studies can be realized in as little as 1–2 weeks. Considering the enormous costs involved in research and development in the pharmaceutical industry, including project team labor "burn" and team resource expenditure, decreasing the length of time for an in vivo efficacy screen, which allows for faster lead candidate selection, can lead to financial savings of up to hundreds of thousands of dollars per month [59]. Thus, a 2-week in vivo efficacy model offers significant advantages in drug development over other more resource intensive models such as drug self-administration.

In addition to low resource investment, another advantage of the CPP model is that CPP studies often include locomotor activity assessments that are typically part of the preclinical abuse potential package [56,60], as is discussed in the next section. Furthermore, the design of CPP experiments provides for the ability to simultaneously assess the effect of repeated drug treatments on locomotor activity that could offer information on behavioral sensitization (see Chapter 2). Taken together, the CPP model offers numerous benefits as part of a preclinical efficacy model.

3.2 CPP in Abuse Liability Studies

The misuse of prescription medications is the fastest growing drug abuse problem in the United States [61]. In 2011, the National Institute on Drug Abuse (NIDA) reported that an estimated 20% of the US population have used prescription drugs nonmedically at least once in their lifetime [62]. Thus, regulatory agencies such as the US Food and Drug Administration (FDA) have increased their focus on abuse potential assessment of new and repurposed drugs. Accordingly, FDA guidance documents highlight more rigorous attention to the testing of abuse potential, both preclinically and clinically. The FDA defines abuse potential as the misuse of a drug for nonmedical reasons for positive psychoactive effects [56]. These positive psychoactive effects are mediated through central nervous system (CNS) activity and range from sedation or euphoria to mood disturbances and hallucinations (see Chapter 2). Since these effects are due to CNS activity, all CNS-active drugs (parent and/or metabolite) as well as drugs that are similar to known drugs of abuse or elicit similar psychoactive effects must be tested for abuse potential and, if appropriate, subsequently subjected to drug scheduling by the Drug Enforcement Agency (DEA) (see Chapters 10 and 12). In addition to new drugs, marketed drugs that are changing routes of administration, switching to over-the-counter designation, or which exhibit unexpected adverse effects related to drug abuse are also subject to abuse potential assessment [56].

While a comprehensive review of the predictive value of various preclinical abuse models was published in 2013 [60], this review did not include CPP. While preclinical drug self-administration is typically used to predict abuse potential reasonably well with respect to DEA scheduling status and human subjective effect studies, the comparative predictive value of CPP is unknown [60]. Nonetheless, given the general alignment of true positives and true negatives in predicting abuse potential between self-administration and CPP [2,6], it is likely that CPP will offer similar predictive value; however, future efforts will be needed to determine the extent of this translation. Despite the concordance of CPP and self-administration, a few exceptions have been noted. Specifically, buspirone and pentylenetetrazole (PTZ) are false positives in this model, as these drugs induce CPP in rodents [63,64] but lack effects in preclinical models of abuse potential [65] and, as of this writing, are not on the DEA schedule list [66]. Potentially even more important from a public health perspective is the avoidance of false negatives that would allow drugs that possess abuse potential to be unscheduled [60]. Two examples of false negatives for the CPP model are pentobarbital and phencyclidine [67,68], which are self-administered [69,70] and are controlled drugs (Schedule II) by the DEA [66]. Interestingly, however, the CPP model is unique compared to other preclinical abuse potential models in that the CPP model correctly identifies lysergic acid diethylamide (LSD) as a true positive [2,71].

Within the drug development process, a typical abuse potential assessment package is comprised of a multitude of data, ranging from in vitro binding and functional studies (see Chapter 2) to in vivo preclinical models (see Chapters 3–6 and 8) and human abuse potential testing (see Chapter 9). Within the framework of animal models used in abuse potential assessment, the FDA highlights the importance of the CPP model in determining the rewarding properties of a drug [56]. While the FDA suggests that CPP is not as "rigorous" as self-administration in determining the rewarding properties of a drug, the CPP model can still provide predictive value in determining if drugs will exhibit abuse potential in humans, suggesting the importance of this model in preclinical testing [56]. Support for this view comes from findings indicating that various drugs of abuse, across a range of pharmacological mechanisms, elicit CPP in rodents [2,6]. As such, the CPP model provides "value added" in the battery of preclinical models used in drug development.

When designing a CPP study to assess abuse potential, careful consideration must be given regarding species selection, drug dose, route of administration, and positive/negative comparators. With regard to species selection, CPP studies are typically performed using rodents; however, as discussed above, CPP has been performed in numerous other species. Rodents represent an appropriate species for preclinical abuse potential assessment, as the majority of preclinical abuse studies typically employ either rodents or primates [56]. Guidance documents from the European Medicines Agency (EMA) [72] and International Council on Harmonization (ICH) [73] advise that preference for rodents should be given over primates unless special circumstances suggest that primates represent a more appropriate species. Nonetheless, the selected species should be responsive to the pharmacological effects of the drug and issues such as metabolites and species-specific pharmacology should be fully considered.

In preclinical abuse potential studies, dose selection is important to ensure that the pharmacological effects of the drug are evaluated across a broad range of doses and exposures. In determining doses for abuse potential studies, it is important to have a clear understanding of the PK/PD relationship of the drug to ensure that systemic exposure meets or exceeds therapeutic exposure in humans. Doses used in CPP should typically target systemic exposures of at least 3- to 5-fold human therapeutic exposures. This will ensure assessment of potential rewarding effects of the drug at representative exposures seen in humans abusing the drug. If the drug to be tested has CNS-active metabolites, this information also needs to be considered and doses should be selected that achieve metabolite exposures similar to or 3- to 5-fold higher than human metabolite exposure. To ensure that adequate exposures of both drug and active metabolite are reached during CPP assessment, PK should be taken during the study or in satellite animals using the same dosing paradigm. Furthermore, the elimination half-life of the drug should be known in the species tested, as potential carryover effects could be observed with drugs that exhibit long half-lives. This is of particular importance for CPP studies, as the acquisition phase requires multiple drug administrations and this could affect the acquisition and expression of CPP. For drugs that exhibit a long half-life, an appropriate washout period must be utilized to allow the drug to be completely cleared prior to dosing of the subsequent vehicle administration.

In CPP studies for abuse potential assessments, an appropriate route of administration also should be used to ensure that the targeted exposures are reached, as PK/PD profiles are dependent upon the route of administration. Given that drugs are typically abused by multiple routes of administration, the intended clinical route of administration as well as other possible routes should be used when possible. One clear advantage of the CPP model over self-administration is the versatility of CPP to various routes of administration. While self-administration studies are limited mainly to the intravenous route, CPP is not. One instance where this is of particular importance is drugs that have poor solubility or drugs that cannot be formulated in solutions or IV preparations. For these situations, drugs can be formulated as suspensions and dosed (e.g., orally, intraperitoneally, etc.) in the CPP model, which represents a distinct advantage over the self-administration assay where the dosing of suspensions is not readily possible.

In addition to the route of administration, the timing of the contextual pairing after drug administration is important in the establishment of CPP or CPA [6]. For example, CPP is reliably established when animals are placed in the paired context 10min after amphetamine administration [9]; however, when amphetamine is given 15min after confining the animal within the context, CPA is obtained [74]. As mentioned previously, in abuse potential assessments using CPP, the timing and duration of context exposure relative to the drug administration depends, at least in part, on the PK/PD characteristics of the drug.

With CPP, as well as other preclinical abuse potential models, studies should be designed to incorporate appropriate positive and negative comparators. Ideally, positive comparators should be drugs with similar pharmacological mechanisms of actions that are known to induce CPP. If the drug to be tested exhibits a novel mechanism of action or a mechanism of action that is not associated with abuse potential, positive comparators that exhibit similar behavioral effects (e.g., CNS depressant or stimulant) should be considered. Conversely, an appropriate negative comparator such as vehicle or, if possible, a drug that does not induce CPP (or lacks abuse potential) that has been approved for the treatment of has been approved for the treatment of the same disease or condition as the drug to be tested. Furthermore, a vehicle control group should also be included to appropriately control for any potential biases within the conditioning procedure and to allow for direct comparison to conditioning produced by the drug of interest.

Similar to the advantages of CPP mentioned for efficacy testing of novel pharmacotherapies, an advantage of CPP for testing abuse liability is the low resource investment required to conduct these studies compared to other preclinical models. As indicated previously, the short amount of time needed for training contrasts with other preclinical models, such as drug discrimination (see Chapter 6) and self-administration (see Chapters 3 and 4), thus yielding higher throughput. This is advantageous for drug discovery programs looking for an early assessment of abuse potential or looking to screen multiple compounds for differentiation on abuse potential. Furthermore, work published since 2011 has focused on the development of the CPP model in zebrafish [41,75] that could offer even less resource investment and higher throughput while providing a benefit in reduction, refinement and replacement (3R's) in animal use [76]. In addition to low resource investment, another advantage of the CPP model is that CPP studies often include locomotor activity assessments which are typically part of the preclinical abuse potential package [56,60]. Taken together, the CPP model offers numerous benefits as part of a preclinical abuse potential assessment.

4. RECENT FINDINGS

To illustrate the utility of CPP toward the development of potential pharmacotherapies for drug abuse, we performed a literature review of different pharmacological agents that have been tested using CPP in either rats or mice. The review was restricted to articles published after 2006, as a comprehensive summary of publications prior to that time has been cataloged by Tzschentke [22]. Articles were segregated into those that assessed the effects of pharmacological treatments on acquisition, expression, or reinstatement of CPP. Three major drug classes yielded a considerable number of articles: (1) stimulants; (2) opiates; and (3) ethanol. Tables 1–3 summarize the results for stimulants, with Table 1 showing the effects on acquisition, Table 2 showing the effects on expression, and Table 3 showing the effects on reinstatement of stimulant seeking. Tables 4–6 summarize the results for both opiates and ethanol, with Table 4 showing the effects on acquisition, Table 5 showing the effects on expression, and Table 6 showing the effects on reinstatement of opiate or ethanol seeking.

Based on the results presented in these tables, the development of pharmacotherapies has examined a multitude of cellular targets. As might be expected, much of the work with CPP has targeted receptor or transporter proteins, including those involved with monoamines, acetylcholine, amino acids, peptides, and endocannabinoids (see Chapter 2). Pharmacotherapies aimed at gene transcription processes and antioxidant activity also have been explored, as has the action of the antibiotic ceftriaxone, which has both neuroprotective and glutamatergic stabilizing properties [77,78]. As an alternative approach, potential pharmacotherapies with mixed or unknown targets have been explored, either as whole plant alkaloids or nonselective synthetics such as aripirazole.

There are a few important points to be extracted from these tabulated studies. First, virtually all of the efficacy assessments have been conducted in male rats. This may represent a significant shortcoming because there is growing evidence that females may be more susceptible to drug abuse [79,80]. In particular, the progress from early experimentation to problematic intake appears to be accelerated in females and the rate of relapse following a period of abstinence is higher in females than in males. The enhanced vulnerability to drug abuse in females is associated with greater levels of estrogen in females

Table 1 Effects of Various Treatment Drugs on the Acquisition of Stimulant CPP

CPP Drug (mg/kg, route)	Species (Strain)	Sex	Age/Weight	Treatment Drug (mg/kg, route)	Mechanism of Action	Effect on CPP	References
				Dopaminergics			
COC (20; ip)	Mouse (C57/6J)	Male	8–14 weeks	YQA14 (50; ip)	D3 antag	↓	[88]
COC (15; ip)	Mouse (Swiss OF-1)	Male	5–6 weeks	AHN-1055 (3, 10; ip)	DAT blocker	↓	[89]
COC (10; ip)	Rat (SD)	Male	200–220 g	RGH-237 (10; po)	D3 partial agonist	↓	[90]
COC (1; iv)	Rat (SD)	Male	275–300 g	cis-flupenthixol (0.5; ip)	D1/D2 antag	↓	[91]
AMP (2; ip)	Rat (Wistar)	Male	175–200 g	Haloperidol (0.1, 0.15; ip)	D2 antag	↓	[92]
AMP (2; ip)	Rat (Wistar)	Male	175–200 g	Nafadotride (0.5, 1; ip)	D3 antag	↔	[92]
MDMA (10; ip)	Mouse (OF1)	Male	21 days	CGS 10746B (10; ip)	Release inhibitor	↓	[93]
MDMA (10; ip)	Mouse (OF1)	Male	21 days	Haloperidol (0.2; ip)	D2 antag	↓	[93]
MDMA (10; ip)	Mouse (OF1)	Male	21 days	Raclopride (0.6; ip)	D2 antag	↓	[93]
MDMA (10; ip)	Mouse (OF1)	Male	21 days	SCH 23390 (0.125, 0.25; ip)	D1 antag	↓	[93]
				Serotonergics			
MDMA (10; ip)	Mouse (OF1)	Male	29 days	Risperidone (0.3; ip)	5-HT2A antag	↓	[94]
MDMA (10; ip)	Mouse (OF1)	Male	29 days	MDL72222 (1, 3; ip)	5-HT3 antag	↓	[95]
				Noradrenergics			
NIC (0.06; sc)	Rat (Wistar AF)	Male	225–245 g	Prazosin (0.5, 1; ip)	α1 antag	↓	[96]
				Cholinergics			
COC (15; ip)	Rat (SD)	Male	250–275 g	18-methoxycoronaridine (40; ip)	Iboga α3β4 antag	↓	[97]
NIC (0.175; ip)	Rat (Wistar)	Male	250–300 g	Varenicline (0.5, 1, 2; sc)	α2β4 partial agonist	↓	[98]
NIC (0.175; ip)	Rat (Wistar)	Male	250–300 g	Mecamylamine (1, 2; sc)	α2β4 antag	↓	[98]
				Glutamatergics			
COC (50; ip)	Mouse (OF-1)	Male	52 days	Memantine (10; ip)	NMDA channel blocker	↓	[99]

COC (50; ip)	Mouse (OF-1)	Male	52 days	CNQX (10; ip)	AMPA antag	↓	[99]
COC (20; ip)	Mouse (C57BL/6)	Male	12–14 weeks	Memantine (0.02–20; ip)	NMDA channel blocker	↓	[100]
COC (20; ip)	Mouse (CD-1)	Male	22–24 g	Nitrous oxide (50%; inhalation)	NMDA antag	↔	[101]
COC (15; ip)	Rat (SD)	Male	10–11 weeks	JNJ16259685 (0.1 ng; intra-VTA)	mGluR1 antag	↓	[102]
COC (10; ip)	Rat (SD)	Male	220–240 g	7-CTKA (5 μg; intra-VTA)	NMDA glycine antag	↓	[103]
COC (10; ip)	Rat (SD)	Male	220–240 g	7-CTKA (5 μg; intra-SN)	NMDA glycine antag	↔	[103]
AMP (2; ip)	Rat (Wistar)	Male	175–200 g	CNQX (1; ip)	AMPA antag	↓	[92]
				Gabaergics			
NIC (0.06; sc)	Rat (Wistar)	?	180–220 g	GS39783 (30, 100; po)	GABA-B modulator	↓	[104]
				Opioids			
COC (10; ip)	Rat (SD)	Male	60 days	CTAP (0.5 μg; intra-NAcore)	μ antag	↓	[105]
COC (10; ip)	Rat (SD)	Male	60 days	CTAP (0.5 μg; intra-NAshell)	μ antag	↔	[105]
COC (10; ip)	Rat (SD)	Male	60 days	CTAP (0.5 μg; intra-rostral VTA)	μ antag	↓	[105]
COC (10; ip)	Rat (SD)	Male	60 days	CTAP (0.5 μg; intra-caudal VTA)	μ antag	↔	[105]
COC (10; ip)	Rat (SD)	Male	60 days	CTAP (0.5 μg; intra-CPu)	μ antag	↔	[105]
COC (10; ip)	Rat (SD)	Male	180–200 g	Ro65-6570 (3.16; ip)	Nociceptin agonist	↓	[106]
AMP (1, 3.16; ip)	Rat (SD)	Male	180–200 g	Ro65-6570 (3.16; ip)	Nociceptin agonist	↔	[106]
AMP (2; ip)	Rat (Wistar)	Male	250–300 g	Naltrexone (0.3–3; ip)	Antag	↔	[107]

Continued

Table 1 Effects of Various Treatment Drugs on the Acquisition of Stimulant CPP—cont'd

CPP Drug (mg/kg, route)	Species (Strain)	Sex	Age/Weight	Treatment Drug (mg/kg, route)	Mechanism of Action	Effect on CPP	References
				Other Neuropeptides			
COC (10; ip)	Mouse (C57BL/6)	Male	?	L-152,804 (3–30; ip)	NPY Y5 antag	↔	[108]
METH (2; ip)	Mouse (Swiss)	Male	28–32 g	Oxytocin (2.5 μg; icv)	Pituitary hormone	↓	[109]
METH (1; ip)	Rat (SD)	Male	200–250 g	Oxytocin (0.6; ip)	Pituitary hormone	↓	[110]
METH (1; ip)	Rat (SD)	Male	200–250 g	Oxytocin (0.6 ng; intra-NAcore)	Pituitary hormone	↓	[110]
METH (1; ip)	Rat (SD)	Male	200–250 g	Oxytocin (0.6 ng; intra-STh)	Pituitary hormone	↓	[110]
				Cannabanoids			
COC (20; ip)	Mouse (Kunming)	Male	18–20 g	Rimonabant (1, 3; ip)	CB1 antag	↓	[111]
METH (2; ip)	Mouse (Kunming)	Male	18–20 g	Rimonabant (1, 3; ip)	CB1 antag	↓	[111]
NIC (0.1; sc)	Mouse (C57BL/6J)	Male	Adult	Rimonabant (3; ip)	CB1 antag	↓	[112]
NIC (1; ip)	Mouse (CD1)	Male	2–3 mo	AM630 (3; ip)	CB2 antag	↓	[113]
NIC (0.4; sc)	Rat (SD)	Male	250–275 g	AM404 (5; ip)	AEA transport blocker	↓	[114]
NIC (0.1–1; ip)	Rat (SD)	Male	250–325 g	URB597 (0.3; ip)	FAAH inhibitor	↓	[115]
NIC (0.1; ip)	Mouse (C57BL/6J)	Male	Adult	URB597 (0.3, 3; ip)	FAAH inhibitor	↑	[112]
				Sigma Drugs			
COC (20; ip)	Mouse (CD-1)	Male	20–22 g	YZ-185 (31.6 μmol; ip)	σ antag	↓	[116]
COC (20; ip)	Rat	Male	Adult	Progesterone (500 μg; sc)	σ antag	↔	[117]
COC (5; ip)	Rat (Fischer)	Female	8 weeks	Progesterone (500 μg; sc)	σ antag	↓	[118]

				Inhibitors			
COC (20; ip)	Mouse (C57BL/6)	Male	Adult	5-aza (0.2, 2 μg; intra-HIPPO)	DNA methyltransferase	↓	[119]
COC (20; ip)	Mouse (C57BL/6)	Male	Adult	5-aza (0.2, 2 μg; intra-PLC)	DNA methyltransferase	↔	[119]
COC (20; ip)	Mouse (Swiss)	Male	8 weeks	3-amino-1,2,4-triazole (1; ip)	Brain catalase	↔	[120]
COC (15; ip)	Rat (SD)	Male	300–350 g	Rolipram (0.5 μg; intra-VTA)	PDE4	↓	[121]
COC (15; ip)	Mouse (C57BL/6J)	Male	6–8 weeks	Rapamycin (10; ip)	mTOR	↔	[122]
COC (12; ip)	Rat (SD)	Male	280–300 g	FN-439 (35 μg; icv)	Matrix metalloproteinase	↓	[123]
METH (1.5; ip)	Mouse (ICR)	Male	28–32 g	Sauchinone (10; po)	NO	↓	[124]
METH (0.5; sc)	Rat	Male	2–4 mo	GZ-793A (15; sc)	VMAT2	↓	[125]
NIC (0.21; sc)	Rat (SD)	Male	30–35 days	Phenylbutyrate (100; ip)	HDAC	↓	[126]
				Miscellaneous			
COC (20; ip)	Mouse (Swiss)	Male	6 weeks	Alpha lipoic acid (100; ip)	H_2O_2 scavenger	↔	[127]
COC (10, 20; ip)	Mouse (C57BL/6)	Male	?	Ceftriaxone (200; ip)	β-lactum antibiotic	↔	[128]
METH (1; ip)	Rat (SD)	Male	Adult	Agmatine (32; ip)	Polyamine	↓	[129]
METH (1; sc)	Mouse (ddY)	Male	?	Gabapentin (10, 30 nmol; icv)	Ca + channel blocker	↓	[130]
NIC (1; ip)	Mouse (NMRI)	Female	20–25 g	Ascorbic acid (1–1000; ip)	Antioxidant	↓	[131]

Table 2 Effects of Various Treatment Drugs on the Expression of Stimulant CPP

CPP Drug (mg/kg, route)	Species (Strain)	Sex	Age/ Weight	Treatment Drug (mg/kg, route)	Mechanism of Action	Effect on CPP	References
				Dopaminergics			
COC (20; ip)	Mouse (C57BL/6J)	Male	8–14 weeks	YQA14 (25, 50; ip)	D3 antag	↓	[88]
COC (15; ip)	Rat (SD)	Male	275–300 g	SKF 81297 (3; sc)	D1 agonist	↓	[132]
COC (15; ip)	Rat (SD)	Male	275–300 g	Quinpirole (1; sc)	D2/3 agonist	↓	[132]
COC (15; ip)	Rat (SD)	Male	200 g	Compound 35 (1–10; ip)	D3 antag	↓	[133]
AMP (2; ip)	Rat (Wistar)	Male	175–200 g	Haloperidol (0.15; ip)	D2 antag	↓	[92]
AMP (2; ip)	Rat (Wistar)	Male	175–200 g	Nafadotride (0.5, 1; ip)	D3 antag	↓	[92]
MDMA (10; ip)	Mouse (OF1)	Male	21 days	CGS 10746B (3, 10; ip)	Release inhibitor	↔	[134]
MDMA (10; ip)	Mouse (OF1)	Male	21 days	Haloperidol (0.1, 0.2; ip)	D2 antag	↓	[134]
MDMA (10; ip)	Mouse (OF1)	Male	21 days	Raclopride (0.3, 0.6; ip)	D2 antag	↔	[134]
MDMA (10; ip)	Mouse (OF1)	Male	21 days	SCH 23390 (0.125, 0.25; ip)	D1 antag	↔	[93]
NIC (0.6; sc)	Rat (SD)	Male	200 g	Compound 35 (1–10; ip)	D3 antag	↓	[133]
				Serotonergics			
COC (5; ip)	Rat (Wistar)	Male	280–300 g	SB 271046 (3, 10; ip)	5-HT6 antag	↓	[134]
COC (5; ip)	Rat (Wistar)	Male	280–300 g	WAY 181187 (3–30; sc)	5-HT6 agonist	↓	[134]
MDMA (10; ip)	Mouse (OF1)	Male	29 days	MDL72222 (1, 3; ip)	5-HT3 antag	↔	[95]
				Noradrenergics			
NIC (0.06; sc)	Rat (Wistar AF)	Male	225–245 g	Prazosin (0.5; ip)	α1 antag	↓	[96]
				Cholinergics			
COC (10; ip)	Mouse (C57BL/6J)	Male	3 mo	Biperiden (10; ip)	M1 antag	↓	[135]
COC (15; ip)	Rat (SD)	Male	250–275 g	18-methoxycoronaridine (40; ip)	Iboga α3β4 antag	↔	[97]
NIC (0.5; sc)	Mouse (C57BL/6J)	Male	8–10 weeks	MII[H9A; L15A] (4.5, 6 pmol; icv)	α6 nACh antag	↓	[136]
NIC (0.17; ip)	Rat (Wistar)	Male	250–300 g	Varenicline (0.5–2; sc)	α2β4 partial agonist	↓	[98]
NIC (0.17; ip)	Rat (Wistar)	Male	250–300 g	Mecamylamine (0.5–2; sc)	α2β4 antag	↓	[98]

				Glutamatergics			
COC (20; ip)	Mouse (CD-1)	Male	22–24 g	Nitrous oxide (50%; inhalation)	NMDA antag	↓	[101]
AMP (2; ip)	Rat (Wistar)	Male	175–200 g	CNQX (0.05–1; ip)	AMPA antag	↓	[92]
				Gabaergics			
NIC (0.06; sc)	Rat (Wistar)	?	180–220 g	GS39783 (30, 100; po)	GABA-B modulator	↔	[104]
				Opioids			
COC (10; ip)	Rat (SD)	Male	60 days	CTAP (0.5 µg; intra-NAcore)	µ antag	↔	[105]
COC (10; ip)	Rat (SD)	Male	60 days	CTAP (0.5 µg; intra-NAshell)	µ antag	↓	[105]
AMP (2; ip)	Rat (Wistar)	Male	?	Naltrexone (0.3–3; ip)	Antag	↔	[107]
NIC (0.5; sc)	Mouse (ICR)	Male	8–10 weeks	JDTic (8, 16; sc)	κ antag	↔	[137]
				Other Neuropeptides			
COC (5; ip)	Rat (Wistar)	Male	?	NPFF (10, 20 nmol; icv)	Antiopioid	↓	[138]
AMP (2; ip)	Rat (Wistar)	Male	270–280 g	SB-334867 (30; ip)	Orexin-1 antag	↓	[139]
METH (2; ip)	Mouse (Swiss)	Male	28–32 g	Oxytocin (0.1–2.5 µg; icv)	Pituitary hormone	↔	[109]
				Sigma Drugs			
COC (20; ip)	Mouse (C57BL)	Male	21–26 g	CM156 (1–20; ip)	σ1 antag	↓	[140]
COC (20; ip)	Rat (Fischer)	Male	Adult	Progesterone (500 µg; sc)	Gonadal hormone	↔	[117]
COC (5; ip)	Rat (Fischer)	Female	8 weeks	Progesterone (500 µg; sc)	Gonadal hormone	↓	[118]
				Inhibitors			
COC (20; ip)	Rat (SD)	Male	200–225 g	CPP-115 (1; ip)	GABA-T inactivator	↓	[141]
COC (15; ip)	Rat (SD)	Male	300–350 g	Rolipram (0.5 µg; intra-VTA)	PDE4	↔	[121]
COC (15; ip)	Mouse (C57BL/6J)	Male	6–8 weeks	Rapamycin (10; ip)	mTOR	↓	[122]
METH (1.5; ip)	Mouse (ICR)	Male	28–32 g	Sauchinone (10; po)	NO	↓	[124]
				Miscellaneous			
METH (1; ip)	Rat (SD)	Male	Adult	Agmatine (10, 32; ip)	Polyamine	↓	[129]
NIC (1; ip)	Mouse (NMRI)	Female	20–25 g	Ascorbic acid (10–1000; ip)	Antioxidant	↓	[131]

Table 3 Effects of Various Treatment Drugs on the Reinstatement of Stimulant CPP

CPP Drug (mg/kg, route)	Species (Strain)	Sex	Age/Weight	Prime	Treatment Drug (dose in mg/kg, route)	Mechanism of Action	Effect on Reinstate	References
					Dopaminergics			
COC (15; ip)	Rat (SD)	Male	275–300 g	**COC (10; ip)**	Quinpirole (0.1–3; sc)	D2/3 agonist	↔	[132]
MDMA (10; ip)	Mouse (OF1)	Male	21 days	MDMA (5; ip)	CGS 10746B (3, 10; ip)	Release inhibitor	↔	[93]
MDMA (10; ip)	Mouse (OF1)	Male	21 days	MDMA (5; ip)	Haloperidol (0.1, 0.2; ip)	D2 antag	↔	[93]
MDMA (10; ip)	Mouse (OF1)	Male	21 days	MDMA (5; ip)	Raclopride (0.3, 0.6; ip)	D2 antag	↔	[93]
MDMA (10; ip)	Mouse (OF1)	Male	21 days	MDMA (5; ip)	SCH 23390 (0.125, 0.25; ip)	D1 antag	↔	[93]
					Serotonergics			
MDMA (10; ip)	Mouse (OF1)	Male	29 days	MDMA (5; ip)	Risperidone (0.1, 0.3; ip)	5-HT2A/D2 antag	↔	[94]
MDMA (10; ip)	Mouse (OF1)	Male	29 days	MDMA (5; ip)	MDL72222 (1; ip)	5-HT3 antag	↓	[95]
					Noradrenergics			
COC (15; ip)	Mouse (C57BL/6J)	Male	8–9 weeks	Stress	Betaxolol (20; ip)	β1 antag	↓	[142]
COC (15; ip)	Mouse (C57BL/6J)	Male	8–9 weeks	Stress	ICI-118,551 (1, 2; ip)	β2 antag	↓	[142]
COC (15; ip)	Mouse (C56BL/6)	Male	8–9 weeks	Stress	Clonidine (0.03; ip)	α2 agonist	↓	[143]
COC (15; ip)	Mouse (C56BL/6)	Male	8–9 weeks	Stress	Prazosin (1, 2; ip)	α1 antag	↔	[143]
COC (15; ip)	Mouse (C56BL/6)	Male	8–9 weeks	Stress	Propranolol (5, 10; ip)	β antag	↓	[143]
COC (15; ip)	Mouse (C56BL/6)	Male	8–9 weeks	Stress	Betaxolol (10; ip)	β1 antag	↔	[143]

COC (15; ip)	Mouse (C56BL/6)	Male	8–9 weeks	Stress	ICI-118,551 (5; ip)	β2 antag	↓	[143]
COC (15; ip)	Mouse (C56BL/6)	Male	8–9 weeks	COC (15; ip)	Clonidine (0.03, 0.3; ip)	α2 agonist	↔	[143]
COC (15; ip)	Mouse (C56BL/6)	Male	8–9 weeks	COC (15; ip)	Prazosin (1, 2; ip)	α1 antag	↔	[143]
COC (15; ip)	Mouse (C56BL/6)	Male	8–9 weeks	COC (15; ip)	Propranolol (5, 10; ip)	β antag	↔	[143]
COC (15; ip)	Mouse (C56BL/6)	Male	8–9 weeks	Yohimbine (2; ip)	Clonidine (0.03, 0.3; ip)	α2 agonist	↔	[143]
COC (15; ip)	Mouse (C56BL/6)	Male	8–9 weeks	Yohimbine (2; ip)	Prazosin (1, 2; ip)	α1 antag	↔	[143]
COC (15; ip)	Mouse (C56BL/6)	Male	8–9 weeks	Yohimbine (2; ip)	Propranolol (10; ip)	β antag	↓	[143]
COC (12; ip)	Rat (SD)	Male	8–9 weeks	Stress	Propranolol (10; sc)	β antag	↔	[144]
					Cholinergics			
NIC (0.175; ip)	Rat (Wistar)	Male	250–300 g	NIC (0.175; ip)	Bupropion (10, 20; ip)	nACh antag/ DAT/NET inhibitor	↓	[145]
NIC (0.175; ip)	Rat (Wistar)	Male	250–300 g	MOR (10; ip)	Bupropion (10, 20; ip)	nACh antag/ DAT/NET inhibitor	↓	[145]
NIC (0.175; ip)	Rat (Wistar)	Male	250–300 g	NIC (0.175; ip)	Varenicline (1, 2; sc)	α2β4 partial agonist	↓	[98]
NIC (0.175; ip)	Rat (Wistar)	Male	250–300 g	NIC (0.175; ip)	Mecamylamine (1, 2; sc)	α2β4 antag	↓	[98]
NIC (0.175; ip)	Rat (Wistar)	Male	250–300 g	MOR (10; ip)	Varenicline (1, 2; sc)	α2β4 partial agonist	↓	[98]
NIC (0.175; ip)	Rat (Wistar)	Male	250–300 g	MOR (10; ip)	Mecamylamine (1, 2; sc)	α2β4 antag	↓	[98]

Continued

Table 3 Effects of Various Treatment Drugs on the Reinstatement of Stimulant CPP—cont'd

CPP Drug (mg/kg, route)	Species (Strain)	Sex	Age/ Weight	Prime	Treatment Drug (dose in mg/kg, route)	Mechanism of Action	Effect on Reinstate	References
					Glutamatergics			
COC (50; ip)	Mouse (OF1)	Male	52 days	COC (25; ip)	Memantine (10; ip)	NMDA channel blocker	↓	[99]
COC (50; ip)	Mouse (OF1)	Male	52 days	COC (25; ip)	CNQX (1, 10; ip)	AMPA antag	↔	[99]
					Gabaergics			
NIC (0.3; sc)	Mouse (C57BL/6)	Male	26–28 g	NIC (0.3; sc)	Baclofen (1.25; ip)	GABA-B agonist	↓	[146]
					Opioids			
COC (15; ip)	Mouse (C57BL/6)	Male	20–30 g	Stress	Norbinaltorphimine (10; ip)	κ antag	↓	[147]
COC (15; ip)	Mouse (C57BL/6)	Male	20–30 g	COC (10; ip)	Norbinaltorphimine (10; ip)	κ antag	↔	[147]
COC (10; sc)	Mouse (C57BL/6J)	Male	20–25 g	Stress	CJ-15,208 (60; po)	κ antag	↓	[148]
COC (10; sc)	Mouse (C57BL/6J)	Male	20–25 g	COC (10; sc)	CJ-15,208 (60; po)	κ antag	↓	[148]
COC (10; sc)	Mouse (C57BL/6J)	Male	19–27 g	Stress	Arodyn (0.3 nmol; icv)	κ antag	↓	[149]
COC (10; sc)	Mouse (C57BL/6J)	Male	19–27 g	COC (10; sc)	Arodyn (0.3 nmol; icv)		↔	[149]
COC (10; sc)	Mouse (ICR)	Male	19–27 g	Stress	PF-04455242 (1, 10; sc)	κ antag	↓	[150]
COC (10; sc)	Mouse (ICR)	Male	19–27 g	COC (10; sc)	PF-04455242 (10; sc)	κ antag	↔	[150]
COC (5; ip)	Rat (SD)	Male	7–9 weeks	COC (3; ip)	Buprenorphine/ Naltrexone (0.3/1; ip)	Partial agonist/ antag	↓	[151]

AMP (2; ip)	Rat (Wistar)	Male	?	AMP (0.5; ip)	Naltrexone (0.3–3; ip)	Antag	↔	[107]
NIC (0.5; sc)	Mouse (ICR)	Male	8–10 weeks	Stress	Norbinaltorphimine (10; sc)	κ antag	↓	[152]
NIC (0.5; sc)	Mouse (ICR)	Male	8–10 weeks	NIC (0.1; sc)	Norbinaltorphimine (10; sc)	κ antag	↔	[152]
					Other Neuropeptides			
COC (10; ip)	Mouse (C57BL/6)	Male	?	COC (5; ip)	L-152,804 (3–30; ip)	NPY Y5 antag	↓	[108]
METH (2; ip)	Mouse (Swiss)	Male	28–32 g	Stress	Oxytocin (0.1–2.5 μg; icv)	Pituitary hormone	↓	[109]
NIC (0.6; sc)	Rat (SD)	Male	Adolescent	Stress	CP-154,526 (20; ip)	CRF-R1 antag	↓	[153]
					Cannabanoids			
COC (20; ip)	Mouse (Kunming)	Male	18–20 g	COC (5; ip)	Rimonabant (3; ip)	CB1 antag	↓	[111]
COC (15; ip)	Mouse (C57BL/6)	Male	8–9 weeks	Stress	AM-251 (3; ip)	CB1 antag	↓	[154]
COC (15; ip)	Mouse (C57BL/6)	Male	8–9 weeks	COC (15; ip)	AM-251 (3; ip)	CB1 antag	↔	[154]
METH (10; ip)	Mouse (Kunming)	Male	18–20 g	METH (5; ip)	Rimonabant (3; ip)	CB1 antag	↓	[111]
NIC (0.5; ip)	Rat (SD)	Male	280–320 g	NIC (0.25; ip)	Rimonabant (3; sc)	CB1 antag	↓	[155]
NIC (0.5; ip)	Rat (Wistar)	Male	250–300 g	NIC (0.5; ip)	Rimonabant (2; ip)	CB1 antag	↓	[156]
NIC (0.5; ip)	Rat (Wistar)	Male	250–300 g	MOR (10; ip)	Rimonabant (0.5, 1; ip)	CB1 antag	↓	[156]
NIC (0.5; ip)	Rat (Wistar)	Male	250–300 g	NIC (0.5; ip)	AM-251 (0.5; ip)	CB1 antag	↓	[157]

Continued

Table 3 Effects of Various Treatment Drugs on the Reinstatement of Stimulant CPP—cont'd

CPP Drug (mg/kg, route)	Species (Strain)	Sex	Age/Weight	Prime	Treatment Drug (dose in mg/kg, route)	Mechanism of Action	Effect on Reinstate	References
NIC (0.4; sc)	Rat (SD)	Male	250–275 g	NIC (0.1; sc)	AM404 (5; ip)	AEA transport blocker	↓	[114]
NIC (0.175; sc)	Rat (Wistar)	Male	250–300 g	ETOH (0.5; ip)	Rimonabant (0.5, 1; ip)	CB1 antag	↓	[158]
					Inhibitors			
METH (1–10; ip)	Rat (SD)	Male	40 days	METH (0.1–10; ip)	γ vinyl-GABA (300; ip)	GABA aminotrans-ferase	↓	[159]
NIC (0.4; ip)	Rat (SD)	Male	250–325 g	NIC (0.4; ip)	URB597 (0.3; ip)	FAAH inhibitor	↓	[115]
					Miscellaneous			
METH (2.5; ip)	Rat (SD)	Male	10 weeks	METH (2.5; ip)	Ceftriaxone (200; ip)	β-lactum antibiotic	↓	[160]
NIC (0.5; ip)	Rat (Wistar)	Male	250–300 g	WIN55, 212–2 (0.5; ip)	Nimodipine (10; ip)	Ca + channel blocker	↓	[158]
NIC (0.5; ip)	Rat (Wistar)	Male	250–300 g	WIN55, 212–2 (0.5; ip)	Flunarizine (5, 10; ip)	Ca + channel blocker	↓	[158]
NIC (0.5; ip)	Rat (Wistar)	Male	250–300 g	ETOH (0.5; ip)	Nimodipine (10; ip)	Ca + channel blocker	↓	[158]
NIC (0.5; ip)	Rat (Wistar)	Male	250–300 g	ETOH (0.5; ip)	Flunarizine (10; ip)	Ca + channel blocker	↓	[158]

Table 4 Effects of Various Treatment Drugs on the Acquisition of Opiate and Ethanol CPP

CPP Drug (mg/kg, route)	Species (Strain)	Sex	Age/ Weight	Treatment Drug (dose in mg/kg, route)	Mechanism of Action	Effect on CPP	References
				Dopaminergics			
MOR (10; ip)	Rat (SD)	Male	220–250 g	L-stepholidine (10, 20; ip)	D2 antag/D1 agonist	↓	[161]
MOR (10; sc)	Rat (SD)	Male	200–250 g	YQA14 (12.5–50; ip)	D3 antag	↔	[162]
ETOH (2; ip)	Mouse (DBA/2J)	Male	8–9 weeks	Raclopride (0.3–1.2; ip)	D2 antag	↔	[163]
ETOH (2; ip)	Mouse (DBA/2J)	Male	8–9 weeks	SCH 23390 (0.1–0.3; ip)	D1 antag	↓	[163]
ETOH (2; ip)	Mouse (DBA/2J)	Male	8–9 weeks	Raclopride (0.5–5 μg; intra-NA)	D2 antag	↔	[164]
ETOH (2; ip)	Mouse (DBA/2J)	Male	8–9 weeks	SCH 23390 (0.05, 0.5 μg; intra-NA)	D1 antag	↓	[164]
ETOH (2; ip)	Mouse (ddY)	Male	40 g	Aripiprazole (3; po)	Mixed D2/5-HT2B/α1A/H1	↓	[165]
ETOH (180 nmol; icv)	Rat (SD)	Male	230–350 g	Fluphenazine (100 μg; intra-NAshell)	D2 antag	↓	[166]
				Cholinergics			
ETOH (2; ip)	Mouse (Swiss)	Male	24–30 g	Mecamylamine (1, 10; icv)	α2β4 antag	↓	[167]
				Glutamatergics			
MOR (10; ip)	Rat (SD)	?	6–8 weeks	MK-801 (0.05; ip)	NMDA antag	↔	[168]
MOR (10; ip)	Rat (SD)	?	6–8 weeks	Ceftriaxone (25; ip)	β-lactum antibiotic	↔	[168]
MOR (10; ip)	Rat (SD)	?	6–8 weeks	MK-801/Ceftriaxone (0.05/25; ip)	NMDA antag/β-lactum antibiotic	↓	[168]

Continued

Table 4 Effects of Various Treatment Drugs on the Acquisition of Opiate and Ethanol CPP—cont'd

CPP Drug (mg/kg, route)	Species (Strain)	Sex	Age/ Weight	Treatment Drug (dose in mg/kg, route)	Mechanism of Action	Effect on CPP	References
MOR (10; sc)	Mouse (CD-1)	Male	22–24 g	Nitrous oxide (50%; inhalation)	NMDA antag	↓	[101]
MOR (7.5; sc)	Rat (Wistar)	Male	200–240 g	MK-801 (1–4 µg; intra-HIPPO)	NMDA antag	↓	[169]
MOR (6; sc)	Rat (Wistar)	Male	240–280 g	MK-801 (0.1–0.5 µg; intra-CeA)	NMDA antag	↓	[170]
MOR (2.5; sc)	Rat (Wistar)	Male	200–240 g	NMDA (0.1–1 µg; intra-HIPPO)	Agonist	↓	[169]
MOR (1; sc)	Rat (Wistar)	Male	240–280 g	NMDA (0.01–1 µg; intra-CeA)	Agonist	↓	[170]
MOR (0.05–5; ip)	Rat (SD)	Male	350–400 g	AP-5 (1 µg; intra-PLC)	NMDA antag	↓	[171]
MOR (3; ip)	Rat (SD)	Male	8 weeks	Ifenprodil (3, 10; ip)	GluN2B antag	↓	[172]
HER (0.05; ip)	Rat (SD)	Male	180–200 g	MPEP (10; ip)	mGluR5 antag	↑	[173]
				Gabaergics			
MOR (5; sc)	Rat (Wistar)	Male	220–250 g	Muscimol (0.5, 1 µg; intra-HIPPO)	GABA-A agonist	↓	[174]
MOR (0.5; sc)	Rat (Wistar)	Male	220–250 g	Bicuculline (0.5, 1 µg; intra-HIPPO)	GABA-A antag	↑	[174]
				Opioids			
MOR (3.16–21.5; ip)	Rat (SD)	Male	180–200 g	Ro65-6570 (3.16; ip)	Nociceptin agonist	↓	[106]
MOR (10; sc)	Rat (SD)	Male	175–199 g	Naltriben (1; ip)	Delta antag	↓	[175]
MOR (2–10; sc)	Rat (SD)	Malc	225 250 g	β-funaltrexamine (5 µg; intra-mTHAL)	Mu antag	↓	[176]
HER (1, 3.16; ip)	Rat (SD)	Male	180–200 g	Ro65-6570 (3.16; ip)	Nociceptin agonist	↓	[106]
ETOH (2; ip)	Mouse (C57BL/6)	Male	18–22 g	TAN-67 (25; sc)	Delta agonist	↑	[177]
ETOH (2; ip)	Mouse (C57BL/6)	Male	18–22 g	SNC80 (20; sc)	Delta agonist	↓	[177]

ETOH (2; ip)	Mouse (C57BL/6)	Male	21–26 g	Naloxone (1, 5; ip)	Antag	↓	[178]
ETOH (2; ip)	Mouse (DBA/2J)	?	6–8 weeks	U50,488H (1, 3; ip)	Kappa agonist	↓	[179]
				Other Neuropeptides			
MOR (5; sc)	Mouse (NMRI)	Male	25–30 g	SB-334867 (10–30; ip)	Orexin-1 antag	↓	[180]
MOR (5; sc)	Mouse (NMRI)	Male	25–30 g	TCS-OX2-29 (5, 10; ip)	Orexin-2 antag	↓	[180]
MOR (10; sc)	Rat (Wistar)	Male	180–200 g	CCK-8 (1; icv)	Anti-opioid	↓	[181]
MOR (3 nmol; icv)	Mouse (Kunming)	Male	18–22 g	Neuropeptide S (1, 3 nmol; icv)	Agonist	↓	[182]
MOR (6 nmol; icv)	Mouse (Kunming)	Male	18–22 g	Neuropeptide S (6, 10 nmol; icv)	Agonist	↓	[182]
ETOH (2; ip)	Mouse (DBA/2)	Male	8–12 weeks	SB-408124 (30; sc)	Orexin-1 antag	↔	[183]
ETOH (2; ip)	Mouse (DBA/2)	Male	8–12 weeks	JNJ-10397049 (10; sc)	Orexin-2 antag	↓	[183]
ETOH (2; ip)	Mouse (DBA/2J)	Male	6–9 weeks	SB-334867 (15, 30; ip)	Orexin-1 antag	↔	[184]
				Cannabanoids			
MOR (6; sc)	Rat (Wistar)	Male	220–270 g	AM251 (90, 120 ng; intra-CeA)	CB1 antag	↓	[185]
MOR (5; sc)	Rat (Wistar)	Male	230–280 g	AM251 (90 µmol; intra-VTA)	CB1 antag	↓	[186]
				Sigma Drugs			
ETOH (2; ip)	Mouse (Swiss)	Male	24–30 g	BD-1047 (1, 10; icv)	σ1 antag	↓	[187]
				Histaminergics			
ETOH (2; ip)	Mouse (DBA/2J)	Male	6–8 weeks	JNJ-10181457 (5; ip)	H3 antag	↓	[188]
ETOH (2; ip)	Mouse (DBA/2J)	Male	6–8 weeks	JNJ-39220675 (0.3; ip)	H3 antag	↓	[188]

Continued

Table 4 Effects of Various Treatment Drugs on the Acquisition of Opiate and Ethanol CPP—cont'd

CPP Drug (mg/kg, route)	Species (Strain)	Sex	Age/ Weight	Treatment Drug (dose in mg/kg, route)	Mechanism of Action	Effect on CPP	References
				Inhibitors			
MOR (16; ip)	Mouse (Swiss)	Male	8 weeks	3-amino-1,2,4-triazole (1000; ip)	Brain catalase	↔	[120]
MOR (7.5; sc)	Rat (SD)	Male	200–250 g	Minocycline (10, 20 μg; intra-NAcore)	Microglia	↓	[189]
MOR (7.5; sc)	Rat (SD)	Male	200–250 g	SB203580 (500 ng; intra-NAcore)	p38	↓	[189]
MOR (3; ip)	Rat (SD)	Male	200–230 g	γV5-3 (1, 10 μg; intra-NAshell)	PKCγ translocation	↓	[190]
ETOH (2; ip)	Mouse (DBA/2J)	Male	8 weeks	SL327 (50; ip)	ERK	↔	[191]
ETOH (2; ip)	Mouse (Swiss)	Male	8 weeks	3-amino-1,2,4-triazole (1000; ip)	Brain catalase	↓	[120]
ETOH (1; ip)	Rat (Wistar)	Male	200–250 g	Milnacipran (40; ip)	5-HT/NET	↓	[192]
				Miscellaneous			
MOR (16; ip)	Mouse (Swiss)	Male	6 weeks	Alpha lipoic acid (100; ip)	H_2O_2 scavenger	↔	[127]
MOR (10; ip)	Mouse (ICR)	Male	6–8 weeks	shRACK1 (20 μl; icv)	Anti-opioid mRNA	↓	[193]
MOR (7.5; sc)	Rat (SD)	Male	300–375 g	Minocycline (50; oral)	Microglial inhibitor	↓	[194]
MOR (5; ip)	Rat (Wistar)	Male	8 weeks	*Nigella sativa* (200, 400; ip)	NO inhibitor/antioxidant	↔	[195]
MOR (5; sc)	Mouse (Wistar)	Male	18–30 g	Cumin fruit oil (0.1–2%; ip)	GABA-A mimetic	↓	[196]
ETOH (2.25; ip)	Mouse (Swiss)	Male	6 weeks	Alpha lipoic acid (100; ip)	H_2O_2 scavenger	↓	[127]
ETOH (2.25; ip)	Mouse (Swiss)	Male	2–3 mo	Berberine (5, 10; ip)	Alkaloid mixed effects	↓	[197]
ETOH (1.25; ip)	Mouse (Swiss)	Male	22–30 g	Agmatine (40; ip)	Polyamine	↓	[198]

Table 5 Effects of Various Treatment Drugs on the Expression of Opiate and Ethanol CPP

CPP Drug (mg/kg, route)	Species (Strain)	Sex	Age/Weight	Treatment Drug (dose in mg/kg, route)	Mechanism of Action	Effect on CPP	References
				Dopaminergics			
MOR (10; ip)	Rat (SD)	Male	220–250 g	L-stepholidine (10, 20; ip)	D2 antag/D1 agonist	↔	[161]
MOR (1 μg; intra-VTA)	Rat (Wistar)	Male	200–300 g	SCH 23390 (0.02–0.5 μg; intra-HIPPO)	D1 antag	↔	[199]
MOR (1 μg; intra-VTA)	Rat (Wistar)	Male	200–300 g	Sulpiride (1.5, 3 μg; intra-HIPPO)	D2 antag	↓	[199]
MOR (10; sc)	Rat (SD)	Male	200–250 g	YQA14 (12.5, 25; ip)	D3 antag	↓	[162]
MOR (5; ip)	Rat (Long Evans)	Male	2.5–3 mo	BP 897 (0.5, 2; ip)	Partial D3 agonist	↔	[200]
MOR (5; sc)	Rat (SD)	Male	200–220 g	Aripiprazole (0.03–0.3; ip)	Mixed D2/5-HT2B/α1A/H1	↔	[201]
ETOH (2; ip)	Mouse (DBA/2J)	Male	8–9 weeks	Raclopride (0.5–5 μg; intra-NAcore)	D2 antag	↔	[164]
ETOH (2; ip)	Mouse (DBA/2J)	Male	8–9 weeks	SCH 23390 (0.05, 0.5 μg; intra-NAcore)	D1 antag	↔	[164]
ETOH (2; ip)	Mouse (DBA/2J)	Male	6–7 weeks	Flupenthixol (1–20 μg; intra-NAcore)	D1/2/3 antag	↔	[202]
ETOH (2; ip)	Mouse (DBA/2J)	Male	6–7 weeks	Flupenthixol (10, 20 μg; intra-AMY)	D1/2/3 antag	↓	[202]
ETOH (2; ip)	Mouse (DBA/2J)	Male	6–7 weeks	Flupenthixol (20 μg; intra-BLA)	D1/2/3 antag	↓	[202]
ETOH (2; ip)	Mouse (DBA/2J)	Male	6–7 weeks	Flupenthixol (20 μg; intra-CeA)	D1/2/3 antag	↔	[202]
ETOH (2; ip)	Mouse (ddY)	Male	40 g	Aripiprazole (3; po)	Mixed D2/5-HT2B/α1A/H1	↓	[165]
ETOH (180 nmol; icv)	Rat (SD)	Male	230–350 g	Fluphenazine (100 μg; intra-NAshell)	D2 antag	↓	[166]

Continued

Table 5 Effects of Various Treatment Drugs on the Expression of Opiate and Ethanol CPP—cont'd

CPP Drug (mg/kg, route)	Species (Strain)	Sex	Age/ Weight	Treatment Drug (dose in mg/kg, route)	Mechanism of Action	Effect on CPP	References
				Serotonergics			
MOR (10; ip)	Rat (SD)	Male	225–250 g	Mirtazapine (5; ip)	5-HT1A agonist/α2 antag	↓	[203]
				Noradrenergics			
MOR (5; ip)	Mouse (NMRI)	Male	20–30 g	Clonidine (0.01–0.04; ip)	α2 agonist	↓	[204]
MOR (5; ip)	Mouse (NMRI)	Male	20–30 g	Tizanidine (0.1–0.4; ip)	α2 agonist	↓	[204]
MOR (5; ip)	Mouse (NMRI)	Male	20–30 g	Xylaxzine (2.5–10; sc)	α2 agonist	↓	[204]
				Cholinergics			
ETOH (2; ip)	Mouse (Swiss)	Male	24–30 g	Mecamylamine (0.1–10; icv)	α2β4 antag	↓	[167]
				Glutamatergics			
MOR (10; sc)	Mouse (CD-1)	Male	22–24 g	Nitrous oxide (50%; inhalation)	NMDA antag	↓	[101]
MOR (7.5; sc)	Rat (Wistar)	Male	200–240 g	MK-801 (1–4 μg; intra-HIPPO)	NMDA antag	↔	[169]
MOR (7.5; sc)	Rat (Wistar)	Male	200–240 g	NMDA (0.1–1 μg; intra-HIPPO)	Agonist	↔	[169]
MOR (6; sc)	Rat (Wistar)	Male	240–280 g	NMDA (0.25–1 μg; intra-CeA)	Agonist	↓	[170]
MOR (6; sc)	Rat (Wistar)	Male	240–280 g	MK-801 (0.25–1 μg; intra-CeA)	NMDA antag	↔	[170]
ETOH (2; ip)	Mouse (DBA/2J)	Male	6–7 weeks	AP-5 (0.5, 1 μg; intra-NAcore)	NMDA antag	↓	[202]
ETOH (0.5; ip)	Rat (Wistar)	Male	200–250 g	EMQMCM (5, 10; ip)	mGluR1 antag	↓	[205]
ETOH (0.5; ip)	Rat (Wistar)	Male	200–250 g	MTEP (2.5, 5; ip)	mGluR5 antag	↓	[205]

				Gabaergics			
MOR (5; sc)	Rat (Wistar)	Male	220–250 g	Muscimol (0.5, 1 μg; intra-HIPPO)	GABA-A agonist	↓	[174]
MOR (5; sc)	Rat (Wistar)	Male	220–250 g	Bicuculline (1, 2 μg; intra-HIPPO)	GABA-A antag	↓	[174]
				Opioids			
MOR (6; sc)	Mouse (C57BL6J)	Male	11 weeks	Nociceptin (0.5, 1.5 nmol; icv)	Agonist	↓	[206]
MOR (2–10; sc)	Rat (SD)	Male	225–250 g	β-funaltrexamine (5 μg; intra-mTHAL)	Mu antag	↔	[176]
ETOH (2; ip)	Rat (SD)	Male	225–250 g	Methylnaloxonium (0.375 μg; intra-ACC)	Antag	↓	[207]
ETOH (2; ip)	Mouse (C57BL/6)	Male	21–26 g	Naloxone (1; ip)	Antag	↓	[178]
				Other Neuropeptides			
MOR (5; sc)	Mouse (NMRI)	Male	25–30 g	SB 334867 (10–30; ip)	Orexin-1 antag	↓	[180]
MOR (5; sc)	Mouse (NMRI)	Male	25–30 g	TCS-OX2-29 (5–10; ip)	Orexin-2 antag	↓	[180]
MOR (10; sc)	Rat (Wistar)	Male	180–200 g	CCK-8 (1; icv)	Anti-opioid	↑	[181]
MOR (6 nmol; icv)	Mouse (Kunming)	Male	18–22 g	Neuropeptide S (0.1–10 nmol; icv)	Agonist	↓	[182]
MOR (5; sc)	Rat (Wistar)	Male	200–250 g	Neuropeptide FF (5–20 nmol; icv)	Anti-opioid	↓	[208]
MOR (5; sc)	Rat (Wistar)	Male	150–220 g	NPFF precursor 85–99 (10, 20 nmol; icv)	Anti-opioid	↓	[209]
ETOH (2; ip)	Mouse (DBA/2)	Male	8–12 weeks	SB-408124 (30; sc)	Orexin-1 antag	↔	[183]
ETOH (2; ip)	Mouse (DBA/2)	Male	8–12 weeks	JNJ-10397049 (10; sc)	Orexin-2 antag	↔	[183]
ETOH (2; ip)	Mouse (DBA/2)	Male	8–12 weeks	SB-334867 (30; ip)	Orexin-1 antag	↔	[184]
ETOH (0.5; ip)	Rat (Wistar)	Male	200–250 g	Neuropeptide FF (5–20 nmol; icv)	Anti-opioid	↔	[208]

Continued

Table 5 Effects of Various Treatment Drugs on the Expression of Opiate and Ethanol CPP—cont'd

CPP Drug (mg/kg, route)	Species (Strain)	Sex	Age/ Weight	Treatment Drug (dose in mg/kg, route)	Mechanism of Action	Effect on CPP	References
				Cannabanoids			
MOR (6; sc)	Rat (Wistar)	Male	220–270 g	AM251 (60–120 ng; intra-CeA)	CB1 antag	↓	[185]
MOR (5; sc)	Rat (Wistar)	Male	230–280 g	AM251 (15–90 μmol; intra-VTA)	CB1 antag	↔	[186]
ETOH (2; ip)	Mouse (HAP)	Male/ Female	62–103 days	LY2183240 (10, 30; ip)	Reuptake blocker	↑	[210]
				Sigma Drugs			
ETOH (2; ip)	Mouse (Swiss)	Male	24–30 g	BD-1047 (1, 10; icv)	σ1 antag	↓	[187]
				Inhibitors			
ETOH (2; ip)	Mouse (DBA/2J)	Male	8 weeks	SL327 (50; ip)	ERK	↔	[191]
ETOH (1.8; ip)	Mouse (DBA/2J)	Male	9–15 weeks	Rapamycin (10; ip)	mTORC1	↓	[211]
				Miscellaneous			
MOR (7.5; sc)	Rat (SD)	Male	200–250 g	Minocycline (10 μg; intra-NAcore)	Microglial inhibitor	↔	[189]
MOR (7.5; sc)	Rat (SD)	Male	200–250 g	SB203580 (500 ng; intra-NAcore)	p38	↔	[189]
MOR (5; ip)	Rat (Wistar)	Male	8 weeks	*Nigella sativa* (200, 400; ip)	NO inhibitor/ antioxidant	↓	[195]
MOR (5; sc)	Mouse (Wistar)	Male	18–30 g	Cumin fruit oil (1, 2%; ip)	GABA-A mimetic	↓	[196]
ETOH (2; ip)	Mouse (Swiss)	Male	2–3 mo	Berberine (5, 10; ip)	Alkaloid mixed effects	↓	[197]
ETOH (2; ip)	Mouse (DBA/2)	Male	?	NP078585 (25; ip)	N/T-type Ca + antag	↓	[212]
ETOH (1.25; ip)	Mouse (Swiss)	Male	22–30 g	Agmatine (20–120; ip)	Polyamine	↔	[198]

Table 6 Effects of Various Treatment Drugs on the Reinstatement of Opiate and Ethanol CPP

CPP Drug (mg/kg, route)	Species (Strain)	Sex	Age/Weight	Prime	Treatment Drug (dose in mg/kg, route)	Mechanism of Action	Effect on Reinstate	References
					Dopaminergics			
MOR (10; sc)	Rat (SD)	Male	200–250 g	MOR (5; sc)	YQA14 (6.25–25; ip)	D3 antag	↓	[162]
MOR (5; sc)	Rat (SD)	Male	200–220g	MOR (3; sc)	Aripiprazole (0.1, 0.3; ip)	Mixed D2/5-HT2B/α1A/H1	↓	[201]
MOR (8; ip)	Rat (SD)	Male	250–300 g	MOR (8, 16; ip)	Modafinil (300; ip)	DAT blocker	↓	[213]
					Cholinergics			
ETOH (2; ip)	Mouse (Swiss)	Male	24–30 g	ETOH (1; ip)	Mecamylamine (0.1; icv)	α2β4 antag	↓	[167]
ETOH (2; ip)	Mouse (Swiss)	Male	24–30 g	Stress	Mecamylamine (0.1; icv)	α2β4 antag	↓	[167]
					Glutamatergics			
MOR (10; ip)	Rat (SD)	?	6–8 weeks	MOR (2; ip)	MK-801 (0.05; ip)	NMDA antag	↔	[168]
MOR (10; ip)	Rat (SD)	?	6–8 weeks	MOR (2; ip)	Ceftriaxone (25; ip)	β-lactum antibiotic	↔	[168]
MOR (10; ip)	Rat (SD)	?	6–8 weeks	MOR (2; ip)	MK-801/Ceftriaxone (0.05/25; ip)	NMDA antag/β-lactum antibiotic	↓	[168]
MOR (3; ip)	Rat (SD)	Male	8 weeks	MOR (2; ip)	Ifenprodil (3, 10; ip)	GluN2B antag	↓	[172]
MOR (3; ip)	Rat (SD)	Male	180–200 g	MOR (2; ip)	Ifenprodil (3, 10; ip)	GluN2B antag	↓	[214]
MOR (3; ip)	Rat (SD)	Male	180–200 g	MOR (2; ip)	Ifenprodil (2 μg; intra-NAshell)	GluN2B antag	↓	[214]
MOR (3; ip)	Rat (SD)	Male	180–200 g	MOR (2; ip)	Ifenprodil (2 μg; intra-HIPPO)	GluN2B antag	↓	[214]

Continued

Table 6 Effects of Various Treatment Drugs on the Reinstatement of Opiate and Ethanol CPP—cont'd

CPP Drug (mg/kg, route)	Species (Strain)	Sex	Age/Weight	Prime	Treatment Drug (dose in mg/kg, route)	Mechanism of Action	Effect on Reinstate	References
MOR (3; ip)	Rat (SD)	Male	180–200 g	Stress	Ifenprodil (1–10; ip)	GluN2B antag	↔	[214]
ETOH (2; ip)	Mouse (C57BL/6)	?	24–36 g	ETOH (2; ip)	AMN082 (5; ip)	mGluR7 agonist	↓	[215]
					Gabaergics			
MOR (10; sc)	Mouse (BALB/c)	Male	5–8 weeks	Stress	Baclofen (2.5; sc)	GABA-B agonist	↓	[216]
MOR (5; sc)	Rat (SD)	Male	225–250 g	Stress	Bicuculline (75 ng; intra-raphe)	GABA-A antag	↓	[217]
MOR (5; sc)	Rat (SD)	Male	225–250 g	Stress	Muscimol (50 ng; intra-raphe)	GABA-A agonist	↑	[217]
					Opioids			
MOR (5; ip)	Rat (SD)	Male	7–9 weeks	MOR (1.25; ip)	Buprenorphine/Naltrexone (0.3/1; ip)	Partial agonist/antag	↓	[151]
					Other Neuropeptides			
MOR (10; sc)	Mouse (C57BL/6J)	Male	7 weeks	Stress	Carbetocin (6.4; ip)	Oxytocin analog	↓	[218]
MOR (10; sc)	Rat (Wistar)	Male	180–200 g	MOR (3; sc)	CCK-8 (0.1, 1 μg; icv)	Anti-opioid	↓	[219]
MOR (10; sc)	Rat (Wistar)	Male	180–200 g	Stress	CCK-8 (0.1, 1 μg; icv)	Anti-opioid	↓	[219]
ETOH (2; ip)	Mouse (DBA/2)	Male	8–12 weeks	ETOH (1; ip)	JNJ-10397049 (10; sc)	Orexin-2 antag	↓	[183]
					Sigma Drugs			
ETOH (2; ip)	Mouse (Swiss)	Male	24–30 g	ETOH (2; ip)	BD-1047 (10; icv)	σ1 antag	↓	[187]

ACC = anterior cingulate cortex; AMP = amphetamine; AMY = amygdala; BLA = basolateral amygdala; CeA = central nucleus of amygdala; COC = cocaine; CPu = caudate putamen; ETOH = ethanol; HER = heroin; HIPPO = hippocampus; MDMA = 3,4-methylenedioxy-*N*-methylamphetamine; MOR = morphine; mTHAL = medial thalamus; NA = nucleus accumbens; NIC = nicotine; PLC = prelimbic cortex; SN = substantia nigra; STh = subthalamic nucleus; VTA = ventral tegmental area; ? = unknown/not supplied.

compared to males [81]. Moreover, females are more sensitive than males to cocaine CPP [82]. These results suggest that pharmacotherapeutic efficacy studies using CPP could benefit by including females.

Second, many of the same pharmacotherapies have been tested against different drugs, including cocaine, amphetamine, nicotine, morphine, and ethanol. One reason for this strategy may be that substance abuse is often viewed as a trait-based factor (e.g., sensation seeking or impulsivity) that predisposes an individual to be at risk for abusing any readily available drug type. At a mechanistic level, this view is consistent with the notion that all drugs of abuse share a common activation of the mesolimbic dopamine reward pathway [83] (see Chapter 2) and thus an effective pharmacotherapy for one type of abused drug may generalize to a different drug. However, an alternative explanation for why a potential pharmacotherapy is often tested against multiple drug types is that it simply reflects the more typical strategy of drug discovery when target identification is largely unknown.

Finally, and perhaps most importantly, evidence provided in these tables clearly demonstrates that CPP alone cannot be used as the go/no-go screen for deciding which pharmacotherapy may have clinical utility. For example, a number of recent studies demonstrate that selective and nonselective antagonists for dopamine receptors (D1-D5) block the acquisition, expression, and reinstatement of stimulant, opiate, and ethanol CPP. However, a meta-analysis from 2013 of randomized placebo-controlled clinical trials has concluded that dopamine antagonists have no effect on cocaine use, abstinence, or craving [84]. Not only are these drugs ineffective as antiabuse medications, but the tolerability of untoward side effects is problematic. This latter finding would be predicted based on preclinical evidence showing that dopamine antagonists produce CPA rather than CPP [85]. Despite the disconnection between preclinical and clinical effectiveness, this disconnection is not unique to CPP. In the case of drug self-administration, for example, preclinical evidence also would predict that dopamine antagonists would be clinically effective for cocaine abuse [86,87]. Thus, it is prudent to use CPP as merely one of multiple behavioral screens for potential pharmacotherapeutic efficacy.

5. CONCLUSION

CPP represents a useful and versatile initial screen for developing medications to treat substance use disorders. In addition, CPP offers value as a preclinical model in determining if a drug has rewarding or reinforcing effects as part of an abuse potential assessment. Similar to other preclinical abuse potential assessments, positive or negative results in this model alone do not mean that a drug will possess or lack abuse potential in humans. Data from CPP experiments provide significant value when used in combination with a larger battery of preclinical models such as self-administration, drug discrimination, physical dependence, and withdrawal studies.

REFERENCES

[1] Childs E, de Wit H. Amphetamine-induced place preference in humans. Biol Psychiatry 2009; 65(10):900–4.
[2] Bardo MT, Bevins RA. Conditioned place preference: what does it add to our preclinical understanding of drug reward? Psychopharmacology 2000;153(1):31–43.
[3] Bardo MT, Rowlett JK, Harris MJ. Conditioned place preference using opiate and stimulant drugs: a meta-analysis. Neurosci Biobehav Rev 1995;19(1):39–51.
[4] Schechter MD, Calcagnetti DJ. Trends in place preference conditioning with a cross-indexed bibliography; 1957–1991. Neurosci Biobehav Rev 1993;17(1):21–41.
[5] Carr GD, Fibiger HC, Phillips AG, editors. Conditioned place preference as a measure of drug reward. Oxford: Clarendon Press; 1989.
[6] Tzschentke TM. Measuring reward with the conditioned place preference paradigm: a comprehensive review of drug effects, recent progress and new issues. Prog Neurobiol 1998;56(6):613–72.
[7] Tombaugh TN, Grandmaison LJ, Zito KA. Establishment of secondary reinforcement in sign tracking and place preference tests following pimozide treatment. Pharmacol Biochem Behav 1982;17(4):665–70.
[8] Huston JP, Silva MA, Topic B, Muller CP. What's conditioned in conditioned place preference? Trends Pharmacol Sci 2013;34(3):162–6.
[9] Spyraki C, Fibiger HC, Phillips AG. Attenuation by haloperidol of place preference conditioning using food reinforcement. Psychopharmacology (Berl) 1982;77(4):379–82.
[10] Monclaro AV, Sampaio AC, Ribeiro NB, Barros M. Time-of-day effect on a food-induced conditioned place preference task in monkeys. Behav Brain Res 2014;259:336–41.
[11] Agmo A, Federman I, Navarro V, Padua M, Velazquez G. Reward and reinforcement produced by drinking water: role of opioids and dopamine receptor subtypes. Pharmacol Biochem Behav 1993;46(1):183–94.
[12] Meisel RL, Joppa MA, Rowe RK. Dopamine receptor antagonists attenuate conditioned place preference following sexual behavior in female *Syrian hamsters*. Eur J Pharmacol 1996;309(1):21–4.
[13] Tenk CM, Wilson H, Zhang Q, Pitchers KK, Coolen LM. Sexual reward in male rats: effects of sexual experience on conditioned place preferences associated with ejaculation and intromissions. Horm Behav 2009;55(1):93–7.
[14] Hughes RN. Behaviour of male and female rats with free choice of two environments differing in novelty. Anim Behav 1968;16(1):92–6.
[15] Bevins RA, Bardo MT. Conditioned increase in place preference by access to novel objects: antagonism by MK-801. Behav Brain Res 1999;99(1):53–60.
[16] Peartree NA, Hood LE, Thiel KJ, Sanabria F, Pentkowski NS, Chandler KN, et al. Limited physical contact through a mesh barrier is sufficient for social reward-conditioned place preference in adolescent male rats. Physiol Behav 2012;105(3):749–56.
[17] Zernig G, Kummer KK, Prast JM. Dyadic social interaction as an alternative reward to cocaine. Front Psychiatry 2013;4:100.
[18] Calcagnetti DJ, Schechter MD. Place conditioning reveals the rewarding aspect of social interaction in juvenile rats. Physiol Behav 1992;51(4):667–72.
[19] Haghparast A, Omranifard A, Arezoomandan R, Ghalandari-Shamami M, Taslimi Z, Vafaei AA, et al. Involvement of dopaminergic receptors of the rat nucleus accumbens in decreasing the conditioned place preference induced by lateral hypothalamus stimulation. Neurosci Lett 2013;556:10–4.
[20] Cahill CM, Xue L, Grenier P, Magnussen C, Lecour S, Olmstead MC. Changes in morphine reward in a model of neuropathic pain. Behav Pharmacol 2013;24(3):207–13.
[21] Navratilova E, Xie JY, Okun A, Qu C, Eyde N, Ci S, et al. Pain relief produces negative reinforcement through activation of mesolimbic reward-valuation circuitry. Proc Natl Acad Sci USA 2012;109(50):20709–13.
[22] Tzschentke TM. Measuring reward with the conditioned place preference (CPP) paradigm: update of the last decade. Addict Biol 2007;12(3–4):227–462.
[23] Lubow RE. Latent inhibition. Psychol Bull 1973;79(6):398–407.
[24] Shoaib M, Stolerman IP, Kumar RC. Nicotine-induced place preferences following prior nicotine exposure in rats. Psychopharmacology (Berl) 1994;113(3–4):445–52.

[25] Lett BT. Repeated exposures intensify rather than diminish the rewarding effects of amphetamine, morphine, and cocaine. Psychopharmacology (Berl) 1989;98(3):357–62.
[26] Randich A, LoLordo VM. Associative and nonassociative theories of the UCS preexposure phenomenon: implications for Pavlovian conditioning. Psychol Bull 1979;86(3):523–48.
[27] Vezina P, Stewart J. Conditioned locomotion and place preference elicited by tactile cues paired exclusively with morphine in an open field. Psychopharmacology (Berl) 1987;91(3):375–80.
[28] Cunningham CL, Ferree NK, Howard MA. Apparatus bias and place conditioning with ethanol in mice. Psychopharmacology (Berl) 2003;170(4):409–22.
[29] Cunningham CL, Patel P, Milner L. Spatial location is critical for conditioning place preference with visual but not tactile stimuli. Behav Neurosci 2006;120(5):1115–32.
[30] Hughes RA, Baker MR, Rettig KM. Cocaine-conditioned place preference in young precocial domestic fowl. Exp Clin Psychopharmacol 1995;3(2):105–11.
[31] Tsibulsky VL, Norman AB. Satiety threshold: a quantitative model of maintained cocaine self-administration. Brain Res 1999;839(1):85–93.
[32] Bardo MT, Valone JM, Bevins RA. Locomotion and conditioned place preference produced by acute intravenous amphetamine: role of dopamine receptors and individual differences in amphetamine self-administration. Psychopharmacology (Berl) 1999;143(1):39–46.
[33] Su ZI, Santoostaroam A, Wenzel J, Ettenberg A. On the persistence of cocaine-induced place preferences and aversions in rats. Psychopharmacology (Berl) 2013;229(1):115–23.
[34] Spyraki C, Nomikos GG, Varonos DD. Intravenous cocaine-induced place preference: attenuation by haloperidol. Behav Brain Res 1987;26(1):57–62.
[35] O'Dell LE, Khroyan TV, Neisewander JL. Dose-dependent characterization of the rewarding and stimulant properties of cocaine following intraperitoneal and intravenous administration in rats. Psychopharmacology (Berl) 1996;123(2):144–53.
[36] Goeders NE, Smith JE. Intracranial cocaine self-administration into the medial prefrontal cortex increases dopamine turnover in the nucleus accumbens. J Pharmacol Exp Ther 1993;265(2): 592–600.
[37] Murray JE, Bevins RA. Cannabinoid conditioned reward and aversion: behavioral and neural processes. ACS Chem Neurosci 2010;1(4):265–78.
[38] Parker LA. Place conditioning in a three- or four-choice apparatus: role of stimulus novelty in drug-induced place conditioning. Behav Neurosci 1992;106(2):294–306.
[39] Levens N, Akins CK. Cocaine induces conditioned place preference and increases locomotor activity in male Japanese quail. Pharmacol Biochem Behav 2001;68(1):71–80.
[40] Huber R, Panksepp JB, Nathaniel T, Alcaro A, Panksepp J. Drug-sensitive reward in crayfish: an invertebrate model system for the study of SEEKING, reward, addiction, and withdrawal. Neurosci Biobehav Rev 2011;35(9):1847–53.
[41] Mathur P, Lau B, Guo S. Conditioned place preference behavior in zebrafish. Nat Protoc 2011; 6(3):338–45.
[42] Rebec GV, Grabner CP, Johnson M, Pierce RC, Bardo MT. Transient increases in catecholaminergic activity in medial prefrontal cortex and nucleus accumbens shell during novelty. Neuroscience 1997;76(3):707–14.
[43] Cunningham CL, Groblewski PA, Voorhees CM. Place conditioning. In: Olmstead MC, editor. Animal models of drug addiction. Humana Press; 2011. p. 167–89.
[44] McBride WJ, Murphy JM, Ikemoto S. Localization of brain reinforcement mechanisms: intracranial self-administration and intracranial place-conditioning studies. Behav Brain Res 1999;101(2):129–52.
[45] Bliss TV, Collingridge GL. A synaptic model of memory: long-term potentiation in the hippocampus. Nature 1993;361(6407):31–9.
[46] Rockstroh S, Emre M, Tarral A, Pokorny R. Effects of the novel NMDA-receptor antagonist SDZ EAA 494 on memory and attention in humans. Psychopharmacology (Berl) 1996;124(3):261–6.
[47] Riedel G, Platt B, Micheau J. Glutamate receptor function in learning and memory. Behav Brain Res 2003;140(1–2):1–47.
[48] Rezvani AH. Involvement of the NMDA system in learning and memory. Boca Raton (FL): CRC Press; 2006.

[49] Cunningham CL, Gremel CM, Groblewski PA. Drug-induced conditioned place preference and aversion in mice. Nat Protoc 2006;1(4):1662–70.
[50] Cherng CG, Tsai CW, Tsai YP, Ho MC, Kao SF, Yu L. Methamphetamine-disrupted sensory processing mediates conditioned place preference performance. Behav Brain Res 2007;182(1):103–8.
[51] Glannon W. Psychopharmacology and memory. J Med Ethics 2006;32(2):74–8.
[52] Crombag HS, Bossert JM, Koya E, Shaham Y. Review. Context-induced relapse to drug seeking: a review. Philos Trans R Soc Lond Ser B, Biol Sci 2008;363(1507):3233–43.
[53] Epstein DH, Preston KL, Stewart J, Shaham Y. Toward a model of drug relapse: an assessment of the validity of the reinstatement procedure. Psychopharmacology (Berl) 2006;189(1):1–16.
[54] Mueller D, Stewart J. Cocaine-induced conditioned place preference: reinstatement by priming injections of cocaine after extinction. Behav Brain Res 2000;115(1):39–47.
[55] Napier TC, Herrold AA, de Wit H. Using conditioned place preference to identify relapse prevention medications. Neurosci Biobehav Rev 2013;37(9):2081–6.
[56] FDA-CDER. Guidance for industry: assessment of abuse potential of drugs (DRAFT guidance). In: Services CfDEaRFUSDoHaH. 2010.
[57] Douaihy AB, Kelly TM, Sullivan C. Medications for substance use disorders. Soc Work Public Health 2013;28(3–4):264–78.
[58] Stinus L, Caille S, Koob GF. Opiate withdrawal-induced place aversion lasts for up to 16 weeks. Psychopharmacology (Berl) 2000;149(2):115–20.
[59] Hughes M, Inglese J, Kurtz A, Andalibi A, Patton L, Austin C, et al. Early drug discovery and development guidelines: for academic researchers, collaborators, and start-up companies. Bethesda (MD): Assay Guidance Manual; 2004.
[60] Horton DB, Potter DM, Mead AN. A translational pharmacology approach to understanding the predictive value of abuse potential assessments. Behav Pharmacol 2013;24(5–6):410–36.
[61] DEA. National drug threat assessment summary. In: Justice USDo. Drug Enforcement Agency; 2013. p. 1–28.
[62] NIDA. Prescription drug abuse. In: Abuse NIoD. Research Report Series: National Institutes of Health; 2011.
[63] Neisewander JL, McDougall SA, Bowling SL, Bardo MT. Conditioned taste aversion and place preference with buspirone and gepirone. Psychopharmacology (Berl) 1990;100(4):485–90.
[64] Gauvin DV, Dormer KN, Holloway FA. Pentylenetetrazole can induce a conditioned place preference. Pharmacol Biochem Behav 1991;40(4):987–90.
[65] Balster RL. Abuse potential of buspirone and related drugs. J Clin Psychopharmacol 1990; 10(3 Suppl.):31S–7S.
[66] DEA. Lists of scheduling actions, controlled substances, regulated chemicals. In: Justice USDo. Drug Enforcement Agency; 2014. p. 1–74.
[67] Lew G, Parker LA. Pentobarbital-induced place aversion. Animal Learn Behav 1998;26(2):219–24.
[68] Acquas E, Carboni E, Garau L, Di Chiara G. Blockade of acquisition of drug-conditioned place aversion by 5HT3 antagonists. Psychopharmacology (Berl) 1990;100(4):459–63.
[69] Carroll ME, France CP, Meisch RA. Intravenous self-administration of etonitazene, cocaine and phencyclidine in rats during food deprivation and satiation. J Pharmacol Exp Ther 1981;217(2):241–7.
[70] Collins RJ, Weeks JR, Cooper MM, Good PI, Russell RR. Prediction of abuse liability of drugs using IV self-administration by rats. Psychopharmacology (Berl) 1984;82(1–2):6–13.
[71] Meehan SM, Schechter MD. LSD produces conditioned place preference in male but not female fawn hooded rats. Pharmacol Biochem Behav 1998;59(1):105–8.
[72] EMA. Guideline on the non-clinical investigation of the dependence potential of medicinal products; 2006.
[73] ICH_M3_(R2). ICH guideline M3 (R2): guidance on non-clinical safety studies for the conduct of human clinical trials and marketing authorisation for pharmaceuticals; 2009.
[74] Hinson RE, Wall AM, Swayze IG. Place avoidance conditioning with D-amphetamine: the effect of screening and the use of preferred and non-preferred sides. J Psychopharmacol 1991;5(3): 207–14.
[75] Collier AD, Echevarria DJ. The utility of the zebrafish model in conditioned place preference to assess the rewarding effects of drugs. Behav Pharmacol 2013;24(5–6):375–83.

[76] Russell WMS, Burch RL. The principles of humane experimental technique. Methuen;1959.
[77] Cui C, Cui Y, Gao J, Sun L, Wang Y, Wang K, et al. Neuroprotective effect of ceftriaxone in a rat model of traumatic brain injury. Neurol Sci: Off J Ital Neurol Soc Ital Soc Clin Neurophysiol 2014;35(5):695–700.
[78] Knackstedt LA, Melendez RI, Kalivas PW. Ceftriaxone restores glutamate homeostasis and prevents relapse to cocaine seeking. Biol Psychiatry 2010;67(1):81–4.
[79] Bobzean SA, Denobrega AK, Perrotti LI. Sex differences in the neurobiology of drug addiction. Exp Neurol 2014;259:64–74.
[80] Anker JJ, Carroll ME. Females are more vulnerable to drug abuse than males: evidence from preclinical studies and the role of ovarian hormones. Curr Top Behav Neurosci 2011;8:73–96.
[81] Carroll ME, Lynch WJ, Roth ME, Morgan AD, Cosgrove KP. Sex and estrogen influence drug abuse. Trends Pharmacol Sci 2004;25(5):273–9.
[82] Zakharova E, Wade D, Izenwasser S. Sensitivity to cocaine conditioned reward depends on sex and age. Pharmacol Biochem Behav 2009;92(1):131–4.
[83] Wise RA. Dopamine and reward: the anhedonia hypothesis 30 years on. Neurotox Res 2008;14(2–3):169–83.
[84] Kishi T, Matsuda Y, Iwata N, Correll CU. Antipsychotics for cocaine or psychostimulant dependence: systematic review and meta-analysis of randomized, placebo-controlled trials. J Clin Psychiatry 2013;74(12):e1169–80.
[85] Manzanedo C, Aguilar MA, Rodriguez-Arias M, Minarro J. Effects of dopamine antagonists with different receptor blockade profiles on morphine-induced place preference in male mice. Behav Brain Res 2001;121(1–2):189–97.
[86] Roberts DC, Loh EA, Vickers G. Self-administration of cocaine on a progressive ratio schedule in rats: dose-response relationship and effect of haloperidol pretreatment. Psychopharmacology (Berl) 1989;97(4):535–8.
[87] Caine SB, Koob GF. Effects of dopamine D-1 and D-2 antagonists on cocaine self-administration under different schedules of reinforcement in the rat. J Pharmacol Exp Ther 1994;270(1):209–18.
[88] Song R, Zhang HY, Peng XQ, Su RB, Yang RF, Li J, et al. Dopamine D(3) receptor deletion or blockade attenuates cocaine-induced conditioned place preference in mice. Neuropharmacology 2013;72:82–7.
[89] Velázquez-Sánchez C, Ferragud A, Hernández-Rabaza V, Nácher A, Merino V, Cardá M, et al. The dopamine uptake inhibitor 3 alpha-[bis(4'-fluorophenyl)metoxy]-tropane reduces cocaine-induced early-gene expression, locomotor activity, and conditioned reward. Neuropsychopharmacology 2009;34(12):2497–507.
[90] Gyertyán I, Kiss B, Gál K, Laszlovszky I, Horváth A, Gémesi LI, et al. Effects of RGH-237 [*N*-{4-[4-(3-aminocarbonyl-phenyl)-piperazin-1-yl]-butyl}-4-bromo-benzamide], an orally active, selective dopamine D(3) receptor partial agonist in animal models of cocaine abuse. J Pharmacol Exp Ther 2007;320(3):1268–78.
[91] Wenzel JM, Su ZI, Shelton K, Dominguez HM, von Furstenberg VA, Ettenberg A. The dopamine antagonist cis-flupenthixol blocks the expression of the conditioned positive but not the negative effects of cocaine in rats. Pharmacol Biochem Behav 2013;114–115:90–6.
[92] Banasikowski TJ, MacLeod LS, Beninger RJ. Comparison of nafadotride, CNQX, and haloperidol on acquisition versus expression of amphetamine-conditioned place preference in rats. Behav Pharmacol 2012;23(1):89–97.
[93] Vidal-Infer A, Roger-Sanchez C, Daza-Losada M, Aguilar MA, Minarro J, Rodriguez-Arias M. Role of the dopaminergic system in the acquisition, expression and reinstatement of MDMA-induced conditioned place preference in adolescent mice. PloS One 2012;7(8):e43107.
[94] Roger-Sanchez C, Rodriguez-Arias M, Minarro J, Aguilar MA. Effects of risperidone on the acquisition and reinstatement of the conditioned place preference induced by MDMA. Brain Res Bull 2013;98:36–43.
[95] Roger-Sanchez C, Rodriguez-Arias M, Minarro J, Aguilar MA. Involvement of 5-hydroxytryptamine 5-HT(3) serotonergic receptors in the acquisition and reinstatement of the conditioned place preference induced by MDMA. Eur J Pharmacol 2013;714(1–3):132–41.
[96] Forget B, Hamon M, Thiebot MH. Involvement of alpha1-adrenoceptors in conditioned place preference supported by nicotine in rats. Psychopharmacology (Berl) 2009;205(3):503–15.

[97] McCallum SE, Glick SD. 18-Methoxycoronaridine blocks acquisition but enhances reinstatement of a cocaine place preference. Neurosci Lett 2009;458(2):57–9.
[98] Biala G, Staniak N, Budzynska B. Effects of varenicline and mecamylamine on the acquisition, expression, and reinstatement of nicotine-conditioned place preference by drug priming in rats. Naunyn-Schmiedeberg's Arch Pharmacol 2010;381(4):361–70.
[99] Maldonado C, Rodriguez-Arias M, Castillo A, Aguilar MA, Minarro J. Effect of memantine and CNQX in the acquisition, expression and reinstatement of cocaine-induced conditioned place preference. Prog Neuro-Psychopharmacol Biol Psychiatry 2007;31(4):932–9.
[100] Lin KY, Cherng CG, Yang FR, Lin LC, Lu RB, Yu L. Memantine abolishes the formation of cocaine-induced conditioned place preference possibly via its IL-6-modulating effect in medial prefrontal cortex. Behav Brain Res 2011;220(1):126–31.
[101] Benturquia N, Le Guen S, Canestrelli C, Lagente V, Apiou G, Roques BP, et al. Specific blockade of morphine- and cocaine-induced reinforcing effects in conditioned place preference by nitrous oxide in mice. Neuroscience 2007;149(3):477–86.
[102] Yu F, Zhong P, Liu X, Sun D, Gao HQ, Liu QS. Metabotropic glutamate receptor I (mGluR1) antagonism impairs cocaine-induced conditioned place preference via inhibition of protein synthesis. Neuropsychopharmacology 2013;38(7):1308–21.
[103] Zhou SJ, Xue LF, Wang XY, Jiang WG, Xue YX, Liu JF, et al. NMDA receptor glycine modulatory site in the ventral tegmental area regulates the acquisition, retrieval, and reconsolidation of cocaine reward memory. Psychopharmacology (Berl) 2012;221(1):79–89.
[104] Mombereau C, Lhuillier L, Kaupmann K, Cryan JF. GABAB receptor-positive modulation-induced blockade of the rewarding properties of nicotine is associated with a reduction in nucleus accumbens DeltaFosB accumulation. J Pharmacol Exp Ther 2007;321(1):172–7.
[105] Soderman AR, Unterwald EM. Cocaine reward and hyperactivity in the rat: sites of mu opioid receptor modulation. Neuroscience 2008;154(4):1506–16.
[106] Rutten K, De Vry J, Bruckmann W, Tzschentke TM. Effects of the NOP receptor agonist Ro65-6570 on the acquisition of opiate- and psychostimulant-induced conditioned place preference in rats. Eur J Pharmacol 2010;645(1–3):119–26.
[107] Haggkvist J, Lindholm S, Franck J. The effect of naltrexone on amphetamine-induced conditioned place preference and locomotor behaviour in the rat. Addict Biol 2009;14(3):260–9.
[108] Sorensen G, Wortwein G, Fink-Jensen A, Woldbye DP. Neuropeptide Y Y5 receptor antagonism causes faster extinction and attenuates reinstatement in cocaine-induced place preference. Pharmacol Biochem Behav 2013;105:151–6.
[109] Qi J, Yang JY, Wang F, Zhao YN, Song M, Wu CF. Effects of oxytocin on methamphetamine-induced conditioned place preference and the possible role of glutamatergic neurotransmission in the medial prefrontal cortex of mice in reinstatement. Neuropharmacology 2009;56(5):856–65.
[110] Baracz SJ, Rourke PI, Pardey MC, Hunt GE, McGregor IS, Cornish JL. Oxytocin directly administered into the nucleus accumbens core or subthalamic nucleus attenuates methamphetamine-induced conditioned place preference. Behav Brain Res 2012;228(1):185–93.
[111] Yu LL, Zhou SJ, Wang XY, Liu JF, Xue YX, Jiang W, et al. Effects of cannabinoid CB(1) receptor antagonist rimonabant on acquisition and reinstatement of psychostimulant reward memory in mice. Behav Brain Res 2011;217(1):111–6.
[112] Merritt LL, Martin BR, Walters C, Lichtman AH, Damaj MI. The endogenous cannabinoid system modulates nicotine reward and dependence. J Pharmacol Exp Ther 2008;326(2):483–92.
[113] Navarrete F, Rodriguez-Arias M, Martin-Garcia E, Navarro D, García-Gutiérrez MS, Aguilar MA, et al. Role of CB2 cannabinoid receptors in the rewarding, reinforcing, and physical effects of nicotine. Neuropsychopharmacology 2013;38(12):2515–24.
[114] Scherma M, Justinová Z, Zanettini C, Panlilio LV, Mascia P, Fadda P, et al. The anandamide transport inhibitor AM404 reduces the rewarding effects of nicotine and nicotine-induced dopamine elevations in the nucleus accumbens shell in rats. Br J Pharmacol 2012;165(8):2539–48.
[115] Scherma M, Panlilio LV, Fadda P, Fattore L, Gamaleddin I, Le Foll B, et al. Inhibition of anandamide hydrolysis by cyclohexyl carbamic acid 3'-carbamoyl-3-yl ester (URB597) reverses abuse-related behavioral and neurochemical effects of nicotine in rats. J Pharmacol Exp Ther 2008;327(2):482–90.

[116] Sage AS, Vannest SC, Fan KH, Will MJ, Lever SZ, Lever JR, et al. *N*-Phenylpropyl-*N'*-(3-methoxyphenethyl)piperazine (YZ-185) attenuates the conditioned-rewarding properties of cocaine in mice. ISRN Pharmacol 2013;2013:546314.

[117] Russo SJ, Sun WL, Minerley AC, Weierstall K, Nazarian A, Festa ED, et al. Progesterone does not affect cocaine-induced conditioned place preference or locomotor activity in male rats. Ethn Dis 2010;20(1 Suppl. 1):S1–73-7.

[118] Russo SJ, Sun WL, Minerly AC, Weierstall K, Nazarian A, Festa ED, et al. Progesterone attenuates cocaine-induced conditioned place preference in female rats. Brain Res 2008;1189:229–35.

[119] Han J, Li Y, Wang D, Wei C, Yang X, Sui N. Effect of 5-aza-2-deoxycytidine microinjecting into hippocampus and prelimbic cortex on acquisition and retrieval of cocaine-induced place preference in C57BL/6 mice. Eur J Pharmacol 2010;642(1–3):93–8.

[120] Font L, Miquel M, Aragon CM. Involvement of brain catalase activity in the acquisition of ethanol-induced conditioned place preference. Physiol Behav 2008;93(4–5):733–41.

[121] Zhong P, Wang W, Yu F, Nazari M, Liu X, Liu QS. Phosphodiesterase 4 inhibition impairs cocaine-induced inhibitory synaptic plasticity and conditioned place preference. Neuropsychopharmacology 2012;37(11):2377–87.

[122] Bailey J, Ma D, Szumlinski KK. Rapamycin attenuates the expression of cocaine-induced place preference and behavioral sensitization. Addict Biol 2012;17(2):248–58.

[123] Brown TE, Forquer MR, Cocking DL, Jansen HT, Harding JW, Sorg BA. Role of matrix metalloproteinases in the acquisition and reconsolidation of cocaine-induced conditioned place preference. Learn Mem (Cold Spring Harb NY) 2007;14(3):214–23.

[124] Kim DH, Yang CH, Hwang M. Sauchinone blocks methamphetamine-induced hyperlocomotion and place preference in mice. Phytomed: Int J Phytother Phytopharm 2013;20(12):1071–5.

[125] Beckmann JS, Denehy ED, Zheng G, Crooks PA, Dwoskin LP, Bardo MT. The effect of a novel VMAT2 inhibitor, GZ-793A, on methamphetamine reward in rats. Psychopharmacology (Berl) 2012;220(2):395–403.

[126] Pastor V, Host L, Zwiller J, Bernabeu R. Histone deacetylase inhibition decreases preference without affecting aversion for nicotine. J Neurochem 2011;116(4):636–45.

[127] Ledesma JC, Aragon CM. Acquisition and reconditioning of ethanol-induced conditioned place preference in mice is blocked by the H(2)O(2) scavenger alpha lipoic acid. Psychopharmacology (Berl) 2013;226(4):673–85.

[128] Ward SJ, Rasmussen BA, Corley G, Henry C, Kim JK, Walker EA, et al. Beta-lactam antibiotic decreases acquisition of and motivation to respond for cocaine, but not sweet food, in C57Bl/6 mice. Behav Pharmacol 2011;22(4):370–3.

[129] Thorn DA, Winter JC, Li JX. Agmatine attenuates methamphetamine-induced conditioned place preference in rats. Eur J Pharmacol 2012;680(1–3):69–72.

[130] Kurokawa K, Shibasaki M, Mizuno K, Ohkuma S. Gabapentin blocks methamphetamine-induced sensitization and conditioned place preference via inhibition of alpha(2)/delta-1 subunits of the voltage-gated calcium channels. Neuroscience 2011;176:328–35.

[131] Sahraei H, Aliabadi AA, Zarrindast MR, Ghoshooni H, Nasiri A, Barzegari-Sorkheh AA, et al. Ascorbic acid antagonizes nicotine-induced place preference and behavioral sensitization in mice. Eur J Pharmacol 2007;560(1):42–8.

[132] Graham DL, Hoppenot R, Hendryx A, Self DW. Differential ability of D1 and D2 dopamine receptor agonists to induce and modulate expression and reinstatement of cocaine place preference in rats. Psychopharmacology (Berl) 2007;191(3):719–30.

[133] Micheli F, Bonanomi G, Blaney FE, Braggio S, Capelli AM, Checchia A, et al. 1,2,4-triazol-3-yl-thiopropyl-tetrahydrobenzazepines: a series of potent and selective dopamine D(3) receptor antagonists. J Med Chem 2007;50(21):5076–89.

[134] Fijal K, Pachuta A, McCreary AC, Wydra K, Nowak E, Papp M, et al. Effects of serotonin (5-HT)6 receptor ligands on responding for cocaine reward and seeking in rats. Pharmacol Rep 2010;62(6):1005–14.

[135] Ramos AC, Andersen ML, Oliveira MG, Soeiro AC, Galduroz JC. Biperiden (M(1) antagonist) impairs the expression of cocaine conditioned place preference but potentiates the expression of cocaine-induced behavioral sensitization. Behav Brain Res 2012;231(1):213–6.

[136] Jackson KJ, McIntosh JM, Brunzell DH, Sanjakdar SS, Damaj MI. The role of alpha6-containing nicotinic acetylcholine receptors in nicotine reward and withdrawal. J Pharmacol Exp Ther 2009;331(2):547–54.

[137] Jackson KJ, Carroll FI, Negus SS, Damaj MI. Effect of the selective kappa-opioid receptor antagonist JDTic on nicotine antinociception, reward, and withdrawal in the mouse. Psychopharmacology (Berl) 2010;210(2):285–94.

[138] Kotlinska J, Pachuta A, Silberring J. Neuropeptide FF (NPFF) reduces the expression of cocaine-induced conditioned place preference and cocaine-induced sensitization in animals. Peptides 2008; 29(6):933–9.

[139] Hutcheson DM, Quarta D, Halbout B, Rigal A, Valerio E, Heidbreder C. Orexin-1 receptor antagonist SB-334867 reduces the acquisition and expression of cocaine-conditioned reinforcement and the expression of amphetamine-conditioned reward. Behav Pharmacol 2011;22(2):173–81.

[140] Xu YT, Robson MJ, Szeszel-Fedorowicz W, Patel D, Rooney R, McCurdy CR, et al. CM156, a sigma receptor ligand, reverses cocaine-induced place conditioning and transcriptional responses in the brain. Pharmacol Biochem Behav 2012;101(1):174–80.

[141] Pan Y, Gerasimov MR, Kvist T, Wellendorph P, Madsen KK, Pera E, et al. (1S, 3S)-3-amino-4-difluoromethylenyl-1-cyclopentanoic acid (CPP-115), a potent gamma-aminobutyric acid aminotransferase inactivator for the treatment of cocaine addiction. J Med Chem 2012;55(1):357–66.

[142] Vranjkovic O, Hang S, Baker DA, Mantsch JR. Beta-adrenergic receptor mediation of stress-induced reinstatement of extinguished cocaine-induced conditioned place preference in mice: roles for beta1 and beta2 adrenergic receptors. J Pharmacol Exp Ther 2012;342(2):541–51.

[143] Mantsch JR, Weyer A, Vranjkovic O, Beyer CE, Baker DA, Caretta H. Involvement of noradrenergic neurotransmission in the stress- but not cocaine-induced reinstatement of extinguished cocaine-induced conditioned place preference in mice: role for beta-2 adrenergic receptors. Neuropsychopharmacology 2010;35(11):2165–78.

[144] Fricks-Gleason AN, Marshall JF. Post-retrieval beta-adrenergic receptor blockade: effects on extinction and reconsolidation of cocaine-cue memories. Learn Mem (Cold Spring Harb NY) 2008;15(9):643–8.

[145] Budzynska B, Biala G. Effects of bupropion on the reinstatement of nicotine-induced conditioned place preference by drug priming in rats. Pharmacol Rep 2011;63(2):362–71.

[146] Fattore L, Spano MS, Cossu G, Scherma M, Fratta W, Fadda P. Baclofen prevents drug-induced reinstatement of extinguished nicotine-seeking behaviour and nicotine place preference in rodents. Eur Neuropsychopharmacol: J Eur Coll Neuropsychopharmacol 2009;19(7):487–98.

[147] Redila VA, Chavkin C. Stress-induced reinstatement of cocaine seeking is mediated by the kappa opioid system. Psychopharmacology (Berl) 2008;200(1):59–70.

[148] Aldrich JV, Senadheera SN, Ross NC, Ganno ML, Eans SO, McLaughlin JP. The macrocyclic peptide natural product CJ-15,208 is orally active and prevents reinstatement of extinguished cocaine-seeking behavior. J Nat Prod 2013;76(3):433–8.

[149] Carey AN, Borozny K, Aldrich JV, McLaughlin JP. Reinstatement of cocaine place-conditioning prevented by the peptide kappa-opioid receptor antagonist arodyn. Eur J Pharmacol 2007;569 (1–2):84–9.

[150] Grimwood S, Lu Y, Schmidt AW, Vanase-Frawley MA, Sawant-Basak A, Miller E, et al. Pharmacological characterization of 2-methyl-*N*-((2'-(pyrrolidin-1-ylsulfonyl)biphenyl-4-yl)methyl)propan-1-amine (PF-04455242), a high-affinity antagonist selective for kappa-opioid receptors. J Pharmacol Exp Ther 2011;339(2):555–66.

[151] Cordery SF, Taverner A, Ridzwan IE, Guy RH, Delgado-Charro MB, Husbands SM, et al. A non-rewarding, non-aversive buprenorphine/naltrexone combination attenuates drug-primed reinstatement to cocaine and morphine in rats in a conditioned place preference paradigm. Addict Biol 2012;19(4):575–86.

[152] Jackson KJ, McLaughlin JP, Carroll FI, Damaj MI. Effects of the kappa opioid receptor antagonist, norbinaltorphimine, on stress and drug-induced reinstatement of nicotine-conditioned place preference in mice. Psychopharmacology (Berl) 2013;226(4):763–8.

[153] Brielmaier J, McDonald CG, Smith RF. Effects of acute stress on acquisition of nicotine conditioned place preference in adolescent rats: a role for corticotropin-releasing factor 1 receptors. Psychopharmacology (Berl) 2012;219(1):73–82.

[154] Vaughn LK, Mantsch JR, Vranjkovic O, Stroh G, Lacourt M, Kreutter M, et al. Cannabinoid receptor involvement in stress-induced cocaine reinstatement: potential interaction with noradrenergic pathways. Neuroscience 2012;204:117–24.

[155] Fang Q, Li FQ, Li YQ, Xue YX, He YY, Liu JF, et al. Cannabinoid CB1 receptor antagonist rimonabant disrupts nicotine reward-associated memory in rats. Pharmacol Biochem Behav 2011;99(4):738–42.

[156] Biala G, Budzynska B, Staniak N. Effects of rimonabant on the reinstatement of nicotine-conditioned place preference by drug priming in rats. Behav Brain Res 2009;202(2):260–5.

[157] Budzynska B, Kruk M, Biala G. Effects of the cannabinoid CB1 receptor antagonist AM 251 on the reinstatement of nicotine-conditioned place preference by drug priming in rats. Pharmacol Rep 2009;61(2):304–10.

[158] Biala G, Budzynska B. Calcium-dependent mechanisms of the reinstatement of nicotine-conditioned place preference by drug priming in rats. Pharmacol Biochem Behav 2008;89(1):116–25.

[159] DeMarco A, Dalal RM, Pai J, Aquilina SD, Mullapudi U, Hammel C, et al. Racemic gamma vinyl-GABA (R,S-GVG) blocks methamphetamine-triggered reinstatement of conditioned place preference. Synap (New York, NY) 2009;63(2):87–94.

[160] Abulseoud OA, Miller JD, Wu J, Choi DS, Holschneider DP. Ceftriaxone upregulates the glutamate transporter in medial prefrontal cortex and blocks reinstatement of methamphetamine seeking in a condition place preference paradigm. Brain Res 2012;1456:14–21.

[161] Wang W, Zhou Y, Sun J, Pan L, Kang L, Dai Z, et al. The effect of L-stepholidine, a novel extract of Chinese herb, on the acquisition, expression, maintenance, and re-acquisition of morphine conditioned place preference in rats. Neuropharmacology 2007;52(2):355–61.

[162] Hu R, Song R, Yang R, Su R, Li J. The dopamine D(3) receptor antagonist YQA14 that inhibits the expression and drug-prime reactivation of morphine-induced conditioned place preference in rats. Eur J Pharmacol 2013;720(1–3):212–7.

[163] Pina MM, Cunningham CL. Effects of dopamine receptor antagonists on the acquisition of ethanol-induced conditioned place preference in mice. Psychopharmacology (Berl) 2014;231(3):459–68.

[164] Young EA, Dreumont SE, Cunningham CL. Role of nucleus accumbens dopamine receptor subtypes in the learning and expression of alcohol-seeking behavior. Neurobiol Learn Mem 2014;108:28–37.

[165] Shibasaki M, Kurokawa K, Mizuno K, Ohkuma S. Effect of aripiprazole on anxiety associated with ethanol physical dependence and on ethanol-induced place preference. J Pharmacol Sci 2012; 118(2):215–24.

[166] Walker BM, Ettenberg A. Intracerebroventricular ethanol-induced conditioned place preferences are prevented by fluphenazine infusions into the nucleus accumbens of rats. Behav Neurosci 2007; 121(2):401–10.

[167] Bhutada P, Mundhada Y, Ghodki Y, Dixit P, Umathe S, Jain K. Acquisition, expression, and reinstatement of ethanol-induced conditioned place preference in mice: effects of exposure to stress and modulation by mecamylamine. J Psychopharmacol 2012;26(2):315–23.

[168] Fan Y, Niu H, Rizak JD, Li L, Wang G, Xu L, et al. Combined action of MK-801 and ceftriaxone impairs the acquisition and reinstatement of morphine-induced conditioned place preference, and delays morphine extinction in rats. Neurosci Bull 2012;28(5):567–76.

[169] Zarrindast MR, Lashgari R, Rezayof A, Motamedi F, Nazari-Serenjeh F. NMDA receptors of dorsal hippocampus are involved in the acquisition, but not in the expression of morphine-induced place preference. Eur J Pharmacol 2007;568(1–3):192–8.

[170] Rezayof A, Golhasani-Keshtan F, Haeri-Rohani A, Zarrindast MR. Morphine-induced place preference: involvement of the central amygdala NMDA receptors. Brain Res 2007;1133(1):34–41.

[171] Bishop SF, Lauzon NM, Bechard M, Gholizadeh S, Laviolette SR. NMDA receptor hypofunction in the prelimbic cortex increases sensitivity to the rewarding properties of opiates via dopaminergic and amygdalar substrates. Cereb Cortex (New York, NY: 1991) 2011;21(1):68–80.

[172] Ma YY, Yu P, Guo CY, Cui CL. Effects of ifenprodil on morphine-induced conditioned place preference and spatial learning and memory in rats. Neurochem Res 2011;36(3):383–91.

[173] van der Kam EL, De Vry J, Tzschentke TM. 2-Methyl-6-(phenylethynyl)-pyridine (MPEP) potentiates ketamine and heroin reward as assessed by acquisition, extinction, and reinstatement of conditioned place preference in the rat. Eur J Pharmacol 2009;606(1–3):94–101.

[174] Rezayof A, Razavi S, Haeri-Rohani A, Rassouli Y, Zarrindast MR. GABA(A) receptors of hippocampal CA1 regions are involved in the acquisition and expression of morphine-induced place preference. Eur Neuropsychopharmacol: J Eur Coll Neuropsychopharmacol 2007;17(1):24–31.
[175] Billa SK, Xia Y, Moron JA. Disruption of morphine-conditioned place preference by a delta2-opioid receptor antagonist: study of mu-opioid and delta-opioid receptor expression at the synapse. Eur J Neurosci 2010;32(4):625–31.
[176] Guo N, Garcia MM, Taylor BK, Zadina JE, Harlan RE. Blockade of micro-opioid receptors in the medial thalamus inhibits acquisition, but not expression, of morphine-induced conditioned place preference. Neuroscience 2008;151(4):948–54.
[177] van Rijn RM, Brissett DI, Whistler JL. Distinctive modulation of ethanol place preference by delta opioid receptor-selective agonists. Drug Alcohol Depend 2012;122(1–2):156–9.
[178] Wrobel M. Acquisition and expression of ethanol-induced conditioned place preference in mice is inhibited by naloxone. Pharmacol Rep 2011;63(1):79–85.
[179] Logrip ML, Janak PH, Ron D. Blockade of ethanol reward by the kappa opioid receptor agonist U50,488H. Alcohol 2009;43(5):359–65.
[180] Tabaeizadeh M, Motiei-Langroudi R, Mirbaha H, Esmaeili B, Tahsili-Fahadan P, Javadi-Paydar M, et al. The differential effects of OX1R and OX2R selective antagonists on morphine conditioned place preference in naive versus morphine-dependent mice. Behav Brain Res 2013;237:41–8.
[181] Wen D, Cong B, Ma C, Yang S, Yu H, Ni Z, et al. The effects of exogenous CCK-8 on the acquisition and expression of morphine-induced CPP. Neurosci Lett 2012;510(1):24–8.
[182] Li W, Gao YH, Chang M, Peng YL, Yao J, Han RW, et al. Neuropeptide S inhibits the acquisition and the expression of conditioned place preference to morphine in mice. Peptides 2009;30(2):234–40.
[183] Shoblock JR, Welty N, Aluisio L, Fraser I, Motley ST, Morton K, et al. Selective blockade of the orexin-2 receptor attenuates ethanol self-administration, place preference, and reinstatement. Psychopharmacology (Berl) 2011;215(1):191–203.
[184] Voorhees CM, Cunningham CL. Involvement of the orexin/hypocretin system in ethanol conditioned place preference. Psychopharmacology (Berl) 2011;214(4):805–18.
[185] Rezayof A, Sardari M, Zarrindast MR, Nayer-Nouri T. Functional interaction between morphine and central amygdala cannabinoid CB1 receptors in the acquisition and expression of conditioned place preference. Behav Brain Res 2011;220(1):1–8.
[186] Rashidy-Pour A, Pahlevani P, Vaziri A, Shaigani P, Zarepour L, Vafaei AA, et al. Involvement of CB1 receptors in the ventral tegmental area in the potentiation of morphine rewarding properties in acquisition but not expression in the conditioned place preference model. Behav Brain Res 2013;247:259–67.
[187] Bhutada PS, Mundhada YR, Ghodki YR, Chaware P, Dixit PV, Jain KS, et al. Influence of sigma-1 receptor modulators on ethanol-induced conditioned place preference in the extinction-reinstatement model. Behav Pharmacol 2012;23(1):25–33.
[188] Vanhanen J, Nuutinen S, Lintunen M, Mäki T, Rämö J, Karlstedt K, et al. Histamine is required for H(3) receptor-mediated alcohol reward inhibition, but not for alcohol consumption or stimulation. Br J Pharmacol 2013;170(1):177–87.
[189] Zhang XQ, Cui Y, Chen Y, Chen Y, Na XD, Chen FY, et al. Activation of p38 signaling in the microglia in the nucleus accumbens contributes to the acquisition and maintenance of morphine-induced conditioned place preference. Brain, Behav Immun 2012;26(2):318–25.
[190] Ping X, Ma Y, Li Y, Qi C, Sun X, Lv X, et al. Essential role of protein kinase C in morphine-induced rewarding memory. Neuropharmacology 2012;62(2):959–66.
[191] Groblewski PA, Franken FH, Cunningham CL. Inhibition of extracellular signal-regulated kinase (ERK) activity with SL327 does not prevent acquisition, expression, and extinction of ethanol-seeking behavior in mice. Behav Brain Res 2011;217(2):399–407.
[192] Simon O'Brien E, Legastelois R, Houchi H, Vilpoux C, Alaux-Cantin S, Pierrefiche O, et al. Fluoxetine, desipramine, and the dual antidepressant milnacipran reduce alcohol self-administration and/or relapse in dependent rats. Neuropsychopharmacology 2011;36(7):1518–30.
[193] Wan L, Xie Y, Su L, Liu Y, Wang Y, Wang Z. RACK1 affects morphine reward via BDNF. Brain Res 2011;1416:26–34.

[194] Hutchinson MR, Northcutt AL, Chao LW, Kearney JJ, Zhang Y, Berkelhammer DL, et al. Minocycline suppresses morphine-induced respiratory depression, suppresses morphine-induced reward, and enhances systemic morphine-induced analgesia. Brain, Behav Immun 2008;22(8):1248–56.
[195] Anvari M, Seddigh A, Shafei MN, Rakhshandeh H, Talebi AH, Tahani MR, et al. *Nigella sativa* extract affects conditioned place preference induced by morphine in rats. Anc Sci life 2012;32(2):82–8.
[196] Khatibi A, Haghparast A, Shams J, Dianati E, Komaki A, Kamalinejad M. Effects of the fruit essential oil of *Cuminum cyminum* L. on the acquisition and expression of morphine-induced conditioned place preference in mice. Neurosci Lett 2008;448(1):94–8.
[197] Bhutada P, Mundhada Y, Bansod K, Rathod S, Hiware R, Dixit P, et al. Inhibitory effect of berberine on the motivational effects of ethanol in mice. Prog Neuro-Psychopharmacol Biol Psychiatry 2010;34(8):1472–9.
[198] Sameer SM, Chakraborty SS, Ugale RR. Agmatine attenuates acquisition but not the expression of ethanol conditioned place preference in mice: a role for imidazoline receptors. Behav Pharmacol 2013;24(2):87–94.
[199] Haghparast A, Esmaeili MH, Taslimi Z, Kermani M, Yazdi-Ravandi S, Alizadeh AM. Intrahippocampal administration of D2 but not D1 dopamine receptor antagonist suppresses the expression of conditioned place preference induced by morphine in the ventral tegmental area. Neurosci Lett 2013;541:138–43.
[200] Vazquez V, Weiss S, Giros B, Martres MP, Dauge V. Maternal deprivation and handling modify the effect of the dopamine D3 receptor agonist, BP 897 on morphine-conditioned place preference in rats. Psychopharmacology (Berl) 2007;193(4):475–86.
[201] Li SX, Zou Y, Liu LJ, Wu P, Lu L. Aripiprazole blocks reinstatement but not expression of morphine conditioned place preference in rats. Pharmacol Biochem Behav 2009;92(2):370–5.
[202] Gremel CM, Cunningham CL. Involvement of amygdala dopamine and nucleus accumbens NMDA receptors in ethanol-seeking behavior in mice. Neuropsychopharmacology 2009;34(6):1443–53.
[203] Graves SM, Persons AL, Riddle JL, Napier TC. The atypical antidepressant mirtazapine attenuates expression of morphine-induced place preference and motor sensitization. Brain Res 2012;1472: 45–53.
[204] Samini M, Kardan A, Mehr SE. Alpha-2 agonists decrease expression of morphine-induced conditioned place preference. Pharmacol Biochem Behav 2008;88(4):403–6.
[205] Kotlinska JH, Bochenski M, Danysz W. The role of group I mGlu receptors in the expression of ethanol-induced conditioned place preference and ethanol withdrawal seizures in rats. Eur J Pharmacol 2011;670(1):154–61.
[206] Sakoori K, Murphy NP. Expression of morphine-conditioned place preference is more vulnerable than naloxone-conditioned place aversion to disruption by nociceptin in mice. Neurosci Lett 2008;443(2):108–12.
[207] Gremel CM, Young EA, Cunningham CL. Blockade of opioid receptors in anterior cingulate cortex disrupts ethanol-seeking behavior in mice. Behav Brain Res 2011;219(2):358–62.
[208] Kotlinska J, Pachuta A, Dylag T, Silberring J. Neuropeptide FF (NPFF) reduces the expression of morphine- but not of ethanol-induced conditioned place preference in rats. Peptides 2007;28(11): 2235–42.
[209] Dylag T, Pachuta A, Raoof H, Kotlinska J, Silberring J. A novel cryptic peptide derived from the rat neuropeptide FF precursor reverses antinociception and conditioned place preference induced by morphine. Peptides 2008;29(3):473–8.
[210] Powers MS, Barrenha GD, Mlinac NS, Barker EL, Chester JA. Effects of the novel endocannabinoid uptake inhibitor, LY2183240, on fear-potentiated startle and alcohol-seeking behaviors in mice selectively bred for high alcohol preference. Psychopharmacology (Berl) 2010;212(4):571–83.
[211] Neasta J, Ben Hamida S, Yowell Q, Carnicella S, Ron D. Role for mammalian target of rapamycin complex 1 signaling in neuroadaptations underlying alcohol-related disorders. Proc Natl Acad Sci USA 2010;107(46):20093–8.
[212] Newton PM, Zeng L, Wang V, Connolly J, Wallace MJ, Kim C, et al. A blocker of N- and T-type voltage-gated calcium channels attenuates ethanol-induced intoxication, place preference, self-administration, and reinstatement. J Neurosci: Off J Soc Neurosci 2008;28(45):11712–9.

[213] Tahsili-Fahadan P, Carr GV, Harris GC, Aston-Jones G. Modafinil blocks reinstatement of extinguished opiate-seeking in rats: mediation by a glutamate mechanism. Neuropsychopharmacology 2010;35(11):2203–10.
[214] Ma YY, Chu NN, Guo CY, Han JS, Cui CL. NR2B-containing NMDA receptor is required for morphine-but not stress-induced reinstatement. Exp Neurol 2007;203(2):309–19.
[215] Bahi A. The selective metabotropic glutamate receptor 7 allosteric agonist AMN082 prevents reinstatement of extinguished ethanol-induced conditioned place preference in mice. Pharmacol Biochem Behav 2012;101(2):193–200.
[216] Meng S, Quan W, Qi X, Su Z, Yang S. Effect of baclofen on morphine-induced conditioned place preference, extinction, and stress-induced reinstatement in chronically stressed mice. Psychopharmacology (Berl) 2014;231(1):27–36.
[217] Li C, Staub DR, Kirby LG. Role of GABAA receptors in dorsal raphe nucleus in stress-induced reinstatement of morphine-conditioned place preference in rats. Psychopharmacology (Berl) 2013;230(4):537–45.
[218] Zanos P, Georgiou P, Wright SR, Hourani SM, Kitchen I, Winsky-Sommerer R, et al. The oxytocin analogue carbetocin prevents emotional impairment and stress-induced reinstatement of opioid-seeking in morphine-abstinent mice. Neuropsychopharmacology 2014;39(4):855–65.
[219] Wen D, Zang G, Sun D, Yang S, Yu F, Li S, Ma C, et al. Effects of CCK-8 on the reinstatement of morphine-induced CPP and expression of behavioral sensitization in rats. Neuroscience 2013;238:230–41.

CHAPTER 8

Utility of Intracranial Self-Stimulation in the Assessment of the Abuse Liability of New Pharmaceuticals

Anton Y. Bespalov[1], Patrick M. Beardsley[2], Mark S. Todtenkopf[3]
[1]Laboratory of Behavioral Pharmacology, Institute of Pharmacology, Pavlov Medical University, St. Petersburg, Russia;
[2]Department of Pharmacology & Toxicology, School of Medicine, Virginia Commonwealth University, Richmond, VA, USA;
[3]Life Sciences and Toxicology Department, Alkermes, Inc., Waltham, MA, USA

Contents

1. INTRODUCTION

The motto "Noli nocere" (Do no harm!) has always been the main guiding principle for those who practice medicine. Safety evaluation is also the main concern for both organizations that aim to develop new drugs and governmental agencies that regulate the progression of novel therapeutic principles into clinical use. Discussions of drug evaluation policies involving physician practitioners, scientists, legislators, and regulatory authorities often call for reevaluation of safety assessment procedures [1]. The scientific assessment of the risks associated with using new drugs is recognized to be at the core of efforts to improve safety, and therefore both drug developers and regulators need to focus on exploring new scientific approaches to detect, understand, predict, and prevent adverse events.

These discussions are driven not only by the discovery of previously unknown adverse reactions to certain drugs, such as cyclooxygenase 2-selective nonsteroidal anti-inflammatory drugs or the multiple sclerosis drug natalizumab, but also by rapid advances in science and the development of novel therapeutic principles. In many areas, existing safety evaluation practices may be expected to be less effective in dealing with newly emerging pharmacological classes and individual drugs. An example of such a field is the nonclinical assessment of drug abuse liability, where concerns have been expressed

Nonclinical Assessment of Abuse Potential for New Pharmaceuticals
http://dx.doi.org/10.1016/B978-0-12-420172-9.00008-4

regarding the availability of adequate methods for the abuse liability assessment of new classes of drugs [2].

Originally, drug abuse potential was defined by the propensity of drugs to induce physical dependence [3]. Hence, one of the core nonclinical procedures during the assessment of the abuse potential of drugs was the determination of spontaneous and precipitated withdrawal effects of drugs (see Chapter 5). As the field developed, the essentiality of physical dependence for the acquisition and maintenance of relapsing addictive behavior became questioned. Additionally, it became recognized that new tools were needed to distinguish drug discontinuation effects that did not drive subsequent drug seeking (e.g., from the SSRIs [selective serotonin reuptake inhibitors]) from abuse-related withdrawal effects that were a component of relapsing drug abuse [2]. Current inventories of diagnostic criteria for drug dependence (e.g., as in DSM-V and ICD-10 [Diagnostics and Statistical Manual-version 5 and International Statistical Classification of Diseases and Related Health Problems-version 10, respectively]) assign much less significance to physical dependence compared to earlier versions. This de-emphasis has been, in part, occasioned by experience with several drugs of abuse for which little or no physical dependence is known to be of clinical importance (e.g., hallucinogens). Partially in recognition of this, the most recently issued draft guidance from the Food and Drug Administration (*Assessment of Abuse Potential of Drugs, January 2010*) outlines the potential of a broad battery of tests, including self-administration (see Chapters 3 and 4), conditioned place preference (CPP) (Chapter 7), drug discrimination (Chapter 6), psychomotor tests (Chapter 2), and tests of physical dependence (Chapter 5) during the nonclinical evaluation of drug abuse liability. For the remaining discussion, it is important to note the definition of "abuse potential" versus "abuse liability" as used in this chapter. "Abuse potential" characterizes the ability of a central nervous system (CNS)-active drug to produce pharmacological effects predictive of the risk of addiction (a main area of interest for a behavioral pharmacologist). "Abuse liability" captures not only the abuse potential of a drug but also other factors, including ease of synthesis, chemical and pharmacokinetic (PK) characteristics, fads in use and abuse, and diversion history.

The discussion below first briefly summarizes the key rationale for the need for alternative or additional methods during the nonclinical assessment of abuse liability for addressing the complexity of emerging drug products, and then examines intracranial self-stimulation (ICSS) as one potential method for addressing this need.

2. RATIONALE FOR THE SEARCH FOR ALTERNATIVE METHODS DURING THE NONCLINICAL ASSESSMENT OF ABUSE POTENTIAL

Current drug abuse liability assessment strategies rely extensively on the prior knowledge about known drugs and our ability to compare effects of these drugs with those of novel compounds. Two of the core nonclinical methods—self-administration and drug discrimination substitution procedures—are currently the "gold standard." For example, in self-administration studies, animals are trained to work (e.g., press levers) for drugs known to maintain responding, such as cocaine. When responding becomes stable, a dose of a test compound or vehicle is substituted. It is expected that substitution with a vehicle results in responding declining to low levels. For a compound to be classified as a positive reinforcer (and by inference, to have abuse potential), substitution has to result in response rates being maintained above those for saline [4]. A limitation of the simple substitution procedure is that it only permits binary predictions, that is, either the test drug serves as a reinforcer and is likely to have abuse potential or it is not self-administered and is unlikely to have abuse potential. The simple substitution procedure is unable to qualitatively rank drugs according to their likely, relative potential for abuse [4]. Drugs that have markedly different levels of abuse in humans can maintain similar levels of responding (e.g., cocaine and diethylpropion, heroin and codeine [4]). Furthermore, substitution patterns can depend on the drug history of the subjects. For example, in PCP-trained monkeys, both memantine and dextromethorphan maintained rates of self-administration above those for saline, indicating PCP-like reinforcing effects [5,6]. However, there is little evidence that these agents would support self-administration behavior in drug-naïve subjects or subjects trained to self-administer drugs other than PCP. For instance, another prototypic NMDA receptor antagonist, MK-801, was found to be self-administered in PCP- but not cocaine-experienced rhesus monkeys [7]. Examples of drugs that have little appreciable abuse liability in humans, but are self-administered by laboratory animals, include procaine and some other local anesthetics [8], antihistamines such as diphenhydramine [9,10], butorphanol [11], nalbuphine [12,13], mazindol [14], nomifensine, and bupropion [15], etc. Such observations suggest that testing in self-administration substitution procedures may occasionally generate predictions of abuse potential when in practice they have little or no abuse liability in humans.

Another reason for the disassociation between predicted and observed abuse potential is that, except for self-administration studies using more complex paradigms such as behavioral economics (e.g., Ref. [16]), current normative methods do not easily support rank-ordering of different drugs in terms of their abuse potential [17]. As the reinforcer is direct stimulation within the reward pathway, ICSS is a direct measure of a drug's effects on the function of brain reward systems [18] and differences in the magnitude of the drug's effects can be ranked relative to known drugs of abuse.

In addition to some false positives, current abuse liability assessment methods may also permit false negatives. Novel drug products often represent pharmacological classes for which limited or no human pharmacology data exist. For example, it may be difficult to relate abuse potential to that of known drug classes and therefore to identify proper training drugs for groups of animals in which substitution tests will be conducted. Further, drug development programs usually aim to identify metabolically stable compounds with longer half-lives. In the context of abuse liability assessment testing, PK properties of drugs can be of critical importance. For drugs with a slow onset of action, delay between the animal's response and the drug's effects may be long enough to prevent successful acquisition of self-administration behavior under standard conditions. For drugs with long half-lives, few drug deliveries would be likely within a test session and at a number that would not easily surpass basal levels of vehicle self-administration. If this is the case, alternative or adjunctive assessment methods may have advantages or may provide additional information to aid in the assessment of abuse potential.

This chapter considers ICSS as an adjunct to more traditional abuse potential assessment methods and argues for it as a potentially valuable tool that could enhance abuse liability assessment of novel pharmaceuticals. ICSS is a paradigm that can be used to quantify brain stimulation reward (BSR). Most drugs of abuse, such as psychostimulants, enhance BSR, while drugs functionally devoid of abuse liability, such as lithium or the neuroleptics, either depress or have irregular effects on BSR. There are several excellent reviews on drug-induced changes in self-stimulation behavior that discuss the utility of this method (e.g., Refs [17,19–24]) and the present chapter does not aim to provide a comprehensive review of the literature. The goal is to briefly review the ICSS paradigm and to identify key factors that distinguish ICSS from drug discrimination and self-administration paradigms in order to highlight how ICSS could contribute to the nonclinical abuse liability assessment of potential drug candidates or existing medications.

3. INTRACRANIAL SELF-STIMULATION

Unlike drug discrimination and self-administration studies, ICSS experiments are conducted almost exclusively in rodents (mostly rats) with virtually no pharmacological studies in primates. ICSS is studied in laboratory animals that have an electrode implanted into the brain. Animals are trained on an operant task (e.g., push a lever, nose [hole] poke, or spin a wheel) that is reinforced by the delivery of electrical stimulation of a specific duration, current frequency, and intensity. There are several brain regions that support operant responding reinforced with ICSS such as the septal area, brainstem, forebrain, and midbrain. Stimulation of so-called brain reward areas such as the medial forebrain bundle (MFB) at the level of the lateral hypothalamus or ventral tegmental area maintain the most robust responding [24–26]. Extensive studies and thorough reviews have discussed the neurobiology underlying the possible mechanisms by which ICSS produces its rewarding effects, and thus, they will not be discussed in great detail here (for additional information readers are referred to Chapter 2 and Refs [20,27–30]).

Briefly, electrical stimulation of the MFB is not thought to result in direct firing of ascending dopaminergic projections, as initially hypothesized, but rather descending firing of myelinated neurons (stage I) that engage stage II dopaminergic dendrites or cell bodies of the VTA and substantia nigra (with possible further projections to the peduculo-pontine and latero-dorsal tegmental nuclei [PPTg and LDTG, respectively]) that subsequently project throughout the mesocorticolimbic system (see Ref. [29] and references within for review).

Drugs of abuse, such as cocaine, amphetamine, opiates, and PCP, enhance BSR, as indicated by a reduction in the threshold frequency or intensity that supports this behavior. That is, it takes less stimulation to support operant responding, and stimulation frequencies or intensities that were previously ineffective are now reinforcing. Conversely, drugs that produce anhedonia or dysphoria, such as neuroleptics, lithium, or κ-opioid receptor agonists [31], decrease BSR, as indicated by an increase in the threshold frequency or intensity that supports this behavior. That is, it takes greater amounts of stimulation to maintain operant responding, and stimulation frequencies or intensities that were previously effective are no longer reinforcing.

A number of methods have been developed for detecting the lowest current intensity of stimulation, train duration, or pulse frequency that maintains response rates above criteria levels. One of the popular discrete-trial titration methods is based on the classical psychophysical method of limits. Within each trial, a response-noncontingent electrical stimulus is presented, followed by a response window of several seconds within which the subject can make a response to receive a second stimulus identical to the initial noncontingent stimulus [32,33]. At each stimulus intensity, there are several trials and, if the subject responds to the majority of the presented stimuli (e.g., at least three out of five trials), the stimulation current intensity is reduced (Figure 8.1). If the subject does not respond sufficiently (e.g., two out of five trials or less) then the current intensity is

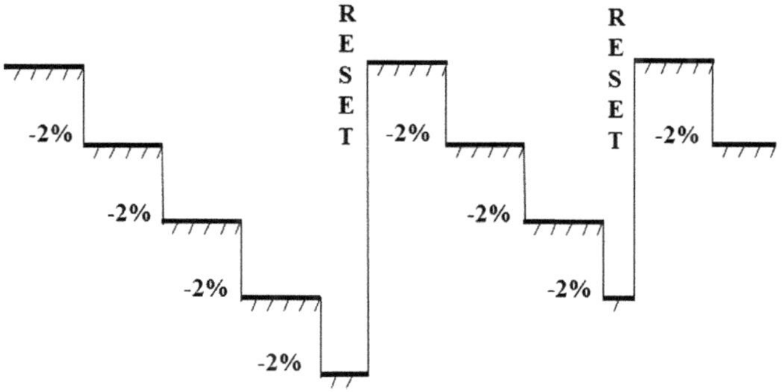

Figure 8.1 ***Auto-titration procedure.*** Based on the classical psychophysical method of limits, within each trial, a noncontingent electrical stimulus is presented. The subject then has a response window of several seconds within which to make a response to receive a second stimulus identical to the initial noncontingent stimulus. At each stimulus intensity, there are several trials and, if the subject responds to the majority of the presented stimuli (e.g., at least three out of five trials), the stimulation current intensity is reduced. If the subject does not respond (e.g., two out of five trials or less) then the current intensity is increased for the next set of trials. Thus, there are several alternating series of descending and ascending current intensities. Stimulation thresholds are defined by analyzing the stimulation intensities at which the current intensity progression changes direction.

increased for the next set of trials. Thus, within each session, there are several alternating series of descending and ascending current intensities (usually starting with the descending series). Stimulation thresholds are defined by analyzing the stimulation intensities at which the progression in current intensity changes direction. This procedure was used to study threshold-lowering effects of various drugs of abuse [23].

An example of the free-operant threshold titration procedure is schematically depicted in Figure 8.2. In a typical auto-titration study of this type, operant conditioning boxes are equipped with two levers and rats are trained to press one of the levers to receive electrical stimulation. Every N^{th} stimulation may be programmed to be followed by the reduction in stimulation intensity (e.g., by 2%, as in Figure 8.2). To return the stimulation intensity to the original level, the subject has to press the second "resetting" lever. Under such a protocol, stimulation thresholds (defined as the last intensity the subject responded for prior to "resetting") can be monitored for long periods of time, providing information on the temporal dynamics of the sensitivity of the brain reward system after the drug injection (e.g., Figure 8.4). This procedure was successfully used to characterize the threshold-lowering effects of various drugs of abuse (e.g., Ref. [34]). However, this auto-titration procedure is associated with failures to observe expected reductions in stimulation thresholds. For instance, diazepam [35] and ethanol [36] did not affect self-titrated thresholds. Furthermore, caffeine was found to elevate self-titrated thresholds [37] but had no effects or facilitated ICSS behavior when thresholds were assessed using other methods [38,39].

An alternative to threshold titration is the curve-shift procedure. Subjects are tested under a range of different stimulation intensities (100–500 μA), train and pulse durations (200–500 ms and 0.1 ms, respectively), or frequencies (18–200 Hz) and the results are plotted as a function relating observed response rates versus the manipulated stimulation parameter (Figure 8.3). This can be considered analogous to a pharmacological

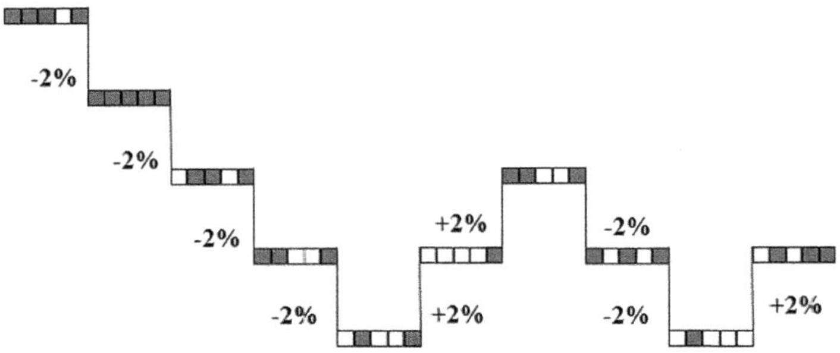

Figure 8.2 ***Discrete-trial titration procedure.*** Operant conditioning boxes are equipped with two operanda (e.g., levers) and rats are trained to press one of the levers to receive electrical stimulation. Every N^{th} stimulation may be programmed to be followed by the reduction in stimulation intensity (e.g., by 2%). To return the stimulation intensity to the original level, the subject has to press the second "resetting" lever. Under such protocol, threshold is defined at the mean intensity in which the rat "resets."

"dose effect" function. The primary dependent variable in these experiments is the stimulation intensity or frequency that is associated with the calculated threshold (Theta-0, T_0) or locus of rise (LOR). These parameters can be calculated [40]. Threshold is defined as the minimum amount of simulation required to maintain operant responding. That is, the stimulation intensity or frequency at which the rate–stimulation curve theoretically crosses the *x*-axis [18]. LOR is the mathematical inflection point of the rate–stimulation curve [28,41,42] (see Figure 8.3). This calculated parameter is highly sensitive to the effects of drugs of abuse that had been repeatedly reported to

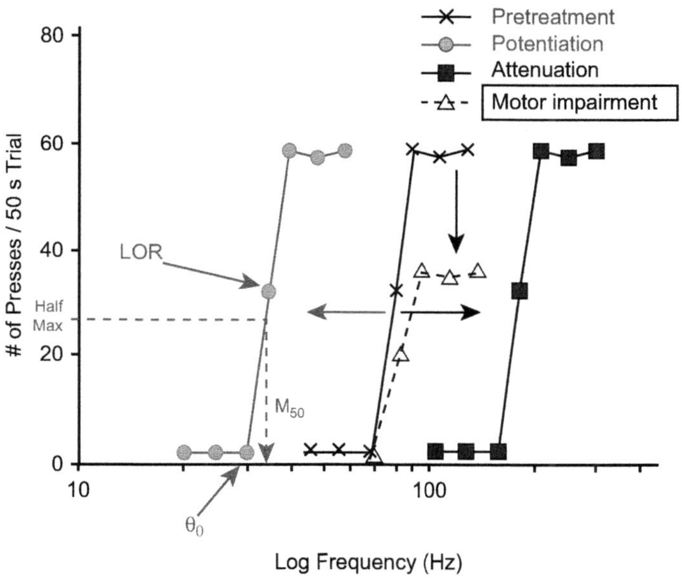

Figure 8.3 ***Curve-shift paradigm.*** In this hypothetical schematic, the center line (X) represents a baseline rate–frequency curve where at high frequencies rats will self-stimulate to receive short 0.5 s bursts of cathodal current. Rats are allowed to self-stimulate for each frequency, beginning with the highest, for 50 s and the number of "presses" is recorded (the number of stimulations is also recorded, but emphasis is placed on how much the rat is willing to work for the stimulation, thus the number of presses is plotted). As the frequency is decreased, the magnitude of the reward is also decreased, resulting in fewer presses until the frequency is no longer rewarding and the rat does not self-stimulate. As indicated by the leftward arrow and left curve (●), when a drug with rewarding properties is administered, the rate–frequency curve is shifted to the left, indicating that frequencies that were previously nonrewarding are rewarding (enhanced or potentiated BSR). Conversely, when a drug with anhedonic properties is administered, as indicated by the rightward arrow and right curve (■), the curve is shifted to the right, indicating that frequencies that were previously rewarding are no longer rewarding. As described in the text, calculations of either M_{50}, LOR, or θ_0 yield a numeric value of BSR from the *x*-axis, and changes in those values directly relate to changes in BSR induced by drug administration. Finally, as indicated by the dashed curve (Δ), a decrease in response rate using this paradigm is less prone to false interpretation as LOR and θ_0 are not appreciably affected. Response rate (M_{50}) is likely to provide a less reliable result, depending on the drug-induced motor impairment, as indicated by the magnitude of the downward arrow.

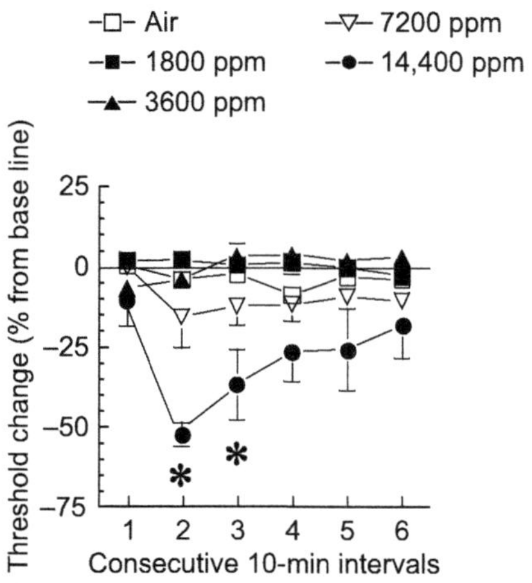

Figure 8.4 ***Time-course of the effects of benzine on stimulation current thresholds for intracranial self-stimulation behavior under an auto-titration procedure.*** Tests were conducted before (10-min pretest) and during the 60-min exposure to the solvents. Data are presented as self-titrated thresholds expressed as the % change from the pretest level. *$P < 0.05$ (Dunnett's test), compared to control exposure to atmospheric air. $n = 5$ for each data point. *Reproduced with permission from Ref. [39].*

shift the curve to the left. This is clearly a response-independent procedure because drugs that reduce operant output—yet have little or no impact on rewarding properties of the stimulation—are expected to produce downward shifts in the curve without affecting T_0 or LOR.

4. PREDICTIVE VALIDITY OF INTRACRANIAL SELF-STIMULATION METHODS

Since the original demonstration of ICSS in 1954 by Olds and Milner [25,43], there have been hundreds of studies conducted with the aim of characterizing the rewarding effects of pharmacological agents. As shown in Table 8.1, drugs that are known to have abuse liability in humans typically facilitate self-stimulation behavior (abuse potential) in animal studies. The list of abused drugs includes nicotine [44], ethanol [45], and THC [46], drugs that are self-administered by animals under certain circumstances (e.g., pretraining to self-administer another drug or under food reinforcement schedule, etc.) and are found to facilitate ICSS behavior only when certain experimental conditions are used (see below). Conversely, self-stimulation behavior is not affected by memantine [47] and butorphanol (Bespalov, Zvartau, unpublished data)—that are known false-positives from self-administration studies. However, similar to self-administration studies, ICSS is not sensitive to LSD-like drugs (Bespalov, unpublished data) but is facilitated by some antihistamine drugs such as tripelennamine [48] as well as by some antidepressants such as bupropion [49]. These examples indicate that, when compared to other methods, ICSS has

Table 8.1 Drugs Abused by Humans

	Abused by Humans[a]	Self-Administration[b]	Self-Stimulation[c]
Psychostimulants			
• Cocaine	Yes	Yes	Yes
• Amphetamine	Yes	Yes	Yes
• MDMA	Yes	Yes	Yes
• Modafinil	No	Yes	Yes
• Methylcathinone	Yes	Yes	Yes
• Ephedrine	No	Yes	No
Antidepressants			
• Tricyclics	(No)	No	No
• MAO inhibitors	No	No	No
• SSRIs	No	No	No
• Bupropion	No	Yes	Yes
Opioids			
• Heroin/morphine	Yes	Yes	Yes
• Methadone	Yes	Yes	Yes
• Butorphanol	No	Yes	No
Sedative-Hypnotics			
• Ethanol	Yes	Yes	Yes
• Benzodiazepines	Yes	Yes	Yes
• Barbiturates	Yes	Yes	Yes
• GHB	Yes	No	Yes
PCP-Like Drugs			
• PCP	Yes	Yes	Yes
• Ketamine	Yes	Yes	No
• Memantine	No	Yes	No
• Dextromethorphan	(Yes)[e]	Yes	No
Hallucinogens			
• LSD	Yes	No	No
• Mescaline	Yes	No	No
Other			
• Nicotine	Yes	Yes	Yes
• Cannabinoids	Yes	Yes	Yes[d]
• Solvents	Yes	Yes?	Yes
• Caffeine	Yes	Yes	No
• Antihistamines	(Yes)[e]	Yes	Yes

[a]Based on reports of nonmedical use/abuse but not human self-administration studies.
[b]Yes–the drug maintains responding at levels above those for saline. Only one, usually the earliest, report is identified unless there have been conflicts.
[c]Ability of the drug(s) to facilitate ICSS behavior acutely (any of the known response-independent estimates).
[d]Conflicting reports exist.
[e](Yes)–may differ for various members of a class; mixed reports; abuse in a narrow population.

comparable ability to predict abuse liability. As mentioned above, the majority of normative self-administration studies have been conducted using a single fixed-ratio schedule of reinforcement, a protocol unable, by itself, to order the relative reinforcing value among drugs. Conversely, there may be more consistency in the predictive validity between ICSS and self-administration studies conducted using a progressive-ratio schedule of reinforcement, as this paradigm examines the motivational aspects of a test compound, that is, how much the subject is willing to work to obtain the drug [17]. In a progressive-ratio schedule, rats are required to press a lever using an incremental fixed ratio, and the highest obtained ratio is considered the "break point," that is, the highest ratio of responding that the subject is willing to perform for a single infusion. As an example, under a fixed-ratio schedule of reinforcement, tramadol is self-administered comparable to morphine, however, when examined under a progressive-ratio schedule of reinforcement, the break point for tramadol is considerably lower than that of morphine [50] (Table 8.2).

Apart from fairly robust predictive validity, a major advantage of ICSS is that the outcome of these studies is usually found to be less affected by PK properties of drugs. First, drugs of abuse reduce ICSS thresholds after their delivery through various routes of administration, including intravenous, subcutaneous, oral, etc. For example, abused solvents such as toluene and benzine are usually abused via inhalation, and laboratory studies have examined ICSS while being conducted in a solvent-enriched atmosphere [39]. The route of administration is not a limiting factor in drug discrimination studies; however, drug discrimination tests require a priori knowledge of the test drug's pharmacodynamics in order

Table 8.2 Self-Stimulation versus Conventional Abuse Liability Assessment Methods

	Drug Discrimination	Self-Administration	Self-Stimulation
Ease of use	High	Low-to-moderate	Low-to-moderate
Cross-lab reliability	High	High	Potentially high[a]
Within-lab reliability	High	High	High
Predictive validity	Moderate	Moderate	Moderate
Face validity	Low	High	Low
Construct validity	Low[b]	High	High
Pharmacological reversal of drug effects	Highly suited	Requires extensive dose–effect analysis	Highly suited
Synergism/additivity between drugs	Detectable	Not under standard conditions	Highly suited
Possibility of abuse liability quantitation	Low	Moderate	Moderate-to-high
Sensitivity to PK properties of drugs[c]	Not sensitive[d]	Sensitive	Not sensitive[d]

[a]Requires standardization of the experimental protocols.
[b]Discrimination behavior is not necessarily based on addiction-related effects of drugs.
[c]Onset of action, half-life.
[d]Experimental protocols can be easily adjusted in response to PK properties of drugs.

to match it with suitable training drugs. Self-administration substitution studies have largely been limited to using intravenous administration to date, and engineering them for other routes of administration would be daunting. Somewhat connected with this observation is that ICSS tests can be conducted with a much broader range of drug formulations, while self-administration studies are limited to those drug formulations that are safe for intravenous administration, can support high enough concentrations of the drug, and permit safe volumes of administration. Second, because ICSS is not satiating like other reinforcers such as food, and is not cumulative, behavioral responding remains stable for long periods of time and allows for the evaluation of test compounds with short or long half-lives and/or slow or long onset of action (Figure 8.4).

Self-stimulation behavior usually remains fairly stable not only within the session but also across days of training and months of testing. Although this may seem counterintuitive based on the current knowledge of the mesolimbic dopaminergic system (see below), there is hardly any evidence of satiation, tolerance, or sensitization to the stimulation. Furthermore, the repeated application of abused drugs does not usually lead to any appreciable signs of tolerance or sensitization when assessed using ICSS methods [51,52]. The reasons underlying this discrepancy are not known, but molecular adaptations could underlie this phenomenon [53]. Regardless, ICSS studies can safely utilize a within-subjects design with multiple tests administered in each subject over long periods of time.

5. FACTORS LIMITING THE USE OF INTRACRANIAL SELF-STIMULATION METHODS FOR ABUSE LIABILITY ASSESSMENT PURPOSES

Given the positive features of ICSS discussed above, the reader may wonder why it does not have more widespread use in the assessment of abuse potential of novel pharmaceuticals during the drug development process, especially given the current rapid expansion of research in ICSS. First, the application of well-established research models to the drug development process is in its infancy. The facilitatory effects of drugs of abuse on self-stimulation behavior appear more difficult to comprehend when compared to the perspective of drug self-administration that can be more readily seen as being homologous to human drug seeking and drug taking. It is usually explained that drugs of abuse "activate" brain reward pathways that facilitate the control of behavior by electrical stimulation of these brain areas. Such interpretation is fully consistent with the current knowledge of neurochemical and neuroanatomical mechanisms of the effects of abused drugs. More specifically, most currently known drugs of abuse are recognized to enhance dopaminergic processes (Chapter 2), and these effects involve, directly or indirectly, projections from dopaminergic cell bodies in the midbrain to the forebrain's ventral striatum, the same pathways that are directly engaged during ICSS experiments [24].

Interestingly, there are a number of nondrug stimuli that also facilitate dopaminergic processes in these pathways (e.g., novelty, acute noxious stimulation). However, at behaviorally nondisrupting exposure levels, these nondrug stimuli have inconsistent effects on ICSS, suggesting that the facilitation of ICSS requires the coapplication of more powerful stimuli that enhance dopaminergic activity but do not interfere with behavioral performance. The need for the stimuli to be fairly strong in order to facilitate ICSS behavior sets certain sensitivity limits.

Second, one of the main obstacles in advancing ICSS as a valid and robust abuse potential assessment method is the lack of standardized procedures that would help to ensure that data generated in different laboratories is comparable and reproducible. There are a number of methodological details that often make an ICSS study unique to the laboratory of origin:

1. Brain site into which the electrode is implanted: Sites along the MFB (including lateral hypothalamus sites) and the ventral tegmental area are associated with the strongest effects of stimulation and the lowest levels of ambivalence [24]. The stimulation site may also determine the pharmacology of the self-stimulation behavior [54].
2. Response rate versus stimulation threshold: While the initial studies primarily assessed changes in response rates induced by drugs, and some laboratories still use this or a variant (likely due to the ease of use in calculations), it is quite clear that changes in response rate often reflect nonspecific changes in operant performance. A hypothetical example that illustrates this confound is if the rate of responding was decreased by increasing the weight of the lever (i.e., increasing the tripping force required) that would unlikely impact the BSR threshold. Thus, if a test drug induced a decrease in response rates, it is quite possible that motor impairment is independent of the rewarding effects of drugs of abuse, such as morphine when initially tested [55]. Instead, more relevant are rate-independent measures such as stimulation thresholds or locus of rise (T0 and LOR; see above) when using a curve-shift paradigm.
3. Reinforcement parameters: Reward magnitude can be controlled as a function of stimulation intensity or frequency. It is argued that the current intensity controls the size of the effective stimulation field (i.e., changing the reinforcer), and the manipulation of the stimulation frequency is often preferred in pharmacological studies (i.e., changing the magnitude of the reinforcer) [24]. It can also be easily envisioned that an increase in the current intensity not only increases the effective stimulation of the intended anatomical pathway (in which the electrode is implanted), but the increased size of an electric field would also affect increasingly larger anatomical regions with neuronal pathways residing in close proximity (which would not be affected by a lower intensity), raising again the issue of anatomical site(s) in question (as detailed in item 1 above).
4. Other manipulated stimulation parameters: The shape of the pulses (e.g., square wave, sine wave), the polarity, the duration of the pulse train, or the manipulandum can, and

often are, different across laboratories. With regard to the manipulandum, the type chosen likely does not significantly affect the impact in measuring BSR. With regard to the shape and polarity of the pulses, it has been fairly well established that square wave cathodal current is preferable as it yields a reliable and consistent rate of responding (see Refs [18,27,28,56,57]).

Such diversity of methodological approaches is certainly a major issue that seriously prevents the implementation of standardized techniques across laboratories and the likely consistency of reported results. However, understanding this problem leads to its solution. With regard to brain sites, there is sufficient evidence, as outlined above, to suggest that stimulation of the MFB at the level of the lateral hypothalamus would be an ideal and universal location. Similarly, there is sufficient evidence to suggest that a model that utilizes a more relevant rate-independent measure, such as a discrete-trial or rate–frequency curve shift paradigm, would be optimal. Lastly, also as outlined above, due to the possibility that changes in the current intensity essentially change the reinforcer, altering the frequency would be preferred as it only changes the magnitude of the reinforcer.

Similar to what was done for the self-administration substitution procedure [4], it needs to be established whether the results generated using a variety of self-stimulation procedures are comparable across different laboratories and whether these procedures need to be standardized. Criteria for evaluating the results of such efforts are fairly easy to define—for example, in terms of quantitative differences within a series of selected reference compounds of interest. Why would someone want to do that? Clearly, the ultimate goal would be to establish the utility of ICSS as an additional method for characterizing the abuse potential of compounds.

Several PK advantages of ICSS procedures were identified above. However, also mentioned above is that as of this writing, ICSS procedures have mainly been confined to rodents, and then mainly to rats, which identifies a PK disadvantage as well. Few successful ICSS attempts have been reported using primates. The near absence of primate ICSS studies is a current limitation of ICSS procedures when involving drugs in which test animal-to-man PK consistency is critical and is most often achieved using nonhuman primates (see Refs [58–60]).

Another potential major limitation of ICSS procedures in abuse potential assessment could pertain to situations in which multiple drugs are administered. In ICSS procedures the subject does not control drug administration as it is administered independent of its behavior by the experimenter. It is well recognized that passive versus active drug administration can result in dramatic differences in neurotransmitter dynamics, gene expression, and protein expression (for review see Ref. [61]). Given the dramatic differences that can result in brain states by passive versus active drug administration, it is unclear what the interpretation of ICSS results should be when one drug is administered and modifies ongoing ICSS-related behavior associated with another drug, such as during the assessment of medications for treating drug abuse disorders.

6. SUMMARY

It is generally accepted that there is a broad range of drugs that potentially warrant abuse liability assessment [62]. Indeed, any drug that enters the CNS or that can affect the CNS may initially be viewed as having a potential risk for abuse and is considered subject to abuse liability testing (FDA Draft Guidance: *Assessment of Abuse Potential of Drugs, January 2010* [63]). As there is no single test or assessment procedure that completely characterizes the abuse liability of a drug (p. S56 in Ref. [64]), nonclinical abuse liability assessment is based on using several experimental approaches. While it is often said that "animal models and procedures for assessing abuse liability are well established" (p. S109 in Ref. [62]), standard and reliable abuse potential assessment algorithms exist only for classical types of abused drugs (e.g., Table 1 in Ref. [2]) but not for potential therapeutic agents with novel mechanisms of action, nor is the intensive, thorough, and open-ended use of models/procedures in a research setting applicable for use in the more constrained and time-sensitive drug development process with differing target goals for medications.

The identification of novel targets for drug discovery and associated novel biology is not the only challenge to safety evaluation methods and not the only argument for searching for novel methods with improved predictive validation. For instance, during drug development an objective could be to modify drug formulation parameters for developing products with more desirable clinical kinetics (e.g., slower onset/protracted effect [62]). Thus, pressures to develop strategies to test the abuse potential of such novel drug formulations will favor evaluations of methods like ICSS that are very well suited for addressing such questions.

One of the research priorities indicated by the Expert Panel of the College on Problems of Drug Dependence [62] was that "research should be undertaken on models for predicting abuse liability in the intended patient population in order to determine abuse risk and determinants of iatrogenic addiction." An important aspect of such models is that the doses and patterns of drug administration should approximate those expected for clinical use. In other words, drugs should be given once or twice daily over a number of days at the doses where therapeutic efficacy is expected. ICSS is a method that is favorable to these treatment regimens and will allow the evaluation of drug effects at clinically relevant exposure levels. However, clinical assessments of abuse liability in the intended patient population that may be naïve to a drug of abuse per se pose other issues (see Chapter 9). Additionally, the potential abuse by the "intended patient population" does not address issues of prescription diversion and misuse/abuse by those who are not the patient (e.g., teenage children of adult patients, abuse in "rave parties," etc. in which the number of pills abused may be multiples of the intended therapeutic dosage). However, ICSS can be used to evaluate both regimens mimicking that of the intended patient population as well as misdirection and potential abuse at multiples of the relevant clinical exposure.

Finally, with more and more compounds going through abuse liability assessment, at some point conclusions on the abuse potential of a given compound should become less qualitative and involve quantitative evaluation, as it is done in other areas of safety evaluation, in order to properly rank and/or categorize the abuse liability of novel pharmaceuticals relative to known drugs of abuse for their respective scheduling (I to V) by the Drug Enforcement Administration (see Chapter 10). ICSS methodology is arguably a paradigm that offers a convenient approach for setting such quantitative criteria; as mentioned above, direct values are quantified in changes in BSR upon drug administration.

The inclusion of ICSS during abuse liability assessment has the potential to enhance our nonclinical ability to assess a drug's abuse potential. As discussed above, standardization of the experimental protocols and assessment of its predictive utility for making regulatory decisions are needed to reach a final conclusion on the utility of ICSS in psychopharmacological research [2], a goal that is relatively easy to obtain in a short-term realm of possibility.

REFERENCES

[1] Food and Drug Administration. The future of drug safety: promoting and protecting the health of the public: FDA's Response to the Institute of Medicine's 2006 Report. US Dept of Health and Human Services; January 2007. http://www.fda.gov/oc/reports/iom013007.html.

[2] Balster RL, Bigelow GE. Guidelines and methodological reviews concerning drug abuse liability assessment. Drug Alcohol Depend 2003;70:S13–40.

[3] Isbell H. The search for the nonaddicting analgesic: has it been worth it? Clin Pharmacol Ther 1977;22:377–84.

[4] Johanson CE, Balster RL. A summary of the results of a drug self-administration study using substitution procedures in rhesus monkeys. Bull Narc 1978;30:43–54.

[5] Nicholson KL, Jones HE, Balster RL. Evaluation of the reinforcing and discriminative stimulus properties of the low-affinity *N*-methyl-D-aspartate channel blocker memantine. Behav Pharmacol 1998;9:231–43.

[6] Nicholson KL, Hayes BA, Balster RL. Evaluation of the reinforcing properties and phencyclidine-like discriminative stimulus effects of dextromethorphan and dextrorphan in rats and rhesus monkeys. Psychopharmacol Berl 1999;146:49–59.

[7] Beardsley PM, Hayes BA, Balster RL. The self-administration of MK-801 can depend upon drug-reinforcement history, and its discriminative stimulus properties are phencyclidine-like in rhesus monkeys. J Pharmacol Exp Ther 1990;252:953–9.

[8] Woolverton WL, Balster RL. Behavioral pharmacology of local anesthetics: reinforcing and discriminative stimulus effects. Pharmacol Biochem Behav 1982;16:491–500.

[9] Bergman J, Spealman RD. Some behavioral effects of histamine H1 antagonists in squirrel monkeys. J Pharmacol Exp Ther 1986;239:104–10.

[10] Beardsley PM, Balster RL. The intravenous self-administration of antihistamines by rhesus monkeys. Drug Alcohol Depend 1992;30:117–26.

[11] Butelman ER, Winger G, Zernig G, Woods JH. Butorphanol: characterization of agonist and antagonist effects in rhesus monkeys. J Pharmacol Exp Ther 1995;272:845–53.

[12] Balster RL, Lukas SE. Review of self-administration. Drug Alcohol Depend 1985;14:249–61.

[13] Steinfels GF, Young GA, Khazan N. Self-administration of nalbuphine, butorphanol and pentazocine by morphine post-addict rats. Pharmacol Biochem Behav 1982;16:167–71.

[14] Wilson MC, Schuster CR. Mazindol self-administration in the rhesus monkey. Pharmacol Biochem Behav 1976;4:207–10.

[15] Bergman J, Madras BK, Johnson SE, Spealman RD. Effects of cocaine and related drugs in nonhuman primates. III. Self-administration by squirrel monkeys. J Pharmacol Exp Ther 1989;251:150–5.
[16] Winger G, Galuska CM, Hursh SR, Woods JH. Relative reinforcing effects of cocaine, remifentanil, and their combination in rhesus monkeys. J Pharmacol Exp Ther 2006;318:223–9.
[17] Negus SS, Miller LL. Intracranial self-stimulation to evaluate abuse potential of drugs. Pharmacol Rev 2014;66:869–917.
[18] Carlezon Jr WA, Chartoff EH. Intracranial self-stimulation (ICSS) in rodents to study the neurobiology of motivation. Nat Protoc 2007;2:2987–95.
[19] Kornetsky C. Brain-stimulation reward: a model for the neuronal bases for drug-induced euphoria. NIDA Res Monogr 1985;62:30–50.
[20] Stellar JR, Rice MB. Pharmacological basis of intracranial self-stimulation reward. In: Cooper SJ, Liebman JM, editors. Topics in experimental psychopharmacology. Oxford: Clarendon Press; 1989. p. 14–65.
[21] Schaefer GJ, Michael RP. Schedule-controlled brain self-stimulation: has it utility for behavioral pharmacology? Neurosci Biobehav Rev 1992;16:569–83.
[22] Liebman JM. Discriminating between reward and performance: a critical review of intracranial self-stimulation methodology. Neurosci Biobehav Rev 1983;7:45–72.
[23] Kornetsky C, Bain G. Brain-stimulation reward: a model for the study of the rewarding effects of abused drugs. NIDA Res Monogr 1992;124:73–93.
[24] Wise RA. Addictive drugs and brain stimulation reward. Annu Rev Neurosci 1996;19:319–40.
[25] Olds J, Milner P. Positive reinforcement produced by electrical stimulation of septal area and other regions of rat brain. J Comp Physiol Psychol 1954;47:419–27.
[26] Olds J. Self-stimulation of the brain; its use to study local effects of hunger, sex, and drugs. Science 1958;127:315–24.
[27] Shizgal P, Murray B. Neuronal basis of intracranial self-stimulation. In: Liebman JM, editor. Neuropharmacological basis of reward. New York: Oxford University Press; 1989. p. 106–63.
[28] Stellar JR, Stellar E. The neurobiology of motivation and reward. New York: Springer-Verlag; 1985. [Ref Type: Book, Whole].
[29] Wise RA. Drug-activation of brain reward pathways. Drug Alcohol Depend 1998;51:13–22.
[30] Yeomans JS. Two substrates for medial forebrain bundle self-stimulation: myelinated axons and dopamine axons. Neurosci Biobehav Rev 1989;13:91–8.
[31] Todtenkopf MS, Marcus JF, Portoghese PS, Carlezon Jr WA. Effects of kappa-opioid receptor ligands on intracranial self-stimulation in rats. Psychopharmacol Berl 2004;172:463–70.
[32] Kornetsky C, Esposito RU. Euphorigenic drugs: effects on the reward pathways of the brain. Fed Proc 1979;38:2473–6.
[33] Markou A, Koob GF. Bromocriptine reverses the elevation in intracranial self-stimulation thresholds observed in a rat model of cocaine withdrawal. Neuropsychopharmacology 1992;7:213–24.
[34] Schaefer GJ, Holtzman SG. Free-operant and auto-titration brain self-stimulation procedures in the rat: a comparison of drug effects. Pharmacol Biochem Behav 1979;10:127–35.
[35] Ichimaru Y, Moriyama M, Gomita Y. Auto-titration technique using intracranial self-stimulation and effects of antianxiety drugs. Jpn J Pharmacol 1985;39:331–8.
[36] Schaefer GJ, Michael RP. Ethanol and current thresholds for brain self-stimulation in the lateral hypothalamus of the rat. Alcohol 1987;4:209–13.
[37] Mumford GK, Neill DB, Holtzman SG. Caffeine elevates reinforcement threshold for electrical brain stimulation: tolerance and withdrawal changes. Brain Res 1988;459:163–7.
[38] Bespalov A, Lebedev A, Panchenko G, Zvartau E. Effects of abused drugs on thresholds and breaking points of intracranial self-stimulation in rats. Eur Neuropsychopharmacol 1999;9:377–83.
[39] Bespalov A, Sukhotina I, Medvedev I, Malyshkin A, Belozertseva I, Balster R, et al. Facilitation of electrical brain self-stimulation behavior by abused solvents. Pharmacol Biochem Behav 2003;75:199–208.
[40] Coulombe D, Miliaressis E. Fitting intracranial self-stimulation data with growth models. Behav Neurosci 1987;101:209–14.
[41] Edmonds DE, Gallistel CR. Parametric analysis of brain stimulation reward in the rat: III. Effect of performance variables on the reward summation function. J Comp Physiol Psychol 1974;87:876–83.

[42] Stellar JR, Kelley AE, Corbett D. Effects of peripheral and central dopamine blockade on lateral hypothalamic self-stimulation: evidence for both reward and motor deficits. Pharmacol Biochem Behav 1983;18:433–42.
[43] Milner PM. The discovery of self-stimulation and other stories. Neurosci Biobehav Rev 1989;13:61–7.
[44] Huston-Lyons D, Kornetsky C. Effects of nicotine on the threshold for rewarding brain stimulation in rats. Pharmacol Biochem Behav 1992;41:755–9.
[45] Kornetsky C, Bain GT, Unterwald EM, Lewis MJ. Brain stimulation reward: effects of ethanol. Alcohol Clin Exp Res 1988;12:609–16.
[46] Gardner EL, Paredes W, Smith D, Donner A, Milling C, Cohen D, et al. Facilitation of brain stimulation reward by delta 9-tetrahydrocannabinol. Psychopharmacol Berl 1988;96:142–4.
[47] Tzschentke TM, Schmidt WJ. Memantine does not substantially affect brain stimulation reward: comparison with MK-801. Brain Res 1999;845:192–8.
[48] Unterwald EM, Kucharski LT, Williams JE, Kornetsky C. Tripelennamine: enhancement of brain-stimulation reward. Life Sci 1984;34:149–53.
[49] Cryan JF, Bruijnzeel AW, Skjei KL, Markou A. Bupropion enhances brain reward function and reverses the affective and somatic aspects of nicotine withdrawal in the rat. Psychopharmacol Berl 2003;168:347–58.
[50] O'Connor EC, Mead AN. Tramadol acts as a weak reinforcer in the rat self-administration model, consistent with its low abuse liability in humans. Pharmacol Biochem Behav 2010;96:279–86.
[51] Bozarth MA, Pudiak CM, KuoLee R. Effect of chronic nicotine on brain stimulation reward. I. Effect of daily injections. Behav Brain Res 1998;96:185–8.
[52] Carlezon Jr WA, Wise RA. Phencyclidine-induced potentiation of brain stimulation reward: acute effects are not altered by repeated administration. Psychopharmacol Berl 1993;111:402–8.
[53] Carlezon Jr WA, Todtenkopf MS, McPhie DL, Pimentel P, Pliakas AM, Stellar JR, et al. Repeated exposure to rewarding brain stimulation downregulates GluR1 expression in the ventral tegmental area. Neuropsychopharmacology 2001;25:234–41.
[54] Herberg LJ, Stephens DN, Franklin KB. Catecholamines and self-stimulation: evidence suggesting a reinforcing role for noradrenaline and a motivating role for dopamine. Pharmacol Biochem Behav 1976;4:575–82.
[55] O'Neill KS, Todtenkopf MS. Using a rate-frequency curve method to assess the rewarding properties of morphine in the intracranial self-stimulation paradigm in rats. J Neurosci Methods 2010;189:75–9.
[56] Vlachou S, Nomikos GG, Stephens DN, Panagis G. Lack of evidence for appetitive effects of Delta 9-tetrahydrocannabinol in the intracranial self-stimulation and conditioned place preference procedures in rodents. Behav Pharmacol 2007;18:311–9.
[57] Yeomans JS. "Temporal summation decay" in hypothalamic self-stimulation: threshold changes at long intrapair intervals due to axonal subnormal periods. Behav Neurosci 1990;104:991–9.
[58] Ward KW, Nagilla R, Jolivette LJ. Comparative evaluation of oral systemic exposure of 56 xenobiotics in rat, dog, monkey and human. Xenobiotica 2005;35:191–210.
[59] Ward KW, Smith BR. A comprehensive quantitative and qualitative evaluation of extrapolation of intravenous pharmacokinetic parameters from rat, dog, and monkey to humans. I. Clearance. Drug Metab Dispos 2004;32:603–11.
[60] Ward KW, Smith BR. A comprehensive quantitative and qualitative evaluation of extrapolation of intravenous pharmacokinetic parameters from rat, dog, and monkey to humans. II. Volume of distribution and mean residence time. Drug Metab Dispos 2004;32:612–9.
[61] Jacobs EH, Smit AB, de Vries TJ, Schoffelmeer AN. Neuroadaptive effects of active versus passive drug administration in addiction research. Trends Pharmacol Sci 2003;24:566–73.
[62] Abuse liability assessment of CNS drugs: conclusions, recommendations, and research priorities. Drug Alcohol Depend 2003;70:S107–14.
[63] Mansbach RS, Feltner DE, Gold LH, Schnoll SH. Incorporating the assessment of abuse liability into the drug discovery and development process. Drug Alcohol Depend 2003;70:S73–85.
[64] Ator NA, Griffiths RR. Principles of drug abuse liability assessment in laboratory animals. Drug Alcohol Depend 2003;70:S55–72.

CHAPTER 9

Clinical Evaluation of Abuse Potential for New Pharmaceuticals: The Assessment of Abuse Potential during Drug Development

Suzanne K. Vosburg, Marta Sokolowska
Grünenthal USA Inc., Bedminster, NJ, USA

Contents

Data generated from animal models are an invaluable source of predictive information that corresponds to human drug-taking behavior [1]. However, these data cannot be fully employed to predict abuse liability without consideration of data collected from the human abuse potential study [2]. Therefore, this chapter focuses on the conduct of the human abuse potential study in the regulatory paradigm.

A conceptual overlap exists between the terms "abuse potential" and "abuse liability." Both terms are used to distinguish the qualities of drugs that may lead to abuse. Here, we refer to abuse potential as the ability of a drug to produce positive subjective or reinforcing effects [3,4]. Thus, a drug having abuse potential in humans suggests that the drug in question may be sought after for nonmedical reasons and taken for the effects that it produces [5–7].

Nonclinical Assessment of Abuse Potential for New Pharmaceuticals
http://dx.doi.org/10.1016/B978-0-12-420172-9.00009-6

As mentioned in the Foreword, the determination as to whether or not a drug has abuse potential is a critical charge both for the pharmaceutical industry and the Food and Drug Administration (FDA). In an effort to clarify this process, the FDA designed a Draft Decision Tree for the Assessment of Abuse Potential ([8,9]; see Figure 1 for a summary graph). This graphic depicts that the decision path may not be linear for every drug, namely because an abuse potential signal can emerge at any time during drug development. An indication that a drug may have abuse potential can occur before it is tested in humans, such as during the establishment of the preclinical in vitro or in vivo profiles. It may be discovered that the chemistry, receptor binding, functional binding, or pharmacokinetic (PK) profile are similar to a known drug of abuse, or the drug may produce an overt abuse-related behavior in animals (such as drug-taking or drug-seeking) prior to an actual abuse potential study [8–12]. Such preclinical discoveries would warrant the conduct of the preclinical abuse liability assessments. If an abuse signal emerges during this set of studies, a human abuse potential trial may be warranted. If the initial preclinical work takes place without the determination of abuse potential, no dedicated abuse potential trials may be required, although evaluation of abuse potential is always ongoing (for instance, via adverse events or drug accountability). Thus, the goal of the decision tree is to depict the process and thinking behind abuse potential assessment and the manner in which the decision points are reached and considered.

Formally, an abuse potential assessment is required by the FDA if the drug acts on the central nervous system (CNS), is chemically or pharmacologically similar to other drugs with known abuse potential, or produces psychoactive effects such as sedation, euphoria, or mood changes in humans ([5], Section IIIB; [13,14]). Although the human abuse potential trial is not the only source of information when characterizing a drug,

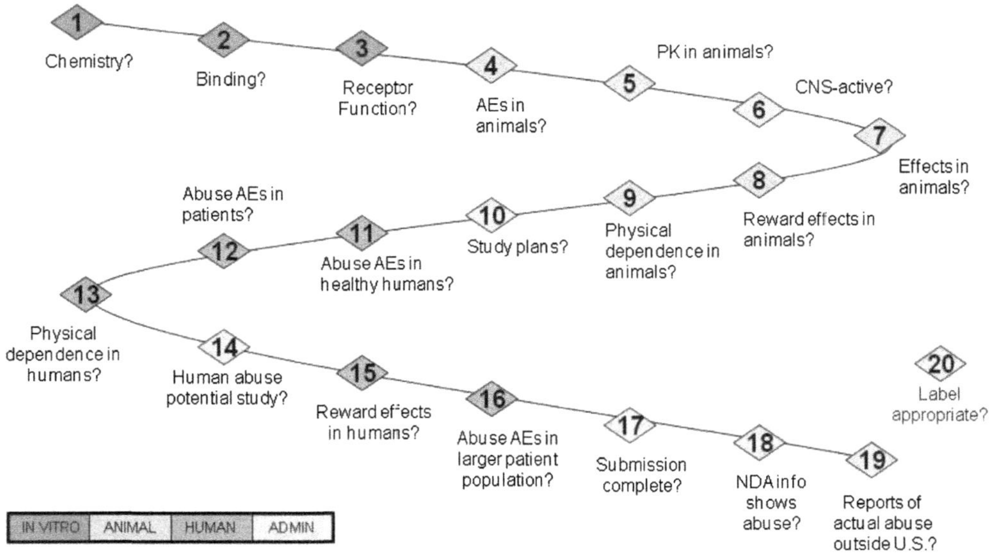

Figure 1 The FDA abuse potential assessment decision tree (ROADMAP).

given the increased awareness of drug abuse and the accompanying public health considerations, an incomplete evaluation of abuse potential in humans in the New Drug Application (NDA) will likely delay the development and perhaps the approval of a drug [4]. Thus, the design and conduct of the human abuse potential trial is a critical piece in any application where it is warranted [4,6,12,13,15,16].

Abuse liability is used as a broader term incorporating abuse potential as well as the assessment of social and economic factors involved in the interplay surrounding human consumption [3,4]. This can include the indication addressed by the drug, the ease of manufacturing the drug, availability, context of use, social perception of use of the drug, or risk of nonmedical use, for example. In toto, abuse liability spans more than the subjective and reinforcing properties of the drug and conveys what happens when the drug comes into contact with humans across multiple situations and environments.

There is a considerable amount of literature addressing the study of abuse liability in humans. It is notable that the 2003 supplement to Drug and Alcohol Dependence is currently one of the most often cited sources in this area (Vol 70, Supplement 3, particularly [6,13,15,17,18]). Also commonly cited are the 1991 issue of the British Journal on Addictions (Vol 86, Issue 12, particularly [12,19–31]), NIDA monographs [32,33], IMMPACT statements [34,35], the 2006 supplemental issue of Drug and Alcohol Dependence on formulations (Vol 83, Supplement 1), and reviews [36–47], to name but a few.

And yet, when considering the conduct of human abuse potential trials and the decisions that must be made within the regulatory paradigm, there are few sources that explicate this process. As such, the need for elucidation still exists [48,49]. Guidelines have been suggested by the FDA, both for abuse liability in general ([5,16], summarized in Table 1), and for abuse deterrent formulations [50]. The remainder of this chapter will

Table 1 General Human Abuse Liability Study Design Parameters as Suggested by the FDA Draft Guidance (2010)

Population	Recreational drug abusers with experience in similar drugs or similar drug class to those being tested. No current addiction or treatment.
Sample size	Specific number not recommended, power should be adequate to detect effects of interest, namely, comparison of test drug to placebo and positive control.
Study design	Single dose administration over a period of time determined by time course of the drug under study. Double-blind, double dummy, placebo and positive comparator controlled, crossover using the recommended repeated Williams square design.
Dose selection	Ranges from minimally effective to supratherapeutic.
Outcome measures	*Three primary measures* are recommended: • drug liking • take drug again • drug identification *Secondary measures* may include: positive effects, negative effects, behavioral measures, physiological measures, other mood state measures, etc.

be a practical consideration and elucidation of the FDA suggestions for human regulatory studies of the abuse potential of medications.

1. DESCRIPTION/OVERVIEW OF THE ABUSE POTENTIAL TRIAL

The standard abuse potential trial is a randomized, double-blind, placebo-controlled, positive-controlled crossover study in which multiple doses of the test drug, positive control, and a placebo are administered to recreational drug abusers in single doses. Typically four to eight treatment arms are conducted [18,48,51,52]. Ratings of subjective drug effects are repeatedly collected with instruments from the field of behavioral pharmacology over various time periods that depend on the complete time course of the drug being tested. No more than three primary outcomes are recommended. A washout period of at least five times the half-life of the longest acting drug is recommended between individual sessions of drug administration [5,48].

This design is considered to be the current standard approach to regulatory human abuse liability across all classes of drugs, even though different CNS drugs may have different modes of action or effects. When modeled upon the FDA guidelines, the outcomes can be used to estimate the likelihood of abuse in recreational drug abusers as well as the likelihood of diversion and use on the street [4,6,18,36].

There are a number of studies incorporating similar types of designs (for instance, opioids: [53–63]; sedatives: [64–73]; and stimulants: [74–76]), however, the regulatory abuse potential trial has a broader purpose than the abuse liability studies in the scientific literature. The abuse potential trial is part of the evaluation of drug safety and is designed to address the question of abuse in the general population, not solely in substance abusers [3]. It is therefore a study that is intended to broadly address public health. As has also been underscored, methodologies have developed and improved over the past 50+ years [16], thus, sponsors may wish to seek out both historical studies and those conducted within the updated regulatory framework for reference.

2. PARTICIPANTS AND SAMPLE SIZE

Participants in the human abuse potential study should be healthy volunteers and have a recent or current history of using drugs recreationally. Recreational use refers to the intermittent use of drugs for reasons other than medical purposes (such as to experiment, to relax, to feel good, to get high, etc. [77]). It follows that recreational users are sought out for human abuse potential studies because they use drugs for their effects but not to a level where they have developed a disruptive addiction disorder. As such, their use is assumed to be accompanied by both a qualified knowledge of the effects and the ability to identify and differentiate these effects.

The characteristics of the study population should be presented in detail, both with respect to past and current drug use and abuse. Details should include the drugs that have been abused, the preferred drugs of abuse, and the duration of abuse as well as abstinence. Although the guidance states that the subjects will not be currently abusing other substances, it is likely that recreational abusers will be using more than one substance. For instance, Shram et al. [78] examined the abuse potential of lorcaserin, a selective and potent centrally acting serotonin 2C receptor subtype agonist. The abuse potential trial was performed because the drug involved a novel mechanism of action, and adverse events (AEs) had been reported sporadically from clinical trials, suggesting possible abuse. Recreational polydrug users with experience with at least one drug class including cannabinoids, hallucinogens, stimulants, depressants, dissociative anesthetics, or opioids were recruited as participants. In studies examining the subjective effects of opioids, recreational opioid users were recruited; however, in addition to opioid use, cannabinoid, stimulant, depressant, hallucinogenic, and dissociative anesthetic use was also reported [79]. Harris et al. [80] examined the relative abuse liability of intranasally administered abuse-deterrent controlled-release oxycodone in recreational users. All reported intranasal recreational use of opioids, while 86.7% reported recreational use of cannabinoids, 30% reported recreational use of depressants, 30% of dissociative anesthetics, and 23.3% of hallucinogens. Thus, recreational use is heterogeneous such that recruitment of a sample where only one drug is used is unlikely.

Recreational use must be reported with the same class of drugs being tested, preferably compounds with similar psychoactive properties or in the same pharmaceutical class as the drug under development. This is not the case in nonregulatory abuse liability studies. For instance, in a study examining the effects of oxycodone, 21% of the sample reported recreational opioid use, yet 100% had used other drugs recreationally (marijuana, stimulants, tranquilizers, hallucinogens, club drugs, and inhalants) [81]. A study that examined the effects of D-amphetamine (AMP) recruited healthy individuals with no drug use other than caffeine, alcohol, or tobacco [82]. Regulatory abuse potential trials would require the recruitment of a full sample of recreational prescription opioid abusers for the first example and recreational prescription stimulant abusers for the second.

Exclusion criteria are described as a current diagnosis of substance dependence, current abuse, or current treatment for a substance-related disorder. As noted previously, the aim of the human abuse potential trial is to determine the likelihood of abuse developing in the broad, heterogeneous population of individuals who may come into contact with or experiment with drugs, versus the smaller and more vulnerable population of individuals struggling with drug addiction [83]. The Draft Guidance was originated prior to the fifth revision of the Diagnostic and Statistical Manual of Mental Disorders (DSM-V [84]). In this regard, the guidance does not incorporate the DSM-V substance use disorder terminology (DSM-IV versus DSM-V diagnoses are presented in Table 2 [84,85]). However, upon review of the 11 criteria that identify substance use disorder in DSM-V (Table 2) it seems questionable that most recreational users will not meet any of the criteria for substance use disorder. Rather, it could be inferred that individuals can still be identified as recreational users when meeting a mild level of substance use disorder (two or three criteria).

Table 2 DSM-IV Substance Abuse and Dependence versus DSM-V Substance Use Disorder (Mild, Moderate, Severe).

DSM-IV		DSM-V
Substance Abuse *(meets 1 or more criteria within a 12-month period)*	**Substance Dependence** *(meets 3 or more criteria within a 12-month period)*	**Substance Use Disorder** *(Mild = meets 2-3 of the criteria; Moderate = meets 4-5 of the criteria; Severe = meets 6 or more of the criteria)*
Recurrent use resulting in failure to fulfill major role obligation at work, home or school	Tolerance, as defined by either of the following: (a) A need for markedly increased amounts of the substance to achieve intoxication or the desired effect or (b) Markedly diminished effect with continued use of the same amount of substance	Taking the substance in larger amounts or for longer than was intended
Recurrent use in physically hazardous situations		Wanting to cut down or stop using the substance but not managing to
Recurrent substance related legal problems	Withdrawal, as manifested by either of the following: (a) The characteristic withdrawal syndrome for the substance or (b) the same (or closely related) substance is taken to relieve or avoid withdrawal symptoms	Spending a lot of time getting, using, or recovering from use of the substance
Continued use despite persistent or recurrent social or interpersonal problems caused or exacerbated by substance		Cravings and urges to use the substance
		Not managing to do what should be done at work, home or school, because of substance use
	The substance is often taken in larger amounts or over a longer period then intended	Continuing to use, even when it causes problems in relationships
	There is a persistent desire or unsuccessful efforts to cut down or control substance use	Giving up important social, occupational or recreational activities because of substance use
	A great deal of time is spent in activities necessary to obtain the substance, use the substance, or recover from its effects	Using substances again and again, even when it leads to danger
	Important social, occupational, or recreational activities are given up or reduced because of substance use	Continuing to use, even when knowledge exists of a physical or psychological problem that could have been caused or made worse by the substance
	The substance use is continued despite knowledge of having a persistent physical or psychological problem that is likely to have been caused or exacerbated by the substance	Needing more of the substance to get the desired effect (tolerance)
		Development of withdrawal symptoms, which can be relieved by taking more of the substance

In addition to recreational drug use, participants should be able to: reliably report "drug liking," rate their own subjective drug experience, rate the similarity of the tested drug effects to specific classes of known drugs of abuse, distinguish between the effects of the test drug and similar drugs, and demonstrate that they can discriminate the effects of the positive control from placebo. This means that participants must be able to identify, characterize, and differentiate multiple drug effects, and they must be able to complete the standardized questionnaires in such a way that properly and validly communicates their experience. Importantly, an ability to differentiate between the positive control drug and the placebo and a favorable response for the positive control is necessary to validate the trial [18,36]. One strategy that is engaged to determine whether this is the case, the prequalification phase, is addressed later in this chapter.

Lastly, the FDA guidance requires regulatory studies to ascertain that participants are not dependent on any substances, with perhaps the exception of caffeine and tobacco. For opioids, this can be established by a naloxone challenge. However, Targiniq, an oxycodone/naloxone formulation, was recently approved for the treatment of moderate-to-severe pain. Some of the studies were conducted in opioid-dependent individuals. Opioid-dependent participants may also be used in evaluation of abuse-deterrent formulations. Thus, as more and varied formulations of medications are developed, this guideline may shift.

The sample size must be sufficient to provide enough power to detect differences of interest and accommodate the number of proposed contrasts [48,51,86,87]. Thus, it is evident that an exact sample size cannot be stated in the guidelines because this will be determined, in part, by the proposed effect size as well as the proposed alpha-levels and the desired power. Examples of abuse potential trial sizes have ranged from 10 to 14 participants and up to and even more than 40 participants [4,18,88,89]. A larger sample size will lead to a more robust power estimate. It is notable that an epidemiological reference source proposed that 90% power is a better alternative to that of the typical 80% commonly found in medical trials [90] because greater power (90%) would be accompanied by the lower probability of a Type II error (10%). In an abuse potential trial, where a false negative result would imply a lack of abuse potential where it really existed, this seems to be a reasonable consideration [48,91].

In any event, sample size estimates should be conducted on clinically meaningful effects or a clinically important difference [92,93]. The study of what constitutes a clinically important difference with regard to the abuse potential trial outcomes is ongoing [92,94,95]. In the regulatory paradigm this estimate is usually derived in part from the expected difference between the positive control and the placebo because it is assumed that there is a lack of information about the size of the difference between the test drug and the placebo [48]. It is expected that the test drug will produce similar outcomes to those produced by the positive control. For example, differences ranging from 20 to 40 points on bipolar "Liking" scales have been reported in comparisons between placebo and multiple positive control drugs [94].

In a comparison between formulations, intranasal administration of reformulated, finely crushed OxyContin® resulted in an average 13.6 point reduction of "Liking" E_{max} measured on the bipolar Visual Analog Scale (VAS) when compared to the original OxyContin® in 27 participants [80]. A subsequent postmarketing study conducted in treatment seekers demonstrated that a reduction in the abuse of OxyContin® followed the reformulation [96,97]. It is thus possible that an approximate 14 point reduction in "Liking" could be considered as a clinically meaningful difference for reformulated opioids, but more data of this nature are required before this can be wholly ascertained.

A study of effect sizes across multiple drugs of abuse revealed that average E_{max} effect sizes for "Liking" ranged from 1 to 3 [94,95] whereas a separate summary of effect sizes for various abuse potential measures for prescription stimulants demonstrated that "Liking" ranged from approximately 0.5–2.0 [16]. Thus, the determination of the size of clinically meaningful effects upon which to power the study and base the sample size must consider the drug and the dose tested. These calculations are most often conducted with the E_{max} value, although E_{max} may not be sensitive to some of the pharmacological characteristics of test drugs and may be subject to variability associated with "expectancy." A potential solution to this problem is using a reflective measure collected the next day for a more reliable estimation [16].

3. STUDY DESIGN

The FDA indicates that the design of the human abuse potential trial should be based on the study objective and the statistical analysis model [5]. Typically the study and statistics are designed to determine whether a difference can be detected between responses produced by the positive control drug and the placebo, whether the test drug produces responses that are different from the positive control, and if the test drug produces responses that are different from placebo [48]. A lack of abuse potential would be suggested by no difference in response between the test drug and the placebo, while at the same time demonstrating a difference in response between the placebo and the positive control (cf. [89]). Conversely, abuse potential would be suggested by a difference in response both between the test drug and the placebo and between the placebo and the positive control.

As mentioned previously, these studies are typically double-blind, double dummy, placebo and positive comparator controlled, and crossover repeated Williams square design for abuse potential testing [50]. Crossover designs are valuable because of their efficiency; they can increase precision due to each person serving as his or her own control, thereby reducing error, and as such, fewer participants are needed than for a between-subjects design [86,87,98]. They are not without potential problems. They can result in longer study periods leading to possible increased drop-out of participants, and the risk of carryover or residual effects from the previous treatments in the design exists [90].

Regardless of their challenges, they are the proposed standard for the design of the human abuse potential trial, namely because of the treatment and variance balances achieved [5,51].

The repeated Williams square design is a generalized Latin square that is balanced for first order carryover effects. Every treatment follows every other treatment the same number of times, ensuring that treatment effects are not due to residual effects from the previous sequence. Further, every sequence of the full Latin square design does not have to be repeated to achieve a balanced design [51,99,100]. This property is desirable when there are more than two treatments under study because it is possible to reduce the number of sequences that must be conducted to achieve uniform, unbiased treatment in the study design [48,51,100]. An odd number of treatments is preferable for Williams square design to achieve sufficient degrees of freedom, allowing for the inclusion of all interaction terms in the model and proper variance balance for analysis enabled by the use of two Latin squares. Investigators should avoid the inclusion of unnecessary treatments and consider the use of hierarchical analytical strategies of this design [51].

As a potential analytical strategy, Chen and Bonson [48] suggest constructing an equivalence margin whereby if a test drug produces an increased score on the VAS positive subjective effect scale that is greater than the 75th percentile of the placebo in more than 50% of study participants, then the test drug could be considered to differ from the placebo and may have abuse potential. An equivalence margin (δ) can be calculated from the normal distribution and the standard distribution of the placebo response and is then added to the placebo response. If the test drug response is significantly lower than the placebo +δ response, then the test drug will be not be considered to have abuse potential. A VAS score that does not differ, or is significantly greater than the placebo +δ response, would be considered as a suggestion of abuse potential in that particular compound. The comparisons can be performed with nonparametric procedures if the distribution of responses is not symmetrical. Chen and Bonson [48] elaborate further detail surrounding these procedures.

4. STUDY SITE

Abuse potential trials should be conducted in controlled laboratory settings, preferably on a closed residential unit [5]. Detailed descriptions of various inpatient laboratory or hospital research units can be found in the abuse liability literature [61,101–104]. Inpatient units are typically within hospitals or research facilities. Participants are monitored around-the-clock for safety purposes, also suggesting that extended data collection is possible. Should there be any AEs after drug administration, or when testing a new entity, it is possible to observe, record, and ensure proper documentation and management. No visitors are allowed, reducing the possibility of outside influence or access to drugs. Once participants are admitted and settled, study participation is straightforward, which removes the possibilities of tardy arrivals, intoxicated arrivals, or simply no arrivals. Inpatient living may reduce one source of nonsystematic variance as participants will have had similar daily living experiences prior to the study's onset.

Frequently, abuse potential trials are conducted in both inpatient and outpatient settings. For safety purposes, the drug is administered during inpatient phases, and participants are released once the psychological and physical effects of the study drug have abated. Washout continues during outpatient phases, and participants are readmitted for each subsequent treatment.

5. SELECTION OF DOSES AND CONTROLS

The selection of doses and controls is a critical piece of a sound abuse potential trial, and there is not an exact formula for this task [24]. The study is typically conducted with doses ranging from minimally effective to maximally tolerated [16], which may span from two to three to even greater multiples of the therapeutic dose range. The dose range must be considered to be safe. Typical procedures from the regulatory paradigm are to consider the maximally tolerated dose as 2-3 times the therapeutic dose if safety is known and precautions are taken to deal with safety concerns.

Broader abuse liability studies often have a larger dose range that is determined in part by Investigators' Brochures but also by dose run-up procedures, the scientific literature, or reports of abuse. A typical recommendation from this literature is to include placebo, up to 3 doses of the test drug, and up to 3 doses of a positive control, where doses are typically a low dose, one or two therapeutic doses, and one or two supratherapeutic doses [6,18,36]. High supratherapeutic doses are often employed for abuse liability testing among drug users due to the rationale that the actual therapeutic doses are of little interest to those who abuse medications, particularly because a lack of sensitivity to subtle effects may exist [18,24]. Within the regulatory paradigm, however, sponsors select their doses based on the preclinical and clinical work they have conducted. It is ultimately recommended that sponsors confer with the Controlled Substance Staff (CSS) at the FDA when choosing appropriate doses of the test drug for abuse potential trials [51].

Positive controls are scheduled drugs that are known to lead to the behavior or rating of interest or have an established pattern of abuse. In the abuse potential trial, these would be drugs that increase ratings of "Liking" or "Take Drug Again." New entities may require novel positive controls. For instance, zolpidem (a benzodiazepine-like drug) was employed as a positive control for a dual orexin receptor antagonist—a novel medication for the treatment of sleep disorders and potentially substance abuse [88]. Dronabinol (synthetic delta-9-tetrahydrocannabinol (THC)) was selected as a positive control for nabiximols (an oromucosal spray primarily containing THC and cannabidiol [105])

Table 3 Selection of Positive Controls across Multiple Drug Classes

Drug Class	Positive Control
Opioid	Hydromorphone
	Morphine
	Oxycodone
Stimulant	D-amphetamine (AMP)
	Mixed amphetamine salts
	Phentermine
	Methylphenidate
Cannabinoid	Dronabinol
Sedative	Alprazolam
	Lorazepam
	Triazolam

and taranabant, a cannabinoid 1 receptor inverse agonist [106]. There are many other examples of thoughtful positive controls, also known as "active controls" across multiple drug classes (cf. [78,89,107,108]). Table 3 presents a sample review of selected positive controls across different drug classes [109]. Standardization of comparators within each drug class where possible would be beneficial for further refinement of the abuse potential paradigm.

5.1 Dose Run up Studies

In addition to consulting with the FDA for dose and study design selections, sponsors may conduct dose run-up or dose escalation pilot studies to provide empirical and safety support for dose selection in the abuse potential study. The conduct of the dose escalation paradigm in the regulatory setting has been discussed in the context of epilepsy medications where it was noted that dose selections for newer medications were frequently not optimal [110,111].

A current preferred model of dose run-up studies is described in the abuse liability literature. Studies are conducted in four to eight individuals [18,24]. As described in Evans et al. ([24]—Principle [3,65]), doses should range from near pharmacologically inactive to high doses and a number of participants should be given the full dose range. Evans et al. [65] evaluated a range of 5–80 mg zolpidem in five research volunteers. Because only two of the five participants tested were able to tolerate the 80 mg dose, the doses used in the main study ranged from 15 to 45 mg zolpidem (with three doses of triazolam as comparators). Preston et al. [68] conducted dose run-up studies of the relaxant methocarbamol in six participants, with doses ranging from 2.25 to 12 g. Because only three of the six participants tested were able to take the highest dose without incident (a fourth took it but was dropped for noncompliance), the study ultimately ended up testing 2.25, 4.5, and 9 g of methocarbamol. Similarly, Preston et al. [69] conducted a dose run-up for diphenhydramine from doses of 50–600 mg. Three of the five participants were able to tolerate the highest dose, whereas two participants became somewhat hypertensive. Thus, the main study included doses of 100, 200, and 400 mg diphenhydramine.

Evans et al. [24] as well as the Draft Guidance [4] note that the dose run-up studies can be considered as an opportunity to evaluate the measures and procedures for the main study. Thus, dose run-up studies share the properties of general pilot studies, which are a useful endeavor for examining the feasibility of proposed study procedures such as screening, recruitment, retention, or assessments and monitoring [93] as well as drug effect, as previously mentioned. They can inform about recruitment and randomization, namely, the proportion of screens that may be eligible to enroll. However, it has been strongly suggested that pilot studies be used solely for these purposes and not for estimates of power or effect size for larger trials [93,112]. This is because the small size of the pilot study may lead to wide overestimates or underestimates of treatment effect. Therefore, while dose run-up studies may provide a good indication of safety or how a larger sample will respond to a drug, they should not be used for further statistical estimation of clinically important effects.

6. PREQUALIFICATION PHASES

Prequalification phases (PQPs), also referred to as enrichment strategies, were addressed in the FDA Draft Guidance for Abuse Deterrent Formulations that was issued in January 2013. Although these guidelines addressed the regulatory principles for abuse-deterrent formulations, general recommendations for an abuse potential trial can be inferred. It was noted that the use of a PQP can increase the power of a study to detect the effects of interest (by ensuring the sample is homogeneous in its abilities to detect drug effect) and familiarize participants with the use of the scales employed in the assay (also perhaps leading to less systematic error).

A PQP should include a positive control and a placebo and establish that participants can discriminate between the two drugs. For instance, Parasrampuria et al. [113] examined the abuse liability of novel formulation (OROS) of extended-release methylphenidate. They employed a PQP to determine enrollment into the primary treatment phase. Participants were required to be able to discriminate a difference between single doses of 20 mg immediate release D-amphetamine and a placebo on at least five of the 10 prespecified items among the VAS, the ARCI, and a subjective drug value procedure. The primary treatment phase studied OROS methylphenidate (54 and 108 mg) compared to IR methylphenidate (50 and 90 mg) with a placebo condition as well.

7. OUTCOME MEASURES: PRIMARY

Numerous instruments have historically and repeatedly been used and recommended for use in abuse liability studies [18,26,28,34,40,47]. There is not as of yet a completely specified set of instruments accepted as a standardized battery to be employed in regulatory abuse potential trials across multiple classes of drugs, although there seems to be a common agreement among most abuse liability studies. Here, we discuss the recommendations for the three primary outcome measures.

The Draft Guidance suggests three primary outcome measures, including the VAS of "Drug Liking," the degree to which the participants would "Take the Drug Again," and drug identification or drug similarity as measures of interest for NCE assessment. The Draft Guidance for Abuse-Deterrent Opioids—Evaluation and Labeling [50] recommends using the bipolar "Drug Liking" VAS as the primary outcome measure on the abuse deterrent formulation (ADF) trials because it appears to correlate most directly with the potential for abuse. From this guidance, we infer that the bipolar "Drug Liking" VAS scale should also be the primary outcome measure used for estimation of clinically important effects in the abuse potential trial.

There is supportive literature for this recommendation. Griffiths et al. [18] suggested that the bipolar scale could be considered as a global evaluation of effect. Building upon this notion, Schoedel [91] suggested that the use of a bipolar scale as the primary outcome measure, with separate unipolar scales employed descriptively, might more thoroughly capture the drug effects. This suggestion takes into account that some drugs are both liked and disliked, and a forced choice between the two may not fully capture these characteristics. Further, the elucidation of the forced or global choice by accompanying separate scales may contribute to a more nuanced understanding of the effect and also render effect sizes across drugs more comparable.

One concern about having both "Liking" and "Take Again" as primary outcome variables is that these measures covary together [18]. This suggests that if a particular pattern in "Liking" is found between treatments, it is likely that a similar pattern will also be found in "Take Again." Thus, there is a need for analytical models that take into account correlated endpoints [114,115]. These data tend to be non-normally distributed, thus, nonparametric procedures are often considered. It is also worth considering whether it would be possible to combine the two measures into a composite endpoint. The use of a composite endpoint with components that are only slightly correlated but not quite dissimilar in their recognized clinical relevance seems to be a preferable balance [116].

There are not widely accepted estimates for clinically relevant "Liking" or "Take again" effect sizes [91,117]. As mentioned previously, retrospective analysis of abuse potential study measures "Liking" and "Take Again" in concert with postmarketing data or national databases with abuse potential signals may be a technique for meaningful primary outcome effect size estimations. It would also be helpful if the FDA–CSS division would make effect size estimates from (de-identified) NDA applications public.

Drug identification is also typically measured with a VAS. These scales are anchored with "0: Not at all similar" and "100: Very Similar." They pose the question, "How similar is the drug you most recently received to…" and then ask the participant to respond to this question for a list of prespecified drugs ("How similar is the drug you most recently received to caffeine?" "How similar is the drug you most recently received to THC?"). Some versions may also ask a second question addressing overall familiarity of the test drug, namely, "How familiar was the effect of the drug you most recently received?", where answers range from "0:Very Unfamiliar" to "100:Very Familiar." Each questionnaire is designed to match the participant's unique drug-taking experience, that is, if a participant has not used a drug enough to meet a standard of comparison (based on the screening assessment) then that drug will not be included in the questionnaire.

8. OUTCOME MEASURES: SECONDARY

Additional measures may be used to further evaluate the subjective effects of drugs. For instance, VAS scales can be used to evaluate the "Strength" of the drug effect, the "High," or "Good/Bad Effects." Behavioral and cognitive performance assessments can be used to capture pharmacologic effects on attributes such as attention or memory (cf. [88,106]). Other measurements can include relevant physiological effects such as pupillometry in the case of opioids or cardiovascular response in the case of stimulants.

The Addiction Research Center Inventory (ARCI) scale has been used to evaluate effects of the drug [118]. The modified ARCI (reduced from 550 to 49 items) produces a set of five indices or scales representing different drug effects. The pentobarbital-chlorpromazine-alcohol group scale (PCAG) provides a measure of sedation, the amphetamine (A or AMP) scale provides a measure of amphetamine-like effects, the benzedrine group scale (BG) also assesses amphetamine-like effects, the lysergic acid diethylamide (LSD) scale is sensitive to somatic and dysphoric changes, and finally, the morphine-benzedrine group (MBG) is often used to describe euphoria [118–120].

The ARCI has been historically used in conjunction with the Single Dose Questionnaire (SDQ) [53], which consists of four primary questions: (1) Do you feel the medicine? (2) This drug is most like what drug listed below (check one): a blank, dope (opiates), cocaine, marijuana, goof balls (barbituates), benzedrine ("Benny"), other; (3) Check each sensation when you feel: normal, "turning of the stomach," skin itchy, relaxed, coasting, "soap box," pleasant sick, drive, sleepy, nervous drunken, other; and (4) My liking for this drug is most nearly described by which of the following: not at all, slight, moderate, a lot, an awful lot, other. The SDQ can be accompanied by an observer form, in which the observer also evaluates the effects of the participant. The ARCI and the POMS (Profile of Mood States) are identified by the Draft Guidance as being assessments of mood state (although it has been our experience that the POMS is not used as widely as the ARCI).

9. AEs: CLINICAL

This section is a broad consideration of AEs and the documenting and reporting thereof. AEs are part of research with human participants. There is no standard definition of AEs across government and nongovernment agencies, however, they are broadly defined by the

US Department of Health and Human Services as "any untoward or unfavorable medical occurrence in a human subject, including any abnormal sign (e.g., abnormal physical exam or laboratory finding), symptom, or disease, temporally associated with the subject's participation in the research, whether or not considered related to the subject's participation in the research (modified from the definition of AEs in the 1996 International Conference on Harmonization E−6 Guidelines for Good Clinical Practice)" (http://www.hhs.gov/ohrp/policy/advevntguid.html). The Code of Federal Regulations, Title 21, Volume 5, Part 312 Investigational New Drug Application, Subpart B, Section 312.32 (http://www.accessdata.fda.gov/scripts/cdrh/cfdocs/cfCFR/CFRSearch.cfm?CFRPart=312&showFR=1) considers them to be "any untoward medical occurrence associated with the use of a drug in humans, whether or not considered drug related." Thus, untoward clinical events that happen during the study are considered AEs whether or not they are related to the specific procedures or drug involved in the study. It is the investigator and/or sponsor's responsibility to classify the AE as expected (anticipated) or unexpected (unanticipated) and then to determine whether the AE is Serious.

9.1 Serious Adverse Events

Serious Adverse Events (SAEs) are defined as occurrences that in the view of the investigator or sponsor result in any of the following outcomes: death, a life-threatening AE, inpatient hospitalization or prolongation of existing hospitalization, a persistent or significant incapacity or substantial disruption of the ability to conduct normal life functions, or a congenital anomaly/birth defect (CFR, 21: 5, Sec 312.32). They suggest that the conduct of the research places participants or others at greater risk of harm or discomfort than was previously known or recognized.

The distinction between expected and unexpected events is also an important characteristic to consider in the conduct of the human abuse potential trial. Events are considered unexpected if they are not listed in the investigator brochure or are not listed at the specificity or severity that has been observed; or, if an investigator brochure is not required or available, they are not consistent with the risk information described in the general investigational plan or elsewhere. The term unexpected also refers to AEs or suspected adverse reactions that might be anticipated from the particular pharmacological properties of the drug but are not specifically mentioned as occurring with the particular drug under investigation (CFR, 21: 5, Sec 312.32).

9.2 Reporting AEs

In the early 1990s, there were multiple AE reporting systems available (including the FDA's Coding Symbols for a Thesaurus of Adverse Reaction Terms (COSTART) as well as the ICD9-CM). Ultimately, it was not possible to standardize terminology across the multiple databases. Thus, the Medical Dictionary for Regulatory Activities (MedDRA) evolved out of a collaborative and collective effort supported by the International Conference on Harmonization of Technical Requirements for Registration of Pharmaceuticals for Human

Use (ICH) to facilitate the sharing of regulatory information internationally ([121], http://www.meddra.org/about-meddra/history).

MedDRA was created as a single, representative source of medical terminology for use of reporting AEs in both pre- and postmarketing phases of the regulatory process in the pharmaceutical industry. It is a hierarchically organized database where Lowest Level Terms (the broadest descriptors/multiple synonyms) are grouped into Preferred Terms (PTs), which are in turn grouped into High Level Terms, which are grouped into High Level Group Terms, which ultimately are organized by System Organ Classes (SOC) [122]. Thus, AEs can be entered via a number of synonyms and ultimately be grouped by the high-level organ system to which they correspond. In general, only terms relevant to pharmaceutical regulatory affairs are included, and it is updated biannually [121–123].

The system is extremely large and changes with great rapidity (version 17 was unveiled in March 2014; the FDA 2010 Draft Guidance references version 12). Inter-rater reliability of AE rating has not been examined, thus, it is not clear how similarly various entities code alike events. In fact, the number of items that have been included for the purpose of precision may lead to a diffusion of identifiable phenomenon because it is possible to use multiple terms for a single event, which may shift the meaning of what the event actually was (there are over 18,000 Preferred Terms in MedDRA). Specific training must be undertaken to use the system, which limits its immediate usefulness (although the ICH provides free training sessions in person or via webinars, so it is accessible). Also, the increase in number of terms may change the statistical frequencies of AEs, rendering historical comparisons difficult [122,124,125].

Standardized MedDRA queries (SMQs) have been developed to identify abuse-related AEs. SMQs are standard, predetermined sets of MedDRA terms that have been grouped together to facilitate searching the database for regulatory needs and retrieving MedDRA coded data. For instance, an SMQ identified as "Drug Abuse, Dependence and Withdrawal" currently exists for the retrieval of AEs related to this category (http://www.meddra.org/standardised-meddra-queries).

The process of identifying and standardizing the reporting of AEs for human abuse potential trials is still ongoing [4,14,126]. AEs may be related to abuse-related behavior and drug administration–intoxication, abrupt discontinuation or withdrawal, diversion or tampering, or overdose on the drug [14]. It has been suggested that writing detailed reports of a participant's experiences in narratives surrounding AEs will enhance the precision of the subsequent coding that must take place to properly identify and code the event by providing context. Recording verbatim comments of participants has been identified as a particularly valuable source of context-specific information that may provide a framework for the detection of other signals of abuse ([4,14]; see also [127] for further elaboration of patient-oriented AE documentation).

The Draft Guidance recommends considering terms broadly categorized by mood elevation (euphoria, euphoric mood, elevated mood, mood alteration, feeling drunk, feeling abnormal), sedation, and psychotomimetic events (hallucination: visual and auditory) for AE identification. They also specify MedDRA 12 lower level terms for inappropriate affect that should be considered when identifying AEs, namely: elation inappropriate, exhilaration inappropriate, feeling happy inappropriately, inappropriate affect, inappropriate elation, inappropriate laughter, or inappropriate mood elevation. The measure of diversion within the context of the abuse potential trial has not yet been standardized.

Recent studies have attempted to improve upon the selection of AEs that are directly related to abuse potential so that they might be more readily employed. At a meeting in 2008, the FDA proposed frequently used MedDRA and verbatim abuse-related terms based on their regulatory experience (Table 4). Love and Sun [128] proposed narrowing

Table 4 The FDA's Abuse-Related Adverse Event Terms

Euphoria-Related Terms	
Euphoric mood	Euphoria, euphoric, exaggerated well-being, excitement excessive, feeling high, felt high[a], high[a], high[a] feeling, laughter
Elevated mood	Mood elevated, elation
Feeling abnormal	Cotton wool in head, feeling dazed, feeling floating, feeling strange, feeling weightless, felt like a zombie, floating feeling, foggy feeling in head, funny episode, fuzzy, fuzzy head, muzzy head, spaced out, unstable feeling, weird feeling, spacey
Feeling drunk	Drunkenness feeling of, drunk-like effect, intoxicated, stoned, drugged
Feeling of relaxation	Feeling of relaxation, feeling relaxed, relaxation, relaxed, increased well-being, excessive happiness
Dizziness	Dizziness and giddiness, felt giddy, giddiness, light headedness, light-headed, light-headed feeling, lightheadedness, swaying feeling, wooziness, woozy
Thinking abnormal	Abnormal thinking, thinking irrational, wandering thoughts
Hallucination	(Auditory, visual, and all hallucination types), illusions, flashbacks, floating, rush, feeling addicted
Terms Often Associated with Drugs of Abuse: Impaired Attention, Psychomotor Events Cognition, Mood	
Somnolence	Groggy, groggy and sluggish, groggy on awakening, stupor
Mood disorders and disturbances	Mental disturbance, depersonalization, psychomotor stimulation, mood disorders, emotional and mood disturbances, deliria, delirious, mood altered, mood alterations, mood instability, mood swings, emotional lability, emotional disorder, emotional distress, personality disorder, impatience, abnormal behavior, delusional disorder, irritability
Mental impairment disorders	Memory loss (excl dementia), amnesia, memory impairment, decreased memory, cognition and attention disorders and disturbances, decreased concentration, cognitive disorder, disturbance in attention, mental impairment, mental slowing, mental disorders

Table 4 The FDA's Abuse-Related Adverse Event Terms—cont'd

Drug tolerance, habituation, drug withdrawal syndrome, substance-related disorders	
Dissociative/Psychotic Terms	
Psychosis	Psychotic episode or disorder
Aggressive	Hostility, anger, paranoia
Confusion and disorientation	Confusional state, disoriented, disorientation, confusion, disconnected, derealization, dissociation, detached, fear symptoms, depersonalization, perceptual disturbances, thinking disturbances, thought blocking, sensation of distance from one's environment, blank stare, muscle rigidity, non-communicative, sensory distortions, slow slurred speech, agitation, excitement, increased pain threshold, loss of a sense of personal identity

[a]Exclude terms that clearly are not pertinent or relevant such as "high blood pressure," "respiratory depression," etc.
From PhRMA-FDA Dialogue Session Abuse Potential Assessments, February 20, 2008.

the MedDRA 16 search terms to 213 terms that are specific to abuse potential from the database. They hypothesized that the employment of this list will result in better sensitivity and specificity of search terms that will ultimately be comparable across multiple studies.

The FDA 2010 guidance further suggests that sponsors carefully categorize and tabulate data that have been collected during safety trials so that they may also be used to establish whether there were any signs of AEs over the course of the drug development. This guidance is in keeping with the extended Consolidated Standards of Reporting Trials (CONSORT) statement addressing specific recommendations for AE reporting in clinical trials [129].

10. AEs: POSTMARKETING SURVEILLANCE

Abuse liability may also be evaluated from postmarketing surveillance. During postmarketing, or any time after a product has been approved and comes on the market, AEs or medication error reports are voluntarily submitted to the Food and Drug Administration Adverse Event Reporting System (FAERS) database by healthcare professionals or individuals [130–135]. If a sponsor or product manufacturer receives an adverse event report, it is transcribed onto a MedWatch form and classified as to the type of event. This information is required to be sent to the FDA, and that report will be entered into the FAERS. Information being entered into the FAERS is coded using terminology from the MedDRA.

There have been concerns regarding this approach ([136–138], as outlined in [139]). Glasser et al. [140] estimated that to discover an AE with a frequency of 0.1%, a sample size of 10,000 individuals would have to be studied in a postmarketing survey, as MedWatch does not target specific AEs. Getz et al. [135] examined 10, 242, 977 events collected between January 2005 and December 2010 and found that patient information was generally complete, and the drug/product name information was complete; however, dosage information, including the dose (31% complete), the start and end dates of use (37% and 23% complete) as well as the lot number (9% complete) and product expiration date (1% complete) were not sufficiently documented. It was also noted that within the information that was submitted, it was not always accurate. For instance, the names of the drug and product, although 100% complete, were only 74% accurate. Thus, while certainly an important data stream, areas of improvement remain. A combination of monitoring MedWatch data and other national data streams along with working with specific programs that collect targeted postmarketing data seems to be a balanced system of gathering these critical data [96,141–144].

11. MEASUREMENT OF ABUSE, MISUSE, AND DIVERSION OF PRESCRIPTION MEDICATIONS

As previously noted, abuse, misuse, and diversion of drugs are problematic behaviors. They may be considered AEs in clinical trials. "Drug abuse," "drug diversion," and "intentional drug misuse" are terms specified in the MedDRA lexicon [128]. However, there are additional sources of data that can contribute to the estimate of abuse, misuse, and diversion.

There are multiple national surveys that are updated annually and address drug abuse. Four are associated with the Substance Abuse and Mental Health Services Administration (SAMSHA). The National Survey on Drug Use and Health (NSDUH; a contract between Research Triangle Institute (RTI) and SAMSHA) provides national and state-level data about the use of licit and illicit drugs in individuals 12 and older. Topics such as percentage of users for various drugs, initiation of use, sources of drugs, youth prevention-related measures, and treatment statistics are covered. Historically, the Drug Abuse Warning Network (DAWN) provided national estimates of drug-related emergency department visits from nonfederal hospitals that operated 24-h emergency departments. DAWN concluded data collection in 2011. The Treatment Episode Data Sets (TEDS) provide estimates of the demographic and substance abuse characteristics of individuals 12 and older who are treated in facilities who report their data to state data collection systems. Lastly, the National Survey of Substance Abuse Treatment Services (N-SSATS) provides an annual census of facilities providing substance abuse treatment in US jurisdictions. In addition to the SAMSHA databases, the National Institute of Drug Abuse (NIDA) sponsors the Monitoring the Future Study (MTF), which is conducted at the University of Michigan. This survey monitors the behaviors, attitudes, and values of secondary school (beginning in eighth grade) and college students as well as young adults and follows many through to their 50s. Lastly, the American Association of

Poison Control Centers' National Poison Data System (NPDS) publishes annual surveillance reports summarizing case report data from individual US poison centers.

Reviewing the summaries of these reports, all of which are publically available, can provide estimates of the scope of drug abuse and misuse in the US, although more product specific data are desirable. The guidelines specify that raw counts and weighted estimates from the databases should be put into the context of relative exposure, especially for purposes of comparisons and assessing trends. They further specify that the ratio of the number of abuse events (numerator) relative to the number of prescriptions or number of patients or amount of drug produced during the specified time period (the denominator) should be calculated to provide an abuse indication corrected for exposure. The databases that have been summarized above adhere to these suggestions.

In addition to these databases, research groups have grown to specialize in the surveillance and collection of prescription drug abuse data required for postmarketing surveillance (among other projects). Two well-known groups are Inflexxion™ and RADARS®. Both groups collect and monitor complex data streams and provide the systematic, large-scale summary reports suggested in the FDA guidance.

For example, RADARS® surveillance systems (www.radars.org) provide reports on data gleaned from programs such as Drug Diversion (approximately 300 prescription drug diversion investigators and regulatory agencies who are asked to report the number of new diversion cases investigated quarterly), Poison Center data (reviews data reports from poison centers for internal validity), Opioid Treatment Programs (administers anonymous questionnaires to patients enrolling in opioid treatment programs regarding drug preferences and use), Survey of Key Informants (patients in treatment at mostly private substance abuse treatment programs are recruited by Key Informants to complete anonymous questionnaires about drug preferences and use), College Survey Program (an online questionnaire collecting data from students who self-identify as being at least a part-time student during a specified period), and StreetRx (a Web site for reporting and viewing street prices of drugs: www.streetrx.com).

These reports appear in published literature. For instance, one report [142] assessed the abuse of the tapentadol immediate release formulation during the first 24 months after it was introduced to the US market. Data were collected from the Poison Center, Drug Diversion, Opioid Treatment, and Survey of Key Informants' Patients programs and revealed low rates of tapentadol abuse. Most notably, and as suggested by the FDA, both summary rate statistics per 100,000 of the population and per 1000 Unique Recipients of Dispensed Drug were provided. Another report [145] described the nonmedical use of tapentadol immediate release and other prescription opioids by college students with both population and URDD rates.

Inflexxion™ (www.inflexxion.com) has developed online clinical instruments, pain assessment services, and screening instruments that can be used with patients who will be prescribed opioids. With regard to postmarketing surveillance activities, they continuously and systematically monitor data collected from the instruments' internet activity for chatter about drugs and also collect and analyze data from the National Addictions Vigilance Intervention and Prevention Program's (NAVIPPRO™) surveillance system. Published reports describe how various data streams contribute to NAVIPPRO surveillance [146] and the postmarketing surveillance of reformulated OxyContin® [96]. They have also reported surveillance data of prescription stimulant abuse [141] and prescription opioid abuse [147].

12. SUMMARY AND CONCLUSION

To conclude, the purpose of this chapter has been to review the conduct of the human abuse potential study from the regulatory perspective. The goal has been to describe why these studies are conducted, how they are conceived and conducted, how they are analyzed, and how abuse liability may continue to be monitored after drug approval. Human abuse potential trials by themselves are not sufficient to bring about drug scheduling; however, they are a critical piece of the abuse liability assessment submitted to the FDA as part of an NDA and are closely evaluated.

We close this chapter with a consideration of other abuse potential paradigms and more specifically human self-administration. Self-administration models are those that estimate the degree to which a drug serves as a reinforcer by measuring the amount increased behavior or "work" emitted by the study subject to obtain the drug, usually in relation to another valuable commodity, such as other drugs or money. When considering models that employ operant schedules, work can be defined as verbal or behavioral responses emitted for a drug [45,148,149]. As described in Comer et al. [148], self-administration paradigms have many variants.

The question at the root of incorporating the self-administration model into the abuse potential paradigm is its capacity to predict drug-taking behavior once a drug has been approved [45]. Regulatory work has been based on the theoretical underpinning that the proxy for risk of abuse is an increased rating of "Liking" or "Take Drug Again" among individuals who do not use drugs to the point of disorder, yet still use drugs because of the effects produced. Thus, a significant difference from the placebo on one or both of these two variables would suggest that the drug has a risk of abuse. However, it has also been demonstrated that within certain drug classes subjective effects and self-administration diverge [45]. The degree to which subjective effects alone or together with self-administration procedures actually estimate a drug's tangible abuse potential has only begun to be methodologically examined.

For instance, Horton et al. [44] addressed this question by the diagnostic capabilities of various components used in abuse-liability assessment to determine how well they predicted the scheduling status of 100 small molecules. Included were a number of assays, including binding, functional activity, locomotor activity, drug discrimination (rats), fixed-ratio self-administration (rats), progressive-ratio self-administration (rats), and human subjective effects paradigms (defined as human abuse potential trials). From each assay, they created a number of summary measures that were used to estimate how well each model predicted scheduling (both sensitivity and specificity or positive and negative prediction), including terms adjusted for the prevalence of the drugs of abuse. In addition to the actual predictive capacities, they also measured how much each index would reduce the uncertainty in the prediction of scheduling.

They found that the preclinical drug discrimination, preclinical self-administration, and human abuse potential trials had the greatest predictive value for scheduling outcome. Specifically, the human abuse potential trials demonstrated a high sensitivity (0.85, 95% CI: 0.70–0.93), moderate specificity (0.52, 95% CI: 0.34–0.70), and a concordance second only to fixed self-administration (rodent) paradigms (0.72 versus 0.78, respectively). In other words, the human abuse potential models predicted 85% of the drugs scheduled (true positives) and 52% of those not scheduled (true negatives). These models were also among the highest predictive assays when taking the prevalence of the drug being abused into account, with an adjusted positive predictive value of 0.43 (range of all assays: 0.31–0.56) and a negative predictive value of 0.89 (range of all assays: 0.73–0.98). Of interest, there was little additional value found in combining measures; for instance, a combination of the human studies with fixed-ratio self-administration rodent studies did not contribute to any better prediction of the scheduling outcome. These data demonstrate both the strengths and the limitations of the human abuse potential in terms of scheduling decisions.

These data [44] lead to an interesting and timely question, namely, how much value would be added to the human abuse potential paradigm by the inclusion of human self-administration studies. A study published in 2013 was the first to statistically evaluate the association between progressive-ratio self-administration models of oral D-amphetamine and subjective effects data and whether there was a general concordance between the two [150]. Across both low and high doses of D-amphetamine, the association between ratings of "Like Drug" and number of capsules earned explained 15% of the variance between the two measures, while the association between ratings of "Willing to Take Again" and number of capsules earned explained 13% of the variance between the two measures. The respective correlations (approximately 0.36 and 0.39) were medium-sized effects, so the association is not inconsequential. However, these data also suggest that there is degree of variability in both measures that is not shared, thus, it is possible to infer that approximately 85–87% of the variability in these measures is accounted for by different aspects of drugs' abuse liability.

Consideration of these studies [44,150] demonstrates a need for an examination of the statistical relationships between self-administration behavioral outcome measures and subjective effects data. Such a study would be an appropriate strategy with which to address the question of whether the behavioral data collected via the self-administration paradigm would contribute additional value to the human abuse potential paradigm beyond that of the already-collected subjective effects data. The resolution to this question will be multifaceted and will likely involve combinations of the mechanism of action and route of administration. Outcomes may also be participant-related: perhaps the nature of the association between the two measures will differ between recreational users and those with a history of disordered or extremely regular use. Few studies in the abuse-liability field employ the progressive-ratio measure in humans; thus, such a review would be limited by a small sample size, yet would be a large contribution to the regulatory area of study.

To conclude, it is clear that self-administration data contribute to the estimate of abuse liability. It has also been repeatedly demonstrated that self-administration and ratings of subjective effects diverge in particular drugs with particular populations. However, it is not clear that a combination of self-administration and subjective effects paradigms will be a synergistic combination that will add additional statistical predictive value or explain enough statistical variance within the regulatory paradigm to justify or support the conduct of both as required procedures for the human abuse potential. The path forward requires a statistical comparison between the self-administration data and the subjective effects studies as well as a comparison to the scheduling information where possible, that is, a combination of the approaches demonstrated in Horton et al. [44] and Bolin et al. [150]. This would be an interesting examination of the role of self-administration in the regulatory paradigm.

REFERENCES

[1] Lynch WJ, Nicholson KL, Dance ME, Morgan RW, Foley PL. Animal models of substance abuse and addiction: implications for science, animal welfare, and society. Comp Med 2010;60(3):177–88.

[2] Epstein DH, Preston KL, Jasinski DR. Abuse liability, behavioral pharmacology, and physical-dependence potential of opioids in humans and laboratory animals: lessons from tramadol. Biol Psychol 2006;73(1):90–9.

[3] Calderon SN, Klein M. A regulatory perspective on the abuse potential evaluation of novel stimulant drugs in the United States. Neuropharmacology 2014;87:97–103.

[4] Schoedel KA, Sellers EM. Assessing abuse liability during drug development: changing standards and expectations. Clin Pharmacol Ther 2008;83(4):622–6.

[5] US. Department of Health and Human Services FDA. Center for drug evaluation and research. Guidance for Industry: assessment of abuse potential of drugs. Silver Spring (MD). 2010.

[6] Balster RL, Bigelow GE. Guidelines and methodological reviews concerning drug abuse liability assessment. Drug Alcohol Depen 2003;70(3 Suppl.):S13–40.

[7] Comprehensive drug abuse prevention and control act of 1970. 1970.

[8] Klein M. FDA guidance for indsutry: assessment of abuse potential of drugs: overview, issues and framework for a decision tree. Rockville (MD): Science of Abuse Liabilty Assessment; 2011.

[9] Bonson K, Sun S. Draft decision tree for abuse potential. Rockville (MD): Science of Abuse Liability Assessment; 2011.

[10] Moser P, Wolinsky T, Castagne V, Duxon M. Current approaches and issues in non-clinical evaluation of abuse and dependence. J Pharmacol Toxicol Methods 2011;63(2):160–7.

[11] Moser P, Wolinsky T, Duxon M, Porsolt RD. How good are current approaches to nonclinical evaluation of abuse and dependence? J Pharmacol Exp Ther 2011;336(3):588–95.
[12] Vocci FJ. The necessity and utility of abuse liability evaluations in human subjects. Br J Addict 1991;86(12):1537–42.
[13] Mansbach RS, Feltner DE, Gold LH, Schnoll SH. Incorporating the assessment of abuse liability into the drug discovery and development process. Drug Alcohol Depend 2003;70(3 Suppl.):S73–85.
[14] Mansbach RS, Schoedel KA, Kittrelle JP, Sellers EM. The role of adverse events and related safety data in the pre-market evaluation of drug abuse potential. Drug Alcohol Depend 2010;112(3):173–7.
[15] Brady KT, Lydiard RB, Brady JV. Assessing abuse liability in clinical trials. Drug Alcohol Depend 2003;70(3 Suppl.):S87–95.
[16] Romach MK, Schoedel KA, Sellers EM. Human abuse liability evaluation of CNS stimulant drugs. Neuropharmacology 2014;87:81–90.
[17] Arfken CL, Cicero TJ. Postmarketing surveillance for drug abuse. Drug Alcohol Depend 2003;70(3 Suppl.):S97–105.
[18] Griffiths RR, Bigelow GE, Ator NA. Principles of initial experimental drug abuse liability assessment in humans. Drug Alcohol Depend 2003;70(3 Suppl.):S41–54.
[19] Bigelow GE. Human drug abuse liability assessment: opioids and analgesics. Br J Addict 1991;86(12):1615–23.
[20] Busto UE, Sellers EM. Anxiolytics and sedative/hypnotics dependence. Br J Addict 1991;86(12):1647–52.
[21] Cami J. Perspectives and future on testing for abuse liability in humans. Br J Addict 1991;86(12):1529–31.
[22] De Wit H. Preference procedures for testing the abuse liability of drugs in humans. Br J Addict 1991;86(12):1579–86.
[23] Farre M, Cami J. Pharmacokinetic considerations in abuse liability evaluation. Br J Addict 1991;86(12):1601–6.
[24] Evans SM, Critchfield TS, Griffiths RR. Abuse liability assessment of anxiolytics/hypnotics: rationale and laboratory lore. Br J Addict 1991;86(12):1625–32.
[25] Fischman MW, Foltin RW. Utility of subjective-effects measurements in assessing abuse liability of drugs in humans. Br J Addict 1991;86(12):1563–70.
[26] Foltin RW, Fischman MW. Methods for the assessment of abuse liability of psychomotor stimulants and anorectic agents in humans. Br J Addict 1991;86(12):1633–40.
[27] Henningfield JE, Cohen C, Heishman SJ. Drug self-administration methods in abuse liability evaluation. Br J Addict 1991;86(12):1571–7.
[28] Jasinski DR. History of abuse liability testing in humans. Br J Addict 1991;86(12):1559–62.
[29] Preston KL. Drug discrimination methods in human drug abuse liability evaluation. Br J Addict 1991;86(12):1587–94.
[30] Roache JD. Performance and physiological measures in abuse liability evaluation. Br J Addict 1991;86(12):1595–600.
[31] Sellers EM, Otton SV, Busto UE. Drug metabolism and interactions in abuse liability assessment. Br J Addict 1991;86(12):1607–14.
[32] Brady JV, Lukas SE. Testing drugs for physical dependence potential and abuse liability. Rockville (MD): National Institute on Drug Abuse; 1984.
[33] Fischman M, Mello N. Testing for abuse liability of drugs in humans. Rockville (MD): National Institute of Drug Abuse; 1989.
[34] Comer SD, Zacny JP, Dworkin RH, Turk DC, Bigelow GE, Foltin RW, et al. Core outcome measures for opioid abuse liability laboratory assessment studies in humans: IMMPACT recommendations. Pain 2012;153(12):2315–24.
[35] O'Connor AB, Turk DC, Dworkin RH, Katz NP, Colucci R, Haythornthwaite JA, et al. Abuse liability measures for use in analgesic clinical trials in patients with pain: IMMPACT recommendations. Pain 2013;154(11):2324–34.
[36] Carter LP, Griffiths RR. Principles of laboratory assessment of drug abuse liability and implications for clinical development. Drug Alcohol Depend 2009;105(Suppl. 1):S14–25.

[37] de Wit H, Griffiths RR. Testing the abuse liability of anxiolytic and hypnotic drugs in humans. Drug Alcohol Depend 1991;28(1):83–111.

[38] Foltin RW, Fischman MW. Assessment of abuse liability of stimulant drugs in humans: a methodological survey. Drug Alcohol Depend 1991;28:3–48.

[39] Isbell H, Fraser HF. Addiction to analgesics and barbiturates. J Pharmacol Exp Ther 1950;99(4:2):355–97.

[40] Jasinski DR. Assessment of the abuse potentiality of morphine like drugs (methods used in man). In: Martin WR, editor. Drug addiction I: morphine, sedative/hypnotic and alcohol dependence. New York: Springer-Verlag; 1977. p. 197–258.

[41] Jasinski DR, Johnson RE, Henningfield JE. Abuse liability assessment in human subjects. Trends Pharmacol Sci 1984;5:196–200.

[42] Jones JD, Comer SD. A review of human drug self-administration procedures. Behav Pharmacol 2013;24(5–6):384–95.

[43] Fischman MW, Johanson CE. Ethical and practical issues involved in behavioral pharmacology research that administers drugs of abuse to human volunteers. Behav Pharmacol 1998;9(7):479–98.

[44] Horton DB, Potter DM, Mead AN. A translational pharmacology approach to understanding the predictive value of abuse potential assessments. Behav Pharmacol 2013;24(5–6):410–36.

[45] Haney M, Spealman R. Controversies in translational research: drug self-administration. Psychopharmacology 2008;199(3):403–19.

[46] Panlilio LV, Goldberg SR. Self-administration of drugs in animals and humans as a model and an investigative tool. Addiction 2007;102:1863–70.

[47] Preston KL, Jasinski DR. Abuse liability studies of opioid agonist-antagonists in humans. Drug Alcohol Depend 1991;28(1):49–82.

[48] Chen L, Bonson KR. An equivalence test for the comparison between a test drug and placebo in human abuse potential studies. J Biopharm Statistics 2013;23(2):294–306.

[49] Rocha BA. Principles of assessment of abuse liability: US legal framework and regulatory environment. Behav Pharmacol 2013;24(5–6):403–9.

[50] US. Department of Health and Human Services FDA, Center for Drug Evaluation and Research. Guidance for industry: abuse-deterrent opioids—evaluation and labeling. Silver Spring (MD). 2013.

[51] Chen L, Tsong Y. Design and analysis for drug abuse potential studies: issues and strategies for implementing a crossover design. Drug Inf J 2007;41(4):481–9.

[52] Chen L, Wang Y. Heat map displays for data from human abuse potential crossover studies. Drug Inf J 2012;46(6):701–7.

[53] Fraser HF, Van Horn GD, Martin WR, Wolbach AB, Isbell H. Methods for evaluating addiction liability. (A) "Attitude" of opiate addicts toward opiate-like drugs. (B) A short-term "direct" addiction test. J Pharmacol Exp Ther 1961;133:371–87.

[54] Jasinski DR, Pevnick JS, Griffith JD. Human pharmacology and abuse potential of the analgesic buprenorphine. Arch Gen Psychiatry 1978;35:501–16.

[55] Jasinski DR, Preston KL. Assessment of dezocine for morphine-like subjective effects and miosis. Clin Pharmacol Ther 1985;38(5):544–8.

[56] Jasinski DR, Preston KL. Evaluation of mixtures of morphine and D-amphetamine for subjective and physiological effects. Drug Alcohol Depend 1986;17(1):1–13.

[57] Jasinski DR, Preston KL. A comparative assay of nefopam, morphine and D-amphetamine. Psychopharmacol Berl 1987;91(3):273–8.

[58] Preston KL, Bigelow GE, Liebson IA. Comparative evaluation of morphine, pentazocine and ciramadol in postaddicts. J Pharmacol Exp Ther 1987;240(3):900–10.

[59] Preston KL, Jasinski DR, Testa M. Abuse potential and pharmacological comparison of tramadol and morphine. Drug Alcohol Depend 1991;27(1):7–17.

[60] Stoops WW, Hatton KW, Lofwall MR, Nuzzo PA, Walsh SL. Intravenous oxycodone, hydrocodone, and morphine in recreational opioid users: abuse potential and relative potencies. Psychopharmacol Berl 2010;212(2):193–203.

[61] Walsh SL, Nuzzo PA, Lofwall MR, Holtman Jr JR. The relative abuse liability of oral oxycodone, hydrocodone and hydromorphone assessed in prescription opioid abusers. Drug Alcohol Depend 2008;98(3):191–202.

[62] Zacny JP, Lichtor JL, Thapar P, Coalson DW, Flemming D, Thompson WK. Comparing the subjective, psychomotor and physiological effects of intravenous butorphanol and morphine in healthy volunteers. J Pharmacol Exp Ther 1994;270(2):579–88.
[63] Zacny JP, Conley K, Marks S. Comparing the subjective, psychomotor and physiological effects of intravenous nalbuphine and morphine in healthy volunteers. J Pharmacol Exp Ther 1997;280(3):1159–69.
[64] Carter LP, Griffiths RR, Suess PE, Casada JH, Wallace CL, Roache JD. Relative abuse liability of indiplon and triazolam in humans: a comparison of psychomotor, subjective, and cognitive effects. J Pharmacol Exp Ther 2007;322(2):749–59.
[65] Evans SM, Funderburk FR, Griffiths RR. Zolpidem and triazolam in humans: behavioral and subjective effects and abuse liability. J Pharmacol Exp Ther 1990;255(3):1246–55.
[66] Evans SM, Troisi 2nd JR, Griffiths RR. Tandospirone and alprazolam: comparison of behavioral effects and abuse liability in humans. J Pharmacol Exp Ther 1994;271(2):683–94.
[67] Johnson MW, Suess PE, Griffiths RR. Ramelteon: a novel hypnotic lacking abuse liability and sedative adverse effects. Arch Gen Psychiatry 2006;63(10):1149–57.
[68] Preston KL, Guarino JJ, Kirk WT, Griffiths RR. Evaluation of the abuse potential of methocarbamol. J Pharmacol Exp Ther 1989;248(3):1146–57.
[69] Preston KL, Wolf B, Guarino JJ, Griffiths RR. Subjective and behavioral effects of diphenhydramine, lorazepam and methocarbamol: evaluation of abuse liability. J Pharmacol Exp Ther 1992;262(2):707–20.
[70] Rush CR, Baker RW, Wright K. Acute behavioral effects and abuse potential of trazodone, zolpidem and triazolam in humans. Psychopharmacol Berl 1999;144(3):220–33.
[71] Troisi 2nd JR, Critchfield TS, Griffiths RR. Buspirone and lorazepam abuse liability in humans: behavioral effects, subjective effects and choice. Behav Pharmacol 1993;4(3):217–30.
[72] Zawertailo LA, Busto U, Kaplan HL, Sellers EM. Comparative abuse liability of sertraline, alprazolam, and dextroamphetamine in humans. J Clin Psychopharmacol 1995;15(2):117–24.
[73] Zawertailo LA, Busto UE, Kaplan HL, Greenblatt DJ, Sellers EM. Comparative abuse liability and pharmacological effects of meprobamate, triazolam, and butabarbital. J Clin Psychopharmacol 2003;23(3):269–80.
[74] Brauer LH, Johanson CE, Schuster CR, Rothman RB, de Wit H. Evaluation of phentermine and fenfluramine, alone and in combination, in normal, healthy volunteers. Neuropsychopharmacology 1996;14(4):233–41.
[75] Heil SH, Holmes HW, Bickel WK, Higgins ST, Badger GJ, Laws HF, et al. Comparison of the subjective, physiological, and psychomotor effects of atomoxetine and methylphenidate in light drug users. Drug Alcohol Depend 2002;67(2):149–56.
[76] Makris AP, Rush CR, Frederich RC, Taylor AC, Kelly TH. Behavioral and subjective effects of D-amphetamine and modafinil in healthy adults. Exp Clin Psychopharmacol 2007;15(2):123–33.
[77] McCabe SE, Cranford JA. Motivational subtypes of nonmedical use of prescription medications: results from a national study. J Adolesc Health Off Publ Soc Adolesc Med 2012;51(5):445–52.
[78] Shram MJ, Schoedel KA, Bartlett C, Shazer RL, Anderson CM, Sellers EM. Evaluation of the abuse potential of lorcaserin, a serotonin 2C (5–HT2C) receptor agonist, in recreational polydrug users. Clin Pharmacol Ther 2011;89(5):683–92.
[79] Schoedel KA, McMorn S, Chakraborty B, Potts SL, Zerbe K, Sellers EM. Positive and negative subjective effects of extended-release oxymorphone versus controlled-release oxycodone in recreational opioid users. J Opioid Manag 2011;7(3):179–92.
[80] Harris SC, Perrino PJ, Smith I, Shram MJ, Colucci SV, Bartlett C, et al. Abuse potential, pharmacokinetics, pharmacodynamics, and safety of intranasally administered crushed oxycodone HCl abuse-deterrent controlled-release tablets in recreational opioid users. J Clin Pharmacol 2014;54(4):468–77.
[81] Zacny JP, Gutierrez S. Subjective, psychomotor, and physiological effects of oxycodone alone and in combination with ethanol in healthy volunteers. Psychopharmacol Berl 2011;218(3):471–81.
[82] Lile JA, Babalonis S, Emurian C, Martin CA, Wermeling DP, Kelly TH. Comparison of the behavioral and cardiovascular effects of intranasal and oral D-amphetamine in healthy human subjects. J Clin Pharmacol 2011;51(6):888–98.

[83] Piazza PV, Deroche-Gamonet V. A multistep general theory of transition to addiction. Psychopharmacol Berl 2013;229(3):387–413.
[84] Diagnostic and statistical manual of mental disorders: DSM-5. Washington (DC): American Psychatric Association; 2013.
[85] Diagnostic and statistical manual of mental disorders. 4th ed. Washington (DC): American Psychiatric Association; 2000.
[86] Piantadosi S. Clinical trials: a methodologic perspective. 1st ed. New York: John Wiley & Sons, Inc.; 1997.
[87] Piantadosi S. Clinical trials: a methodologic perspective. 2nd ed. New York: John Wiley & Sons, Inc.; 2005.
[88] Cruz HG, Hoever P, Chakraborty B, Schoedel K, Sellers EM, Dingemanse J. Assessment of the abuse liability of a dual orexin receptor antagonist: a crossover study of almorexant and zolpidem in recreational drug users. CNS Drugs 2014;28(4):361–72.
[89] Schoedel KA, McMorn S, Chakraborty B, Zerbe K, Sellers EM. Reduced cognitive and psychomotor impairment with extended-release oxymorphone versus controlled-release oxycodone. Pain Physician 2010;13(6):561–73.
[90] Woodward M. Epidemiology: study design and data analysis. 3rd ed. Boca Raton: CRC Press/Taylor & Francis Group; 2014.
[91] Schoedel KA. Interpretation of human abuse potential studies and clinically important responses to ADFs. In: Abuse deterrent formulation science meeting. 2013. North Bethesda (MD).
[92] Guyatt GH, Osoba D, Wu AW, Wyrwich KW, Norman GR. Clinical Significance Consensus Meeting G. Methods to explain the clinical significance of health status measures. Mayo Clin Proc 2002;77(4):371–83.
[93] Leon AC, Davis LL, Kraemer HC. The role and interpretation of pilot studies in clinical research. J Psychiatric Res 2011;45(5):626–9.
[94] Schoedel K, Shram MJ, Levy-Cooperman N, Chen N, Mills C, Setnik B, et al. Defining clinically important differences in subjective abuse potential measures. Palm Springs (CA): The College on Problems of Drug Dependence; 2012.
[95] Shram M, Levy-Cooperman N, Chen N, Mills C, Bartlett C, Setnik B, et al. Sensitivity and performance of derived parameters from human abuse potential studies. Palm Springs (CA): The College on Problems of Drug Dependence; 2012.
[96] Butler SF, Cassidy TA, Chilcoat H, Black RA, Landau C, Budman SH, et al. Abuse rates and routes of administration of reformulated extended-release oxycodone: initial findings from a sentinel surveillance sample of individuals assessed for substance abuse treatment. J Pain Off J Am Pain Soc 2013;14(4):351–8.
[97] Severtson SG, Bartelson BB, Davis JM, Munoz A, Schneider MF, Chilcoat H, et al. Reduced abuse, therapeutic errors, and diversion following reformulation of extended-release oxycodone in 2010. J Pain Off J Am Pain Soc 2013;14(10):1122–30.
[98] Jones B, Kenward MG. Design and analysis of cross-over trials. 2nd ed. Boca Raton (FL): Chapman & Hall/CRC Press; 2003.
[99] Williams EJ. Experimental designs balanced for the estimation of residual effects of treatments. Aust J Sci Res 1949;Series A2:149–68.
[100] Wang B, Wang X, Gong L. The construction of a Williams design and randomization in cross-over clinical trials using SAS. J Stat Softw 2009;29(1):1–10.
[101] Foltin RW, Ward AS, Haney M, Hart CL, Collins ED. The effects of escalating doses of smoked cocaine in humans. Drug Alcohol Depend 2003;70(2):149–57.
[102] Haney M, Ward AS, Comer SD, Foltin RW, Fischman MW. Abstinence symptoms following oral THC administration to humans. Psychopharmacol Berl 1999;141(4):385–94.
[103] Haney M, Ward AS, Comer SD, Foltin RW, Fischman MW. Abstinence symptoms following smoked marijuana in humans. Psychopharmacol Berl 1999;141(4):395–404.
[104] Strain EC, Walsh SL, Preston KL, Liebson IA, Bigelow GE. The effects of buprenorphine in buprenorphine-maintained volunteers. Psychopharmacol Berl 1997;129(4):329–38.
[105] Schoedel KA, Chen N, Hilliard A, White L, Stott C, Russo E, et al. A randomized, double-blind, placebo-controlled, crossover study to evaluate the subjective abuse potential and cognitive effects of nabiximols oromucosal spray in subjects with a history of recreational cannabis use. Hum Psychopharmacol 2011;26(3):224–36.

[106] Schoedel KA, Addy C, Chakraborty B, Rosko K, Dunbar S, Maes A, et al. Human abuse potential and cognitive effects of taranabant, a cannabinoid 1 receptor inverse agonist: a randomized, double-blind, placebo- and active-controlled, crossover study in recreational polydrug users. J Clin Psychopharmacol 2012;32(4):492–502.
[107] McColl SL, Burstein AH, Reeves KR, Billing Jr CB, Stolar M, Sellers EM. Human abuse liability of the smoking cessation drug varenicline in smokers and nonsmokers. Clin Pharmacol Ther 2008;83(4):607–14.
[108] Setnik B, Roland CL, Cleveland JM, Webster L. The abuse potential of Remoxy((R)), an extended-release formulation of oxycodone, compared with immediate- and extended-release oxycodone. Pain Med 2011;12(4):618–31.
[109] Sokolowska M. Human abuse liability studies: discussions of various applications and limitations during testing. Rockville (MD): Science of Abuse Liability Assessment; 2011.
[110] Pledger G. Proof of efficacy trials: choosing the dose. Epilepsy Res 2001;45(1–3):23–8. Discussion 9–30.
[111] Schwabe S. Proof of efficacy trials: choosing the dose. Epilepsy Res 2001;45:29–30.
[112] Kraemer HC, Mintz J, Noda A, Tinklenberg J, Yesavage JA. Caution regarding the use of pilot studies to guide power calculations for study proposals. Arch Gen Psychiatry 2006;63(5):484–9.
[113] Parasrampuria DA, Schoedel KA, Schuller R, Gu J, Ciccone P, Silber SA, et al. Assessment of pharmacokinetics and pharmacodynamic effects related to abuse potential of a unique oral osmotic-controlled extended-release methylphenidate formulation in humans. J Clin Pharmacol 2007;47(12):1476–88.
[114] Borm GF, Houben RM, Welsing PM, Zielhuis GA. An investigation of clinical studies suggests those with multiple objectives should have at least 90% power for each endpoint. J Clin Epidemiol 2006;59(1):1–6.
[115] Neuhauser M. How to deal with multiple endpoints in clinical trials. Fundam Clin Pharmacol 2006;20(6):515–23.
[116] Sankoh AJ, Li H, D'Agostino Sr RB. Use of composite endpoints in clinical trials. Statistics Med 2014;33(27):4709–14.
[117] Kraemer HC, Kupfer DJ. Size of treatment effects and their importance to clinical research and practice. Biol Psychiatry 2006;59(11):990–6.
[118] Martin W, Sloan J, Sapira J, Jasinski D. Physiologic, subjective, and behavioral effects of amphetamine, methamphetamine, ephedrine, phenmetrazine, and methylphenidate in man. Clin Pharmacol Ther 1971;12(2):245–58.
[119] Haertzen CA, Hill HE, Belleville RE. Development of the addiction research center inventory (Arci): selection of items that are sensitive to the effects of various drugs. Psychopharmacologia 1963;4:155–66.
[120] Haertzen CA. Development of scales based on patterns of drug effects, using the addiction Research Center Inventory (ARCI). Psychol Rep 1966;18(1):163–94.
[121] Brown EG, Wood L, Wood S. The medical dictionary for regulatory activities (MedDRA). Drug Saf 1999;20(2):109–17.
[122] Schroll JB, Maund E, Gotzsche PC. Challenges in coding adverse events in clinical trials: a systematic review. PLoS One 2012;7(7):e41174.
[123] Wood K. The medical dictionary for drug regulatory affairs (MEDDRA) project. Pharmacoepidemiol Drug Saf 1994;3:7–13.
[124] Bousquet C, Lagier G, Lillo-Le Louet A, Le Beller C, Venot A, Jaulent MC. Appraisal of the MedDRA conceptual structure for describing and grouping adverse drug reactions. Drug Saf 2005;28(1):19–34.
[125] Brown EG. Methods and pitfalls in searching drug safety databases utilising the Medical Dictionary for Regulatory Activities (MedDRA). Drug Saf 2003;26(3):145–58.
[126] Richesson RL, Fung KW, Krischer JP. Heterogeneous but "standard" coding systems for adverse events: issues in achieving interoperability between apples and oranges. Contemp Clin Trials 2008;29(5):635–45.
[127] Basch E. Beyond the FDA PRO guidance: steps toward integrating meaningful patient-reported outcomes into regulatory trials and US drug labels. Value Health J Int Soc Pharmacoeconomics Outcomes Res 2012;15(3):401–3.
[128] Love LA, Sun S. Proposed query to capture abuse-related adverse events. San Diego (CA): The College on Problems of Drug Dependence; 2013.

[129] Ioannidis JP, Evans SJ, Gotzsche PC, O'Neill RT, Altman DG, Schulz K, et al. Better reporting of harms in randomized trials: an extension of the CONSORT statement. Ann Intern Med 2004;141(10):781–8.

[130] Kessler DA. MEDWatch: the new FDA medical products reporting program. Clin Pharm 1993;12(7):529–32.

[131] Kessler DA. Introducing MEDWatch. A new approach to reporting medication and device adverse effects and product problems. JAMA 1993;269(21):2765–8.

[132] Kessler DA. MEDWatch: the new FDA medical products reporting program. Am J Hosp Pharm 1993;50(6):1151–2.

[133] Kessler DA, Kennedy DL. MedWatch: FDA's new medical products reporting program. J Clin Eng 1993;18(6):489–92.

[134] Klein E, Bourdette D. Postmarketing adverse drug reactions: a duty to report? Neurol Clin Pract 2013;3(4):288–94.

[135] Getz K, Stergiopoulos S, Kaitin K. Evaluating the completeness and accuracy of MedWatch data. Am J Ther 2014;21(6):442–6.

[136] Wood AJ. The safety of new medicines: the importance of asking the right questions. JAMA 1999;281(18):1753–4.

[137] Wood AJ, Stein CM, Woosley R. Making medicines safer–the need for an independent drug safety board. N Engl J Med 1998;339(25):1851–4.

[138] Brewer T, Colditz GA. Postmarketing surveillance and adverse drug reactions: current perspectives and future needs. JAMA 1999;281(9):824–9.

[139] Woody GE, Senay EC, Geller A, Adams EH, Inciardi JA, Schnoll S, et al. An independent assessment of MEDWatch reporting for abuse/dependence and withdrawal from Ultram (tramadol hydrochloride). Drug Alcohol Depend 2003;72(2):163–8.

[140] Glasser SP, Salas M, Delzell E. Importance and challenges of studying marketed drugs: what is a phase IV study? Common clinical research designs, registries, and self-reporting systems. J Clin Pharmacol 2007;47(9):1074–86.

[141] Cassidy T, McNaughton E, Varughese S, Russo L, Zulueta M, Butler S. Nonmedical use of prescription ADHD stimulant medications among adults in a substance abuse treatment population: early findings from the NAVIPPRO surveillance system. J Atten Disord 2015;19(4):275–83.

[142] Dart RC, Cicero TJ, Surratt HL, Rosenblum A, Bartelson BB, Adams EH. Assessment of the abuse of tapentadol immediate release: the first 24 months. J Opioid Manag 2012;8(6):395–402.

[143] Sembower MA, Ertischek MD, Buchholtz C, Dasgupta N, Schnoll SH. Surveillance of diversion and nonmedical use of extended-release prescription amphetamine and oral methylphenidate in the United States. J Addict Dis 2013;32(1):26–38.

[144] Zosel A, Bartelson BB, Bailey E, Lowenstein S, Dart R. Characterization of adolescent prescription drug abuse and misuse using the Researched Abuse Diversion and Addiction-related Surveillance (RADARS((R))) System. J Am Acad Child Adolesc Psychiatry 2013;52(2):196–204.e2.

[145] Dart RC, Bartelson BB, Adams EH. Nonmedical use of tapentadol immediate release by college students. Clin J Pain 2014;30(8):685–92.

[146] Butler SF, Budman SH, Licari A, Cassidy TA, Lioy K, Dickinson J, et al. National addictions vigilance intervention and prevention program (NAVIPPRO): a real-time, product-specific, public health surveillance system for monitoring prescription drug abuse. Pharmacoepidemiol Drug Saf 2008;17(12):1142–54.

[147] Cassidy TA, DasMahapatra P, Black RA, Wieman MS, Butler SF. Changes in prevalence of prescription opioid abuse after introduction of an abuse-deterrent opioid formulation. Pain Med 2014;15(3):440–51.

[148] Comer SD, Ashworth JB, Foltin RW, Johanson CE, Zacny JP, Walsh SL. The role of human drug self-administration procedures in the development of medications. Drug Alcohol Depend 2008;96(1–2):1–15.

[149] Richardson NR, Roberts DC. Progressive ratio schedules in drug self-administration studies in rats: a method to evaluate reinforcing efficacy. J Neurosci Methods 1996;66(1):1–11.

[150] Bolin BL, Reynolds AR, Stoops WW, Rush CR. Relationship between oral D-amphetamine self-administration and ratings of subjective effects: do subjective-effects ratings correspond with a progressive-ratio measure of drug-taking behavior? Behav Pharmacol 2013;24(5–6):533–42.

CHAPTER 10

Regulatory Framework and Guidance to the Evaluation of the Abuse Liability of Drugs in the United States and Europe

Silvia Calderon[1,*], Alessandra Giarola[2], David Heal[3]
[1]Center for Drug Evaluation and Research, Food and Drug Administration, Silver Spring, MD, USA; [2]Safety Pharmacology Department, GlaxoSmithKline, Ware, Hertfordshire, UK; [3]RenaSci Ltd., BioCity, Nottingham, UK

Contents

1. INTRODUCTION

The quantity of safety testing of new drugs for use in humans that is required to support drug registration has been steadily increasing over the last 20–30 years, and this trend shows no signs of abating. The evaluation of the potential for recreational abuse and/or liability to induce tolerance, physical dependence, and a withdrawal (or

* Opinions and assertions contained herein are those of the author, and they are not to be construed as representing those of the Food and Drug Administration.

Nonclinical Assessment of Abuse Potential for New Pharmaceuticals
http://dx.doi.org/10.1016/B978-0-12-420172-9.00010-2

discontinuation) syndrome is a mandatory part of testing that is required by the FDA (Food and Drugs Administration) and EMA (European Medicines Agency) for new central nervous system (CNS) drug candidates. It is now fair to state that any new chemical entity (NCE) that extensively crosses the blood–brain barrier (irrespective of whether or not the brain is the primary site of therapeutic action) will have to undergo a preclinical assessment to determine its potential for recreational abuse (its subjective effects and positive reinforcing potential) and its liability to induce tolerance and/or physical dependence.

Abuse liability assessment is the application of scientific methods to determine the extent to which a drug has the pharmacological and chemical properties predictive of its likelihood to produce abuse and dependence. This is needed for existing products that become subject to abuse, in which case information about their actual nonmedical use can be used to help identify problems as they emerge. It is also important to be able to predict abuse liability for new drugs during the development and approval process so additional drug controls set by the legal framework of the country where the drug will be marketed could be considered if the drug is shown to have abuse potential. These important goals have led to the development of a scientific field of abuse liability assessment. An abuse potential assessment requires an understanding of all properties of a drug predictive of the abuse of the drug, and this multidisciplinary approach ranges from preclinical pharmacology (in vitro and in vivo studies) through human pharmacology studies to postmarketing surveillance. There is not a single study that in isolation will address the abuse potential of a drug. This assessment is carried out as part of the general safety and efficacy evaluation for all new drugs under development with CNS activity, and in the USA, for all psychoactive drugs with new or significantly altered formulations. There are numerous published reviews of methods and approaches and some scientific organizations and regulatory authorities have developed guidelines and recommendations. The EMA [1], Health Canada [2], and the FDA [3] issued guidance on accepted approaches and methodologies used in the evaluation of the abuse potential of new drugs, for which there is no marketing history.

Abuse potential refers to the likelihood that a drug with psychoactive or CNS effects will sustain nonmedical self-administration that results in disruptive or undesirable consequences (regardless of whether or not this is associated with dependence). Examples of the psychoactive effects that drugs may produce include sedation, euphoria, perceptual and other cognitive distortions, hallucinations, and mood changes [3]. The terms abuse potential and abuse liability have often been used interchangeably because they represent similar concepts. However, the term abuse liability captures the human social and environmental factors that reflect the consequences or liability of abuse and can be difficult to predict prior to marketing of the drug and difficult to recreate in a laboratory environment.

Dependence liability is not only its potential to induce psychological dependence, which is the driver of drug-seeking behavior, but also tolerance and a syndrome of physical and/or psychological dependence on withdrawal. The latter is not only a risk for the nonmedical recreational abuse of the compound (the unintended population), but also for patients being medically prescribed the drug (the intended population). The evaluation, that is a mandatory part of the testing that is required by the FDA for USA regulatory approval, focuses on predicting the risks that the drug will pose for misuse and recreational abuse liability. In Europe, the scope of the evaluation set out by EMA for new CNS drug candidates is much wider and is not restricted to an assessment of its potential risk for recreational abuse. In addition, the assessment must also predict its liability to produce physical and/or psychological dependence in subjects who misuse or abuse the drug, and in patients who will be medically treated with the drug, and its potential to induce a syndrome of physical or psychological dependence on withdrawal.

The next sections provide an overview of the scientific aspects of the evaluation of the abuse potential of new drugs, as well as the regulatory framework and criteria applied in making recommendations for scheduling in the United States of America (USA) and in the European Union (EU).

2. REGULATORY FRAMEWORK AND GUIDANCE TO THE EVALUATION OF THE ABUSE POTENTIAL OF DRUGS IN THE UNITED STATES

In the USA, the assessment of the abuse potential of a drug is performed to fulfill the requirements of two laws. These laws are the Federal Food, Drug, and Cosmetic Act (FFD&CA) and the Controlled Substances Act (CSA). Within this regulatory framework, the FDA is the organization that evaluates the scientific and medical data related to the abuse potential of a new drug. Determination of the abuse potential of a drug provides important safety information and ensures that the drug is appropriately labeled and, if needed, subject to appropriate drug controls under the CSA. Under the regulations of the FFD&CA, Sponsors developing a drug with potential for abuse must submit as part of the new drug application (NDA) "a description and analysis of studies or information related to abuse of the drug, including a proposal for scheduling under the Controlled Substances Act." In addition, the NDA must include a description "of any studies related to overdose, including information on dialysis, antidotes, or other treatments, if known" [21 CFR 314.50(d)(5)(vii)].

The CSA establishes five schedules for control (Schedules I–V), and a recommendation for scheduling a drug in one of the five schedules is based upon the relative abuse potential, accepted medical use for treatment in the USA, and dependence liability of the drug. Each schedule under the CSA includes a set of regulations that are most restrictive for the Schedule I and II substances and relatively less restrictive for the Schedule III–V drugs (see Table 1). Before a drug with a potential for abuse can be

Table 1 Schedules and Criteria for Control under the US Controlled Substances Act (CSA)

Schedule	Criteria for Control
I (CI)	**1.** The drug or other substance has a high potential for abuse. **2.** The drug or other substance has not currently accepted medical use in the treatment in the United States. **3.** There is a lack of accepted safety for use of the drug or other substance under medical supervision.
II (CII)	**1.** The drug or other substance has a high potential for abuse. **2.** The drug or other substances has a currently accepted medical use in treatment in the United States or a currently accepted medical use with severe restrictions. **3.** Abuse of the drug or other substances may lead to severe psychological or physical dependence.
III (CIII)	**1.** The drug or other substance has a potential for abuse less than the drugs or other substances in Schedules I and II. **2.** The drug or other substance has a currently accepted medical use in the treatment in the United States. **3.** Abuse of the drug or other substance may lead to moderate or low physical dependence or high psychological dependence.
IV (CIV)	**1.** The drug or other substance has low potential for abuse relative to the drugs or other substances in Schedule III. **2.** The drug or other substance has a currently accepted medical use in the treatment in the United States. **3.** Abuse of the drug or other substance may lead to limited physical dependence or psychological dependence relative to the drug or other substances in Schedule III.
V (CV)	**1.** The drug or other substance has low potential for abuse relative to the drugs or other substances in Schedule IV. **2.** The drug or other substance has a currently accepted medical use in treatment in the United States. **3.** Abuse of the drug or other substance may lead to limited physical or psychological dependence relative to the drugs or other substances in Schedule IV.

Controlled Substance Act, Title 21 U.S.C. 812- Schedules of Controlled Substances.

controlled under the CSA, the Secretary of the Department of Health and Human Services (HHS), must make a recommendation for scheduling the drug under the CSA to the Drug Enforcement Administration (DEA), based on the available abuse-related data. The regulatory responsibilities for scheduling are described in 21 US.C. 811 and 812, as well as in 21 CFR Part 1300, with delegation of authority from the Secretary of the Department of HHS to the FDA. Within the FDA, this authority was delegated to the Center for Drug Evaluation and Research (CDER), and within CDER to the Controlled Substance Staff (CSS). CSS performs the scientific evaluation of the abuse potential of a drug for HHS. The National Institute on Drug Abuse (NIDA) provides advice on the recommendation. In this process, FDA determines what level of controls a drug needs, and it will recommend to the Assistant Secretary for Health (the designee of the Secretary of HHS, ASH/HHS) to submit a scheduling recommendation to the DEA [3]. The DEA has the final authority in scheduling actions. Each schedule under the CSA carries specific regulatory requirements relating to the drug's labeling, prescribing, advertising, manufacturing, promotion and marketing, use in the practice of medicine, and the institution of criminal penalties.

The abuse potential assessment is submitted as a section of the original NDA. The data for this assessment may be collected throughout all phases of development including the research and development stage. The findings are reported in the "8-Factor analysis" document that is submitted to FDA as part of the NDA.

FDA's current understanding of the type of studies recommended when evaluating the abuse potential of a drug is outlined and described in the draft FDA Guidance for Industry on the Assessment of Abuse Potential of Drugs [3]. The approaches for assessing abuse potential described in this guidance have been developed, applied, and tested for their reliability by the scientific community through the years [4]. While this guidance describes current accepted methodology used in the assessment of abuse potential, it offers a considerable degree of scientific flexibility regarding models and methodology because the assessment of abuse potential is an evolving area of research.

The FDA/CDER guidance [3], comparable to the Canadian guidance [2], emphasizes that the abuse potential assessment of a drug relies not only on preclinical studies but on the assessment of abuse potential in humans as well. In general, it is accepted that human data will be given a greater weight than nonhuman data in the assessment. For example, a positive signal in human abuse potential studies will be given more consideration than a negative signal in preclinical animal behavioral studies, such as self-administration and drug discrimination. Preclinical animal and human models have proven to be predictive of the abuse potential of drugs that fall within well-defined pharmacological classes, such as stimulants, opioids, and depressants. However, the assessment of the abuse potential of novel substances that do not fit within these well characterized classes is challenging.

A decision-making conceptual framework is depicted in Figure 1. A systematic assessment of the potential for abuse of a drug should be considered when the drug or NCE, or its active metabolites, has CNS activity, behaving as a stimulant or depressant, or producing other effects that are centrally mediated. The abuse potential of human metabolites that are present at 10% or greater of parent drug systemic exposure at steady state also need to be characterized [5]. The chemical and pharmacological similarity of the NCE or its active metabolites to other drugs of known abuse potential will also prompt the need for an abuse potential assessment. Drugs with known abuse potential fall within any of the following drug classes: opioids (analgesics and anesthetics), depressants (sedative-hypnotics, benzodiazepines, and others), stimulants (cocaine, amphetamines,

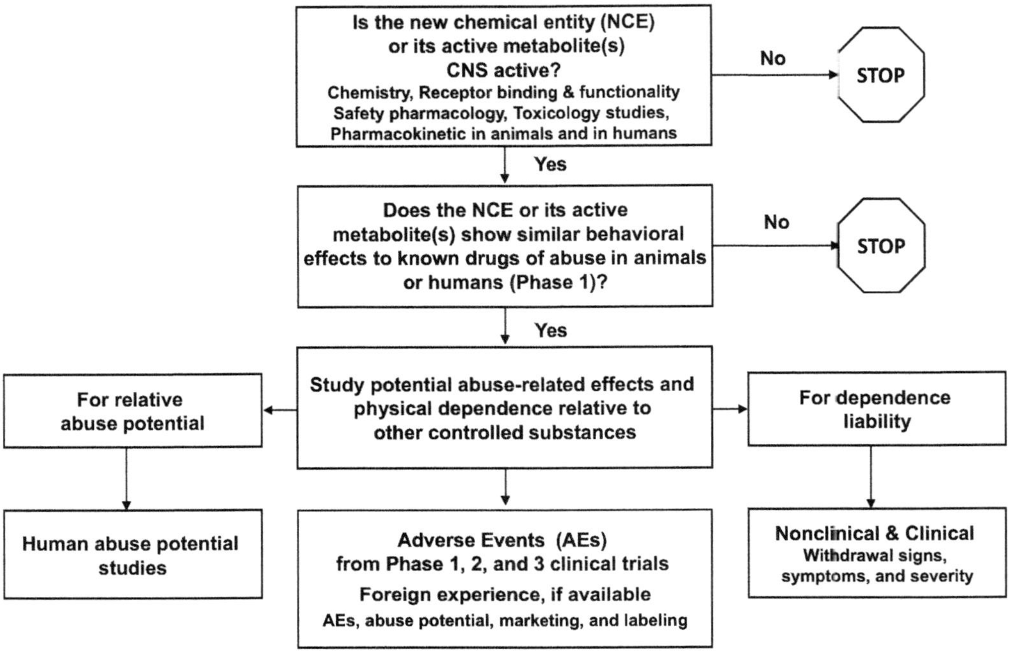

Figure 1 Decision-making conceptual framework in the assessment of the abuse potential of a new chemical entity (NCE).

and others), hallucinogens, phencyclidine and similar drugs active at the NMDA receptor, cannabinoids (marijuana and related compounds), and nicotine-like drugs. Abuse potential assessments are not limited to the study of new chemical entities (NCEs), as these assessments may be required as part of the characterization of new dosage forms of a drug substance or for a marketed drug product that presents an unexpected adverse event (AE) profile. For example, in the early 1990s, the abuse potential of butorphanol was reevaluated, when significant abuse of the substance was associated with the introduction of a novel nasal spray formulation. Up until the introduction of the nasal spray, butorphanol was available as a nonscheduled drug in an injectable form. As a result of this reevaluation and based on the new data available at the time, butorphanol was placed in Schedule IV of the CSA [6].

The assessment of the abuse potential of a drug requires a multidisciplinary approach and consists of a comprehensive evaluation of the chemistry, pharmacology (preclinical and clinical), pharmacokinetics, and pharmacodynamic profiles of the drug, AEs observed in clinical trials, as well as anticipated public health risks that may follow introduction of the drug into the market [3]. Data related to the chemistry, pharmacology, toxicology, metabolism, and pharmacokinetics are collected for all drugs under development, and these studies are often conducted early in the development scheme. The abuse potential of a drug is measured relative to that of a known drug of abuse. Consequently, the selection of the appropriate comparators or positive controls is based not only on the pharmacological properties of the positive controls, but the abuse potential of these controls and their scheduling status as well.

In reviewing the abuse potential of a drug, the focus is on all data related to the following properties of the drug:

1. Chemistry
2. Preclinical pharmacology (animal and in vitro receptor binding studies)
3. Animal behavioral and dependence pharmacology
4. Pharmacokinetics and pharmacodynamics
5. Human abuse potential laboratory studies
6. Clinical trial data relative to abuse and dependence potentials
7. Integrated summaries of safety and efficacy
8. Foreign experience with the drug if the drug is marketed in other countries (AEs, abuse potential, marketing, and labeling)

1. Chemistry

Chemical and structural similarity of the drug to other drugs with known abuse potential will also prompt the need for an abuse potential evaluation. Observation of such structure activity similarities can be made as early as the time of drug discovery. For example, a morphinan or a β-phenylethylamine structure may indicate a similar activity to that of an opioid or stimulant, respectively. FDA does not suggest any particular method or analysis to be used for the chemical structure similarity assessment; therefore, Sponsors have no limitations in using the currently available method/analysis or in developing novel ones. The most commonly used analysis is the Tanimoto similarity index. The Tanimoto index accounts for the number of shared features (i.e., common fragment substructures) between the two compounds. Features in compounds can be expressed as binary fingerprints where each bit represents the presence or absence of a substructure (chemical group, particular bond, atom, etc.) in the compound. Once the fingerprints for the compounds to compare (i.e., compound A versus compound B) have been created, the Tanimoto index is expressed as follows:

$$T = Nab/(Na + Nb - Nab)$$

where Nab is the number of features common to both compounds, Na is the number of features in compound A, and Nb is the number of features in compound B. Tanimoto similarity coefficient is accepted by regulatory authorities, but it is not a validated method and presents some weaknesses and limitations. Tanimoto coefficient should be used as early screening to identify gross chemical structure similarities with any compounds scheduled by DEA and should be followed by a more precise analysis on the compounds that are closer to the cut-off value [7,8].

The chemical assessment should include information related to the synthesis of the drug, physicochemical properties of the substance and proposed drug product and data related to alternate synthesis pathways and drug characteristics including yields and impurity profiles. In addition, information on extractability and solubility of the drug is relevant for the abuse potential assessment.

Other chemical properties of a drug that may impact its abuse potential include physicochemical characteristics such as high water solubility or stability at vaporization temperatures of the NCE on its salt or base form, because they indicate that the drug may be suitable for abuse intravenously or by smoking, thus facilitating the rapid delivery of the drug into the brain. It is known that drugs that rapidly reach the brain are more rewarding and are associated with high levels of abuse [9–14]. The high water solubility of salts of opioids such as oxycodone, or salts of amphetamine and methylphenidate allow for abuse of these substances through the intravenous route, whereas the low water solubility of benzodiazepines limits their intravenous abuse. The stability of a drug at high temperatures allows for smoking or inhalation of the drug, increasing its abuse potential.

2. Preclinical pharmacology (animal and in vitro receptor binding studies)

Data on the general pharmacology and toxicology of the drug are collected early on in the development program. Conducted as part of the general pharmacology assessment of the drug, the receptor binding profile and study results from in vitro and ex vivo studies provide data to evaluate the interaction of the novel drug at various receptor systems and receptor subtypes known to mediate the effects of many drugs of abuse (see Chapter 2 of this volume). The interaction of the drug at these abuse-related sites, either as primary sites of the pharmacological action or as "off target" sites will determine the need for assessment, and it will inform the design of additional studies in animals to further characterize the abuse potential of the drug.

Progressing from structure to effect initially involves the in vitro characterization of the effects of a compound predicting its equivalence to a known abused drug. Concern is justified if the NCE belongs to or shares relevant CNS activity with a pharmacological class of drugs associated with abuse liability or if it has a new mechanism of CNS action for which there is no previous experience.

Useful preliminary information can be gained from ligand-binding studies and functional in vitro/ex vivo assays. The first signals can be derived from binding of the active NCE to known targets involved in drug dependence (e.g., opioid receptors, dopamine/serotonin/noradrenaline receptors/transporters, NMDA, GABA, cannabinoids, etc.; See Chapter 2). Functional assays are needed to clarify the relevance and nature of such binding (e.g., agonist, antagonist, partial agonist, etc.). For example, a novel drug that targets the noradrenergic system, but also binds with high affinity and acts as a full agonist at the $5HT_{2A}$ and $5HT_{2C}$ receptors should be studied for its potential hallucinogenic properties, and its abuse potential should be compared to that of other hallucinogenic drugs that interact with the same serotonin receptor subtypes. Test agents with novel mechanisms of action may pose the risk of abuse potential that is entirely unknown. This situation, therefore, requires a careful assessment to be performed.

AEs in the preclinical studies can also be indicative of abuse potential. Typically, they can arise during standard clinical observations conducted during repeat-dose general toxicity studies or from the neurobehavioral observations performed during Irwin studies (e.g., increased locomotor activity, withdrawal signals like agitation following interruption of treatment). The effect of a novel drug on locomotor activity in animals (see Chapter 2) constitutes a basic parameter indicative of stimulant (increase in locomotor activity) or sedative (decrease in locomotor activity) pharmacology. The evaluation of the effect of a drug on motor activity is one of the effects measured as part of the safety pharmacology core evaluation of drugs [15].

3. Animal behavioral and dependence pharmacology

If a positive abuse potential signal arises after evaluating the chemistry, general pharmacology, safety pharmacology, and toxicology of the drug or its active metabolites, more specific studies (such as behavioral studies) will need to be performed. Behavioral studies constitute the core of the preclinical abuse potential assessment and are an integral component in the abuse potential assessment of drugs. Drug discrimination (see Chapter 6) and self-administration (see Chapters 3 and 4) are well accepted and widely used models for the evaluation of the reinforcing and discriminative properties of drugs, and they are relevant studies in predicting the abuse potential of many classes of drugs [16–20]. Other behavioral models used to measure the rewarding properties of drugs in laboratory animals include conditioned place preference (CPP) (see Chapter 7) and intracranial self-stimulation (see Chapter 8), though these models have been used less frequently for regulatory purposes [21,22]. For a complete review of these behavioral study procedures and the relevant methodological variables, we refer the reader to previous chapters in this book, as indicated. It is recommended that behavioral studies be conducted after the therapeutic dose of the drug has been established because, in general, the dose selection is based on the maximum plasma levels (C_{max}) achieved in humans at the therapeutic dose.

Animal self-administration studies have good predictive validity in assessing the abuse potential of several drug classes. Drugs that are self-administered by animals are typically self-administered by humans and have a potential for abuse [18,23,24]. However, there are limited data on the self-administration of novel drugs that are chemically and pharmacologically dissimilar from prototypical drugs of abuse such as opioids, benzodiazepines, and cocaine-like stimulants. Indeed the predictive validity of self-administration studies in assessing the abuse potential of novel drugs may be completely unknown. Typically, self-administration studies employ the intravenous route of administration, which may be limited by the solubility of the drug being studied. Another limitation is that self-administration studies may not be applicable to the evaluation of drugs that produce effects broadly characterized as "psychedelic." As a class, serotonergic hallucinogens are not self-administered by animals despite their abuse by humans. Similarly, cannabinoids are only self-administered under relatively specific laboratory conditions. Taken together, hallucinogens and cannabinoids are well-known false negatives in the self-administration paradigm.

Drug discrimination is also viewed as a traditional behavioral model used in the abuse potential evaluation of drugs. Drug discrimination studies indicate whether the drug being studied produces similar effects (interoceptive cues) to a known drug of abuse, and they help predict the subjective effects of the drug in humans. Drug discrimination is a sensitive and pharmacologically specific behavioral assay, in that more general behavioral effects such as euphoria or somnolence do not appear to determine the outcome of the test [18]. The predictive value of this model depends on the selection of the training drug, which can be challenging when evaluating the abuse potential of a drug with a novel mechanism of action. In this situation, one of two approaches is recommended. In the first approach, the novel NCE is used as a training drug and known drugs of abuse are tested for their ability to substitute for the NCE. In the second approach, the novel drug is tested for its ability to substitute for the training drug in several groups of animals, with each group trained to discriminate a prototypical drug of abuse (a hallucinogen, a cannabinoid, a stimulant, or other drug of abuse) from saline. These studies generally use the intraperitoneal, intramuscular, or subcutaneous injection or the proposed therapeutic route of administration. Drug discrimination data may provide data for certain classes of drugs that are not self-administered or where self-administration occurs under very specific conditions (e.g., hallucinogens and cannabinoids). In addition, drug discrimination data may help determine the positive control to be used in human abuse potential studies. One of the limitations of this model is that a negative result only indicates that the test drug is not like the training drug. In general, negative signals in drug discrimination or self-administration studies are not conclusive of a lack of abuse potential.

Physical dependence studies are conducted as part of the overall abuse potential assessment of drugs. These studies are conducted to determine the presence of a withdrawal syndrome and to assess the safety and health consequences associated with discontinuation or a significant dose reduction of the drug. Physical dependence studies are also used to support one of the three required findings for a scheduling recommendation. However, physical dependence per se is not considered a sign of abuse potential because it constitutes a physiological state of adaptation in response to repeated drug abuse [25]. Information on physical dependence is incorporated in the drug product label to inform health care practitioners about the safety risks associated with drug withdrawal. In general, physical dependence is assessed in animal models or in the clinical environment through the evaluation of signs or symptoms following discontinuation of the drug [18].

4. Pharmacokinetics and pharmacodynamics

Pharmacokinetic studies in animals and humans are conducted early on in the abuse potential evaluation program. These studies allow for an evaluation of the systemic exposure to the drug and metabolites and will aid in the selection of the appropriate species for behavioral studies. The abuse potential of human metabolites that are present at 10% or greater of parent drug systemic exposure at steady state also need to be characterized [5]. Pharmacokinetic studies provide data on the maximum concentration, time to onset, time to maximum concentration, and total exposure. In addition, when conducted in humans, these studies also capture safety-related pharmacodynamic outcomes of the NCE. It is accepted that drugs rapidly delivered into the brain have greater abuse potential [9–14]. This association between abuse potential and kinetics has been demonstrated for different pharmacological classes. Changes in routes of administration from those producing slow drug delivery and absorption to those promoting faster kinetics can promote illicit use of the drug. Therefore, characterization of the pharmacokinetic and pharmacodynamic properties of a substance and product are important for determining the abuse potential [26–28].

A drug's formulation can often influence the setting in which it is used/abused, and thereby the population who has access to it. A substance that is incorporated into several dosage forms may exhibit varying abuse liabilities based upon the principles of onset and duration of actions. The route of administration and physical dosage form can affect abuse liability because of differences in commercial distribution or marketing of various drug products. These factors can influence the extent of risk exposure of the general population. Consideration must be given to whether the active drug could be extracted from the proposed dosage form with the purpose of abuse through alternative routes of administration (special attention should be given to the feasibility of preparing suitable solutions for intravenous use) [29,30].

5. Human abuse potential laboratory studies

Clinical abuse potential studies and evaluation of abuse-related AEs captured in clinical trials (Chapter 9) are used to complement the aforementioned preclinical studies. Human abuse potential studies constitute an accepted methodology to assess the relative abuse potential of a new drug in humans [31–35]. The objectives of these studies are to provide information on the relative abuse potential of a new drug in humans and to predict the likelihood of abuse when the drug becomes available for marketing. These studies are typically conducted in participants experienced in the recreational use of drugs that are pharmacologically similar to the NCE. The selection of the appropriate positive comparators should be based on pharmacological similarity; for example, the selection of phentermine as a positive control might not be adequate when trying to study the abuse potential of a novel stimulant drug that does not show the same activity at monoaminergic sites.

6. Clinical trial data relative to abuse and dependence potentials

The evaluation of the AEs profile of a drug from clinical trials is also taken under consideration when evaluating the abuse potential of drug as they present an opportunity to collect information about effects in humans, which might not have been predicted by preclinical work. The systematic categorization, tabulation, and analysis of safety data related to mood elevation, as well as events that mirror those of typical drugs of abuse, can provide relevant information on the overall abuse potential assessment. The AE profile of the drug may be different depending on the population being studied and the doses being tested. Phase 1 safety and pharmacokinetic studies provide data on the AEs profile of the drug in healthy volunteers and also provide data on the effects of doses higher than the therapeutic dose. Phase 2 and Phase 3 studies can provide data on the AE profile of the NCE on the target therapeutic population, and a different AE profile might be observed for the same NCE in different populations. Data from all phases of development contributes to the AE database (MedDRA), and there are standard AE terms (e.g., euphoria, feeling drunk) that could possibly be associated with abuse liability. Pertinent data can include measurements of tolerance, physical dependence, or withdrawal symptoms, and the presence of signs or symptoms of drug abuse, misuse, diversion, tampering, or overdose [31,35,36].

2.1 Abuse Potential and Drug Scheduling

The USA CSA establishes five schedules for control of drugs and categorizes drugs in one of the five schedules based on relative abuse potential, medical usefulness, and dependence liability of the drug. Table 1 describes the criteria for control associated with each of these five schedules. For example, a drug is placed in Schedule II of the CSA if (1) the drug has a high potential for abuse, (2) it has a currently accepted medical use in treatment in the USA or a currently accepted medical use with severe restrictions, and (3) abuse of the drug may lead to severe psychological or physical dependence.

Each schedule under the CSA includes a set of regulations or measures required to protect the public health via minimizing abuse and diversion while allowing access to the drug for legitimate therapeutic purposes. The controls and regulations of the CSA are most restrictive for the Schedules I and II substances, and they are relatively less restrictive for the Schedules III–V drugs. Drugs in Schedule I have no accepted medical use in treatment in the United States. Depending on the Schedule (from II to V), controls may include manufacturing and production quotas, varying degrees of manufacturing and distribution site security requirements, dispensing and prescribing limitations, a range of record-keeping and reporting requirements, and import/export regulations. Prescribers, dispensers, drug manufacturers, and distributors are required to register with the USA DEA. In addition to the regulations, different penalties are associated with the various Schedules.

A recommendation for scheduling is a legal document based on scientifically sound and legally defensible data relevant to each substance considered for scheduling. This recommendation is also referred to as an 8-Factor Analysis, because it addresses the

eight factors established by the CSA when determining the need for scheduling a drug [21 US.C. 811 (c)]. These factors are the following:
1. Its actual or relative potential for abuse
2. Scientific evidence of the drug's pharmacological effects, if known
3. The state of current scientific knowledge regarding the drug or other substance
4. Its history and current patterns of abuse
5. The scope, duration, and significance of abuse
6. What, if any, risk there is to the public health
7. Its psychic or physiological dependence liability
8. Whether the substance is an immediate precursor of a substance already controlled.

As described in the Introduction, the DEA has final authority regarding scheduling decisions and makes the ultimate decision on the schedule of a drug after receiving input from FDA and NIDA through the ASH/HHS. Two recent articles have addressed various aspects of the drug scheduling process [37,38]. These articles describe the legal framework of drug scheduling, the roles of FDA and DEA in the process, the complexity of the scheduling process, and the scientific and medical data needed to support a recommendation for scheduling.

3. THE EUROPEAN UNION AND EMA

Although there had been an economic alliance between various European countries dating back as far as 1952, strictly speaking, the EU (European Union) only came into effect in November 1993 when the Treaty on EU was ratified. The EU has grown from its initial six Member States, viz Belgium, France, Italy, Luxemburg, Netherlands, and West Germany, to its current total of 28 members and now includes in its greatly expanded membership many of the former Eastern Bloc countries.

EMA, formerly known as the European Agency for the Evaluation of Medicinal Products (EMEA), is an EU organization that came into existence in 1995. EMA was set up to undertake a role across the EU that was analogous to the one performed by the FDA in the USA. The major difference is that EMA operates as a decentralized agency that recruits expertise from all EU Member States as required, as opposed to operating as a self-standing, regulatory authority. The main responsibilities of EMA are the protection and promotion of public and animal health through the evaluation and supervision of medicines for human and veterinary use. The Committee for Medicinal Products for Human Use (CHMP) is the division within EMA that is responsible for evaluating applications for the approval of new drugs for use in humans, for preparing opinions on questions concerning these medicines, and monitoring and advising on the safety of marketed drugs. Consistent with its decentralized model, EMA performs its scientific assessment of human medicinal products by working with a network of ~4500 experts throughout the EU. The agency draws on these resources via 40 National Competent Authorities (NCAs) within the EU Member States. In the UK, the responsible NCA is the Medicines and Healthcare Products Regulatory Agency (MHRA). In addition to evaluating and supervising medicines for human use in the 28 members of the EU, EMA also performs this role for affiliated countries, viz Iceland, Liechtenstein, and Norway, which are not EU Member States.

3.1 European Regulatory Procedures

There are four separate and distinct regulatory routes for submitting a Marketing Authorisation Application (MAA) for a new medicine for prescription use in humans in one or more EU Member States.

3.1.1 Centralized Procedure

In the EU, a pharmaceutical or biotechnology industry Sponsor is able to submit a single MAA to EMA that will, if granted, provide a license that is simultaneously valid in all EU countries, together with Iceland, Liechtenstein, and Norway (the "Community"). The Centralized Procedure is optional for many of the CNS-active drugs, which require an assessment of the risks they pose for abuse and/or dependence liability. However, this route is compulsory for medicinal products manufactured using biotechnology processes, for orphan medicinal products, and for human products containing a new active substance that was not authorized in the Community before May 20, 2004 that are intended for the treatment of neurodegenerative disorders. In the Centralized Procedure, the MAA is evaluated by expert representatives from two EU Member States, that is, a Rapporteur and Co-Rapporteur. Their opinion on the benefit/risk for the drug-candidate is presented to an expert panel of representatives from all of the EU Member States who then vote on whether or not to grant approval. The yes/no decision is made on a simple majority vote. From the Sponsor's perspective, the advantage of the Centralized Procedure is marketing authorization can be granted in all EU Member States plus the three affiliates based on a single decision-making procedure. The disadvantage of this route to market is if the majority vote goes against approval, then marketing authorization is denied in all EU Member States, including those which voted in favor of approval.

3.1.2 The Decentralized Procedure

The Decentralized Procedure allows Sponsors to apply for simultaneous marketing authorizations for a new human medicine in more than one, but not all, EU Member States, providing the drug has not yet been authorized in any EU country and does not fall within the mandatory scope of the Centralized Procedure (see previous). In the

Decentralized Procedure, the yes/no decision on approval for a marketing authorization is made on a country-by-country basis.

3.1.3 The National Procedure

Each EU Member State also has its own procedures for the authorization of new human medicines that fall outside of the scope of the Centralized Procedure. Sponsors from within the pharmaceutical and biotechnology sectors can submit the MAA to the NCA of an individual Member State. In the UK, the Medicines and Healthcare products Regulatory Agency (MHRA) is the organization that will evaluate and provide an opinion on MAA submissions from Sponsors. A marketing authorization is granted exclusively for use in the approving Member State. In this procedure, the opinion of one Member State is independent of all others and the yes/no decision on marketing approval applies only to that specific country.

3.1.4 The Mutual Recognition Procedure

When a medicine is first authorized in one EU Member State in accordance with its own approval procedures, the Sponsor can apply for further marketing authorizations from other EU countries using a procedure in which these countries agree to recognize the validity of the original, national marketing authorization. In this case, the yes/no decision is made on a country-by-country basis with the possibility that the MAA will be approved in some EU Member States, but not in others.

3.2 Product Labeling, Controlled Drug Status, and Scheduling for New CNS-Active Drugs

All of the four routes to European regulatory approval described in the previous section result in the creation of a single product label, that is, the Summary of the Product Characteristics (SPC). This SPC applies across all EU Member States where the drug has been approved for human use. SPCs for drugs approved for human use in the EU can be obtained from the EMA Website (www.ema.europa.eu/ema/) and are available for download in multiple languages. The European procedures for evaluating abuse/dependence liability for new CNS-active drug-candidates and the legislative framework for Controlled Drugs (CDs) differ significantly from those in the USA. These differences have important implications for the development of CNS-active drugs for the European market. Analogous to the situation in the USA, CD legislation covers both the medical use and also judicial penalties for misuse/abuse of the particular CD (see Figure 2).

Even for countries that are part of the EU, the laws and penalties relating to the non-medical use and abuse of CNS-active drugs differs from one country to another for historical reasons. There is no overarching legal framework for CD drugs set under EU Law. For this reason, although there is a single SPC for each approved drug on the EMA

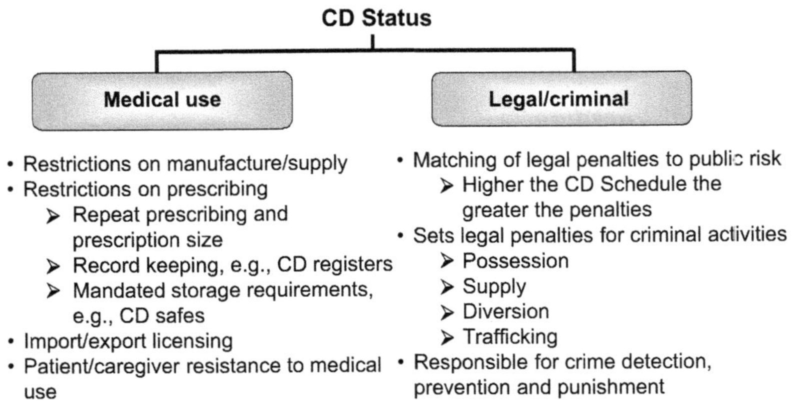

Figure 2 Legal and administrative requirements relating to the medical use of Controlled Drugs (CDs).

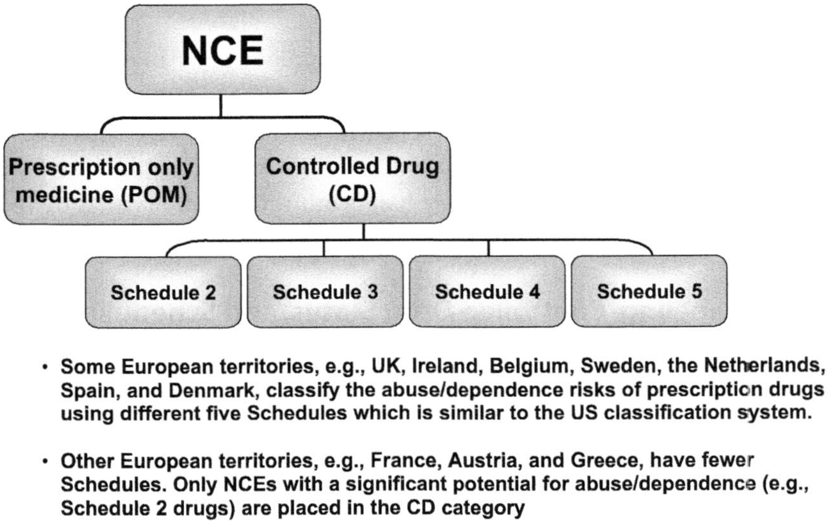

Figure 3 Scheduling of Controlled Drugs in the Summary of Product Characteristics (SPCs) across different EU Member States.

Website, the SPC is silent on the issue of CD status. Unlike the USA where FDA/DEA set the CD Schedule that applies across all US states, in Europe, the decision on whether or not a particular drug is a CD status is taken at the national level by individual EU Member States. The reasons for this are clearly apparent in Figure 3.

Hence, CD status and scheduling are viewed as a labeling issue and are not generally considered as part of the benefit/risk assessment performed by EMA in its decision to approve or decline the MAA for a particular drug-candidate. One possible exception to this view would probably apply to a hypothetical, novel, CNS-active NCE that offered no therapeutic improvements over existing approved drugs, but

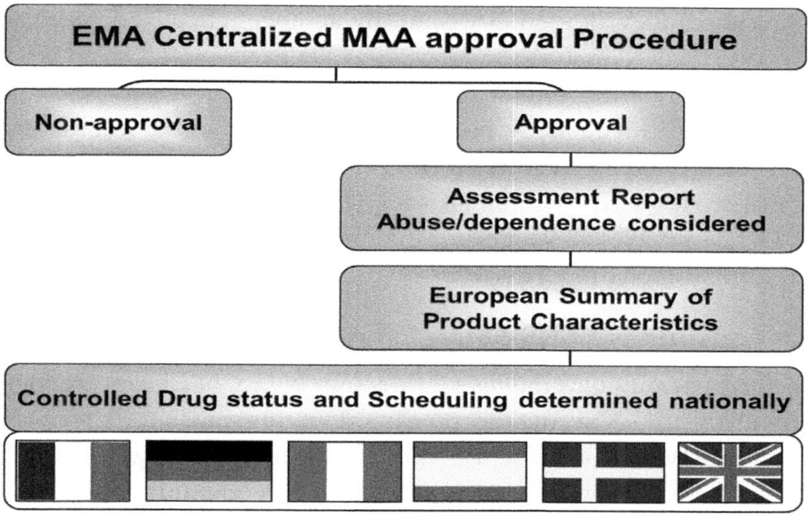

Figure 4 Regulatory procedures for determining the CD status of new drugs in individual EU Member States.

posed considerably greater risks in terms of its potential for recreational abuse and/or dependence.

The package of preclinical and clinical data on abuse/dependence liability has to be provided in the appropriate sections of the MAA for the NCE. These sections are contained within the body of the MAA and are not submitted to the agency as a separate document, cf. the 8-Factor Analysis that is submitted to FDA. The specialists on this subject from within the EMA, together with experts from various EU member states, will evaluate the evidence on abuse/dependence and if the Centralised Procedure has been used, then they will publish their opinion in the Assessment Report that appears on the EMA Website when the MAA is approved. The SPC is also published at this time. Either subsequent to or in parallel with this procedure, the CD status/Scheduling is determined by each country within the EU where the drug is to be marketed (see Figure 4).

The opinions on abuse/dependence liability offered by EMA and the resulting decisions taken by individual EU countries are generally less conservative in nature than those taken by CSS/FDA/DEA. The approval and CD status of pregabalin (Lyrica®) and lacosamide (Vimpat®) provides support for this opinion. Pregabalin, which was developed by Park-Davis/Pfizer for the prevention of complex partial seizures, is structurally related to the inhibitory amino acid γ-aminobutyric acid (GABA). It is a close analogue of another Park-Davis/Pfizer antiepileptic drug, that is, gabapentin (Neurontin®), which had been approved as a nonscheduled drug for the same indication by the FDA in 2002. Pregabalin was approved as an antiepileptic drug in Europe in 2000, and it was not classified as a CD. For the US approval 2 years later, Pfizer conducted a clinical trial in drug-experienced, human volunteers. The final outcome of the abuse/dependence evaluation was classification as C-V in the USA. Similarly, another antiepileptic drug, lacosamide (Vimpat®), was approved by EMA in June 2008 [39]. It was not classified as a CD in the UK and other EU countries. On the other hand, when this drug was reviewed 6 months later in the USA, CSS requested data for lacosamide from a trial in drug-experienced human volunteers to complete its evaluation. The final decision was to place lacosamide into C-V, making it the first sodium channel blocker ever to be a classified as a CD in the USA. These examples also highlight the importance that CSS/FDA places on the value of data from studies of CNS-active NCEs in human abuse liability trials.

3.3 What Constitutes a CNS-Active Drug?

Guidance for Sponsors developing CNS-active NCEs has been produced by the CHMP of EMA to advise on the preclinical testing procedures that are recommended for the evaluation of abuse and dependence liability. This guidance was issued in final form in March 2006 [1]. Because EMA does not require a determination of abuse/dependence liability in drug-experienced, human volunteers, this topic is not included in CHMP's guidance. Although CHMP/EMA does make use of AE reporting from Phase 1 and Phase 2/3 human trials in making its assessment, the agency has issued no formal guidance on how this objective is to be achieved. As described earlier in this chapter, the CDER of the FDA has issued a more wide-ranging guidance on the subject that offers advice and recommendations on both preclinical and clinical procedures for evaluating the abuse/dependence liability of CNS-active drug-candidates.

EMA defines a CNS-active drug in the "Scope" section of the document on page four of its guidance [1]. "The need for dependence potential testing should be considered for all new CNS-active medicinal products. See also Note 1. [Note 1: In general, only CNS active substances are of concern. However, active substances with peripheral targets may enter the brain as well either as parent active substance or as a metabolite at relevant concentrations and interact at central targets. This could be a concentration-dependent phenomenon, the result of applying different routes of administration or a consequence of metabolism. When available data give rise to a concern in this respect, studies as explained in this document should be considered to further clarify the pharmacological profile of the product.]" However, the guidance also issues the following warning to Sponsors "If no studies are performed, the lack of these studies should be justified." If the NCE sits in a gray area, the statement strongly suggests that the advice on whether it will be necessary to perform a package of abuse/dependence studies should be sought from CHMP/EMA by the Sponsor.

In summary, an NCE does not need to be in development for a psychiatric, neurological, analgesic, or anesthetic indication to be eligible for an abuse/dependence assessment; all that is necessary for it to require evaluation is for it to enter the brain in sufficient quantity at doses within or above the pharmacological and clinical range to an extent where they can evoke behavioral and/or psychoactive effects.

3.4 EMA-Recommended Preclinical Package of Abuse/Dependence Studies for CNS-Active New Chemical Entities

The preclinical experimental studies are set out in "Guideline on the Non-Clinical Investigation of the Dependence Potential of Medicinal Products" [1]. It should be noted that the term dependence is used in the title of the guideline, and this covers an assessment of the risks posed by the drug-candidate for misuse, recreational abuse, psychological dependence, and physical dependence on withdrawal. The scope of the evaluation of dependence is extremely broad, which it defines as the propensity of a CNS-active drug-candidate to give rise to a need for repeated doses of the substance to "feel good" or to avoid "feeling bad." The guideline indicates that dependence potential can be measured in animal and human drug testing procedures, although data from studies in drug-experienced, human volunteers are not required for European drug registration. The testing procedures should include assessments of psychological dependence (drug-seeking or craving) and physiological or physical dependence, which refers to tolerance and withdrawal symptoms (as a result of neuro-adaptation). In its guidance, EMA clearly states that "Drug dependence is not the same as drug abuse." EMA accepts that there are situations in which treatment with a dependence-producing drug needs to be continued, even after the patient has become dependent on it, citing opiates, cocaine, and barbiturates as examples. In addition, EMA is keen to learn about the potential risks for "drug withdrawal syndromes" (cf. those produced by the SSRIs [selective serotonin reuptake inhibitors] and benzodiazepines) that are posed by new CNS-active drugs that often have novel pharmacological mechanisms.

The testing procedures are divided into "First tier," that is, in vitro and in vivo pharmacology, and "Second tier," that is, specific behavioral pharmacology tests to investigate abuse/dependence potential. Typical in vitro pharmacology studies include a determination of the affinity of the drug candidate for a range of abuse-related molecular targets, for example, receptors, binding sites, ion channels and transporters (see Chapter 2). In vivo studies are likely to include assessments of motor activity (Chapter 2) including sedation or activation/stimulation, relevant specific behaviors, for example, head-twitches [a model for detecting serotonergic hallucinogens], and in addition, intracerebral microdialysis in freely moving rodents to investigate the effect of the drug-candidate on the efflux of dopamine in the mesolimbic system, which is believed to mediate the rewarding and reinforcing effects of a wide range of known substances of abuse (see Chapter 2). These in vivo studies can be sophisticated and provide a wealth of information to link the pharmacokinetic profile of the drug candidate, for example, plasma drug concentrations, with CNS neurochemistry, for example, dopamine efflux, and functional outcomes, for example, locomotor activity [40].

The package of Second tier preclinical studies has to address the following issues:

- Discriminative effect (subjective experience) (Chapter 6). Is the subjective experience evoked by the drug candidate similar to that of any known substance of abuse?
  - Rats, but other species, for example, primates, pigeons, etc., are occasionally used.
- Reinforcing effect (psychological dependence, craving). Is the subjective effect of the drug-candidate rewarding or reinforcing? Does it lead to drug-seeking behavior?
  - Intravenous self-administration in rats (Chapter 3).
  - The guidance also states that a progressive ratio schedule of reinforcement and break-point analysis should be used to determine the reinforcing effect of the drug-candidate relative to reference active comparators (page 7 of the CHMP/EMA Guideline).
  - Drug-reinforced conditioned place preference (CPP) studies (Chapter 7) are given as an alternative technique for assessing drug reinforcement. Its use can be justified in some situations, for example, where the solubility of the drug-candidates precludes testing in an intravenous self-administration model.
- Physical dependence (withdrawal) (see Chapter 5). Does repeated exposure to the NCE induce tolerance that leads to a syndrome of physical dependence when treatment is stopped?
  - Generally rats.
  - Tolerance can be assessed during the dosing phase.
  - For some drug-candidates, results from several ≥ 1-month good laboratory practice (GLP) toxicology studies can be subjected to a rigorous, specialized post hoc re-analysis to create a Study Report tolerance and physical dependence liability (e.g., see the EMA Assessment Report on Vimpat) [39].

All of the above studies need to be well designed and incorporate the use of at least one positive control, that is, reference comparator substance of abuse, and negative control, that is, placebo.

The choice of reference comparator substance(s) of abuse for use in the evaluation of the abuse/dependence potential of NCEs has to be supported by a good scientific rationale.

1. The chemical structure of the drug-candidate is similar to that of a known substance of abuse or known class of abuse substances.
2. The pharmacological mechanism of action of the drug-candidate is similar or identical to that of a known substance of abuse, for example, μ-opioid receptor agonist or dopamine releasing agent.
3. If the drug-candidate has a novel pharmacological mechanism, then the reference comparator could be another drug used in the intended therapeutic indication, which is subject to diversion and recreational abuse or is known to produce dependence and/or addiction.

The CHMP/EMA recommends that where rodent or other nonprimate models are available, they should be used in preference to primate models subject to the usual caveats, for example, validity of the model, technical feasibility, DMPK profile, etc. Although the primate was previously considered to be the species of choice for intravenous self-administration studies, a recent critical analysis by Horton et al. has revealed that the predictive validity results from rodent self-administration experiments is at least as good as that obtained from primates [19].

The requirement for GLP compliance in the nonclinical testing of drugs for abuse and/or dependence liability is a difficult subject. CHMP/EMA states that First tier pharmacology studies need not be performed to GLP (see Section 7, [1]). However, Second tier tests are part of the Safety Pharmacology package and should comply with GLP wherever possible (see Section 7, [1]). However, EMA does not mandate GLP for abuse/dependence liability testing because these experiments are seen as investigative studies, are extremely difficult to design, conduct, and interpret, and the expertise to conduct them often resides in research laboratories that are not GLP-accredited. If a study is not performed to GLP, then a justification for this decision needs to be provided. The study itself needs to be rigorously designed, conducted, reported, audited, and archived (GLP-like). Also, an impact assessment must be performed on the study and included in the Study Report to show that there has been no significant adverse consequence of not performing the study to GLP (see Section 7, [1]). The preclinical abuse/dependence package to support the successful European registration of the D-amphetamine (AMP) prodrug, lisdexamfetamine (Vyvanse®, Elvanse®, Tyvanse®), is an example of GLP-like drug-discrimination and self-administration testing in rats [41]. In addition, most of the advances in research in the abuse/dependence field have been generated by scientists from academic research laboratories. Although most academic laboratories are not configured for GLP or GLP-like study conduct, it is possible to set up collaborations with eminent academic scientists in the abuse/dependence filed to achieve the dual objectives of engaging the best scientists to conduct a particular abuse/dependence study and attain the level of reporting, data collection, and archiving mandated by the regulatory agency [41,42].

3.5 Reporting Results from Preclinical Abuse/Dependence Assessments in the European MAA

The results from the preclinical and clinical evaluations of abuse/dependence liability are reported in the appropriate sections of the MAA, that is, Secondary Pharmacodynamics, Safety Pharmacology, and Clinical Safety. This piecemeal approach differs from the USA procedure where the evidence on the potential risk of abuse/dependence is also reported separately from the NDA in the Sponsor's own evaluation of the evidence that will be contained in the 8-Factor Analysis. Because, in

Europe, decisions on CD status and Scheduling are taken at a national level, it is often useful to Sponsors to have all of the preclinical and clinical information on abuse/dependence potential of its drug candidate drawn together in a single document to facilitate the evaluation and decision making by national authorities. However, the 8-Factor Analysis is not well suited to this task because of the heavy emphasis placed on data obtained in drug-experienced human abuse studies and the redundancy of some of the factors.

4. A COMPARISON OF THE EUROPEAN AND US REGULATORY APPROACHES TO ABUSE/DEPENDENCE EVALUATION, REPORTING, AND DECISION MAKING

The similarities and differences between the European and US regulatory approaches to evaluating the potential risks of abuse/dependence are illustrated in Figure 5.

Overall, the objectives of the exercise are identical, that is, to make realistic predictions of the risks for abuse and dependence that novel CNS-active drugs are likely to pose to patients and wider society after they have received marketing approval and are widely available in a real-world setting. As shown by the text in green and blue of Figure 5, there is a high degree of consensus between the approaches adopted by CHMP/EMA and CSS/FDA. The major area of difference is the reliance of CSS/FDA on evidence on recreational abuse liability obtained from trials performed in drug-experienced human volunteers. The other difference is the mechanisms for reporting the results in the submission dossier. Although it is

	CHMP/EMA Guidance	FDA (CSS) Guidance
Phasing of testing	Prior to Phase I	In parallel with clinical development → (Phases I-III)
Species of choice	Rodents	Primates or rodents
Safety pharmacology	Yes	Yes
GLP	Preferred/ Not mandated	Preferred/ Not mandated
Reliance on drug-experienced volunteer studies	No	Yes
Reporting	Appropriate sections of the MAA	Separate filing to CSS* as part of the NDA

*CSS = Controlled Substances Staff

Consensus Growing consensus Divergence

Figure 5 Differences between the European and US approaches to the evaluation of abuse liability.

necessary to take these differences into account when designing abuse/dependence evaluation programs for CNS-active drug candidates seeking US and European approval, the high degree of overlap between the two regulatory approaches ensures that it is feasible to design and perform one set of preclinical studies to meet the needs of both regulatory agencies.

REFERENCES

[1] EMA/CHMP, European Medicine Agency, Committee for Medicinal Products for Human Use. Guidance on the non-clinical investigation of the dependence potential of medicinal products; 2006. http://www.ema.europa.eu/docs/en_GB/document_library/Scientific_guideline/2009/09/WC500003360.pdf [accessed 23.02.14].
[2] Health Canada, Minister of Health. Guidance document on the clinical assessment of abuse liability for drugs with central nervous system activity; 2007. http://www.hc-sc.gc.ca/dhp-mps/alt_formats/hpfb-dgpsa/pdf/prodpharma/abuse_liability_abusif_usage_clin-eng.pdf [accessed 24.02.14].
[3] FDA/CDER, US Department of Health and Human Services, Food and Drug Administration, Center for Drug Evaluation and Research. Guidance for industry on the assessment of abuse potential of drugs; 2010. http://www.fda.gov/downloads/Drugs/GuidanceComplianceRegulatoryInformation/Guidances/UCM198650.pdf [accessed 20.10.13].
[4] Balster RL, Bigelow GE. Guidelines and methodological reviews concerning drug abuse liability assessment. Drug Alcohol Depend 2003;70:S13–40.
[5] FDA/CDER, US Department of Health and Human Services, Food and Drug Administration, Center for Drug Evaluation and Research. Guidance for industry on the safety testing of metabolites; 2008. http://www.fda.gov/OHRMS/DOCKETS/98fr/FDA-2008-D-0065-GDL.pdf [accessed 20.10.13].
[6] Schedule of controlled substances. Placement of butorphanol into Schedule IV. October 1, 1997. Final rule. 62 FR 51370.
[7] Martin YC, Kofron JL, Traphagen LM. Do structurally similar molecules have similar biological activity? J Med Chem 2002;45:4350–8.
[8] Willett P. Similarity searching using 2D structural fingerprints. In: Bajorath Jurgen, editor. Chemoinformatics and computenional chemical biology, methods in molecular biology, vol. 672. Springer Science+Business Media; 2011. p. 133–57.
[9] Gossop M, Griffiths P, Powis B, Strang J. Severity of dependence and route of administration of heroin, cocaine and amphetamines. Br J Addict 1992;87:1527–36.
[10] Henningfield JE, Keenan RM. Nicotine delivery kinetics and abuse liability. J Consult Clin Psychol 1993;61:743–50.
[11] Hatsukami DK, Fischman MW. Crack cocaine and cocaine hydrochloride. Are the differences myth or reality? JAMA 1996;276:1580–8.
[12] Volkow ND, Wang GJ, Fischman MW, Foltin R, Fowler JS, Franceschi D, et al. Effects of route of administration on cocaine induced dopamine transporter blockade in the human brain. Life Sci 2000;67:1507–15.
[13] Samaha AN, Robinson TE. Why does the rapid delivery of drugs to the brain promote addiction? Trends Pharmacol Sci 2005;26:81–7.
[14] McColl S, Sellers EM. Research design strategies to evaluate the impact of formulations on abuse liability. Drug Alcohol Depend 2006;83:S52–62.
[15] FDA/CDER/CBER/ICH. Guidance for industry S7A safety pharmacology studies for human pharmaceuticals; 2001. http://www.fda.gov/downloads/Drugs/GuidanceComplianceRegulatoryInformation/Guidances/ucm074959.pdf [accessed 20.10.13].
[16] Balster RL. Drug abuse potential evaluation in animals. Br J Addict 1991;86:1549–58.
[17] Brady JV. Animal models for assessing drugs of abuse. Neurosci Biobehav Rev 1991;15:35–43.
[18] Ator NA, Griffiths RR. Principles of drug abuse liability assessment in laboratory animals. Drug Alcohol Depend 2003;70:S55–72.

[19] Horton DB, Potter DM, Mead AN. A translational pharmacology approach to understanding the predictive value of abuse potential assessments. Behav Pharmacol 2013;24:410–36.
[20] Huskinson SL, Naylor JE, Rowlett JK, Freeman KB. Predicting abuse potential of stimulants and other dopaminergic drugs: overview and recommendations. Neuropharmacology March 22, 2014. [Epub ahead of print].
[21] Bardo MT, Bevins RA. Conditioned place preference: what does it add to our preclinical understanding of drug reward? Psychopharmacology (Berl) 2000;153:31–43.
[22] Watterson LR, Watterson E, Olive MF. Abuse liability of novel 'legal high' designer stimulants: evidence from animal models. Behav Pharmacol 2013;24:341–55.
[23] Schuster CR, Thompson T. Self-administration of and behavioral dependence on drugs. Annu Rev Pharmacol 1969;9:483–502.
[24] Johanson CE, Balster RL. A summary of the results of a drug self-administration study using substitution procedures in rhesus monkeys. Bull Narc 1978;30:43–54.
[25] O'Brien CP. Drug addiction and drug abuse. In: Hardman JG, Limbird LE, Molinoff PB, Ruddon RW, Goodman Gilman A, editors. Goodman & Gilman's The Pharmacological Basis of Therapeutics 9th ed. New York: McGraw-Hill Professional; 1996. p. 557–80.
[26] de W it H, Dudish S, Ambre J. Subjective and behavioral effects of diazepam depend on its rate of onset. Psychopharmacology (Berl) 1993;112:324–30.
[27] Comer SD, Collins ED, MacArthur RB, Fischman MW. Comparison of intravenous and intranasal heroin self-administration by morphine-maintained humans. Psychopharmacology (Berl) 1999;143:327–38.
[28] Woolverton WL, Wang Z. Relationship between injection duration, transporter occupancy and reinforcing strength of cocaine. Eur J Pharmacol 2004;486:251–7.
[29] Schuster CR, Henningfield J. Conference on abuse liability assessment of CNS drugs. Drug Alcohol Depend 2003;70:1–4.
[30] Sellers EM, Schuster CR. Conference on drug formulations and abuse liability. Drug Alcohol Depend 2006;83:1–3.
[31] Brady KT, Lydiard RB, Brady JV. Assessing abuse liability in clinical trials. Drug Alcohol Depend 2003;70:87–95.
[32] Griffiths RR, Bigelow GE, Ator NA. Principles of initial experimental drug abuse liability assessment in humans. Drug Alcohol Depend 2003;70:S41–54.
[33] Chen L, Tsong Y. Design and analysis for drug abuse potential studies: issues and strategies for implementing a crossover design. Drug Inf J 2007;41:481–9.
[34] Carter LP, Griffiths RR. Principles of laboratory assessment of drug abuse liability and implications for clinical development. Drug Alcohol Depend 2009;105:14–25.
[35] Mansbach RS, Schoedel KA, Kittrelle JP, Sellers EM. The role of adverse events and related safety data in the pre-market evaluation of drug abuse potential. Drug Alcohol Depend 2010;112:173–7.
[36] Schoedel KA, Sellers EM. Assessing abuse liability during drug development: changing standards and expectations. Clin Pharmacol Ther 2008;83:622–6.
[37] Rocha BA. Principles of assessment of abuse liability: US legal framework and regulatory environment. Behav Pharmacol 2013;24:403–9.
[38] Calderon SN, Klein M. A regulatory perspective on the abuse potential evaluation of novel stimulant drugs in the United States. Neuropharmacology 2014;87:97–103.
[39] EMA assessment report on Vimpat. 2008. http://www.ema.europa.eu/docs/en_GB/document_library/EPAR_-_Public_assessment_report/human/000863/WC500050341.pdf.
[40] Rowley HL, Kulkarni R, Gosden J, Brammer R, Hackett D, Heal DJ. Lisdexamfetamine and immediate release D-amfetamine – differences in pharmacokinetic/pharmacodynamic relationships revealed by striatal microdialysis in freely-moving rats with simultaneous determination of plasma drug concentrations and locomotor activity. Neuropharmacology 2012;63:1064–74.
[41] Freeman KB, Heal DJ, McCreary AC, Woolverton WL. Assessment of ropinirole as a reinforcer in rhesus monkeys. Drug Alcohol Depend 2012;125:173–7.
[42] Heal DJ, Buckley NW, Gosden J, Slater N, France CP, Hackett D. A preclinical evaluation of the discriminative and reinforcing properties of lisdexamfetamine in comparison to D-amfetamine, methylphenidate and modafinil. Neuropharmacology 2013;73:348–58.

CHAPTER 11

Risk Management Implications of Abuse Potential Assessment

Jack E. Henningfield[1,2], August R. Buchhalter[1], Edward J. Cone[1], Michelle D. Ertischek[1], Reginald V. Fant[1], Karen K. Gerlach[1], Sidney H. Schnoll[1]
[1]PinneyAssociates, Bethesda, MD, USA; [2]School of Medicine, Johns Hopkins University, Baltimore, MD, USA

Contents

1. INTRODUCTION: RISK MANAGEMENT IN THE CONTEXT OF CONTROLLED SUBSTANCE SCHEDULING

Risk management can be broadly considered as any and all of the strategies implemented to minimize the risks and therefore enable the realization of the benefits of medications. For decades, risk management has been promulgated primarily through the approved drug label that is generally, but not always precisely, harmonized by drug regulatory agencies across countries and regions [1]. This labeling includes special controls (often referred to as "drug scheduling" or "controlled substance scheduling") for medications that have the potential for abuse and dependence ("addiction"). Drug scheduling places the medication in a schedule that is intended to be commensurate with the risk it poses for abuse and dependence [2–6] (see also Chapter 10).

Controlled substance scheduling includes several key elements that are also increasingly being included in risk management programs or plans (RMPs) or the legislatively defined versions used in the US, which are called Risk Evaluation and Mitigation Strategies (REMS) [7,8]. Scheduling determinations are based on a scientific foundation that includes abuse potential assessment, as described in this book and elsewhere [9,10], evaluation of public effects, chemistry, and other factors (see Chapter 10) and elsewhere

Nonclinical Assessment of Abuse Potential for New Pharmaceuticals
http://dx.doi.org/10.1016/B978-0-12-420172-9.00011-4

[5,6]. As is the case with RMPs, drug scheduling is intended to enable appropriate access for patients by employing structured predefined elements that are intended to be commensurate with and appropriate to the risks posed by the drug or drug class. The drug schedules therefore include special warnings and guidance in the labeling, restrictions on prescribing and marketing, and often legal requirements for handling and distributing the drug substance and pharmaceutical products that contain that substance.

Formal RMPs include two additional components that are discussed in this chapter: a plan for postmarketing surveillance and a plan for interventions to address unintended consequences [11,12]. As discussed elsewhere, in the context of controlled substances, the RMP is in addition to the risk management provisions imposed by controlled substance scheduling [13].

1.1 Recent History and Evolution

Since the 1990s, many countries have added special labeling, placing restrictions on use, marketing and distribution, and/or requiring dedicated surveillance efforts to monitor for, manage, and mitigate potential risks that might be posed by a legal drug (e.g., [8,14,15]). Together, these requirements have evolved into RMPs, including REMS in the US. These plans may be required as a condition of drug approval or added postapproval to address unintended consequences posed by drug use. In the US, REMS programs are a special category of risk management that has been legally defined and includes enforceable elements codified in the Food and Drug Administration Amendments Act (FDAAA) of 2007. As described in Section 4 and elsewhere [7,8], REMS is a generally more burdensome and legally enforceable form of risk management that is required when the Food and Drug Administration (FDA) makes the determination that special procedures must be implemented to ensure safe use of a drug.

In the case of drugs that act on the central nervous system (CNS) with abuse and addiction potential, the risks primarily are related to people other than patients who generally have not been prescribed the drug (i.e., people who abuse drugs or are at risk of developing drug abuse and dependence). Addressing risks in the nonpatient population involves a delicate balance so as not to unduly restrict legitimate access and use by those in need of the medicine while simultaneously minimizing the risks to people who illegitimately obtain the drug [13,16–20].

The scientific foundation for risk management of CNS drugs includes many of the same types of scientific data that factor into national and international controlled substance scheduling recommendations, specifically, data on drug chemistry, mechanism of action, preclinical and clinical abuse potential assessments, epidemiology, and public health consequences, as described in this book (see Chapters 2, 9, 10 and 12) and elsewhere [9,10,13,21,22]. As discussed in the foregoing papers and reports, the science of abuse liability assessment is done largely according to models and procedures used globally and relied upon for national, regional, and international drug control according to the laws and regulatory frameworks promulgated internationally [6], nationally, and regionally (e.g., [5,10,22,23,24]).

Risk management must now also address issues related to the drug dosage form or formulation (e.g., pill, transdermal patch, extended-release mechanisms). Whereas abuse potential assessment and drug scheduling may consider the formulation of the drug, determination of the schedule is primarily based on the active chemical entity and its pharmacology, as discussed by Calderon et al. in this volume (Chapter 10). Drug products that differ in formulation but contain the same chemical entity, in the same drug schedule, may be treated very differently with respect to their risk management burdens, as is the case for various formulations of oxycodone, buprenorphine, and certain stimulants indicated for the treatment of attention deficit hyperactivity disorder (ADHD) in the US [18]. The importance of the opioid dosage form as a determinant of abuse and risk to patients and nonpatients led the US FDA to develop a draft guidance for the industry: Abuse-Deterrent Opioids—Evaluation and Labeling. The draft guidance was released for comments in 2013 and it was finalized in 2015. This guidance provides a basis for assessing as well as for "incentivizing" the development of abuse deterrent opioid drug products [22]. This topic is discussed in greater detail later in this chapter as it has important implications for risk management.

For CNS-acting drugs, many aspects of risk management strategies flow from the abuse potential science foundation and are intended to supplement the provisions of drug scheduling to mitigate the risk of abuse and dependence. Whereas there are many variants on the frameworks for assessing abuse potential data, including those relied upon by the World Health Organization (WHO) Expert Committee on Drug Dependence [25,26], our analysis will follow the more recently promulgated framework of the US FDA because it is relied upon by many drug developers, reflects input from many of the leading scientists and institutions involved in such research, and is in general harmony with systematic international approaches for the evaluation of drug dependence potential. The US FDA approach to the assessment of abuse liability is described in the form of two guidance documents: draft 2010 guidance on Assessment of Abuse Potential of Drugs [10] and 2015 guidance on Abuse-Deterrent Opioids—Evaluation and Labeling [22]. These two documents were intended to guide recommendations for drug scheduling and labeling, including potential drug claims, but they also provide information that is vital to the development of risk management approaches for CNS-acting drugs.

The 2010 guidance is reflected in many of the chapters in the present volume and includes guidance for the design of studies and interpretation of data concerning the chemistry (Chapter 10), mechanism of action (Chapter 2), and preclinical (Chapters 2–8) and clinical (Chapter 9) abuse liability studies. It briefly discusses the importance of chemistry studies of the "ease or risk of extraction," potential routes of nonmedical administration, and mechanisms of abuse deterrence. These mechanisms may include formulations and added substances intended to resist and discourage inappropriate use and routes of abuse as well as pro-drugs and chemical entities that limit the speed of delivery and/or onset of effects so as to reduce reinforcing and euphoria-inducing effects that contribute to the risk of abuse and dependence. The 2015 guidance substantially expanded this area of drug evaluation and provided much more extensive guidance on the evaluation of potentially abuse deterrent and abuse enabling features of drug products. Although the 2015 guidance is opioid-focused and its offering of potential for abuse-deterrent claims ("tiered label claims") is specific to the regulation of opioids by the FDA, it is generally applicable to most CNS-acting drugs.

The types of studies recommended in the 2010 and 2015 guidance documents are highly relevant for assessing the need for and design of drug- and drug class-specific RMPs because of the level of attractiveness or, conversely, the magnitude of deterrence against abuse conferred by the molecule and/or formulation. These factors may be critical determinants of the degree and nature of abuse likely to be associated with the drug in the real world.

Prior to the availability of these guidance documents, abuse potential assessment was largely focused on the abuse potential conferred by the molecule and its pharmacology, which are the primary data informing controlled substance scheduling recommendations and placement. However, over the past few decades there has been increasing attention given to the importance of the speed of delivery of the drug to the CNS and to drug-specific factors that influence the speed of onset of effects as additional determinants of abuse potential (e.g., [27–36]).

Abuse potential and other factors influencing use and dependence risk have also been studied for tobacco and medicinal nicotine-delivering products, and this research has yielded valuable information concerning the importance of product design, ingredients, and formulation factors that are relevant to the regulation of these products under national and international regulatory conventions (e.g., [8,37–44]). Tobacco and nicotine-related research and emerging regulation merits attention by those focused on pharmaceutical development and evaluation. This area of research and regulation is highly relevant for understanding the potential abuse and dependence risks of nicotine-containing products that range from traditional tobacco products and nicotine medicines to products that contain and deliver nicotine but do not contain tobacco (e.g., electronic cigarettes) [45,46]. These different products contain the same active chemical entity (i.e., nicotine), but the assessment of their abuse potential may vary greatly based on formulation and product design.

The science foundation guiding the development of RMPs is discussed in Sections 2 and 3. Section 2 focuses on laboratory-based in vitro manipulation and extraction studies to assess tamperability and potential abuse deterrent or enabling features of the product (i.e., Category 1 studies discussed in FDA's 2015 guidance). Section 3 focuses on abuse liability studies (Category 2 and 3 studies in FDA's 2015 guidance) of pharmacokinetics, pharmacodynamics, and abuse potential and how these data are brought together in an overall abuse potential assessment to inform drug scheduling and risk evaluation and management. Implications of abuse liability assessment research findings for RMP development are discussed in Section 4. Risk management also includes postmarketing surveillance strategies (Category 4 studies in the 2015 guidance and discussed in greater detail in FDA guidance documents specific to risk management [7,11,12,47,48]).

2. ABUSE POTENTIAL ASSESSMENT FOR DRUG SCHEDULING AND RISK MANAGEMENT DEVELOPMENT

As most of this volume describes the rationale and methods of abuse potential assessment, this chapter focuses on key concepts that are important to consider in developing and implementing RMPs, including REMS. Historically, abuse potential (often referred to as "abuse liability") assessment had focused almost exclusively on the "active pharmaceutical ingredient" (API), also referred to as the "chemical entity" or "new chemical entity" (NCE), the "molecular entity," or the "drug substance." This practice is consistent with and largely flows from the International Drug Control conventions of 1961 and 1971 that recognized the indispensable need for appropriate medical access to certain addictive drugs for the treatment of people with a wide range of diseases, including pain [6,49]. National parties to the treaty developed their own frameworks to be in harmony with this approach such as in the case of the US Controlled Substances Act (CSA). These approaches provide the basis for determining whether a given chemical entity should be controlled ("scheduled") and ensuring that the restrictiveness of the schedule is consistent with the risks of abuse (see Chapter 10) and elsewhere [5,6].

The FDA [50] described an approach to Premarketing Risk Assessment that provides a prototype for the subsequent REMS approach in the US and also reflects the premarket risk assessment strategies employed by the European Medicines Agency (EMA) [14] and Health Canada [15]. In the case of controlled substances, this assessment includes consideration of many of the same factors used to determine the controlled substance schedule placement of the drug. In the US, this similar approach provides the basis for harmonization of the REMS with the scheduling provisions of the CSA to mitigate the risks of misuse, abuse, and dependence. The comprehensive assessment of abuse potential used to inform appropriate labeling, scheduling, and risk management includes an analysis of eight factors laid out in the CSA [10,21]:

1. its actual or relative potential for abuse;
2. scientific evidence of its pharmacological effect, if known;
3. the state of current scientific knowledge regarding the drug or other substance;
4. its history and current pattern of abuse;
5. the scope, duration, and significance of abuse;
6. what, if any, risk there is to the public health;

7. its psychic or physiological dependence liability; and
8. whether the substance is an immediate precursor of a substance that is already controlled under the CSA.

When a New Drug Application (NDA) is submitted to the FDA, these eight factors are analyzed following the format described in the FDA's Draft Guidance on the "Assessment of Abuse Potential of Drugs" [10,21]. This analysis presents the preclinical, animal, and the clinical human data conducted on the drug product that are relevant to the abuse or dependence potential of the drug. All abuse liability data, including public health risks and benefits, are relevant to both scheduling and the REMS (see chapter 10). Additional guidance is available for the assessment of the relative abuse potential of new drug formulations [22].

As discussed elsewhere in this volume, preclinical data are highly relevant to the assessment of abuse potential and dependence and therefore to the development of a Premarketing Risk Assessment and Risk Management Plan or REMS. Animal discrimination (Chapter 6) and self-administration (Chapters 2 and 3) data provide an initial insight into whether the drug has abuse potential and whether additional human data are needed. Animal data can inform the design of the human abuse liability study(ies) in that they can help to determine [1] the appropriate positive control (or reference) drug (particularly in cases in which the drug is from a novel pharmacological class) [2]; doses of test and control drugs; and [3] the safety profile of the drug at supratherapeutic doses, suggesting the need for an REMS.

3. IN VITRO ASSESSMENT OF PRODUCTS FOR TAMPERABILITY, ABUSE RISK, AND DETERRENCE

As discussed in the introduction, the drug dosage form or formulation itself may be a critical determinant of the risk and nature of abuse (e.g., ease of converting an oral dosage form for use by smoking or injecting) and consequences (e.g., speed and dose of delivery and the importance of these factors in producing euphoric effects and overdose). Although such factors are likely relevant for all categories of abuseable CNS drugs, the increasing rates of prescription opioid abuse and overdose death in the US led to the FDA's development of the 2015 guidance, in order to incentivize the development of safer and less abusable opioids [22]. In principle, the drug dosage form can function to mitigate the potential risks intrinsic to the active ingredient. Although much of the following discussion will be about drug formulation, there are other approaches that can also function to mitigate the risk such as the inclusion of an opioid antagonist along with the therapeutic agonist, prodrugs, and approaches that slow drug entry into the brain regardless of how it was systemically delivered [10,51].

The development of opioid drug products with abuse-deterrent properties is intended to improve patient safety and reduce abuse. Abuse-deterrent properties can be introduced into a formulation in a number of ways and may differentially impact abuse by different routes of administration. For example, a tablet that is formulated to resist crushing by forming a gel when hydrated with a small amount of water would be expected to mitigate abuse

Table 1 General Framework for Categorization of Abuse-Deterrent Formulations

Category	Principle	Examples
Physical/chemical barriers	Physical barriers that prevent chewing, crushing, or grinding (e.g., tablet hardness); chemical barriers that resist extraction and injection (e.g., gelling in water)	OxyContin®, Nucynta®, Exalgo®, Opana® ER, Hysingla™ ER
Agonist/antagonist combinations	Addition of an opioid antagonist (e.g., naloxone, naltrexone) that is without activity if taken orally, but reduces or eliminates euphoria or drug "high" by other routes	Embeda™, Suboxone®, Targeniq®
Aversion	Addition of a substance (e.g., niacin, sodium lauryl sulfate) that produces an unpleasant effect	
Delivery system	Drug depots and implants	Probuphine®
New molecular entities and prodrugs	Properties could include need for enzymatic activation, different receptor binding profiles, slower penetration into the CNS	Vyvanse®
Combination	More than one method incorporated into the formulation	
Novel approaches	Novel approaches or technologies not captured previously	

by intranasal and injection routes but would not impact oral abuse of intact tablets. As outlined in Table 1, the 2015 FDA guidance provides a general framework for categorization of abuse-deterrent formulations based on different deterrence strategies. A brief review of the major elements of this guidance will be followed by a discussion of the design and rationale of Category 1 in vitro laboratory studies and how these studies are fundamental for understanding the overall abuse potential of a new formulation or NCE.

Abuse-deterrent formulations must be evaluated at various stages of development for regulatory approval and appropriate labeling. The 2015 FDA guidance lists three types of premarketing studies (Categories 1–3) that may be necessary "...to obtain a full and scientifically rigorous understanding of the impact of a technology or technologies on a product's abuse potential..." and postmarketing studies (Category 4) to assess the impact of an abuse-deterrent formulation on real-world abuse:

- Category 1: Laboratory-based in vitro manipulation and extraction studies
- Category 2: Pharmacokinetic studies
- Category 3: Clinical abuse potential studies
- Category 4: Postmarketing studies to determine whether the abuse-deterrent product produces a significant reduction in population-based estimates of abuse

The FDA encourages the development of abuse-deterrent technologies and intends to take a "flexible, adaptive approach to labeling of these products." Data from the four category assessments are intended to lead to label claims reflecting the level of abuse deterrence that the FDA determines are supported by the evidence.

FDA provides examples of claims that might be considered for inclusion in the labeling of the product. The following summary of the FDA examples illustrates the intent of the FDA to provide stronger claims reflective of stronger benefits: (i) the product is formulated with physicochemical barriers to abuse; (ii) the product is expected to reduce or block effect of the opioid when the product is manipulated; (iii) the product is expected to result in a meaningful reduction in abuse; (iv) the product has demonstrated reduced abuse in the community. Claims that imply demonstrated reduced abuse and other benefits in the "community" (often termed "real world") require strong evidence from post marketing studies including surveillance termed "Category 4" studies by FDA (see Section 3.1), whereas the other claims might be based on evidence from premarket Category 1, 2 and 3 studies (Section 3.1).

3.1 Design and Rationale of Category 1 Studies

Many drug misusers/abusers resort to physical and chemical manipulation ("tampering") of opioid formulations in attempts to alter the properties of the drug or the formulation. Cone [52] reported that the perceived motives for tampering by nonmedical users include enhancement of psychoactive effects, enhancement of drug availability, faster onset of effects, and elimination of undesirable excipients (i.e., those ingredients other than the active ingredient). Such manipulations could expose abusers to larger, potentially toxic doses. In addition, such manipulations, if successful, may make the product more suitable for abuse by alternate routes of administration (injection, intranasal, sublingual, smoking, and rectal).

The design of scientifically rigorous in vitro laboratory studies of abuse-deterrent products should begin with considerations from multiple knowledge domains encompassing the following areas:

- physico-chemical properties of the API and formulation excipients;
- abuse potential of API; and
- abuse patterns relating to tampering practices and preferred routes of administration.

A valid Category 1 assessment should challenge a product in ways that are known to be practiced or may plausibly be used by drug abusers in "real-world" settings. Generally, simple one-step methods are preferred in most abuse attempts, but highly motivated abusers sometimes attempt complex, multistep procedures. The complex methods of manipulation would most likely be attempted by individuals with experience and access to suitable chemicals and solvents that are less commonly found in the household. Conceptually, Category 1 studies consist of the following general types of assessments:

- Physical manipulations
  - Tablets and capsules: crushing/grinding tablets, particle size determinations, band uniformity, effects of heating and freezing
  - Transdermal systems: cutting/separating layers

- Extraction experiments
  - One-step extraction with solvents displaying a variety of chemical properties
  - Multistep extraction and isolation procedures
- Injectability
  - Extraction in small aqueous-based solvents for injection
  - Effects of heat, agitation, and extraction time on quantity and quality of extract
- Smokeability
  - Vaporization studies to determine optimized conditions
- "Dose dumping" studies
  - Dissolution studies to determine effects of coingestion of alcoholic beverages
- Specialized assessments that may be needed for specific APIs and formulations
  - Thermal stressing effects (effects of heat on excipients and polymeric matrices) on extraction efficiency, viscosity, and injectability
  - Solution viscosity measurements
  - Chemical challenges that may separate/inactivate antagonists/irritants
  - Chemical and enzymatic challenges that may convert prodrugs or new chemical entities to another molecular species with greater activity or more desirable characteristics
  - Free-base isolation studies
  - Solubility studies of APIs and excipients

Although some of the elements of Category 1 studies could be standardized (e.g., extraction studies), major differences in the chemical and physical properties of various abuse-deterrent technologies require a "tailoring" approach in study design of a specific formulation. A comprehensive assessment must take into consideration the nature of the API(s), formulation excipients, and the intended mode and rate of drug delivery.

It is well established that both dose and speed of delivery are important determinants of a drug's reinforcing properties. Consequently, tampering efforts are frequently directed toward changing the product into a form suitable for administration by a faster delivery route with a resultant faster onset of drug effects. Because most tampering procedures are relatively simple to perform, a successful abuse-deterrent formulation is expected to impart a substantial "barrier" to tampering efforts, greatly increasing the work required (time, effort, and resources) for a successful outcome. Tampering efforts appear to be based primarily on individual experience, trial and error experimentation, and upon information found in Internet postings by other individuals engaged in tampering. Many efforts at purification of API and/or manipulation for use by alternate routes of administration are not successful, and it is difficult to determine, based on Internet postings, the frequency at which successful outcomes are achieved. Complex tampering efforts, when attempted, are accompanied by highly uncertain outcomes.

Hence, Category 1 studies can be conceptualized as a means of determining the amount of work that must be expended (under standardized conditions) to either

Table 2 Interpretation of the Results of Category 1 Studies on Various Routes of Administration

Category 1 Studies	Route of Administration
Physical manipulations (cutting, grinding, powdering)	Oral (chewing, "parachute"), nasal
Aqueous and alcoholic extractions in large volume; dissolution	Oral (drink), rectal
Extractions studies in small volumes; syringeability studies	Injection, nasal, rectal, transmucosal
Dissolution studies with ethanol	Oral with alcohol coingestion
Simulated smoking studies with formulation	Smoking
Free-base studies: extraction and precipitation experiments	Smoking

overcome the formulation barrier or alternately the extent of formulation failure. Set endpoints for judging whether a tampering attempt (either simple or complex multistep procedures) is successful or not are a function of how much purified drug can be isolated (dose and concentration) and how much work must be expended. Use of comparators (approved products with and without abuse-deterrent features) in these studies serve a vital role in the interpretative process and often serve as guideposts for defining the strengths and weaknesses of the new product.

As many tampering efforts are directed toward altering administration to a nonintended route, Category 1 findings provide data relative to the ease of conversion of a product to a form suitable for nonintended routes of administration. Table 2 summarizes how the results of Category 1 studies can be interpreted relative to different routes of administration.

3.2 Implications of Category 1 Findings

Over the lifetime of the development of an abuse-deterrent product, information from one developmental phase can inform study designs in other phases. For example, preclinical findings in animal self-administration studies help establish dose requirements by different routes of administration relevant to the reinforcing and euphoriant properties of the API. In a similar manner, Category 1 findings provide the foundation for understanding the strengths and weakness of a formulation and inform the design of Category 2 pharmacokinetic studies (how much drug is released and the speed of delivery) and Category 3 clinical abuse potential studies (ethical and relevant routes of administration, basis for production of a "standardized" tampered product). Finally, Category 1–3 findings may have predictive value regarding the potential for obtaining stronger claims such as "demonstrated to be less abused in the community" through Category 4 studies following product commercialization.

Category 1 findings may also provide information relevant to risk management requirements. Some delivery systems contain drug amounts that would be toxic to a nontolerant individual. If manipulations (e.g., chewing or crushing) increase the speed of drug release, the risk of overdose/death would also increase. Other formulations containing an excess of the drug (e.g., transdermal patches) may also contain large amounts of the drug even as "residual drug" after use. One of the nonpatient issues that has come to the forefront is disposal, both of unused product and used transdermal systems. Consequently, risk management requirements for access, storage, and disposal of drug products become important. In the context of risk management, this challenge highlights the need to balance desired behaviors by patients and caregivers and the undesired behaviors of potential nonmedical users, abusers, and diverters. Appropriate storage and tracking of used transdermal systems is an important step in risk management for these products, as these systems generally retain large quantities of the drug even after they have been used appropriately. Improper disposal provides an opportunity for access by an abuser as well as accidental exposure of a child or household pet. The use of child-resistant storage containers is one method for addressing unintentional exposure to children, but these containers also need to be patient friendly, readily permitting even those with poor dexterity to access their medication. This ready access for patients must be balanced with the concern about storage containers becoming targets for drug abusers seeking to steal product [19].

Overall, Category 1 studies provide a detailed, comprehensive picture of the strengths and weaknesses of an abuse-deterrent formulation across a broad range of conditions when subjected to physical manipulations by patients and caregivers and tampering attempts by abusers. These studies may have predictive value in assessing the vulnerabilities of the product and identifying relevant concerns to be addressed in RMPs.

4. RMPs TO ADDRESS ABUSE AND DEPENDENCE-RELATED RISKS

The US FDA increasingly applied risk management to address abuse-related and other use-related risks of medications in the 1990s as a tool to support approval of medications that posed a range of risks. In an attempt to balance the benefit/risk ratio to permit otherwise risky medications to be approved, the FDA imposed certain requirements prior to granting approval. Among the earliest examples of risk management is the patient package insert distributed with oral contraceptives in the 1970s [7]. Examples of other drugs for which the FDA required risk management include the acne medicine Accutane (isotretinoin), over-the-counter (OTC) nicotine gum and patches, and the opioid-related analgesic Ultram (tramadol).

The FDA was aware that exposure to isotretinoin during pregnancy could result in significant fetal deformity and potentially death. To address this concern while also allowing women in need of the medication to use it, a RMP was put in place in 2005 to ensure that women receiving prescriptions for the medication were not pregnant and that they were using appropriate methods of birth control while taking the medication. The program has since been strengthened to further enhance patient protection.

Other early RMPs were established to control the risks associated with use by those for whom the medication was not intended—in particular, to mitigate abuse and misuse. One example is OTC nicotine replacement therapies (gum and patch). At the time these medications were being considered for OTC availability, the concern was raised that young people would become addicted to nicotine through the use of these products. The company that marketed these products as OTC medications was required to conduct surveillance to assess whether these products were being abused by people under the age of 18 and to report its findings to the FDA [53].

The analgesic tramadol was first approved in the US in 1995 as a noncontrolled substance, based on data suggesting a low risk of abuse. The manufacturer committed to implementation of a comprehensive postmarketing surveillance program to collect and analyze data on abuse within high-risk populations [54], providing an example of how risk management can function as an extension of scheduling, sometimes replacing and, in other cases, complementing it [7,13]. More recent RMPs tend to go further, applying risk management on top of scheduling. (Based on the resulting data, as of July 2014, the US Drug Enforcement Administration (DEA) has placed tramadol into Schedule IV of the CSA.)

Since 2004, the FDA has published a series of draft and final guidance documents on the topic of risk management. Labeling, including directions for safe and effective use and any special warnings, forms the basis for any risk management activities and is of the upmost importance [47,48]. Scheduling of controlled substances emerged as a more specialized tool, based in labeling, for drugs that carried risks of abuse and addiction. The approach to risk management described below evolved from the observed need and desire to take steps to improve the benefit and risk balance for certain drugs.

In 2004, in the US, the FDA began with a series of three guidance documents describing risk management as a process of premarketing risk assessment, pharmacovigilance (PV), and the selection and assessment of specific tools to minimize risk as part of a Risk Minimization Action Plan (RiskMAP) [47,48]. Since there was continued concern that some drugs required increased vigilance to enable their safe use, the US Congress passed the FDAAA of 2007 which, modeled on the FDA's 2005 final guidance, gave the FDA the legal authority to direct and enforce risk management in the form of REMS if the FDA considered an REMS "necessary to ensure that the benefits of the drug outweigh the risks of the drug" [55]. In the case of both RiskMAPs and REMS, postmarketing surveillance generally goes far beyond traditional routine PV, particularly in the case of serious safety risks and inadequate study of at-risk populations. The surveillance undertaken under these RMPs is proactively conducted and manufacturers are expected to address issues with proper mitigation steps.

Both the RiskMAP and REMS approaches were required to be developed and implemented on a scientific foundation based on the patient population, the seriousness of the indication, the anticipated benefits and likely duration of treatment with the drug,

Table 3 Examples of Elements to Assure Safe Use

- Training or certification of health care providers
- Special certification of pharmacies, practitioners, and health care settings dispensing the drug
- Limiting settings for dispensing of the drug
- Dispensing only after documentation of evidence of safe use conditions
- Monitoring of patients receiving the drug
- Patient registry

and the risks that may be associated with the drug. Of concern when developing, implementing, and assessing any risk management activity is maintaining a balance between safety and ensuring patient access to medicines. Ongoing development and methodological assessment have been emphasized in both public meetings and expert conferences, although many feel this has not been thoroughly implemented [7,19].

In addition to surveillance, both the RiskMAP and REMS provided for the identification and implementation of tools to mitigate risks. The 2007 law that created REMS gave the FDA the authority to require implementation of Elements to Assure Safe Use (ETASU) (Table 3) to mitigate specific risks [55].

While the specific components included in individual RMPs required by the FDA vary widely across drugs, this is considered to be appropriate since it allows the FDA and manufacturers to address and monitor the issues of specific concern for the product(s) (e.g., sodium oxybate versus tramadol versus transdermal methylphenidate) or class of products (e.g., extended release and long acting (ER-LA) opioids) [18]. While historically the risks to nonpatients were not considered to be under the purview of the FDA (with the exception of children and fetuses), in the case of scheduled substances in particular there has been a shift toward RMPs that also aim to protect nonpatients from the risks of misuse, abuse, and overdose [7]. However, even in the case of scheduled substances, the nature of risk management varies depending on the product(s) and associated risks [18].

In addition to single-product RMPs, the FDA has begun requiring manufactures of certain classes of drugs to develop and implement shared RMPs. One example of a shared REMS involves products that are all classified as ER-LA opioids. This shared REMS was approved by the FDA with the goal of reducing serious adverse events associated with inappropriate prescribing as well as misuse and abuse of ER-LA opioids while permitting appropriate patient access to these pain medications.

Another application of risk management in the US is "Subpart H regulations." These regulations provide for accelerated approval of drugs for serious or life-threatening diseases and serve to provide a path to approval and access to drugs that bring a meaningful benefit to patients (21 CFR 314.500). In 2002 the FDA approved Xyrem (sodium oxybate), the sodium salt of gamma-hydroxybutyrate (GHB), for treatment of cataplexy and excessive daytime sleepiness in patients with narcolepsy. The required RiskMAP supported the scheduling of sodium oxybate GHB [25] and reflects the pharmacology, preclinical, and clinical data as well as public health concerns about illicit use, including poisoning of others in conjunction with assault [18].

Outside of the US, risk management follows a PV life cycle approach. Applications for marketing authorization submitted in the EU must include a RMP that addresses the medicine's safety profile based on the product and patient population and nonclinical and clinical data as well as steps intended to mitigate risks, studies planned to gather more information about the risks, and measures to determine the effectiveness of risk management [14]. Significant changes to existing marketing authorization may trigger a request from the EMA for a RMP, and any individual EU national authority may also request an RMP to address concerns about the benefit and risk balance of a medicine. European RMPs are subject to ongoing review and revision as new safety information becomes available during the life cycle of a medicine. Health Canada, the Canadian agency responsible for the oversight of pharmaceuticals, has adopted the EU approach and format for RMPs with minor revisions to provide the necessary Canadian context, although Canada has yet to pass legislation requiring RMPs [15]. The Therapeutic Goods Administration of Australia has also adopted the EU legislation but requires an EU RMP to be accompanied by a supplementary annex with appropriate Australia-specific risk information [56]. Since the RMP is not issue based but rather based on product profile and safety concerns, there are no specific requirements for controlled substances. If a product has an abuse liability issue, it will be one of the safety concerns for which the marketing authorization holder (MAH) will be requested to develop and submit a PV and risk minimization (RM) plan.

One example of an EU RMP put into place after approval is that of methylphenidate. In the EU, a review of the safety of methylphenidate by the EMA's Committee for Medicinal Products for Human Use (CHMP) was triggered by concerns about cardiovascular and cerebrovascular safety. Following this review, an RMP was put into place to monitor and support the safe use of methylphenidate, with the participation of all MAHs of methylphenidate-containing products in the EU [57].

All of these various examples of risk management around the world point to a series of steps and actions through which a beneficial medicine that also has abuse potential can pass from development to approval and marketing. These steps include (1) information on the active ingredient (e.g., pharmacology, preclinical and clinical data, abuse potential assessment); (2) regulatory actions (e.g., controlled substance scheduling, risk management, reviews of New Drug Applications and Marketing Authorization Applications); and (3) postmarketing surveillance and mitigation actions.

5. CONCLUSIONS

Existing preclinical methods of abuse potential assessment developed, along with clinical methods, largely from the search for less addictive opioids that emerged in the 1930s [5,6,58–61]. These methods provide the primary scientific foundation for determining if chemical entities should be regulated as controlled substances and, if so, which level of control is appropriate. Increasingly, since the dawn of the twenty-first century, such studies are also used to guide risk management and the development of specific RMPs. More recently, they are used to assess the risk of abuse by various routes of administration that may be facilitated or deterred by characteristics of the dosage form.

Pharmaceutical developers might increasingly be able to use RMPs to differentiate products. For example, tramadol remained unscheduled in the US for more than a decade under the auspices of an RMP. Various formulations of oxycodone now fluctuate in the US regarding their labeling claims and the nature of their RMPs even though they are all regulated as Schedule II drugs.

Although clinical research, as discussed by Vosburg and Sokolowska in this volume (Chapter 9) and in vitro tamper assessment, as discussed in this chapter and elsewhere [62], have prominently served in risk management development and drug labeling, preclinical methods should be adaptable to guide drug development, providing the foundation for RMPs as well as drug scheduling decisions. How preclinical abuse potential research can guide product development and regulation to provide the basis for product differentiation is thus a challenge to researchers but one that may serve pharmaceutical development (see the discussion by Kallman (Chapter 12) in this volume).

Finally, an important question for the regulatory process in the future is the extent to which risk management should be considered in drug scheduling recommendations. In the US, propofol remains unscheduled in part because of the defacto RMP entailed by its very restrictive labeling whereas the prodrug form, fospropofol, is placed in schedule IV, in part due to its water solubility and the assumption that it will be more widely available [63]. As the science and technology of drug dosage forms improve, differential scheduling of the same active molecular entity may emerge as an incentive for such development. The offering of tiered labeling claims by the FDA [22] is the primary incentive at this time. However, products considered substantially more resistant to particularly addictive and dangerous methods of use may also warrant differentiation by less burdensome RMPs than competitors and/or less restrictive drug scheduling.

The twentieth century international drug control conventions and national frameworks such as the US CSA did not anticipate such developments, but the drug development technology of the twenty-first century offers a much broader range of options for controlling therapeutic action, side effects, and abuse potential than the more narrow chemical-specific approach that dominated much of drug development in the twentieth century. Drug regulation and research methods need to evolve more quickly to provide important incentives for drug development and evaluation of the products resulting from innovations in drug development, which are emerging with increasing frequency. This book brings much of this together and hopefully will be an equal asset for pharmaceutical researchers, regulators, and developers.

DISCLOSURE

The authors provide consulting services through Pinney Associates to pharmaceutical companies regarding preclinical and clinical abuse potential assessment, risk management, postmarketing surveillance, drug scheduling, and other regulatory requirements for CNS-acting drugs with a potential for abuse and dependence. This manuscript was independently prepared without support for or input from any such commercial interests.

ACKNOWLEDGMENT

The authors thank Christine Sweeney and Daniel Wang for their editorial assistance in the preparation of this manuscript.

REFERENCES

[1] European Commission. A Guideline on summary of product characteristics. 2005. Available at: http://ec.europa.eu/health/files/eudralex/vol-2/c/spcguidrev1-oct2005_en.pdf [accessed 22.09.2014].
[2] United Nations. Single convention on Narcotic drugs, 1961 New York. March 30, 1961.
[3] United Nations. Convention on psychotropic substances Vienna. February 21, 1971.
[4] Title 21 USC 801. Controlled substances act, 1970. Title 21—food and drugs. Chapter 13—drug abuse prevention and control. 1970.
[5] Balster RL, Bigelow GE. Guidelines and methodological reviews concerning drug abuse liability assessment. Drug Alcohol Depend 2003;70(Suppl. 3):S13–40.
[6] Spillane J, McAllister WB. Keeping the lid on: a century of drug regulation and control. Drug Alcohol Depend 2003;70(Suppl. 3):S5–12.
[7] Liederman DB. Risk management of drug products and the US Food and Drug Administration: evolution and context. Drug Alcohol Depend 2009;105S:S9–13.
[8] Food and Drug Administration. Guidance for industry. Format and content of proposed risk evaluation and mitigation strategies (REMS), REMS assessments, and proposed REMS modifications. Rockville, MD: US Department of Health and Human Services Food and Drug Administration, Center for Drug Evaluation and Research (CDER), Center for Biologics Evaluation and Research (CBER); September 2009.
[9] Carter LP, Griffiths RR. Principles of laboratory assessment of drug abuse liability and implications for clinical development. Drug Alcohol Depend 2009;105(Suppl. 1):S14–25.
[10] Food and Drug Administration. Guidance for industry. Assessment of abuse potential of drugs. Silver Spring, MD: US Department of Health and Human Services, Food and Drug Administration, Center for Drug Evaluation and Research (CDER); January 2010.
[11] Dart RC. Monitoring risk: post marketing surveillance and signal detection. Drug Alcohol Depend 2009;105(Suppl. 1):S26–32.
[12] Dasgupta N, Schnoll SH. Signal detection in post-marketing surveillance for controlled substances. Drug Alcohol Depend 2009;105(Suppl. 1):S33–41.
[13] Schnoll SH, Ertischek MD, Henningfield JE. Risk management programs: a supplement to the controlled substances act. Update Food Drug Law Regul Educ 2006;(Issue 4):19–23.
[14] European Medicines Agency. Guidance on format of the risk management plan (RMP) in the EU—in integrated format. 2014. EMA/465932/2013 Rev.1. Available at: http://www.ema.europa.eu/docs/en_GB/document_library/Regulatory_and_procedural_guideline/2012/11/WC500134650.pdf.
[15] Health Canada. Notice regarding implementation of risk management planning including the adoption of ICH guidance pharmacovigilance planning—ICH topic E2E. 2009. File number 09-103644-626. Available at: http://www.hc-sc.gc.ca/dhp-mps/alt_formats/hpfb-dgpsa/pdf/prodpharma/notice_avis_rmp_pgr_e2e-eng.pdf.

[16] Balster RL, Johanson CE, Walsh SL. Risk management and post-marketing surveillance of CNS drugs: an introduction. Drug Alcohol Depend 2009;105(Suppl. 1):S1–3.
[17] Schuster CR, Barthwell AG, Henningfield JE. Introduction to college on problems of drug dependence special conference on risk management and post-marketing surveillance of CNS drugs. Drug Alcohol Depend 2009;105(Suppl. 1):S4–8.
[18] McCormick CG, Henningfield JE, Haddox JD, Varughese S, Lindholm A, Rosen S, et al. Case histories in pharmaceutical risk management. Drug Alcohol Depend 2009;105S:S42–55.
[19] Henningfield JE, Schuster CR. Risk management and post-marketing surveillance of CNS drugs. Drug Alcohol Depend 2009;105S:S56–64.
[20] Johanson CE, Balster RL, Henningfield JE, Schuster CR, Anthony JC, Barthwell AG, et al. Risk management and post-marketing surveillance for the abuse of medications acting on the central nervous system: expert panel report. Drug Alcohol Depend 2009;105(Suppl. 1):S65–71.
[21] Calderon SN, Klein M. A regulatory perspective on the abuse potential evaluation of novel stimulant drugs in the United States. Neuropharmacology 2014. pii: S0028-3908(14) 00126-9.
[22] Food and Drug Administration. Guidance for industry. Abuse-deterrent opioids—evaluation and labeling. Silver Spring, MD: US Department of Health and Human Services, Food and Drug Administration, Center for Drug Evaluation and Research (CDER); April 2015.
[23] Health Canada. Clinical assessment of abuse liability for drugs with central nervous system activity. 2007. Available at: http://www.hc-sc.gc.ca/dhp-mps/prodpharma/applic-demande/guide-ld/abus/abuse_liability_abusif_usage_clin-eng.php [accessed 21.09.2014].
[24] European Medicines Agency. Non-clinical safety studies for the conduct of human clinical trials and marketing authorization for pharmaceuticals. 2008. Available at: http://www.ema.europa.eu/docs/en_GB/document_library/Scientific_guideline/2009/09/WC500002941.pdf [accessed 21.09.2014].
[25] World Health Organization. Thirty-fifth meeting of the Expert Committee on Drug Dependence. 2012. Available at: http://www.who.int/medicines/areas/quality_safety/35thecddmeet/en/ [accessed 21.09.2014].
[26] World Health Organization. Thirty-sixth meeting of the Expert Committee on Drug Dependence. 2014. Available at: www.who.int/medicines/areas/quality_safety/36thecddmeet/en/ [accessed 21.09.2014].
[27] Abreu ME, Bigelow GE, Fleisher L, Walsh SL. Effect of intravenous injection speed on responses to cocaine and hydromorphone in humans. Psychopharmacol Berl 2001;154:76–84.
[28] Balster RL, Schuster CR. Fixed-interval schedule of cocaine reinforcement: effect of dose and infusion duration. J Exp Anal Behav 1973;20:119–29.
[29] Beardsley PM, Balster RL. The effects of delay of reinforcement and dose on the self-administration of cocaine and procaine in rhesus monkeys. Drug Alcohol Depend 1993;34:37–43.
[30] de Wit H, Dudish S, Ambre J. Subjective and behavioral effects of diazepam depend on its rate of onset. Psychopharmacol Berl 1993;112:324–30.
[31] Foltin RW, Fischman MW. Smoked and intravenous cocaine in humans: acute tolerance, cardiovascular and subjective effects. J Pharmacol Exp Ther 1991;257:247–61.
[32] Griffiths RR, McLeod DR, Bigelow GE, Liebson IA, Roache JD. Relative abuse liability of diazepam and oxazepam: behavioral and subjective dose effects. Psychopharmacology 1984;84:147–54.
[33] Marsch LA, Bickel WK, Badger GJ, Rathmell JP, Swedberg MD, Jonzon B, et al. Effects of infusion rate of intravenously administered morphine on physiological, psychomotor, and self-reported measures in humans. J Pharmacol Exp Ther 2001;299:1056–65.
[34] McColl S, Sellers EM. Research design strategies to evaluate the impact of formulations on abuse liability. Drug Alcohol Depend 2006;83(Suppl.1):S52–62.
[35] Nelson RA, Boyd SJ, Ziegelstein RC, Herning R, Cadet JL, Henningfield JE, et al. Effect of rate of administration on subjective and physiological effects of intravenous cocaine in humans. Drug Alcohol Depend 2006;82:19–24.
[36] Strang J, Bearn J, Farrell M, Finch E, Gossop M, Griffiths P, et al. Route of drug use and its implications for drug effect, risk of dependence and health consequences. Drug Alcohol Rev 1998;17: 197–211.
[37] Evans SE, Hoffman AC. Electronic cigarettes: abuse liability, topography and subjective effects. Tob Control 2014;23(Suppl. 2):ii23–9.

[38] Henningfield JE, Hatsukami DK, Zeller M, Peters E. Conference on abuse liability and appeal of tobacco products: conclusions and recommendations. Drug Alcohol Depend 2011;116(1–3):1–7.

[39] Henningfield JE, Keenan RM. Nicotine delivery kinetics and abuse. J Consult Clin Psychol 1993;61(5):743–50.

[40] Houtsmuller EJ, Fant RV, Eissenberg TE, Henningfield JE, Stitzer ML. Flavor improvement does not increase abuse liability of nicotine chewing gum. Pharmacol Biochem Behav 2002;72:559–68.

[41] Schuh KJ, Schuh LM, Henningfield JE, Stitzer ML. Nicotine nasal spray and nicotine vapor inhaler: abuse liability determination. Psychopharmacology 1997;130:352–61.

[42] Vansickel AR, Cobb CO, Weaver MF, Eissenberg TE. A clinical laboratory model for evaluating the acute effects of electronic "cigarettes": nicotine delivery profile and cardiovascular and subjective effects. Cancer Epidemiol Biomarkers Prev 2010;19(8):1945–53.

[43] Vansickel AR, Weaver MF, Eissenberg T. Clinical laboratory assessment of the abuse liability of an electronic cigarette. Addiction 2012;107(8):1493–500.

[44] World Health Organization. The scientific basis of tobacco product regulation. 2007. Available at: http://www.who.int/tobacco/global_interaction/tobreg/9789241209458.pdf. [accessed 21.09.2014].

[45] WHO Framework Convention on Tobacco Control. Electronic nicotine delivery systems. Conference of the Parties to the WHO Framework Convention on Tobacco Control. Sixth Session. Moscow, Russian federation; October 13–18, 2014. Available at: http://apps.who.int/gb/fctc/PDF/cop6/FCTC_COP6_10-en.pdf?ua=1 [accessed 21.09.2014].

[46] Farsalinos KE, Polosa R. Safety evaluation and risk assessment of electronic cigarettes as tobacco cigarette substitutes: a systematic review. Ther Adv Drug Saf 2014;5(2):67–86.

[47] Food and Drug Administration. FDA guidance for industry: good pharmacovigilance practices and pharmacoepidemiologic assessment (Pharmacovigilance guidance). March 2005. Available at: http://www.fda.gov/downloads/regulatoryinformation/guidances/ucm126834.pdf. [accessed 21.09.2014].

[48] Gerlach KK, Dasgupta N, Schnoll SH, Henningfield JE. Epidemiology of stimulant misuse and abuse: implications for future epidemiologic and neuropharmacologic research. Neuropharmacology 2014;87:91–96. Available at: http://dx.doi.org/10.1016/j.neuropharm.2014.04.020, in press.

[49] World Health Organization. Ensuring balance in national policies on controlled substances—guidance for availability and accessibility of controlled medicines. 2011. Available at: http://www.who.int/medicines/areas/quality_safety/GLs_Ens_Balance_NOCP_Col_EN_sanend.pdf. [accessed 21.09.2014].

[50] Food and Drug Administration. FDA guidance for industry: premarketing risk assessment. Available at: http://www.fda.gov/downloads/RegulatoryInformation/Guidances/ucm126958.pdf; March 2005 [accessed 21.09.2014].

[51] Webster LR, Smith S, Silowsky J, Gogas K, Odinecs A, Eldon M, et al. Abuse potential assessment of a novel opioid analgesic NKTR-181: implications for labeling and scheduling. San Diego, CA: College on Problems of Drug Dependence; 2013.

[52] Cone EJ. Ephemeral profiles of prescription drug and formulation tampering: evolving pseudoscience on the Internet. Drug Alcohol Depend 2006;83(Suppl. 1):S31–9.

[53] Shiffman S, Sweeney CT. Ten years after the Rx-to-OTC switch of nicotine replacement therapy: what have we learned about the benefits and risks of non-prescription availability? Health Policy 2008;86:17–26.

[54] Cicero TJ, Adams EH, Geller A, Inciardi JA, Munoz A, Schnoll SH, et al. A postmarketing surveillance program to monitor Ultram (tramadol hydrochloride) abuse in the United States. Drug Alcohol Depend 1999;57:7–22.

[55] Food and Drug Amendments Act of 2007 (2007). Public L. 110-85, § 505–1, 121 STAT. 823.

[56] Therapeutic Goods Administration. Risk management plan (RMP) questions & answers. Version 1.3 October 2012. Available at: http://www.tga.gov.au/pdf/pm-risk-management-plans-qa-121004.pdf.

[57] European Medicines Agency. European medicines agency makes recommendations for safer use of Ritalin and other methylphenidate-containing medicines in the EU. 2009. See http://www.ema.europa.eu/ema/index.jsp?curl=pages/news_and_events/news/2009/11/news_detail_000218.jsp&mid=WC0b01ac058004d5c1 [accessed 21.09.2014].

[58] Campbell ND. Discovering addiction the science and politics of substance abuse research. University of Michigan; 2007. See http://www.press.umich.edu/269246/discovering_addiction/sthash.HB8LhLY9.dpuf. [accessed 21.09.2014].

[59] Campbell ND, Olsen JP, Walden L. The narcotic farm: the rise and fall of America's first prison for drug addicts. New York: Abrams; 2008.

[60] Schuster CR, Henningfield JE. Conference on abuse liability assessment of CNS drugs. Drug Alcohol Depend 2003;70:S1–4.

[61] Expert Panel. Abuse liability assessment of CNS drugs: conclusions, recommendations, and research priorities. Drug Alcohol Depend 2003;70(Suppl. 3):S107–14.

[62] Cone EJ, Giordano J, Weingarten B. An iterative model for in vitro laboratory assessment of tamper deterrent formulations. Drug Alcohol Depend 2013;131(1–2):100–5.

[63] Drug Enforcement Administration. Schedules of controlled substances; placement of fospropofol into schedule IV2009. FR Doc E9–23971[Federal Register: October 6, 2009 (Volume 74, Number 192)] [Rules and Regulations] [Page 51234–51236] From the Federal Register Online via GPO Access [wais.access.gpo.gov] [DOCID:fr06oc09-3].

CHAPTER 12

Future Directions in Abuse Potential Assessment

Mary Jeanne Kallman
Preclinical Neuroscience, Covance Laboratories, Lead Optimization, Greenfield, IN, USA

Contents

The establishment of the Controlled Substance Staff (CSS) at the Food and Drug Administration (FDA) in 2001 and the publication of the European Guidelines in 2006 [1] and the US draft guidance in 2010 [2] have contributed to the current interest in the evaluation of the abuse liability potential of central nervous system compounds in development. The M3 Guidance on Nonclinical Safety Studies for the Conduct of Human Clinical Trials and Marketing Authorization for Pharmaceuticals published in 2013 [3] also includes a section on preclinical liability studies (also see Chapter 10 for regulatory considerations). The application of drug abuse science to preclinical drug development for meeting regulatory requirements has matured in the past 13 years. As this book describes, there are still unmet needs for the pharmaceutical industry and the continued development of models for assessment and how data from those models should be applied for decision making. What will the future bring?

One area anticipated for future growth is the development of a strong scientific database for the rodent. The rodent database in drug discrimination is quite expansive and diverse but the rodent database for dependence assessment and self-administration is more limited. The current emphasis in the European Medicines Agency (EMA) guideline and the FDA draft guidance on the use of rodents for abuse potential evaluations whenever possible has driven the need for expansion of the current database on abuse profiles. The scientific literature has always focused on drugs with known abuse profiles rather than evaluations of pharmaceuticals with unknown profiles that could impact the initial compound scheduling. Pharmaceutical companies are primarily interested in drug development for compounds that will be scheduled below a Schedule 2. The identification of borderline compounds with the techniques available is much more difficult for a Schedule 4 compound. Pfizer has published information on the concordance of rodent and primate data for self-administration data with human known abuse and US Drug Enforcement Administration (DEA) scheduling decisions [4,5]. They have reported strong predictability

Nonclinical Assessment of Abuse Potential for New Pharmaceuticals
http://dx.doi.org/10.1016/B978-0-12-420172-9.00012-6

of both rodent and primate models to each other and to the human situation. The discussion in their papers also addresses the value of rodent studies in providing preclinical data for assessing potential drug abuse. A broader rodent database could be helpful for selecting appropriate comparators and training compounds for the models used in the laboratory. In the development of compounds with unknown abuse liability profiles that are most typically for oral administration there is a need for a broader scientific database on rodent self-administration to provide perspective for data analysis. Well defined oral comparator compounds are not always characterized in rodent dependence models. This database is growing and will be broader in the future if pharmaceutical companies continue to publish comparator compound data from their abuse liability assessments.

More discussion about the adequacy of rodent data for potential abuse liability decisions should probably occur. One excellent publication on the potential differences in data generated in the three standard models with rodents and primates is the 2007 Weerts et al. paper [6] (see also Chapters 3 and 4 on rodent and nonhuman primate self-administration, respectively, as well as Chapters 5 and 6 on physical dependence [withdrawal] and drug discrimination, respectively). The authors do an excellent job of summarizing the literature where species differences are known (see also Refs [5,7,8]) for specific compounds. The Weerts et al. paper [6] also describes the neuroanatomical and pharmacokinetic differences between rats and monkeys that could account for differences in data generated for novel compounds for scheduling decision making. Some future wisdom about the exceptional situations when primate data would be valuable could be considered. The compounds that require primate data might include compounds with significant kappa opioid receptor activity and cocaine analogues. Another design issue for further discussion is the trigger for conducting progressive ratio or choice evaluations to understand and or compare the reinforcing strength of a novel compound. These data can clearly enhance the conclusions made about the reinforcing strength of a compound but they should only be conducted when a compound is first observed to be significantly reinforcing in comparison with a vehicle (see Chapter 3).

The "gold standard" core studies for abuse liability assessment—dependence, drug discrimination (Chapter 6), and self-administration (Chapters 3 and 4)—will probably remain the core of the abuse liability evaluations with minor adjustments to study design. The real future challenge is how to assess compounds that do not have characteristics that permit drug delivery that is workable in the gold standard models. The best example of this problem is a compound that cannot be administered intravenously for conducting a traditional self-administration study. A number of researchers have developed self-administration models that do not require IV self-administration. Inhalational [7–12], subcutaneous [13], and oral self-administration are all routes for drug exposure [14–16] that have been used in academic research environments to characterize compounds that are delivered by non-IV routes. Much of the research in this area compared different routes of drug administration for a single compound and was intended to better understand how the abuse process might be altered by the parameters associated with the route of administration. Moreover, the nonintravenous (non-IV) approaches have been used to evaluate specific types of compounds such as solvents or inhalational compounds that are abused. These non-IV models have not been used to characterize most pharmaceutical compounds in development and they may be more difficult to execute in the industry or contract research organization (CRO) setting where equipment can be costly. Oral and inhalational models might be worth considering for some compounds in drug development that will be administered in the clinic by a route other than intravenous. Another approach might be to use nontraditional models (instead of self-administration) like conditioned place preference (CPP) (see Chapter 7) or intracranial self-stimulation (ICSS) (see Chapter 8) to evaluate potential abuse liability. These less traditional models have been recommended by the CSS on occasion and have received discussion in multiple drug abuse liability symposiums at scientific meetings. CPP and ICSS are not currently considered "gold standard" but could be acceptable alternative models in the future with more validation and a better understanding of positive and negative control data from the models. To bring these models into the forefront will require summarizing validation data and standardizing protocols to support better integration and communication of the risks associated with assessment with these models, as suggested in Chapter 8 in this volume in the case of ICSS. Continued efforts to challenge the traditional approaches will be required to increase the industry's dependence on the nontraditional models. The future will include more of the nongold standard data coupled with the publication and discussion of these nontraditional models because the industry is focused on the development of compounds with diverse pharmacokinetics, chemistry, and nonoral routes of administration that will require different approaches for determining the potential for abuse.

One consideration where we assume that there is agreement is the preference for rodents as subjects for these evaluations. This perspective has been driven to some extent by regulatory documents and by the 3Rs directives to reduce, reuse, and recycle. Overall the selection of the rodent for these studies is probably the best approach, but are there circumstances where primate data are necessary for understanding specific compounds? Review of the predictability of the rodent data for scheduling decisions and predictability to the human abuse situation is a good method for a better understanding of the best approach for subject selections for these studies. The publication by Horton et al. and others [5,6] addresses both types of predictability of classic preclinical abuse liability assessments. Some discordance does exist for the rodent to primate data based on historical archives, as discussed in Chapter 4 of this volume by Nadar et al.

As has been described in the chapters that are core to this book, standard designs for the three primary models have been identified and we understand the implications of basic technical manipulations of those paradigms. The execution of these evaluations does include multiple manipulations, sometimes within a single study. For drug discrimination studies is it not uncommon to vary pretreatment times and the route of exposure. For dependence/withdrawal studies the duration of the dependence phase and the withdrawal phase or the frequency of compound dosing may be specific to the half-life of the compound evaluated. The data generated during the withdrawal phase may direct an extension of the assessment period to determine when a return to normal behavior occurs. In the execution of the self-administration model there is no consensus on the use of "priming" or the delivery of a small drug injection prior to the first response in testing. The determination of the infusion concentration for a single injection of the novel compound and potential extension of the duration of drug availability are some variables of importance for the type of data generated. Continued efforts to discuss and share approaches for defining the study parameters will provide a greater degree of consistency in the future. One definitive development for the future that would be helpful would be to develop a solubility decision tree for compounds that could provide direction for choosing a traditional IV self-administration model over CPP or ICSS.

Another area that deserves future attention and discussion is screening in early drug development. Most companies currently conduct abuse potential assessments when their compound is in Phase 2 clinical development, as recommended by the CSS of the FDA. This package of studies is required for the 8-factor analysis and scheduling by the DEA of a new compound. Toward the end of Phase 2 there should be good information about the highest clinical dose that will be developed therapeutically that is required to set doses for these preclinical studies. Sometimes companies need to make earlier "go/no-go" decisions to conserve the expenditures for clinical trials with compounds that would be considered unacceptable for FDA submission due to an abuse liability profile. Sometimes the competition in a particular drug development niche would preclude the development of a compound that required scheduling or scheduling as a level 2 compound. Some companies have actually considered or executed abuse liability assessments early in drug development and again later when clinical doses have been defined. Conducting identical assays (at different doses and prior to understanding intended therapeutic doses) is costly and has the potential of generating data with conflicting conclusions that will require resolution. The identification of screening strategies is a unique industry consideration and not an area of academic interest. We are already doing binding panels and slice preparations. Are those sufficient? Some possibilities for earlier in vivo screening could be determined from the basic neurochemistry (see Chapter 2) of a compound determined from receptor binding data in conjunction with a general behavioral assessment (e.g., locomotor activity; see also Chapter 2) as well as more specific "reward" assessing techniques like the CPP model, imaging techniques to identify typical dopamine involvement in the compound's activity, or even conducting self-administration at a single dose/concentration of the compound to support go/no-go decision making. Selection of a dose or concentration would be made as a multiple of the in vivo efficacy dose of the compound in rodents. Depending on the level of reassurance desired, a multiple of 5× or maybe 10× of the efficacy dose could be sufficient for a go/no-go decision. Some consideration of the goal of early testing would definitely contribute to the decision-making algorithm adopted. Data generated in the early screening models, especially with CPP, could be correlated with the completed self-administration data collected later in the drug development process for surviving compounds. The development of these correlational data would support the growth of a database on nontraditional models. More discussion on potential abuse liability screening would seem appropriate since a single approach for screening has not been adopted.

The future will definitely bring increased awareness of how to deal with atypical compounds in abuse liability assessment. This type of assessment will include compounds that typically do not work in the classic models. Examples of compounds that are not active in the classical self-administration model are peripherally active obesity compounds and other peripherally active compounds like steroids, compounds that build muscle mass, growth hormone, and compounds intended to treat frailty. These compounds all require nontraditional approaches for understanding abuse potential and many are, or will be, scheduled in the future. Will paper scientific arguments/discussions be sufficient?

For a number of companies, the concept of abuse and misuse of a new chemical entity (NCE) has expanded to include misuse in sports—aka doping. Doping exhibits many of the aspects of a "standard" abused drug: nonmedical use that may be rewarded by enhanced performance, diversion, illicit use, and in many cases, overuse to the point of harm. While addressing the "doping potential" of an NCE is a very different concern and type of assessment versus abuse potential, and though not necessarily subject to scrutiny by the CSS of the FDA, there are means to do so [17].

Several companies have agreements with the World Anti-Doping Agency (WADA) to share information about new chemical entities to allow for detection in athletes. Such agreements serve the role of good corporate citizenship, regard for the safety of athletes, and minimization of diversion from patients who have a medical need for the drug. The International Federation of Pharmaceutical Manufactures (IFPMA) working group on anti-doping has established guidelines [17] for assisting companies in addressing the potential for doping of a NCE. While such an agreement with WADA by a company is purely voluntary, some regard to the potential for unwanted press should a company's substance be misused, especially if there is resultant harm to the athlete, should be considered. This growing area of interest from both the public and athletes' perspectives will lead to more formal requirements for companies working in this drug development space.

The future will include many challenges related to the diversity of compounds in drug development and even the increased efforts to develop compounds to treat drug abuse per se and/or develop abuse deterrent formulations. The move in drug development away from traditional small molecules creates many issues for the future of abuse liability assessment. Specifically, we will have to develop seamless approaches in some situations for the evaluation of biologics, large molecules, molecules with long duration of activity, and insolubility. There have even been some recent citations on the development of a vaccine approach for the treatment of drug abuse by administering an antidrug monoclonal antibody (mAb) to block the specific drug from binding to the receptor of interest (i.e., the antidrug mAb binds/sequesters the drug peripherally, thus limiting central nervous system penetration and receptor binding). The longer half-life of mAbs compared to currently used abuse-limiting medications would be a benefit for therapeutic application of this technique but still impermanent, so the search is on for adeno-associated virus (AAV) gene transfer vector encoding proteins (such as antidrug mAbs) that might be more therapeutically durable. This possibility has been discussed for the potential treatment of cocaine [18] and nicotine/smoking abuse [19].

How does a laboratory approach the challenges of working with atypical molecules for the assessment of abuse and the treatment of drug abuse? No single laboratory approach exists for testing atypical molecules, therefore different perspectives will be required. More discussion on these issues and the best approaches is imperative for designing abuse liability assessments. Large molecules that were thought to not cross the blood–brain barrier are under scrutiny for evaluation of at least dependence/withdrawal assessments. Some are taking the position that this is not necessary but there are probably specific drivers for the inclusion of large molecules in some abuse liability evaluations. The burden will be on the industry to provide logic and detailed approaches for evaluating or not evaluating these compounds as we move forward. A 2014 presentation by DeZafra [20] at the Safety Pharmacology Society Meeting discussed some of the issues related to the abuse liability evaluation of large molecules. We can anticipate a continuation of this dialogue as industry thoughts on large molecule testing evolve.

Another future area of development will be in the clinical realm. There are no standards for "abuse related terms," and each company can employ its own set of terms that will ultimately be coded into the MEDRA classification system. Standardization of the term that each company employs, with the agreement of the FDA, will ensure greater consistency in identification and interpretation of abuse-related signals. Such an effort at standardization is currently underway.

A final area for future direction is the continued effort of the pharmaceutical industry to develop and maintain strong relationships and communication with government and regulatory agencies like the CSS at the FDA, National Institute on Drug Abuse (NIDA), and the DEA. Interactions with organized scientific groups such as College on Problems of Drug Dependence (CPDD), Cross Company Abuse Liability Consortium (CCALC), and others will also be important for maintaining a scientific and drug development role in the future of drug abuse liability assessments. A working amicable relationship builds the most productive and informed environment. A recollection of some comments made by Dr Throckmorton of the FDA in a talk titled "Integrating Clinical and Nonclinical

Pharmacology in Drug Development" at the Safety Pharmacology Society Meeting in 2011 [21] provides strong support for regulatory/industry relationships. The essence of the comment was that the CCALC/CSS relationship of interacting to generate discussion of abuse liability issues in an open forum was one of the best integrated relationships for the FDA. These types of activities are critical for the future development of abuse liability assessment. A collaborative discussion of Abuse Deterrent Formulations occurred in the fall of 2013. Another collaborative discussion between the CCALC and the CSS was in the planning for an April 2015 FDA-Industry Dialogue with a variety of both clinical and preclinical topics for discussion. Interactions with NIDA and CPDD have also been reasonably successful, with joint support for programming at annual meetings and involvement in the face-to-face Dialogue discussions with the CSS. One area where improved communication should be a goal for the future is continued efforts from the DEA to educate the industry about their requirements and scheduling pressures. The recent dissatisfaction of Eisai, Inc. over the delayed scheduling of Fycompa as a schedule III treatment for epilepsy might be reduced by the three-way interactions between the sponsor and FDA/DEA in the future drug registration/scheduling process.

ACKNOWLEDGMENTS

Special thanks to Dr Thomas Hudzik, AbbVie Ltd., for the text around the current efforts to coordinate abuse liability efforts with "doping" evaluations and to Dr Dave Compton for discussions on the Fycompa scheduling and AAV-gene therapy.

REFERENCES

[1] EMA (EMEA/CHMP/SWP/94227/2004). Guideline on the non-clinical investigation of the dependence potential of medicinal products. March 2006.
[2] FDA. Guidance for industry – assessment of abuse potential of drugs Draft guidance. January 2010.
[3] M3. ICH M3(R2). Guidance on nonclinical safety studies for the conduct of human clinical trials and marketing authorization for pharmaceuticals. June 2009.
[4] O'Connor EC, Chapman K, Butler P, Mead AN. The predictive validity of the rat self-administrative model for abuse liability. Neurosci Biobeh Rev 2011;35:912–38.
[5] Horton DB, Potter DM, Mead AN. A translational pharmacology approach to understanding the predictive value of abuse potential assessments. Behav Pharmacol 2013;24(5–6):410–36.
[6] Weerts EM, Fantegrossi WE, Goodwin AE. The value of nonhuman primates in drug abuse research. Exp Clin Psychopharmacol 2007;15(4):309–27.
[7] Collins RJ, Weeks JR, Cooper MM, Good PL, Russell RR. Prediction of abuse liability of drugs using IV self-administration by rats. Psychopharmacol 1984;82:6–13.
[8] Balster RL, Bigelow GE. Guidelines and methodological reviews concerning drug abuse liability assessment. Drug Alcohol Depend 2003;70:513–40.
[9] Bowen SE. Increases in amphetamine-like discriminative stimulus effects of the abused inhalant toluene in mice. Psychopharmacology 2006;186:517–24.
[10] Weiss B, Wood RW, Macys DA. Behavioral toxicology of carbon disulfide and toluene. Environ Health Perspect 1979;30:39–45.
[11] Wood RW, Grubman J, Weiss B. Nitrous oxide self-administration of the squirrel monkey. J Pharmacol Exp Ther 1977;202:491–9.

[12] Shelton KL, Slavova-Hernandez G. Characterization of an inhaled toluene drug discrimination in mice: effects of exposure conditions and route of administration. Pharmacol Biochem Behav 2009;92: 614–20.
[13] Shelton KL, Nicholson K. Benzodiazepine-like discriminative stimulus effects of toluene vapor. Eur J Pharmacol November 15, 2013;720(1–3):131–7.
[14] Shelton KL. Inhaled toluene vapor as a discriminative stimulus. Behav Pharmacol 2007;18(3):219–29.
[15] Newman JL, Carroll ME. Reinforcing effects of smoked methamphetamine in rhesus monkeys. Psychopharmacology 2006;188:193–200.
[16] Shelton RL, Grant KL. Effects of naltrexone on Ro 15-4513 on multiple schedule of ethanol and tang self-administration. Clin Exp Res 2001;25(11Z):1576–85.
[17] IFPMA Points to Consider Document. Identification of compounds with potential for doping abuse and sharing of information with WADA. 2012. Available online at http://www.ifpma.org/ethics/doping-in-sport.html.
[18] Rosenberg JB, Hicks MJ, De BP, Pagovich O, Frenk DG, Janda KD, et al. AAVrh.10-mediated expression of an anti-cocaine antibody mediates persistent passive immunization that suppresses cocaine-induced behavior. Hum Gen Ther 2012;23:451–9.
[19] Hicks MJ, Rosenberg JB, De BP, Pagovich O, Young CN, Qiu J-P, et al. AAV-directed persistent expression of an anti-nicotine antibody gene for smoking cessation. Sci Transl Med 2012;4(140):140–87.
[20] DeZafra C. Considerations for abuse liability assessment. In: Presentation at the safety pharmacology society annual meeting. 2014.
[21] Throckmorton D. Integrating clinical and non-clinical pharmacology in drug development. In: Presentation at the safety pharmacology society annual meeting. 2010. Boston, MA.

INDEX

Note: Page numbers followed by "f" and "t" indicate figures and tables, respectively.

F

G

H

I

L

M

N

S

T

U

V

W

Edwards Brothers Malloy
Ann Arbor MI. USA
July 24, 2015